THE HOME BEYOND

OR,

VIEWS OF HEAVEN,

AND ITS RELATION TO EARTH,

BY

Over Four Hundred Prominent Thinkers and Writers.

BY THE

Rt. Rev. SAMUEL FALLOWS, D. D.,

AUTHOR OF "BRIGHT AND HAPPY HOMES," "LIBERTY AND UNION," "SYNONYMS AND ANTONYMS," "SYNONYMS DISCRIMINATED," "ABBREVIATIONS AND CONTRACTIONS," ETC.

DETROIT, MICH.
R. D. S. TYLER & CO.
1885.

COPYRIGHTED BY
SAMUEL FALLOWS,
1883, 1884.

In the interest of creating a more extensive selection of rare historical book reprints, we have chosen to reproduce this title even though it may possibly have occasional imperfections such as missing and blurred pages, missing text, poor pictures, markings, dark backgrounds and other reproduction issues beyond our control. Because this work is culturally important, we have made it available as a part of our commitment to protecting, preserving and promoting the world's literature. Thank you for your understanding.

INTRODUCTION.

No subject is of such paramount or absorbing interest to man as that of death and the future life. "If a man die shall he live again?" is the question springing from every heart, and trembling on every lip. To every home death comes. To every one it is appointed once to die. Does death then, end all? Shall we write over our cemeteries, "Death is an eternal sleep"?

Thank God we are not left in darkness on this intensely practical and important theme. Light, somewhat dim and struggling, it is true, comes from the fact that all the phenomena of mind are different from those of the perishable body, that our instincts and aspirations are for continued existence, that the best and longest life on earth is an imperfect and therefore an incomplete life, that our sense of justice demands a future state for the vindication of right and the punishment of wrong, that the almost universal sentiment or conviction of the race has been in favor of a life to come of some kind or character.

But these considerations and others of a similar nature afford a mere probability only of the reality of an existence beyond the grave. The Christian Revelation makes that probability an assured certainty. Out of the region of wishful hope, of a strong foreboding, of a reasonable peradventure, it transports us to a world of glorious fact. Death is but a passage to another life. Death is but the vestibule to the house not made with hands, eternal in the heavens. Death is but a shadow, not a substance. The dead are the truly living. From the skies, the world's Prophet, Priest and King has come, incarnated in a human body, enshrining a human soul. From Joseph's tomb He rose, the body the same, yet changed, the manhood changed, yet the same. Back to his native skies has He gone with the same body and the same manhood that manifested His divine nature while on the earth. By His life, death, resurrection and ascension, He hath abolished death and brought life and immortality to light.

With him the departed saints have life in richness and fullness inconceivable to us who are still amid the turmoils of this mortal existence. The personality they possessed here, they have there. They are the same, and yet changed. They know us still. They sympathize with us still. They love us still. They help us still. To that heavenly home they are waiting to welcome us when our warfare is accomplished.

The aim of the author of the "Home Beyond" has been to set forth through the aid of the best thinkers and writers of the centuries, the grand truth of immortality, and the reality and glory of the Home in Heaven. The value of such a work, so carefully compiled, is well nigh inestimable. To any who are beset with doubts and fears it will prove an armory from which bright and shining weapons can be taken to put to flight these enemies of their comfort and peace. It will be precious solace to those who are laying away to rest the loved of their homes and hearts. It will help their faith lift up the tearful eye to the land of beauty, bountifulness, and blessedness, where the redeemed walk in white. It will stimulate them to live nobler lives on earth, that they may through the grace of God secure at last, the rest and rewards of Heaven.

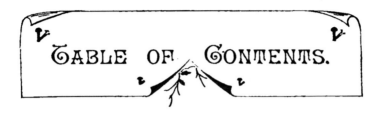

I. MAN.

Man the Child of God—Man a Temple of Heaven—Man a Reed that Thinks—Man's Nobility—Man and Nature—Man, Body and Spirit—Man not a Mere Animal—Man Animal and Rational—God Imaged in Man—Self and Ego—General Facts of Mind—Darwinism and Man—Definitions of Man—The Divine Element in Evolution—Man, Body, Soul and Spirit—Nature and Man - Man Redeemable.............. 33–62

II. LIFE.

Life a Journey—Evolution and Life—Material Processes and Life—Atoms and Consciousness—Life One Great Ritual—The Peril of Life—Not One Life Destroyed—Live and Help Live—Life the Time for Work—The Present Life in View of the Future—Longevity of Studious and Busy Men—Excitement and Short Life—The Blessings of a Short Life—Building up Life—Life New and Old—Life and Death—Life a River—Life's Discipline a Training for Heaven—Life a Stream—Life is Passing—John Wesley's Old Age—The Sooner We Go the Better—Brevity of Life—Farewell Life—To Live is Christ—Life is for Character, and Character is for Immortality 63–132

III. DEATH.

The Deathday Better than the Birthday—The Evening of Death—Death and its Warnings—Death is Yours—Death is Life Death an Angel of Light—What is Death?—Right and Wrong Views of Death—The Dead are the Living—Death the Destroyer and the Restorer—Death Does not End All—Destruction of the Assyrians—The Voices of the Dead—The Spirit Survives in its Completeness—Death Overcome—Death and Immortality—Contrasts in Death—Our Burial Places Sacred—Toward Evening—Death the Gate of Life—Two Funerals—Death Pangs, Birth Pangs—We Love to Visit Our Cemeteries—Jesus the Precious Name in Death—The Death of Death—The Death of a Good Man—A Stingless Death—Death has Lost its Terror—The Dead and the Living—I Would not Live Alway—Nearer my Rest—No Fear of Death—The Right View of Death—Death According to

Philo—The Soul Does not Sleep—We Shall Reach the Haven—The Soul Departing—The Historic Dead—Death a Transition—If we Could all Die Together—The Dead are Ours Still—Death Binds us Together—Victor over Death—Death a Divine Message—Asleep in Jesus—Fill up the Ranks—Into Thy Hands I Commend my Spirit—Mozart's Requiem—Burial of Moses—On the Death of a Mother—The Dying Mother—Death of Garfield—Man's Mortality—Thy Will be Done. 133-180

IV. THE DYING.

(I.) GLIMPSES OF THE FUTURE BY THE DYING.

The Dying Seeing Departed Friends—Visions of a Dying Youth—Only a Little Brook—The Dying Child and Her Departed Mother—Dr. Lowell Mason—Bishop D. W. Clark—Rev. Alfred Cookman—The Dying Dauphin—On the River's Verge—Daughter of Rev. T. A. Goodwin, D. D.—The Peak in Darien—The Revelations to the Dying—Heaven not Far Away...134-149

(II.) DYING TESTIMONIES AND EXPERIENCES.

The Dying Husband—Sir Isaac Newton—Dr. Guthrie—Rev. Edward Payson, D. D.—Rev. Prof. Henry Smith, D. D.—Folding the Lambs in His Bosom—Bring the Children Home—Going to Jesus—Whitefield's Death—Grateful Testimony—What Message to Jesus?—Felicia Hemans—John Locke—The Mother and Her Dying Boy—Sir Walter Raleigh—Joseph Addison—Sir Matthew Hale—John Wesley—Isaac Watts, D. D.—Rev. John Fletcher—Sir Thomas Fowell Buxton—Rev. Charles Simeon—Rev. Charles Wesley—Charlotte Elizabeth—Matthew Henry—John Howard...150-172

(III.) THE MARTYRS.

Martyred Heroes—Bishops Ridley and Latimer—John Huss—Jerome of Prague—Lawrence Saunders—Rev. George Wishart—Dr. Rowland Taylor—Lord Viscount Winceslaus—Archbishop Cranmer—Polycarp...173-180

V. THE DEATH OF CHILDREN.

The Child is Dead—The Blossom Transplanted—Little Bessie—Can I Wish it Back?—One Year Ago—Death of a Child—The Angels of Grief—The King Hath Sent for the Children—The Good Shepherd—Regret, but not Murmur—The Shepherd Carrying the Lambs Before—Over the River—The Death of a Young Girl—A Child's Death—The Little Child and the Ferryman—Passing under the Rod—The Cheerful Giver—The Buds Opening in Heaven—Infant Choirs in Heaven—A Mother's Lament—The Children Coming and Going—Calling His Children Home—Only Sleeping—The Present, Past and Future—Grandfather's Pet—Death of an Infant—Gone Before—Death

of an Infant—Low she Lies—On the Death of my Son—Lucy—The
Death Angel—The Reaper and the Flowers—Bear Them to their Rest
—Of Such is the Kingdom—Christ Receives Children into Heaven—
The Child is with God—Don't Pray to Keep me, Mother Dear—Tears
for the Departed Children—Say not 'Twere a Keener Blow—Lambs
Safely Folded—One Link Gone—The Death of the First-born Child
—Baby's Shoes—Which shall Go ?—Heaven is Full of Children—The
Death of a Child—My Child—Would you Call Him Back ?—Be Reconciled in the Death of a Child........ 181–230

VI. IMMORTALITY.

Immortality—Hope Beyond the Grave—The Dynasty of the Future—The
Upward Tendencies of the Soul—The Hope of Immortality—Insurance and the Future Life—The Desire for Continued Existence—The
Great Hereafter—Little Concern for the Future—The Immortal Life
—The Idea of Man's Immortality Divinely Impressed—Immortality
and Death—The Strain of Immortality—Moral Life Beyond Earth—
This Life an Argument for the Next—A Second Life—Immortal
Flowers—Argument for Immortality from the Heart-life—The Arguments of Plato—The Immortal Spirit—Immortal Light—Through a
Glass Darkly—Christ Brings Immortality to Light—The Immortal
Mind...231–259

VII. THE RESURRECTION.

The Resurrection of Christ—Christ is Risen—The Resurrection of Christ
Attests the Incarnation—Faith in Christ's Resurrection—The Resurrection Morning—A Changed Body—A Risen Christ Victorious—We
do not Worship a Dead Saviour—Raised on the Last Day—Christ's
Resurrection Body—Christ Conquered Death for Us—The Dead Glorified Through Christ—Proof of Christ's Resurrection—Behold
the Place Where They Laid Him—The Resurrection Body—He is not
Here; He is Risen—The Resurrection Morning—The Evening Cloud
—The Resurrection Illustrated—Christ Rose by His own Power—
The Magi and the Resurrection—Christ's Return to Heaven—Jewish
Rabbis on the Resurrection—The Ascension of Christ—Weaving of
Easter Flowers............ 259–290

VIII. HEAVEN.

Heaven—Christ is in Heaven—Reminiscences of the Past in Heaven—
Heaven a Place Prepared by Christ—Heaven a Place—The Eternal
Life Indescribable—Zion our Home—Heaven Indescribable—The Future will Clear up Many Mysteries—The Many Mansions—Future
Revelations—Moral Heroes in Heaven—Who are in Heaven?—From
Glory to Glory—Heaven not a Strange Place—What Makes Heaven
for Us?—They Love us Still—The Better Home—Telegraphing Ahead

to Heaven—The Glories to Come—Heaven a Locality—Heaven a Home Circle—Heaven Above Us—Not Wrong to Speculate About Heaven—Heaven God's Dwelling Place—Who are Fit for Heaven?—At Evening Time it Shall be Light—The City of God for Me—Jesus Interceding in Heaven — Citizens of Heaven — Views of Heaven Changed—The Aristocracy of Heaven—The Heavenly City—The "Open Sesame" to Heaven—Jesus in Heaven—Heaven Sought Through Trouble—Progression in Heaven—Saints in Full View of Heaven—Harriet Newell, Rev. David Simpson, Henry Martyn, Richard Baxter, Rev. Wilbur Fisk, D. D., Lord Bacon, Rev. Richard Watson, Samuel Rutherford, Mr. McLaren, Rev. S. R. Bangs, John Howard—Various Views of Future Happiness—Money Cannot Buy Heaven—Many Mansions—Joy in Heaven—Heaven and Eternal Life—New Powers in Heaven—Martyrs in Heaven—No Night in Heaven—Worship in Heaven—The Soul's Power in Heaven—The New Song—No Regret in Heaven—The Heavenly Country—Scripture Names in Heaven—No Death in Heaven—The True Heaven—Beyond the Grave—Employments of Heaven—Knowing By-and-by—Joys of Heaven—No Night in Heaven—Jesus is Present in Heaven—No Fear in Heaven—No Sorrow in Heaven—Paradise—Heaven our Home—Heaven a Happy Place—Heaven—Attractions of Heaven—No More Sea—The Shore of Eternity—The New Jerusalem..............291–378

IX. RECOGNITION.

Recognition of Friends in Heaven—Summary of Reasons for Recognition—Isolation and Future Union—Shall we Know Each Other?—Expectation of Meeting Friends—Friends will be Known in Heaven—Calvin—We Live in Hope of Seeing Friends Again—The Strong Immortal Hope—The Future Life—Friends and Enemies Meet in Heaven—Our Departed Friends are in Heaven—Recognition a Truly Catholic Idea—Dying Friends Pioneers—The Departed Preserve their Integrity—More Friends in Heaven than on Earth—Joy of Pastor and People in Heaven—Belief of the Hebrews—The Upward Procession—Remembrance of the Dead—I See Thee Still—Messages to the Other Side—We Shall Know One Another—Gone, but not Lost—Not Lost, but Gone Before—What a Meeting in Heaven—We Mourn not without Hope—Heaven a Place of Joy—Recognition not a Fancy—We Shall Know Each Other in Heaven—Belief of Melancthon, Cruciger, Olevianus, Scaliger—The Question of Recognition Unnecessary—We Shall Know Each Other in Glory—I Shall Know Him—How Shall we Know Each Other in Heaven?—The Belief of the Fathers—The Departed Remember—Heaven and Earth—But a Little While—Friends not Lost—The Separation Short—The Pleasing Hope of Recognition—A Well-founded Hope—Recognition in Heaven a Fact—Recognition no Day-dream—Love Indestructible—Heathen Views of Recognition—What shall we Be?—Not Strangers to Each Other..379–422

X. ANGELIC MINISTRY.

Angels the Escort to Heaven—The Interest of Angels in Men—The Angels Desire to Look into Salvation—Why Men Deny Angelic Existence—The Poor Dying Girl—Views of Wesley, Oberlin, and Clark—Children under Care of Angels—Earth-angels and Heaven-angels—The Nation's Guardian Angels—The Bodies of Angels—An Angel Standing by—Angels are in Heaven—Angelic Sympathy—Three Little Angels—Heliodorus Punished in the Temple—The Angels Coming for St. Cecilia—Hooker's Meditation on the Angels—The Heavenly Host of Angels—Angels Attendant upon Man—Angelic Sympathy Needed—Unseen Companions—Guardian Angels—Sympathy of Angels—Angels not Unembodied Spirits—How Loving are the Angels to Men—Ministering Angels in Holy Scriptures—The Angel of Patience—Fallen Angels.......................... ...423-456

XI. SAINTLY SYMPATHY.

Our Beloved—Communion of the Dead with the Living—The Sainted Dead Lead us Heavenward—The Sainted Dead Interested in Us—The Shining Ones—Degrees of Bliss in Heaven—Sainted Friends—The Sainted Watchers—The Sainted Dead Interested in the Living—Communion with the Departed—The Departed Anxious for Us—The Memory of the Sainted Dead—The Cloud of Witnesses—Communion with the Departed—They are Perfectly Blest—My Two Angel Boys—Our Coming Life—The Grafted Bud—Help from those Fallen Asleep—The Heavenly Host—Entering at the Celestial Gates—Personality and Consequent Sympathy of the Departed—The Sympathy of the Two Worlds—The Departed Remember—What a Meeting in Heaven—The Dear Love of Old—Saintly Sympathy—Love Unites us Again—Come up Hither—Will you Write About me, Mother?—A Blind Girl's Dream—I am the Mother, 'tis Best—The Spirit Retains its Human Form—The Dead are with Us—The Departed Still Ours—Cowper's Grave—Departed Friends near Us—The Departed Employed on Ministries of Love—We do not Lose Departed Friends—The Voices of the Dead—The Family in Heaven and Earth—The Child and the Mourners—The Happier Sphere—Ties not Broken in Death—The Family in Heaven and in Earth—The Sainted Dead..457-512

THE REV. T. DE WITT TALMAGE, D. D.

ILLUSTRATIONS.

	PAGE.
The Rt. Rev. Samuel Fallows, D. D	2
The Rev. T. DeWitt Talmage, D. D.	12
Metropolitan Tabernacle, Spurgeon's	34
D. L. Moody	42
John G. Whittier	54
Alfred Tennyson	62
The Rev. Charles H. Spurgeon	70
The Pastor's College, Spurgeon's	80
Death on the Pale Horse	88
The Destruction of the Assyrians	100
The Rev. W. Augustus Muhlenburg, D D	114
Death of the Widow's Daughter	134
Moses. (By Michael Angelo)	154
Rev. David Swing, D. D.	159
Joseph Addison	166
Bishop Gilbert Haven, D. D.	172
The Rev. Arthur Penryhn Stanley, D. D. (Late Dean of Westminster)	174
The Brooklyn Tabernacle, T. DeWitt Talmage	182
The Rev. Charles Wesley	192
William Cowper	196
Henry W. Longfellow	220
Edmund Spenser	230
The Raising of Jairus' Daughter	232
David Freidrich Strauss	250
Ecce Homo	260
The Agony in the Garden	270
The Burial of Christ	276
He is not Here, He is Risen	280
The Coming Forth of Lazarus	284
The Ascension of Christ	288
The Land Which is Afar off	292

LIST OF ILLUSTRATIONS.

	PAGE.
The Rev. Theodore L. Cuyler, D. D.	300
The Rev. John Keble	316
The Rev. F. W. Farrar, D. D, Canon of Westminster	324
Henry Kirke White	340
The Cottage in Which Mr. Spurgeon Preached his First Sermon	352
There Shall be no More Sea	372
William Cullen Bryant	380
The Rev. Wm. Ormiston, D. D	390
William Shakespeare	396
Dante	414
Robert Southey	418
Jacob's Dream	424
The Angel Announcing the Birth of Christ	432
The Angels Coming for St. Cecilia	438
Heliodorus Punished in the Temple	440
The Angelic Host	444
Attendant Angels	448
The Rev. John Hall, D.D.	453
Westminster Abbey	456
Jacob Wrestling with the Angel	466
The Guardian Angel	468
Rev. Henry W. Bellows, D. D.	484
John Milton	492
The Translation of Elijah	494
Bishop D. W. Clark, D. D.	502

AUTHORS AND WRITERS QUOTED.

A

Achilles	420
Adams, John Quincy	230
Addison, Joseph	165
Adkins, E., Rev. Dr.	368
Adler, Felix	64, 66
Aiken	331
Aiken, Wm., Rev. Dr.	505
Ajax	420
Akenside	241
Alger, W. R.	110, 118, 248, 295, 334
Antigone	420
Aristotle	72
Augustine, St.	39
Anaxagoras	72
Angelo, Michael	73
Anquetil	74
Arbuthnot, Dr.	49
Arch, John	395
Arnold, Edwin (Light of Asia)	202, 203

B

Bacon, Francis, Lord	73, 328
Bacon, Roger	73
Bailey, Philip James	66
Bangs, S. B., Rev.	330
Barnes, Albert	75, 443
Barton, Bernard	371
Bascom, H. Bishop	301
Bateman, Dr	148
Baxter, Richard	327, 385
Bayne, Peter	49
Bayly, T. H.	219
Becon, Thomas	400
Beale, Prof.	285
Beattie, James, Dr.	241
Beecher, Henry Ward	77, 306, 497
Bellows, H. W., Rev. Dr.	485
Bennett, William C.	224
Bentham	73
Bentley, Richard	72
Bernard of Clairvaux	107
Bethune, Geo. W., Rev. Dr.	211, 213, 431
Beza	72
Bickersteth, E. H., Rev	299
Blackwood's Magazine	222
Blair, Hugh, Rev. Dr.	165, 256
Blumhart	148
Bolingbroke, Lord	234
Bonar, Horatius, Rev.	210, 378
Brown, J. B.	76
Browne, Thomas, Sir	53
Browning, Elizabeth Barrett	69, 498
Bryant, William Cullen	75, 195, 392
Buffon	73
Bulmer	326, 328
Bunsen, Baron	266
Bunyan, John	467
Burgess, Geo., Rt. Rev. Dr.	404, 405, 475
Burleigh, William H.	194
Burns	53
Bushnell, Horace, Rev. Dr.	342
Brozurgi	95
Byron	73, 99

C

Caird, John, Rev.	93
Calvin, John	386
Camerarius	405
Campbell, Thomas	255, 331
Campbell, Dr.	420
Cardan	74
Carlyle, Thos.	36
Carneades	71
Carpenter, W. B., Dr.	40
Cato	75, 420
Cecil, Richard	325

LIST OF AUTHORS AND WRITERS QUOTED.

Chalmers, Thomas, Dr. 74, 184
Chambers' Journal. 205
Cherubini 74
Chrysippus. 71
Cicero. 333, 420
Clark 245
Clark, D. W., Bishop . 148, 430, 431, 495
Clarke, James Freeman, Rev. Dr. . 489
Clarke, Rufus W., Rev. Dr. 373
Clarke, James F., Rev. 202
Claude. 73
Cobbe, Frances Power 142
Coke, Lord. 73
Coleridge, Samuel Taylor. 60
Conder 180
Cook, Joseph. 277
Cookman, Alfred, Rev. 140
Cooper, W. H., Rev. Dr., 310, 397,
.... 420, 422, 480
Copernicus 73
Cornaro, Lewis. 71
Collins, Anthony. 162
Cornoval. 148
Cotton 179
Cowper, William 165, 190
Coxe 162
Cranmer, Archbishop 179
Crebillon. 73
Crocker, B. F., Prof. 254
Crosby, Howard, Rev Dr. ... 296, 445
Cruciger 405
Cumberland 73
Cumming, John, Rev. Dr. 125
Cunningham, Allan. 226, 230
Cuyler, T. L., Rev. 124, 203, 302
Cyprian. 387

D

Damiani, Peter. 388
Dana, Mary S. B., Mrs. 198, 214
Dana, Jas. B., Prof. 37, 38
Dante. 215
Davies, John, Sir. 41
Davy, Humphrey, Sir 78
Democritus. 71
Denison, Mrs. 494
Dewey, Orville, Rev. Dr. .. 97, 1 1, 105

Dickens, Charles. 132
Dick, Thos., Rev. Dr. . 320, 405, 435, 447
Diogenes. 71
Dix, Morgan, Rev. Dr. 44
Dobell, Sidney. 488
Doddridge, Philip, Dr. 186, 215, 413, 415
.... 451
Drelincourt, Charles, Rev. 400
Duff, Mc., Rev. Dr. 469
Durer, Albert. 73
Dyer, Sidney, Rev. Dr 95, 104
Dykes, J. Oswald, Rev. Dr. ... 111, 307

E

Eadie, John, Rev. Dr. 274
Edmeston 508
Edmonson, J. E., Rev. 348, 353, 361,
.... 365, 366, 369, 406, 410
Edwards, Jonathan, Rev. Dr. 411
Elam, Charles, Dr. 39, 50, 71
Elliott, Charlotte. 119
Elizabeth, Charlotte. 170
Emerson 53
Epimenides 71
Erasmus 74
Erskine 204
Eudemus. 285
Euripides 71, 333
Evans, Christine, Rev. ....
Everett, Edward 237

F

Faber. 303
Faber, F. W., Rev. Dr. 377, 412
Fallows, Samuel, Rt. Rev., 140, 142,
155, 233, 261, 264, 266, 268, 270,
.... 381, 425, 429
Farel 386
Farningham, Marianne. 478
Farrar, F. W., Rev. Dr. 43, 279
Fenelon. 402
Ferguson, Adam. 73
Fisk, Wilbur, Rev. Dr. 328
Fleury, Cardinal. 74
Fontenelle. 73, 74
Forrester, Fanny. 178, 200
Foss, Cyrus, Bishop. 427
Foster, R. S., Bishop. .. 35, 51, 355, 503

LIST OF AUTHORS AND WRITERS QUOTED.

Fowler, Chas. H., Rev. Dr., 358, 430, 492
Franklin, Dr. 52
Fuerbach 109
Fuseli 73

G

Galen 71
Galileo 73
Gascoigne 103
Gerok, Charles, Rev. Dr. 317
Gill, T. H. 500
Goethe 73, 287
Goldoni 73
Goodell, C. L., Rev. Dr. 63
Goodwin, E. P., Rev. Dr. 268
Goodwin, T. A., Rev. Dr. 142
Gorgias 71
Gough, John B. 59
Grant 330
Gray, John 101
Greenwood, F. W. P., Rev. Dr., 394, 490
Gregory, Nyssen 39
Guthrie, Rev. Dr., 94, 103, 107, 109, 155, 200, 273, 285

H

Hale, Matthew, Sir 165
Hall, John, Rev. Dr. 454
Hall, Robert, Rev. 413
Halley 74
Halsey, Leroy J., Rev. 191
Hamilton, William, Sir 45
Hamline, L. L., Bishop 345
Handel 74
Harbaugh, H., Rev. Dr., 395, 433, 464, 470, 471, 475
Harvey 73
Hastings, Elizabeth, Lady 148
Haven, Gilbert, Bishop 123
Havergal, R., Frances, Miss 110
Haydn 74
Hayne, Paul E. 354
Hazlitt 52
Heber, Reginald, Bishop, 79, 214, 435
Heberden 73
Hedge, F. H., Prof. 482
Hemans, Mrs. 162, 190, 391

Henry, Matthew 170
Hepworth, George H., Rev. Dr. 370
Heraclitus 333
Herbert, George 415
Herodicus 71
Herodotus 234
Herschel 73
Heyne 72
Hickok, Laurens B., Rev. Dr. 45
Hippocrates 71
Hitchcock, R. D., Prof. 64
Hobart, John Henry, Bishop, 271, 420
Hobbes 72, 73
Homer 420
Hood, Thomas 84
Howard, John 331
Huie, Richard, Dr. 209, 402, 415
Hunt, Leigh 151
Huntington, C. 323
Huss, John 176
Hutton 73
Huxley, Prof. 50

I

Isocrates 71

J

James, John, Rev. Dr. 403
Jameson, Mrs. 446
Jay, William, Rev. 388
Jerekiah, Rabbi 287
Jerome 334
Jerome of Prague 176
Johnson, Dr. 74
Julian, Emperor 333

K

Kant 73
Keble, John, Rev. 313
Ken, Bishop 417
King, Thomas Starr, Rev. 59, 122
Kinney, Elizabeth C., Mrs. 225
Kipp, P. E., Rev. 252
Klopstock 177
Knapp, George C., Dr. 391
Kneller 73

LIST OF AUTHORS AND WRITERS QUOTED.

L

Lamartine	398
Landor	164
Laplace	73
Latimer, Bishop	175
Lavel	402
Leighton, Archbishop	203
Leroy, M.	73
Le Sage	73
Leyburn, John, Rev. Dr.	57
Lickenback, W. H., Rev.	315
Liddon, H. P., Canon, Rev. Dr., 102,	112, 244
Linnæus	73
Locke, John	73, 162
Longfellow, Henry W.	121, 157, 212
Longfellow, Marian	116
Lordat, M.	73
Lowell, Maria W.	190
Lowenhoeck	73
Luther	385

M

MacLeod, Norman, Rev. Dr.	249
Macrobius	333
MacDonald, George, Rev.	126
Madden, Dr.	72
Mahomet	64
Mahan, Asa, Rev. Dr.	356
Mansfield, Lord	73
Mant, Bishop	419
Martineau, James, Rev.	124
Martyn, Henry	327
Mather, Cotton	189
McClelland, Alexander, Rev. Dr.	104
McDuff, J. R., Rev. Dr.	323
McLain, Dr.	148
McLaren, Mr.	330
Melancthon	405
Melville, H., Rev. Canon	275, 447
Metastasio	73
Methusaleh	75
Miller, Hugh	241
Millman, Dean	469
Milton, John	73, 229, 333, 429, 436
Minos	420
Mivart	40
Mondalesco	75
Monsell, John S. B.	224
Montgomery, James	180, 201, 401
Moody, D. L., 92, 103, 117, 156, 158, 197, 267, 269, 272, 297, 298, 312, 313, 318, 319, 320, 335, 344, 386, 389, 431, 436	
Moore, Daniel, Rev.	308
Moore, Henry	247
Morata, Olympia	148
More, Hannah	149, 325
Morgagni	74
Muhlenberg, Wm. Augustus, Rev.,	115

N

Naude	73
Neander	72, 458, 473
Neoptholemus	420
Nevin, J. W., Rev. Dr.	391
Newell, Harriet	326
Newman	215
Newman, J. H., Cardinal	85
Newton, Isaac, Sir	73, 153
Newton, John, Rev.	229, 402
Nollekens	73
Norris, John	164
Norton, Mrs.	208

O

Oberlin	430
Olevianus, Casper	405
Olin, Dr.	155
Opie, Amelia	130
Ormiston, Wm., Rev. Dr.	317
Orpheus	420

P

Paley, Wm., Archdeacon	394
Paul, Jean	239, 242
Parker, Theodore	249
Parr	72
Pascal	36
Payson, Edward, Rev. Dr.	155
Peabody, A. P., Prof.	393, 459
Philo	118
Phrenological Journal	207
Pierpont, John	227
Pighius	72
Pinchas, Rabbi	287

Pindar 71
Pinel 74
Planche, J. R. 153
Plato 52, 71, 234, 254
Pliny 72
Pollok, Robert 426
Polybius 71
Polycarp 180
Porphyry 333
Porter, Noah, President 257
Potts, J. H., Rev. Dr. 140
Power 303
Priestly, Dr. 334
Priest, N. A. W., Mrs. 193, 366
Prime, S. I., Rev. Dr. 229, 496
Prior 86
Punshon, William Morley, Rev. Dr. 416
Pythagoras 71, 333

Q

Quarles, Francis 83
Quatrefages, Prof. 38
Quersonnieres, des M. 73
Quintillian 71

R

Rabelais 73
Rabrichebbo, Rabbi 287
Raleigh, Walter, Sir 164
Randolph, A. D. F. 185
Reid, D. M., Rev. 323
Reid, T. 73
Reylance, J. H., Rev. Dr. 53
Rhadamanthus 420
Richards, William C. 217
Ridley, Bishop 175
Robertson, F. W., Rev. 55
Rollin 74
Rowe, Mrs. 329
Rutherford, Samuel 329
Ruysch 74

S

Sanderson, N. I. M., Mrs. 491
Saunders, Lawrence 177
Scaliger, Joseph 72, 405
Schaff, Philip, Rev. Dr. 112
Schmacker, S. S., Rev. Dr. 403

Scott, Rev. Dr. 215
Scott, Sir Walter 253
Scudder, H., Rev. Dr. 99
Seneca 72
Shakespeare 37
Shauffler, D., Rev. 191
Shelton, John, Sir 178
Sheridan, R. B. 195
Shillaber, B. P. 479
Sigourney, L. H., Mrs. 199, 207
Simpson, David, Rev. 326
Simpson, Matthew, Bishop, 117, 246,
.... 401, 428, 472, 476, 487, 501
Sirmond, Father 73
Smiles, Samuel 122
Smith, Adam 52
Smith, Henry B., Rev. Dr. 156
Smyth, Thomas, Rev. Dr. 403
Socrates 71
Sophocles 71
South, Dr. 74
Southern, Thomas 73
Southey, Mrs. 67
Southey, Robert 52, 417, 419
Spear, Sam T., Rev. Dr. 120
Spenser 207
Spitta, Charles J. P. 421
Sprague, Charles 398
Spring, Gardner, Rev. Dr. 278
Spurgeon 79, 89, 106, 110, 449, 486
Stanley, Dean 84, 119, 441, 442
Steele, Annie 258
Stevens, Abel, Rev. Dr. 160
Stevens, R. S., Rev. Dr. 313
Stewart, D. 73
Stilling 412, 487
Stone, Ellen, Mrs. 400
Storrs, R. S., Rev. Dr. 307, 315
Stowe, Harriet Beecher 186
Swift, Dean 74
Swing, David, Prof. 242, 251

T

Talmage, T. DeWitt, Rev. Dr., 75, 82,
91, 105, 108, 121, 131, 156, 157, 243,
277, 286, 304, 305, 309, 311, 313, 320,
321, 334, 384, 390, 399, 434, 438.

LIST OF AUTHORS AND WRITERS QUOTED.

Taylor, George Lansing, Rev. Dr.. 266
Taylor, Isaac..................... 334
Taylor, Rowland, Dr............. 178
Tennyson, Alfred..........68, 409
Theophilus...................... 333
Theophrastus..................71, 75
Theopompus...................... 289
Thomas, H. W., Rev. Dr.....252, 283
Thompson, J. P., Rev. Dr........ 41
Thucydides...................... 72
Tillotson, Archbishop............ 389
Tissot, M....................... 71
Titian.......................... 74
Trench, Archbishop.............. 366
Trumbull, H. Clay............... 504
Tully........................... 39
Turner, Rev. Dr................. 161

U

Ursinus......................... 405

V

Varro........................... 71
Vaughn, C. J., Rev. Dr.......... 482
Virgil..................333, 392
Voltaire........................ 73
Vossius......................... 72

W

Walker.......................... 52
Waller................74, 153, 327
Wastell, Samuel................. 131
Watson, Richard, Rev.......329, 341

Watts, Dr 74, 167
Watts, James.................... 74
Webster, Daniel.............204, 237
Weed, Thurlow................... 75
Wesley, Charles........169, 176, 188
Wesley, John................73, 167
Whiston......................... 73
White, Henry Kirke.............. 170
Whitfield....................... 160
Whittier, J. G........55, 188, 452, 480
Wilcox.......................... 167
Wild, Joseph, Rev. Dr........... 272
Williams........................ 187
Williams, W. R., Rev. Dr........ 98
Willis, N. P.................... 69
Wilmot.......................... 73
Wilson, Bishop.................. 148
Wilson, John, Prof.............. 282
Winceslaus, Viscount............ 178
Winslow......................... 74
Wishart, George, Rev............ 177
Wordsworth 328

X

Xenophon........................ 71

Y

Young, Edward,73, 77, 149, 164,165,
175, 176, 180, 248, 330, 331, 391, 454

Z

Zeno............................ 71
Zwinger......................... 329

General Index.

A

A Blind Girl's Dream	493
A Changed Body—Rev. E. P. Goodwin, D. D.	267
A Child's Death—R. B. Sheridan	195
A Mother's Lament—James Montgomery	201
An Angel Standing By—Bishop Heber	435
Angelic Ministry	425
Angelic Sympathy—John Milton	436
Angelic Sympathy Needed—Harbaugh	443
Angels Attendant upon Man—Rev. Albert Barnes	442
Angels in Heaven—D. L. Moody	436
Angels not Unembodied Spirits—Rev. Dr. Dick	447
Angels our Escort to Heaven—Rt. Rev. Samuel Fallows, D. D.	425
Archbishop Cranmer	179
Argument for Immortality from the Heart-Life—H. W. Thomas, D. D.	252
A Risen Christ Victorious—Bishop Fallows	268
A Second Life—Prof. David Swing	251
Asleep in Jesus—Rev. Theodore L. Cuyler, D. D.	124
A Stingless Death—Rev. J. Oswald Dykes, D. D	111
At Evening Time It Shall be Light—Rev. W. K. Lickenback	314
Atoms and Consciousness—Felix Adler	65
Attractions of Heaven—Bernard Barton	371
A Well-Founded Hope—George Herbert	415

B

Baby's Shoes—Wm. C. Bennett	224
Bear Them to Their Rest—Rev. George W. Bethune, D. D.	213
Belief of Melancthon, Cruciger, Olevianus, and Scaliger—Rt. Rev. Geo. Burgess, D. D.	405
Belief of the Hebrews—John Arch	395
Behold the Place Where They Laid Him—Rev. Canon H. Melville, D. D.	275
Be Reconciled in the Death of the Child.—Rev. John Newton	229
Beyond the Grave—Bishop R. S. Foster, D. D	355
Bishop D. W. Clark—Bishop Fallows	139
Bishops Ridley and Latimer	175
Body and Soul—Rev. Thos. Starr King	59
Brevity of Life—Francis Quarles	83

Bringing the Children Home—D. L. Moody............................. 157
Building up Life—J. B. Brown 76
Burial of Moses............. 128
But a Little While—Melville 413

C

Calling His Children Home—Rev. T. L. Cuyler, D. D.............. 203
Calvin—John Calvin's Letter to Farel.................................. 386
Can I Wish It Back—Philip Doddridge, D. D........................... 186
Charlotte Elizabeth—Henry Kirke White............................. 170
Children Under Care of Angels—Rev. Dr. Bethune............ 431
Christ Brings Immortality to Light.—President Noah Porter, D. D. LL. D. 257
Christ Conquered Death for Us.—Rev. Joseph Wild, D. D.............. 272
Christ Is in Heaven.—D. L. Moody........ 295
Christ is Risen.—Rt. Rev. Samuel Fallows, D. D.... 264
Christ Receives Children Into Heaven.—Rev. Dr. Doddridge............ 215
Christ's Return to Heaven.—Rev. T. DeWitt Talmage, D. D........ 286
Christ Rose By His Own Power.—Rev. Dr. Guthrie........ 285
Christ's Resurrection Body.—D. L. Moody............................. 273
Citizens of Heaven.—Charles Gerok, D. D. (Germany)........... 317
Come Up Hither.—Rev. F. W. P. Greenwood, D. D................. 490
Communion of the Dead with the Living—Rev. Prof. A. P. Peabody, D. D. 459
Communion with the Departed—Bishop Pearson................ 473
Communion with the Departed.—Rt. Rev. Geo. Burgess, D. D 475
Contrasts in Death.—Rev. Sidney Dyer, D. D......... 104
Cowper's Grave—Elizabeth Barrett Browning... 498

D

Darwinism and Man.—Peter Bayne 49
Daughter of Rev. T. A. Goodwin, D. D.—Bishop Fallows................ 142
Death According to Philo.—Quoted by Alger............................ 118
Death a Divine Message—Rev. James Martineau....................... 123
Death an Angel of Light.—Rev. Sidney Dyer, D. D..................... 95
Death and Immortality.—George Gascoigne............................ 103
Death and its Warnings.—D. L. Moody....   92
Death a Transition.—Longfellow.. 120
Death Binds us Together.—Samuel Smiles......... 122
Death Does Not End All.—Rev. H. Scudder, D. D. 98
Death Has Lost its Terror.—Rev. Philip Schaff, D. D................... 111
Death is Life.—Rev. Dr. Guthrie.. 94
Death is Yours.—Rev. John Caird, D. D................................. 93
Death of a Child.—Charles Wesley....................................... 188
Death of an Infant......... 206
Death of an Infant.—Mrs. L. H. Sigourney........................ 207
Death of Children 181
Death of Garfield.—Talmage...... 131
Death of the Good Man.—Robert Blair................................... 106

GENERAL INDEX.

Death Overcome.—Rev. Dr. Guthrie.................................... 103
Death Pangs, Birth Pangs.—Rev. Dr. Guthrie........................ 107
Death the Destroyer and the Restorer —Rev. W. R. Williams, D. D...... 98
Death the Fiat of God.—Rev. Canon H. P. Liddon, D. D............... 112
Death the Gate of Life—Rev. Orville Dewey, D. D.................... 105
Definitions of Man. —Adam Smith..................................... 52
Degrees of Bliss in Heaven.—Rev. J. A. McDuff, D. D................ 469
Departed Friends Near Us.—Bishop M. Simpson....................... 501
Destruction of the Assyrians.—Byron................................. 99
Don't Pray to Keep Me, Mother Dear.—William C. Richards........... 217
Dr. Guthrie.—Bishop Fallows... 155
Dr. Lowell Mason—Bishop Fallows.................................... 139
Dr. Rowland Taylor.. 178
Dying Friends Pioneers.—Young....................................... 391

E

Earth Angels and Heaven Angels.—Rev. H. Harbaugh, D D............. 433
Employments of Heaven.—Rev. Asa Mahan.............................. 356
Entering in at the Celestial Gates.................................. 483
Evolution and Life.—Prof. R. D. Hitchcock, D. D.................... 64
Excitement and Short Life... 74
Expectation of Meeting Friends.—Rev. Richard Baxter................ 385

F

Faith in Christ's Resurrection.—Bishop Fallows..................... 266
Fallen Angels.—Rev. John Hall, D.D.................................. 455
Farewell Life.—Thomas Hood.. 84
Felicia Hemans.. 162
Fill up the Ranks.—Rev. John Cumming, D. D......................... 125
Folding the Lambs in His Bosom.—Talmage............................ 157
Friends and Enemies Meet in Heaven.—Archbishop Tillotson........... 389
Friends not Lost.—Rev. Robert Hall.................................. 413
Friends Will be Known in Heaven.—D. L. Moody....................... 386
From Glory to Glory.—H. W. Beecher.................................. 306
Future Revelations.—Power... 303

G

General Facts of Mind.—Rev. Laurens B. Hickok, D. D................ 45
God Imaged in Man.—Canon Farrar..................................... 43
Going to Jesus.—D. L. Moody... 158
Gone Before.—Phrenological Journal.................................. 206
Gone But not Lost.—Mrs. Ellen Stone................................. 400
Grandfather's Pet.—Chambers' Journal................................ 205
Grateful Testimony.—Rev. Dr. Turner.................................. 161
Guardian Angels —Mrs. Jameson....................................... 446

H

Hannah More.. 325
Harriet Newell.. 326
Heathen Views of Recognition.—R. W. H. Cooper, D. D. 420
Heaven.—Rev. Geo. H. Hepworth, D. D 370
Heaven Above Us.—D. L. Moody............................... 311
Heaven a Happy Place.—Rev. J. Edmonson..................... 369
Heaven a Home Circle.—Talmage............................... 311
Heaven a Locality.—Rev. W. H. Cooper, D. D.................. 310
Heaven and Earth.—F. W. Faber............................... 412
Heaven and Eternal Life.—Rev. Wm. Morley Punshon, D. D. 336
Heaven a Place.—D. L. Moody................................. 297
Heaven a Place of Joy.—Rev. S. S. Schmacker, D. D., Rev. Thos. Smith, D. D.. 403
Heaven a Place Prepared by Christ.—Rev. Howard Crosby, D. D... 296
Heaven God's Dwelling Place.—D. L. Moody.................... 312
Heaven Indescribable.—Bishop Bascom, D. D................... 301
Heaven is Full of Children 226
Heaven not a Strange Place.—Unknown 306
Heaven not Far Away 149
Heaven Our Home.—Rev. E. Adkins, D. D...................... 368
Heaven Sought Through Trouble.—Rev. T. DeWitt Talmage, D. D... 321
He is Not Here: He has Risen.—Canon F. W. Farrar, D. D 280
Heliodorus Punished in the Temple............................ 439
Help from Those Fallen Asleep.—Rev. C. J. Vaughn, D. D...... 482
Henry Martyn.. 327
Hooker's Meditation on the Angels.—Dean Stanley............. 441
Hope Beyond the Grave.—James Beattie, LL. D................ 240
How Loving are the Angels to Men.—Rev. C. H. Spurgeon...... 449
How Shall We Know Each Other in Heaven.—Rev. J. Edmonson, D. D.. 410

I

I am the Mother, 'Tis Best.—Mrs. Denison..................... 494
If We Could all Die Together.—Rev. T. DeWitt Talmage, D. D.... 121
Immortal Flowers 251
Immortality.—Rt. Rev. Samuel Fallows, D. D.................. 233
Immortality and Death.—Edward Young........................ 247
Immortal Light.. 255
Incorrect Views of the Soul—Sir John Davies................. 41
Infant Choirs in Heaven 200
Inseparable Fellowship.—Neander 392
Insurance and the Future Life.—Rev. T. DeWitt Talmage, D. D.. 243
Into Thy Hands I Commend My Spirit.—Geo. MacDonald......... 126
Isaac Watts, D. D... 167
I Shall Know Him.—Tennyson................................. 409
Is Memory Annihilated.—Rev. Wm. Jay........................ 388

Isolation and Future Union...... 383
I Would not Live Alway.—William Augustus Muhlenburg, D. D........ 115

J

Jerome of Prague.—Young... 176
Jesus in Heaven.—Rev. Dr. Talmage.. 320
Jesus Interceding in Heaven.—Rev. Wm. Ormiston, D. D............... 317
Jesus is Present in Heaven.. 363
Jesus the Precious Name in Death.—Talmage............................... 108
Jewish Rabbis on the Resurrection... 287
John Howard.. 331
John Huss.—C Wesley.. 176
John Locke.—Coxe 162
John Wesley's Old Age.. 81
John Wesley.—Wilcox... 167
Joseph Addison... 165
Joy in Heaven.—D. L. Moody 335
Joys of Heaven.—Nancy A. W. Priest....................................... 360
Joy of Pastor and People in Heaven.—Rev. H. Harbaugh, D. D.......... 395

K

Knowing By and By.—Rev. C. H. Fowler, LL.D........................... 358

L

Lambs Safely Folded.—Rev. Dr. Bethune.................................... 219
Lawrence Saunders.—Klopstock... 177
Life a Journey.—Rev C. L. Goodell, D. D................................... 63
Life and Death.—Edward Young... 77
Life a River.—Sir Humphrey Davy... 78
Life a Stream.—Bishop Heber.. 79
Life is for Character, and Character for Immortality.—Cardinal J. H. Newman.. 85
Life is Passing.—Spurgeon... 79
Life, New and Old.—H. W. Beecher.. 77
Life One Great Ritual.—Philip James Bailey............................... 66
Life's Discipline a Training for Heaven.—Sir Humphrey Davy.......... 78
Life the Time for Work.—Elizabeth Barrett Browning..................... 69
Little Bessie.—A. D. F. Randolph 184
Little Concern for the Future.—Bishop M. Simpson....................... 246
Live and Help Live.—Alice Cary... 68
Longevity of Studious and Busy Men.—Charles Elam, M. D. M. R. C. P. 71
Long Life and Hard Study.. 74
Lord Bacon... 328
Lord Viscount Winceslaus... 178
Love Indestructible.—Robert Southey....................................... 419
Love Unites Us Again.—Rev. James Freeman Clarke, D. D............... 489

Low She Lies.—Mrs. Norton... 208
Lucy.—Rev. Horatius Bonar, D. D..................................... 210

M

Man and Nature.—Prof. James D. Dana................................ 37
Man, Animal and Rational.—Mivart................................... 40
Man a Reed that Thinks.—Pascal..................................... 36
Man a Temple of Heaven.—Carlyle.................................... 36
Man, Body and Spirit.—Prof. James D. Dana.......................... 37
Man, Body, Soul and Spirit.—Rev. F. W. Robertson................... 55
Man Not a Mere Animal.—Prof. Quatrefages........................... 38
Man on the Darwinian Theory.—Bishop Randolph Foster, D. D.......... 51
Man Redeemable.—Samuel Taylor Coleridge............................ 60
Man Separated from the Animals.—Rev. J. P. Thompson, D. D.......... 41
Man's Mortality.—Simon Wastell..................................... 131
Man's Nobility.—Shakespeare.. 37
Man Superior to the Brute.—Rev. Morgan Dix, D. D................... 43
Man the Child of God—Bishop R. S Foster, D. D...................... 35
Many Mansions.—Isaac Taylor.. 334
Martyred Heroes.—William Cowper.................................... 173
Martyrs in Heaven.—Rev. T. DeWitt Talmage.......................... 337
Material Processes and Life.—Felix Adler........................... 64
Matthew Henry.—Young... 170
Messages to the Other Side.—Rev. Dr. Talmage....................... 399
Metaphors of Life.—Prior... 86
Mind Not the Result of Organization.—Rev. John Leyburn, D. D....... 57
Mind Preserves its Integrity Amid the Decay of the Body.—C. Elam, M. D. 50
Ministering Angels in Holy Scriptures.—Philip Doddridge, D. D...... 451
Money Cannot Buy Heaven.—Talmage................................... 334
Moral Heroes in Heaven. Rev. Dr. Talmage........................... 304
Moral Life Beyond Earth.—Rev. Norman MacLeod, D. D................. 249
More Friends in Heaven than on Earth.—Rev. F. W. P. Greenwood, D. D. 394
Mozart's Requiem.—Rufus Dawes...................................... 127
Mr. McLaren of Edinburgh... 330
My Child—John Pierpont... 227
My Two Angel Boys.. 479

N

Nature and Man.—John B. Gough...................................... 59
Nearer My Rest—Marian Longfellow................................... 116
New Powers in Heaven.—Rev. Andrew R. Bonar, D. D................... 337
No Death in Heaven.—Rev. J. Edmonson, A. M......................... 353
No Fear in Heaven.—Rev. J. Edmonson, A. M.......................... 365
No Fear of Death.—Bishop M. Simpson, D. D.......................... 117
No More Sea.—Rev. Rufus W. Clark, D. D............................. 373
No Night in Heaven.—Rev R. W. Clark, D. D.......................... 339
No Night in Heaven.—Rev. J. Edmonson............................... 361

No Regret in Heaven.—Bishop L. L. Hamline.................... 345
No Sorrow in Heaven —Edmonson.................................. 365
Not Lost, but Gone Before —Montgomery......................... 401
Not One Life Destroyed.—A. fred Tennyson...................... 67
Not Strangers to Each Other.—Rev. W. H. Cooper, D. D......... 422
Not Wrong to Speculate About Heaven.—D. L. Moody............. 312

O

Of Such is The Kingdom.—Mrs. Mary S. B. Dana.................. 214
One Link Gone.—Unknown.. 221
One Year Ago.—Mrs. H. B. Stowe.................................. 186
Only a Little Brook.—Bishop Fallows............................. 137
Only Sleeping.—Archbishop Leighton.............................. 203
On the Death of a Child.—Allan Cunningham...................... 230
On the Death of a Mother.—Amelia Opie 130
On the Death of My Son.—Richard Huie, M. D..................... 209
Our Beloved... 458
Our Burial Places Sacred.—Rev. Alexander McClelland, D D...... 104
Our Coming Life.—John G. Whittier............................... 480
Our Departed Friends are in Heaven.—D. L. Moody................ 389
Over the River.—Mrs. N. A. W. Priest............................ 193

P

Paradise.—Archbishop Trench..................................... 366
Passing under the Rod.—Mrs. Mary S. B. Dana.................... 198
Personality and Consequent Sympathy of the Departed.—Rev. H. W.
    Bellows, D D.. 485
Polycarp.—Conder 180
Prof. Huxley's One-Sided View.—Prof. Huxley.................... 50
Progression in Heaven.—Rev. D. M. Reid.......................... 325
Proof of Christ's Resurrection.—Rev. John Eadie, D. D. LL. D... 274

R

Raised on the Last Day.—Rt. Rev. Bishop John Henry Hobart, D. D..... 271
Recognition a Truly Catholic Idea.—Rev. J. W. Nevin, D. D...... 391
Recognition of Friends in Heaven................................ 381
Recognition in Heaven.—Peter Damiani............................ 388
Recognition in Heaven a Fact.—Rev. Wm. Morley Punshon, D. D.
    Bishop Ken. Southey... 416
Recognition No Day Dream.—Bishop Mant........................... 419
Recognition Not a Fancy.—Rev. John James, D. D................. 403
Regret but Not Murmur.—William Cowper........................... 190
Remembrances of the Dead.—Lamartine 398
Reminiscences of the Past in Heaven.—Rev. R. S. Storrs, D. D... 295
Rev. Alfred Cookman.—Bishop Fallows 140
Rev. Charles Simeon... 169
Rev. Charles Wesley... 169

GENERAL INDEX.

Rev. David Simpson.. 326
Rev. George Wishart... 177
Rev. Edward Payson, D. D.—Bishop Fallows........................... 155
Rev. Prof. Henry B. Smith, D. D..................................... 156
Rev. Richard Watson... 329
Rev. S. R. Bangs.—Young... 170
Rev. Wilbur Fisk, D. D.. 328
Richard Baxter.. 327
Richard Cecil... 325
Right and Wrong Views of Death.—Prof. A. P. Peabody, D. D........... 96

S

Sainted Friends.—Rev. H. Harbaugh, A. M............................. 470
Saintly Sympathy.—Unknown... 488
Samuel Rutherford.—T. H. Bayly...................................... 169
Say Not 'Twere a Keener Blow.. 218
Scripture Names of Heaven.—Rev. J. E. Edmonson, A. M................ 348
Self and Ego.—Sir Wm. Hamilton...................................... 44
Shall We Know Each Other.—Rev. T. DeWitt Talmage, D. D.............. 384
Shall We Know Each Other.—Luther's Conversation..................... 385
Sir Isaac Newton —Waller.. 153
Sir Matthew Hale.—Blair... 165
Sir Walter Raleigh —Lander.. 164
Summary of Reasons for Recognition.—Rt. Rev. Sam'l Fallows, D. D... 381
Sympathy of Angels—Rev. H. Melville................................. 446

T

Tears for the Departed Children.—Talmage............................ 218
Telegraphing Ahead to Heaven.—D. L. Moody........................... 308
The Angel of Patience.—John G. Whittier............................. 452
The Angels Coming for St. Cecilia................................... 439
The Angels Desire to Look into Salvation.—Bishop M. Simpson, D. D... 428
The Angels of Grief.—J. G. Whittier................................. 188
The Arguments of Plato.—Prof. B. F. Crocker, D. D................... 254
The Aristocracy of Heaven.—D. L. Moody.............................. 318
The Ascension of Christ.—D. L. Moody................................ 289
The Belief of the Fathers—Dr. Edwards............................... 411
The Better Home.—Rev. Daniel Moore, A. M............................ 308
The Blessings of a Short Life.—Rev. T. DeWitt Talmage, D. D......... 75
The Blossom Transplanted.—Dr. Thomas Chalmers....................... 184
The Bodies of Angels.—Rev. Dr. Dick................................. 434
The Body Wrongly Viewed.—Charles Elam, M. D......................... 39
The Buds Opening in Heaven.—Rev. Dr. Guthrie........................ 200
The Cheerful Giver.—Mrs. L. H. Sigourney............................ 199
The Child is Dead.—Rev. Irenæus Prime............................... 183
The Child is with God.—Henry Ward Beecher........................... 216
The Children Coming and Going.—James Freeman Clarke................. 202

GENERAL INDEX.

The City of God for Me.—Rev. R. S. Storrs, D. D.	315
The Cloud of Witnesses.—Rev. H. Harbaugh, D. D.	475
The Cloud of Witnesses.—Bishop Mattnew Simpson, D. D.	476
The Dead and the Living.	113
The Dead are Ours Still—Thomas Starr King	122
The Dead are the Living.—Rev. Orville Dewey, D. D.	97
The Dead are with Us.—Rev. S. I. Prime, D. D.	496
The Dead Glorified through Christ.—Rev. Dr. Guthrie.	273
The Dear Love of Old.—Sydney Dobell.	488
The Death Angel—Geo W. Bethune, D. D.	211
The Death-Day better than the Birth-Day.—Rev. C. H. Spurgeon.	89
The Death of a Child.—Cunningham.	226
The Death of a Good Man.—Spurgeon.	110
The Death of a Young Girl.—William H. Burleigh.	194
The Death of Death.—Rev. Dr. Guthrie, W. R. Alger.	109
The Death of the Apostles.	174
The Death of the First Born Child.—Blackwood's Magazine.	222
The Departed Anxious for Us.—Neander.	473
The Departed Employed on Ministries of Love.—Bishop R. S. Foster.	503
The Departed Preserve Their Integrity.—Prof. A. P. Peabody, D. D.	393
The Departed Remember.—Stilling.	487
The Departed Still Ours.—Rev. H. W. Beecher, D. D.	497
The Desire for Continued Existence.—Rev. Canon H. P. Liddon, D. D.	244
The Divine Element in Evolution.—Rev. J. H. Reylance, D. D.	52
The Dying Child and Her Departed Mother.—Rev. H. Harbaugh, D. D.	138
The Dying Dauphin.—Rev. J. H. Potts, D. D.	140
The Dying Husband.—Leigh Hunt.	151
The Dying Mother.—Robert Pollok.	130
The Dying Seeing Departed Friends.—Rev. T. DeWitt Talmage, D. D.	135
The Dynasty of the Future.—Hugh Miller.	241
The Eternal Life Indescribable.—D. L. Moody.	298
The Evening Cloud.—Professor Wilson	282
The Evening of Death.—Rev. T. DeWitt Talmage.	91
The Family in Heaven and Earth—Edmeston.	508
The Future Life.—W. C. Bryant.	392
The Future Will Clear up Many Mysteries.—Rev. Theo. L. Cuyler, D. D.	302
The Glories to Come.—Dr. Talmage.	309
The Good Shepherd.—Maria W. Lowell.	189
The Grafted Bud	481
The Great Hereafter.—Clark.	245
The Happier Sphere.	509
The Heavenly City.—D. L. Moody.	319
The Heavenly Country.	347
The Heavenly Host—Prof. Frederick H. Hedge, D. D.	482
The Heavenly Host of Angels—Dean Stanley.	441
The Historic Dead.—Rev. Samuel T. Spear, D. D.	120
The Hope of Immortality.—Prof. David Swing.	242

GENERAL INDEX.

The Idea of Man's Immortality Divinely Impressed.—Henry Moore	247
The Immortal Life	246
The Immortal Mind.—Anne Steele	258
The Immortal Spirit.—Thomas Campbell	255
The Interest of Angels in Men.—Bishop Cyrus Foss, D. D	427
The King Hath Sent for the Children.—Cotton Mather	189
The Little Child and the Ferryman.—D. L. Moody	197
The Magi and the Resurrection.—W. R. Alger	285
The Many Mansions.—Faber	303
The Martyrs	173
The Materialistic Hypothesis Repugnant.—Dr. W. B. Carpenter	40
The Memory of the Sainted Dead.—Rev. H. Harbaugh, A. M.	474
The Mother and Her Dying Boy	163
The Nation's Guardian Angels.—Talmage	434
The New Jerusalem.—Rev. Horatius Bonar, D. D	378
The New Song.—D. L. Moody	344
The Open "Sesame" to Heaven.—D. L. Moody	320
The Peak in Darien.—Frances Power Cobbe	142
The Peril of Life—Mrs. Southey	67
The Pleasing Hope of Recognition.—Dr. Doddridge.—R. Hule	415
The Poor Dying Girl.—Rev. C. H. Fowler, D. D	430
The Present Life in View of the Future.—N. P. Willis	69
The Present, Past, and Future.—Daniel Webster	204
The Question of Recognition Unnecessary.—Rev. Dr. Dick	405
The Reaper and the Flowers.—Henry W. Longfellow	212
The Resurrection	259
The Resurrection Body.—Joseph Cook	277
The Resurrection Illustrated.—H. W. Thomas, D. D	283
The Resurrection Morning.—D. L. Moody	266
The Resurrection Morning.—Dr. Talmage	281
The Resurrection of Christ.—Rt. Rev. Samuel Fallows, D. D	261
The Resurrection of Christ Attests the Incarnation.—Rev Geo. Lansing Taylor, D. D	265
The Revelations to the Dying.—Bishop D. W. Clark, D. D	148
The Right View of Death.—D. L. Moody	117
The Sainted Dead	422
The Sainted Dead Interested in the Living.—Bp. Matthew Simpson, D. D.	472
The Sainted Dead Interested in Us.—Rev. H. Harbaugh, A. M	465
The Sainted Dead Lead Us Heavenward.—Rev. H. Harbaugh, A. M.	464
The Sainted Watchers.—Rev. H Harbaugh, A. M	471
The Separation Short.—Dr. Philip Doddridge	413
The Shepherd Carrying the Lambs Before.—Rev. Leroy J. Halsey	191
The Shining Ones—John Bunyan	467
The Shore of Eternity.—Rev. F. W. Faber, D D	377
The Sooner We Go, the Better.—Rev. T. DeWitt Talmage, D. D.	82
The Soul Departing.—Charlotte Elliot	119
The Soul Does Not Sleep.—D. L. Moody	118

The Soul's Power in Heaven.—Rev. Horace Bushnell, D. D............. 342
The Spirit Retains its Human Form.—Bishop D. W. Clark, D. D........ 495
The Spirit Survives its Completeness.—Rev. Canon H. P. Liddon, D. D... 102
The Strain of Immortality.—W. R. Alger............................ 248
The Strong Immortal Hope.. 387
The Sympathy of the Two Worlds.—Rev. C. H. Spurgeon............ 486
The True Heaven.—Paul E. Hayne................................ 354
The Upward Procession.—Rev. W. H. Cooper, D. D................ 397
The Upward Tendencies of the Soul.—Akenside..................... 241
The Voices of the Dead.—Rev. Wm. Aiken, D. D 505
The Voices of the Dead.—Rev. Orville Dewey, D. D............... 101
They are Perfectly Blest.—Marianne Farningham.................... 478
They Love Us Still.—Rev. J. Oswald Dykes, D. D................... 307
This Life an Argument for the Next.—Theodore Parker............... 249
Three Little Angels... 437
Through a Glass Darkly.—Rev. Hugh Blair, D. D 256
Thy Will be Done.. 132
Ties not Broken in Death.—Rev. H. Harbaugh, D. D................ 509
To Live is Christ.—Dean Stanley................................... 84
Toward Evening.—Talmage.. 105
Two Funerals.—Spurgeon.. 106

U

Unseen Companions.—Rev. Howard Crosby, D. D.................. 445

V

Various Views of Future Happiness................................. 333
Victor over Death.—Bishop Gilbert Haven, D. D.................... 123
Views of Heaven Changed... 318
Views of Wesley, Oberlin, and Clark.—D. L. Moody................. 430
Visions of a Dying Youth.—Rev. Thos. Binney, D. D................. 136

W

Weaving of Easter Flowers.—Bishop Fallows........................ 290
We Do Not Lose Departed Friends.—H. Clay Trumbull.............. 504
We Do Not Worship a Dead Saviour.—D. L Moody................ 269
We Live in Hope of Seeing Friends Again.—Cyprian................. 387
We Love to Visit Our Cemeteries.—Rev. Dr. Guthrie 108
We Mourn Not without Hope.—Lavel, Rev. John Newton, Fenelon, R. Huie... 402
We Shall Know Each Other in Glory.—Rev. J. Edmonson............ 406
We Shall Know Each Other in Heaven.—Rt. Rev. Geo. Burgess, D. D... 404
We Shall Know One Another.—Thos. Becon........................ 400
We Shall Reach the Haven.—Dean Stanley......................... 119
What a Meeting in Heaven.—Bishop M. Simpson, D. D.............. 487
What Am I?—Dr. Arbuthnot....................................... 48
What is Death?—Buzurgi (The Persian Poet)....................... 95

What Makes Heaven for Us?—D. L. Moody................................ 307
What Message to Jesus?... 161
What Shall We Be?—Charles J. P. Spitta................................... 421
Which Shall Go?—Mrs. Elizabeth C. Kinney............................... 225
Whitefield's Death.—Rev. Abel Stevens, D. D.............................. 160
Who Are Fit for Heaven?—Rev. R. S. Stevens, D. D...................... 313
Who Are in Heaven?—Rev. Dr. Cummings................................. 305
Why Men Deny Angelic Existence.—Bishop Fallows 429
Will You Write About Me, Mother?—Mrs. N. I. M. Sanderson........... 491
Worship in Heaven.—Rev. Richard Watson................................ 341
Would You Call Him Back?—Rev. S. J. Prime, D. D...................... 228

Z

Zion Our Home.—Rev. E. H. Bickersteth.................................. 299

METROPOLITAN TABERNACLE—SPURGEON'S.

MAN, THE CHILD OF GOD.

BISHOP R. S. FOSTER, D. D.

NOW let us go back to this Artist of the universe, alone; I would like to show how the first infinitesimal stone was laid, and stone upon stone reared, building up in sublime beauty through the millions of years; how He stood before it and viewed it, and compared it with the original. Now I shall go back to that condition of things when there were no forms, no voices, no spirits palpitating with rapturous emotion. God is alone the unoriginated, eternal God, who is now about to disclose what He is, to unfold Himself. There is no intelligence to see Him, but He will make one; He has the thought now of an intelligence that will stand spellbound before that which He will make; that will trace His power, see His wisdom, delight in His order, revel in His glory: He is going to make such a soul as that. He now begins His project: fixes systems of worlds that shall hang upon nothing, that shall flame and flash in fixed orbits, clothed with fashion and forms of beauty and delight to spirits like His own, that shall bow before Him as the Lord that has created all things, thereby manifesting His skill, wisdom, power and eternal Godhead. Now, if you will study Him, you will find that there is something within His soul that is within your soul. See the flowers of creation, carpets of verdure, of beauty; there was that beauty in His mind. See He is designing a complex of confections; He forms the refreshing waters and the delicious fruits. He is kind, thoughtful and loving, more so than a delicate, loving mother to her child.

MAN A TEMPLE OF HEAVEN.

THE essence of our being, the mystery in us that calls itself "I"—ah, what words have we for such things?—is a breath of Heaven; the Highest Being reveals Himself in man. This body, these faculties, this life of ours, is it not all as a vesture for that Unnamed? "There is but one temple in the universe," says the devout Novalis, "and that is the body of man. Nothing is holier than that high form. Bending before men is a reverence done to this revelation in the flesh. We touch heaven when we lay our hand on a human body." This sounds much like a mere flourish of rhetoric; but it is not so. If well meditated, it will turn out to be a scientific fact; the expression, in such words as can be had, of the actual truth of the thing. *We* are the miracle of miracles—the great inscrutable mystery of God. We cannot understand it, we know not how to speak of it; but we feel and know, if we like, that it is verily so.

CARLYLE.

MAN A REED—THAT THINKS.

MAN is but a reed, the frailest in nature; but he is a reed that thinks. It needs not that the whole universe should arm itself to crush him—a vapor, a drop of water, will suffice to destroy him. But should the universe crush him, man would yet be nobler than that which destroys him: for he knows that he dies; while of the advantage which the universe has over him, the universe knows nothing.

PASCAL.

MAN'S NOBILITY.

WHAT a piece of work is a man! How noble in reason! how infinite in faculties! in form and moving, how express and admirable! in action, how like an angel! in apprehension, how like a god! the beauty of the world! the paragon of animals.

SHAKSPEARE.

MAN AND NATURE.

BESIDES these beneficial provisions, the forces and laws of Nature were particularly adapted to Man, and Man to those laws so that he should be able to take the oceans, rivers and winds into his service, and even the more subtle agencies, heat, light and electricity; and the adjustments were made with such precision that the face of the earth is actually fitted hardly less than his own to respond to his inner being; the mountains to his sense of the sublime; the landscape, with its slopes, its trees, its flowers, to his love of the beautiful, and the thousands of living species, in their diversity, to his various emotions and sentiments. The whole world, indeed, seems to have been made almost a material manifestation, in multitudinous forms, of the elements of his own spiritual nature, that it might thereby give wings to the soul in its heavenward aspirings. It may therefore be said with truth that Man's spirit was considered in the ordering of the earth's structure as well as in that of his own body.

PROF. JAMES D. DANA.

MAN—BODY AND SPIRIT.

WITH the creation of man a new era in geological history opens. In earliest time only *matter* existed—dead matter. Then appeared *life*, unconscious life in the plant, conscious and intelligent life in the animal. Ages rolled by, with varied exhibitions of animal and vegetable life. Finally Man appeared, a being made of *matter* and endowed with *life*, but more than this, partaking of a *spiritual nature*. The systems of life belong essentially to time ; but Man, through his spirit, to the opening and infinite future. Thus gifted, Man is the only being capable of reaching toward a knowledge of himself, of nature, or of God. He is, hence, the only being capable of conscious obedience or disobedience of any moral law, the only one subject to degradation through excesses of appetite and violation of moral law, the only one with the will and power to make nature's forces his means of progress.

Prof. James D. Dana.

MAN NOT A MERE ANIMAL.

Like all organic and living beings, man has a body. This body will furnish a first class of characters—the physical characters. Like animals, man is endowed with instinct and intelligence. Though infinitely more developed in him, these characters are not changed in their fundamental nature. They appear in the different human groups in phenomena, sometimes very different, as for instance the different languages. The differences of manifestation of this intelligence will constitute the second class of characters—the intellectual characters.

Finally, it is established that man has two grand faculties, of which we find not even a trace among animals. He alone has the moral sentiments of good and evil; he alone believes in a future existence succeeding this natural life; he alone believes in beings superior to himself, that he has never seen, and that are capable of influencing his life for good or evil.

In other words, man alone is endowed with morality and religion. These two faculties are revealed by his acts, by his institutions, by facts that differ from one group to another, from one race to another. From these is drawn a third class of characters—that of moral and religious characters.

Prof. Quatrefages.

THE BODY WRONGLY VIEWED.

CHARLES ELAM, M. D.

EPICTETUS may well illustrate the views of the philosopher. When severely treated by his master, Epaphroditus, under the most intense agony he smiled, and told him that he would break his leg with twisting it. This actually did occur, but without disturbing his equanimity. On being questioned as to the cause of his astonishing composure, he merely replied that the body was *external*."

THE BODY UNDULY DEPRECIATED.

In the early centuries of the Christian era, the body seemed to be ever of less and less estimation. There is something even amusing in the excess of contempt in which it was held, and the abuse heaped upon it. A prison-house, a cage, a weary load of mortality,—these were, by comparison, complimentary terms. Gregory Nyssen calls it "a fuliginous ill-savored shop, a prison, an ill-savored sink," as the words are translated by an old divine. It is "a lump of flesh which mouldereth away, and draweth near to corruption whilst we speak of it." St. Augustine defines the two natures thus, "Domine, duo, creasti; alterum prope te, alterum prope nihil." At the best, the body was considered a workshop for the soul. The torments of the body were so utterly despised, as scarcely to be considered personal matters:—

> " Tormenta, carcer, ungulæ,
> Stridensque flammis lamina,
> Atque ipsa pœnarum ultima,
> Mors."

In fine, the body was considered the source of all evil, and, as such, worthy of no consideration. The Platonists, as St. Augustine says, "hold that these our mortal members do produce the effects of fear, desire, joy, and sorrow, in our bodies; from which four perturbations (as Tully calls them), or passions, the whole inundations of man's enormities have their source and spring."

The Manicheans put the climax to these reproaches cast upon the body. They maintained that the body was so evil that its creation cannot be ascribed to the same author as that of the soul. Farindon says: "The Manichee, observing that war which is betwixt it (the body) and the soul, alloweth it no better maker than the Devil;" and Ludovicus Vives, to the same effect says: "They held all flesh the work of the Devil, not of God, and therefore they forbade their hearers to kill any creatures, lest they should offend the Prince of Darkness whence they said all flesh had originated.

THE MATERIALISTIC HYPOTHESIS REPUGNANT.

To WHATEVER extent we may be ready to admit the dependence of our Mental operations upon the organization and functional activity of our Nervous System, we must also admit that there is *something beyond and above* all this, to which, in the fully-developed and self-regulating Intellect, that activity is subordinated: whilst, in rudely trampling on the noblest conceptions of our Moral Nature as mere delusions, the purely Materialistic hypothesis is so thoroughly repugnant to the intuitive convictions of Mankind in general, that those who really experience these are made to *feel* its fallacy, with a certainty that renders logical proof unnecessary.

DR. W. B. CARPENTER.

MAN, ANIMAL AND RATIONAL.

THE lesson, then, concerning man, which we seem to gather from nature, as revealed to us in our own consciousness, and as externally observed, is that man differs fundamentally from every other creature which presents itself to our senses. That he differs absolutely, and therefore differs in origin also. * * * He is manifestly "animal," with the reflex functions, feelings, desires and emotions of an animal. Yet equally manifest is it that he has a special nature, "looking before and after," which constitutes him rational. Ruling, comprehending, interpreting and completing much in nature, we also see in him that which manifestly points above nature.

MIVART.

MAN SEPARATED FROM THE ANIMALS.

MAN has been defined as an Intelligence served by organs; and his reasoning intelligence is a characteristic that separates him from the brute creation by a chasm that they can never cross. The contrast is most striking when the human mind is directed to a point where the instinct of an animal is exhibited in the highest perfection. Only by the refined and severe method of the calculus was it ascertained that to secure the most room and strength upon a given space, with the least waste of material, the builder must adopt the exact angles which the bee forms by instinct. But how much greater the mind of Newton that grasped the principles, and defined the laws, and gave the rules of calculation, than the instinct of the bee in doing its work.

REV. J. P. THOMPSON, D. D.

INCORRECT VIEWS OF THE SOUL.

SIR JOHN DAVIES.

> Musicians think our souls are harmonies;
>   Physicians hold that they complexions be;
> Epicures make them swarms of atomies;
>   Which do by chance into our bodies flee.
>
> One thinks the soul is air; another fire;
>   Another blood, diffus'd about the heart;
> Another saith the elements conspire,
>   And to her essence each doth yield a part.
>
> Some think one gen'ral soul fills every brain,
>   As the bright sun sheds light in every star;
> And others think the name of soul is vain,
>   And that we only well-mixed bodies are.
>
> Thus these great clerks their little wisdom show,
>   While with their doctrines they at hazard play;
> Tossing their light opinions to and fro,
>   To mock the lewd, as learn'd in this as they;
>
> For no craz'd brain could ever yet propound,
>   Touching the soul so vain and fond a thought;
> But some among these masters have been found,
>   Which, in their schools, the self-same thought have taught.

DWIGHT L. MOODY.

GOD IMAGED IN MAN.

SO it ever is. The true Man is at once Shekinah and Commentary; and the Augustest Verities take form and find expression not less in what he is than what he says. The seer as well as what is seen, the prophet as well as the prophecy, the messenger as well as the message, the apostle as well as the epistle, are freighted with revelations of God. And in watching the ebb and flow of the blood in lofty, devout souls, there comes in upon one a better sense of the rhythm and meaning of the pulse-beatings of the Great Divine Heart. By every throb of a life which has been cast in the mould of the Spirit, and by every utterance which has leaped from the lips in answer to the broodings and movings of the Holy Ghost upon a responsive nature, the Everlasting Gates are being lifted up, and we have a nearer and clearer view of the King of Glory, who waits for the faith and love, for the pure heart and the clean hand, which shall one day usher him in.

CANON FARRAR.

MAN SUPERIOR TO THE BRUTE.

BEFORE man was formed animals were created. Some of these animals were greatly superior to others, yet none showed the possession of reason or conscience, or the power of speech. The symbol of this entire order of creation is *dust*. Now, from out of dust God created man. This is the basis. As an animal man has the wants, the passions of brutes. We admit all that may be claimed in the way of analogy. We *touch* the lower world. But we find in us much that is other than we have in common with the brutes. It is one of the greatest of fallacies to say, that because of these analogies all that we have in the way of conscience, mind, spiritual powers, have been evolved out of the animal.

God breathed into man's nostrils the breath of life. In the original it is the breath of *lives*. This may be but the plural of excellence, or it may refer to the intellectual, the moral, and the spiritual life. The grand old fathers of the church, the latchets of whose shoes no moderns are worthy to unloose, declared that by breathing into the nostrils of man, God superadded to the animal nature a higher one which could not have come to it otherwise. The conscience, the mind, the soul was now added. Now we have articulate, intelligent speech. All this was built on the animal base. It is impossible for any man long to believe these higher powers spring from the animal. They sprang from, and belong to the immortal world. We are taught then that man is two-fold. He touches the animal, as he touches the spiritual. This removes the objections that arise from analogy.

REV. MORGAN DIX, D. D.

SELF AND EGO.

SIR WM. HAMILTON

AS the best preparative for a proper understanding of these terms, I shall translate to you a passage from the *First Alcibiades* of Plato. The interlocutors are Socrates and Alcibiades.

Socr. Hold, now, with whom do you at present converse? Is it not with me?—*Alcib.* Yes.

Socr. And I also with you?—Alcib. Yes.

Socr. It is Socrates then who speaks?—Alcib. Assuredly.

Socr. And Alcibiades who listens?—Alcib. Yes.

Socr. Is it not with language that Socrates speaks?—Alcib. What now? of course.

Socr. To converse, and to use language, are not these then the same?—Alcib. The very same.

Socr. But he who uses a thing, and the thing used,—are these not different?—Alcib. What do you mean?

Socr. A currier,—does he not use a cutting knife, and other instruments?—Alcib. Yes.

Socr. And the man who uses the cutting knife, is he different from the instrument he uses?—Alcib. Most certainly.

Socr. In like manner, the lyrist, is he not different from the lyre he plays on?—Alcib. Undoubtedly.

Socr. This, then, was what I asked you just now,—does not he who uses a thing seem to you always different from the thing used? —Alcib. Very different.

Socr. But the currier, does he cut with his instruments alone, or also with his hands?—Alcib. Also with his hands.

Socr. He then uses his hands?—Alcib. Yes.

Socr. And in his work he uses also his eyes?—Alcib. Yes.

Socr. We are agreed, then, that he who uses a thing, and the thing used, are different?—Alcib. We are.

Socr. The currier and lyrist are, therefore, different from the hands and the eyes, with which they work?—Alcib. So it seems.

Socr. Now, then, does not a man use his whole body?—Alcib. Unquestionably.

Socr. But we are agreed that he who uses, and that which is used, are different?—Alcib. Yes.

Socr. A man is, therefore, different from his body?—Alcib. So I think.

Socr. What then is the man?—Alcib. I cannot say.

Socr. You can at least say that the man is that which uses the body?—Alcib. True.

Socr. Now, does anything use the body but the mind?—Alcib. Nothing.

Socr. The mind is, therefore, the man?—Alcib. The mind alone."

To the same effect, Aristotle asserts that the mind contains the man, not the man the mind. "Thou art the soul," says Hierocles, "but the body is thine." So Cicero—"Mens cujusque is est quisque, non ea figura quæ digito demonstrari potest;" and Macrobius—"Ergo qui videtur, non ipse verus homo est, sed verus ille est, a quo regitur quod videtur."

GENERAL FACTS OF MIND.

REV. LAURENS B. HICKOK, D. D.

WE are not conscious of what mind is, as we are conscious of what an exercise is; we know a thought, an emotion, and a volition, as we do not know the mind which thinks, feels and wills. The mind itself cannot appear in consciousness, as does its acts. But, while the mind itself does not appear in consciousness, and the different exercises are successively appearing and disappearing, there is that which does not come and go as the exercises arise and depart. One consciousness remains, and holds within itself all these fleeting appearances of thoughts, feelings and choices. There is also, in this one conciousness, the additional testimony that these exercises are not thrown in upon its field, as shadows passing over a landscape, but that they come up from some *nisus* or energy that produces them from beneath; and that when the thought appears, there has been a conscious energizing in its production; and when the thought vanishes and an emotion or a volition appears, there has been something which did not pass away with the thought, but energizes again in the emotion or the volition; and thus that there is some entity as opposed to non-being, which abides and energizes in consciousness.

Something *is*, while the varied exercises successively come and go upon the field of human consciousness. *What* this something is, the consciousness does not reveal; but *that* it permanently is, in its unchanged identity, the consciousness does testify. It is as if the mirror could feel itself, and its repeated throes of reflection, while it can by no means envisage itself, but only that which stands before it. This conscious perduring of somewhat, as opposed to non-entity, we now take as a fact in experience, and call it MIND. We do not attempt to determine what it is, though negatively we may say in many things what it is not; all we need is to affirm, that it is; and we then have permanent being which does not arise and vanish with its acts.

2. *This existence is not phenomenal nor ideal.*

The phenomena appear and disappear, arise and vanish; this does not appear, nor does it lose itself when they depart; but it holds them though successive, still within its own unity, and determines them all to be its own. It perpetually is, in all its phenomena, and these phenomena are all from it.

3. *It has its conscious identity through all changes.*

The exercises of the mind arise and vanish, and are each separate and distinct from others in their appearance, but the same mind is in, and through, them all, and holds them all in its one consciousness. The thought which was yesterday, or last year, in consciousness, and the conscious thought of to-day, are both recognized as being in the same self-consciousness. The self-consciousness has not changed, while the exercises have been continually coming and departing. The mind, thus, remains in its own identity, yesterday, to-day, and onward into the future, perpetually the same mind. Through all development of its faculties; in all its states; the mind itself neither comes nor goes, but retains its self-sameness through all changes. Its phenomenal experience varies *in* time, but itself perdures *through* time.

4. *Mind is esentially self-active.*

All matter is essentially inert, except as acted on by outward forces. Its inner constituting forces are balanced in exact counteraction, and hold itself in its own position, with a *vis inertiæ* that resists all action which would displace it. The movement of matter must be traced up, through all its propagations, to some first mover in a mind; and out of this mind only, could the impulsive moving energy have originated. Nature, thus, acts upon nature, in its different parts, mechanically, as its different forces balance themselves in their own action, or in unbalanced movement obtrude one upon another. One portion of matter, impinging upon another, is a *percussive* force; when suddenly expelling others that surround its own center, is an *explosive* force; and when coming in combination with another, and giving off a third, is an *effervescive* force. But when we have superadded to all the forces in matter, whether gravitating, chemical, or crystalline, a proper *vital* force—which takes up matter, penetrates it, assimilates, and incorporates it, and thus builds up about itself its own organized body—we have an existence selfactive, self-developing, spiritual; which originates motion from itself, and spontaneously uses inert matter for its own ends. When this vital force rises from simple spontaneity in the plant, to that of sensation in the animal, and from this to distinct self-consciousness in man, we have the higher forms of the spiritual; and, in the human mind, attain to a manifest discrimination of it from all that is material, in its inherent self-activity.

The human mind has the consciousness of this self-energizing. Its agency is properly its own, and originates in its own causalty. As a created being, the original ground of the mind's existence is in God its Maker. It is dependent upon its Creator both, that it is, and for what it is; but as created by God, it is endowed by Him with a proper causalty. It originates its own thoughts, emotions, and purposes; and needs only the proper occasions for its activity, and this activity is spontaneously originated by it. This activity is circumscribed within given limits, and in its sphere of action it must have, also, certain occasions for action; yet within this sphere, and supplied with these occasions, it originates its own acts, and is conscious of its own *nisus* as it goes out in exercise. The occasions for thought do not cause the thinking; the mind thinks from its own spontaneous casualty. Within such limits, and under such occasions, it is cause for originating thought and feeling.

    5. *The mind discriminates itself from Its objects.*

We say nothing here of the particular facts in the process of discriminating one object from another, and all objects from the mind itself; and nothing of the awakening in self-consciousness, which is consequential upon such discrimination; but only mark the general fact itself, that the mind separates itself from all of its objects action. All mental action is conditioned to some object or end of action. We cannot think, without some content of thought; nor feel, without some object of emotion; any more than we can see, or hear, without something to be seen or heard. There must be the agent acting, and the object as end of action; and between these, the mind discriminates, and assigns to each, its own distinct identity. The object is known as other than the agent; and thus the mind has the fact that it is, and that some other than it is, and that there is a separating line between them.

Of itself, as acting being, it affirms that it is the *subject* of the activity. The mind *lies under* the act, and is a ground for it. Of that which is the end of its action, it affirms that it is the object of the action. It *lies directly* in the way of the act, and meets it face to face. The act springs from the mind itself, as subject, and terminates in its end, as object.

WHAT AM I.

W HAT am I, whence produced, and for what end?
  Whence drew I being, to what period tend?
Am I th' abandon'd orphan of blind chance,
Dropp'd by wild atoms in disordered dance?
Or, from an endless chain of causes wrought,
And of unthinking substance, born with thought?
Am I but what I seem, mere flesh and blood,
A branching channel with a mazy flood?
The purple stream that through my vessels glides,
Dull and unconscious flows, like common tides,

The pipes, through which the circling juices stray,
Are not that thinking I, no more than they;
This frame, compacted with transcendent skill,
Of moving joints, obedient to my will;
Nursed from the fruitful glebe, like yonder tree,
Waxes and wastes,—I call it mine, not me,
New matter still the mould'ring mass sustains;
The mansion chang'd, the tenant still remains;
And, from the fleeting stream, repair'd by food,
Distinct, as is the swimmer from the flood.

Dr. Arbuthnot.

DARWINISM AND MAN.

No one, in my opinion, who does not maintain that Hebrew chronology enables us to fix the date of the appearance of man in the world is compelled to admit the irreconcilability of Darwin's new volumes with Revelation. In point of fact, there are large sections of his argument which seem to lend strength to these positions: First, that man is a fallen creature; second, that without positive Divine aid, given by inspiration or otherwise, man could never become what he is. If Darwin makes out anything, he makes out that savage man is a more selfish, more cruel, more licentious, and more miserable being than the highest tribes of the animal kingdom. On my mind, also, the statements of Mr. Darwin have very deeply impressed the idea that our species could not have passed the *bridge* between animalism and humanism without the interposition of a Divine hand. So far as we know, all savage races are dying out. To the best of my information, Whately, if he were alive to-day, could challenge Darwin to point, in the history of the past, to any one savage race which had risen by its unaided energies to civilization. If, then, all known savage races are dying out, and no historical race can be shown to have risen direct from savagery, is it not mere hypothisis and imagination to say that a beast, admitted to have stood lower in intellect than the lowest known savage, improved itself into man. Mr. Darwin's book does not seem to me to prove that man has become what he is without Divine impulse (Goethe called it *steigerung;* and this *steigerung,* or impulse of progress, he held to be an indispensable factor in solving the problem of universal existence).

Peter Bayne.

PROF. HUXLEY'S ONE-SIDED VIEW.

"ALL vital action may be said to be the result of the molecular forces of the protoplasm which displays it. And if so, it must be true, in the same sense and to the same extent, the thoughts to which I am now giving utterance, and your thoughts regarding them, are the expression of the molecular changes in that matter of life which is the source of our other vital phenomena.....After all, what do we know of that "*spirit*" over whose threatened extinction by matter a great lamentation is arising,....except that it is a name for an unknown and hypothetical cause or condition, of states of consciousness? In other words, matter and spirit are but names for the imaginary substrata of groups of natural phenomena." And again: "In itself it is of little moment whether we express the phenomena of matter in terms of spirit, or the phenomena of spirit in terms of matter; matter may be regarded as a form of thought; thought may be regarded as a property of matter; each statement has a certain relative truth. But with a view to the progress of science the materialistic terminology is in every way to be preferred.

PROF. HUXLEY.

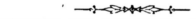

MIND PRESERVES ITS INTEGRITY AMID THE DECAY OF THE BODY.

NOTHING can be more certain than this, that however dependent mind may be for its manifestations upon a material organ, it is essentially different in nature. Were there no presumptive evidence of this from the phenomena of memory, imagination, &c., it would be supplied abundantly by the frequent instances of persistent integrity of the mind amid the utter decay of the bodily organs. "*My friends*," said Anquetil, when his approaching end was announced to him by his physicians, "*you behold a man dying full of life!*" On this expression M. Lordat remarks: "It is indeed an evidence of the duplicity of the dynamism in one and the same individual; a proof of the union of two active causes simultaneously created, hitherto inseparable, and the survivor of which is the biographer of the other.

CHARLES ELAM, M. D.

MAN ON THE DARWINIAN THEORY.

BISHOP RANDOLPH FOSTER, D. D.

THE Darwinian theory is, that life in its most primitive forms appeared in minute particles of matter, cells, or germs; and thence expanded into an indefinite number of organisms, the highest of which is man; that each quickened seed contains potentially all possible existences; that the order of evolution is as follows—first, lichens and fungi; second, mosses, liverworts, and alga; third, ferns, and other cryptogamia; fourth, flowers, plants, and trees; that animal life appears in the rudimental cell, and is developed, first, in the protozoa, foraminifera, etc.; next, in the radiata; third, in the mollusca; fourth, in the articulated dwellers in seas, and on the borders of lakes and rivers; and lastly, in the vertebrata —mammals, from the mouse to man. The doctrine that our immediate ancestors are the simia, and our remote progenitors the protozoa, is not particularly flattering to human pride. It surrenders the differentiated spiritual nature. It positively affirms that our grandfathers were pollywogs, and our fathers, are apes, and assign as reasons for the dictum, the variability of species, the struggle for existence among animated forms, and the survival of the fittest together with the fact that nature reveals a constantly ascending scale of being.

Some of these reasons are formed in truth; others are manifestly fallacious. If all the alleged facts of Darwinism be true, its conclusions are inevitable. But there is a fatal fallacy in the fourth predicate, which breaks the Darwinian chain of logic in the middle; where ascending divergence from the parent stock is perpetual, it only needs time to reach man from moss. So Darwin claims. But he affirms that while the variations of species are perpetual, those variations run on longitudinally. This is not true to observed facts. Variation runs in a circle, and not along a right line. This simple fact shatters all systems founded on the contrary proposition.

Geology demonstrates the truth of this principle. Darwin may have varied the pigeon species by careful labor, as others have varied, the species, horse, dog, man. But in all their variations, the species is the same,—horse, dog, pigeon, man. The pigeon has never been changed into the dog, nor the horse into man. Darwin confesses the utter absence of evidence to the truth of his theory. It is fanciful, imaginative, but not scientific, not inductively true.

Because Carlo barks in his sleep, he concludes that Carlo has imagination, and that his remote descendants may write tragedies like Shakespeare, or epics like Paradise Lost. Carlo has a hang-dog look when chided. Therefore, Carlo is capable of shame or moral feeling, and his descendants may write ethical treatise, such as Hopkin's Law of Love, or the Ten Commandments. The ape cracks nuts with a stone, or builds nests on boughs. Therefore he is an inventor, and his children centuries hence may build steamships. A pigeon carried in darkness to a great distance, when loosed, rising in circles to a great height, then flies in a line to its owner. Therefore the pigeon is an astronomer, and some future evolution from the pigeon may write a new Principia.

DEFINITIONS OF MAN.

MAN is a two-legged animal without feathers.—*Plato.*——It is said, Socrates brought a cock despoiled of his feathers into Plato's school, exclaiming, "Behold the man of Plato!" Again: he has been called "a laughing animal," "a cooking animal," "an animal with thumbs," "a lazy animal." A travelled Frenchman being asked to name one characteristic of all the races he had visited, replied, "Lazy."——A tool-making animal.—*Dr. Franklin*——A cultivating animal.—*Walker.*——A poetical animal.—*Hazlitt*——Man is a dupable animal. Quacks in medicine, quacks in religion, and quacks in politics, know this, and act upon that knowledge. There is scarcely any one who may not, like a trout, be "taken by tickling."—*Southey.* ——Man is an animal that makes bargains. No other animal does this: no dog exchanges bones with another.—*Adam Smith.*

THE DIVINE ELEMENT IN EVOLUTION.

FOR myself I will say, frankly, that evolution will no doubt be found to explain many of the phenomena of nature, which not only theologians, but experts in natural science, have misunderstood. It has given us and will probably fortify, new conceptions of the methods of divine operation, teaching us to look upon natural progress, not as attained by sudden leaps, but by gradual ascent. It may require us to dismiss our notions of frequent creations, and accept the idea of a primal creation, having inherent energies, or deposits of force, adequate to all natural functions and effects; subject to the inspection and rule of the Maker and Lord, but requiring no rude infractions of power in the way of help or correction. In accepting such views of the economy of nature, however, we shall find not less, but more and mightier, occasions to magnify and adore the great Author, who so "ordereth all things after the counsel of His own will." But *material matter* is one thing, and *spiritual life* is another, and at some point in the upward ascent from the "fire mist," or the "sea slime," there must have been an inspiration from above of intelligence, reason, will, which the sea slime never having had, as I just now said, it never could give. We may talk of "nature's great progression.... from blind force to conscious intellect and will;" but it is little more than rhetoric. There are gulfs which still yawn, wide as ever before, between inorganic and organic nature; between living and dead matter; between blind force and force directed by intellect; between animal instinct and moral feeling; between the semi-automatic intelligence of the brute and the pure reason of the mind of man. These gulfs *may* be bridged, but as they are *not* bridged, and it is to practice delusion upon the credulous to cover them with a flimsy covering of speculation or assumption, and to call such covering solid ground.

Rev. J. H. Reylance, D. D.

The whole Creation is a mystery, and particularly that of man.
Sir Thomas Browne.

A man is the whole encyclopedia of facts. The creation of a thousand forests in one acorn, and Egypt, Greece, Rome, Gaul, Britain and America, lie folded already in the first man.
Emerson.

A man's a man for a' that.
Burns.

> Lord, what is man, whose thoughts, at times,
> Up to they seven-fold brightness climbs,
> While still his grosser instincts cling
> To earth, like other creeping things!
> So rich in words, in acts so mean;
> So high, so low; chance-swung between
> The foulness of the penal pit
> And truth's clear sky millenium-lit.
>
> WHITTIER.

MAN, BODY, SOUL AND SPIRIT.

REV. F. W. ROBERTSON.

The apostle Paul divides human nature into a three-fold divisions. This language of the apostle, when rendered into English, shows no difference whatever between "soul" and "spirit." We say, for instance, that the soul of man has departed from him. We also say that the spirit of a man has departed from him. There is no distinct difference between the two; but in the original two very different kinds of thoughts, two very different modes of conception, are presented by the two English words "soul" and "spirit." When the apostle speaks of the body, what he means is the animal life—that which we share in common with beasts, birds, and reptiles; for our life, our sensational existence, differs but little from that of the lower animals. There is the same external form,—the same material in the blood vessels, in the nerves, and in the muscular system. Nay, more than that, our appetites and instincts are alike, our lower pleasures like their lower pleasures, our lower pain like their lower pain; our life is supported by the same means, and our animal functions are almost indistinguishably the same.

But, once more, the apostle speaks of what he calls the "soul.' What the apostle meant by what is translated "soul" is the immortal part of man—the immaterial as distinguished from the material; those powers, in fact, which man has by nature—powers natural, which are yet to survive the grave. There is a distinction made in

Scripture by our Lord between these two things. "Fear not," says He, "them who can kill the body; but rather fear Him who can destroy both body and soul in hell."

We have, again, to observe, respecting this, that what the apostle called the "soul" is not simply distinguishable from the body, but also from the spirit. By the soul the apostle means our powers natural—the powers which we have by nature. Herein is the soul distinguishable from the spirit. In the Epistle to the Corinthians we read, "But the natural man receiveth not the things of the Spirit of God; for they are foolishness unto him; neither can he know them, because they are spiritually discerned. But he that is spiritual judgeth all things." Observe, there is a distinction drawn between the natural man and the spiritual. What is there translated "natural" is derived from precisely the same word as that which is here translated "soul." So that we may read, just as correctly, "The man under the dominion of the soul receiveth not the things of the Spirit of God; for they are foolishness unto him; neither can he know them, because they are spiritually discerned. But he that is spiritual judgeth all things." And again, the apostle, in the same Epistle to the Corinthians, writes: "That is not first which is spiritual, but that which is natural;" that is, the endowments of the soul precede the endowments of the spirit. You have the same truth in other places. The powers that belong to the spirit were not the first developed; but the powers which belong to the soul, that is, the power of nature. Again, in the same chapter, reference is made to the natural and spiritual body. "There is a natural body, and there is a spiritual body." Literally, there is a body governed by the soul, that is, powers natural; and there is a body governed by the Spirit, that is, higher nature. Let, then, this be borne in mind, that what the apostle calls "soul" is the same as that which he calls, in another place, the "natural man." These powers are divisible into two branches—the intellectual powers and the moral sense. The intellectual powers man has by nature. Man need not be regenerated in order to possess the power of reasoning, or in order to invent. The intellectual powers belong to what the apostle calls the "soul." The moral sense distinguishes between right and wrong. The apostle tells us, in the Epistle to the Romans, that the heathen—manifestly natural men—had the law "work of the written in their hearts; their conscience also bearing witness."

The third division of which the apostle speaks he calls the "spirit;" and by the spirit he means that life in man which, in his natural state, is in such an embryo condition that it can scarcely be said to exist at all,—that which is called out into power and vitality by regeneration, the perfections of the powers of human nature. And you will observe that it is not merely the instinctive life, nor the intellectual life, nor the moral life, but it is principally our nobler affections,—that existence, that state of being, which we call love. That is the department of human nature which the apostle calls the spirit; and accordingly, when the Spirit of God was given on the day of Pentecost, you will remember that another power of man was called out, differing from what he was before. That Spirit granted on the day of Pentecost did subordinate to Himself, and was intended to subordinate to Himself, the will, the understanding, and the affection of man; but you often find these spiritual powers were distinguished from the natural powers, and existed without them. So, in the highest state of religious life, we are told, men prayed in the spirit. Till the spirit has subordinated the understanding, the gift of God is not complete—has not done its work. It is abundantly evident that a new life was called out. It was not merely the sharpening of the intellectual powers; it was calling out powers of aspiration and love to God; those affections which have in them something boundless,—that are not limited to this earth, but seek their completion in the mind of God Himself.

MIND NOT THE RESULT OF ORGANIZATION.

REV. JOHN LEYBURN, D. D.

WHERE, in all the researches of physiology, has there been discovered the first trace of mind or thought resulting from combinations or laws of matter? Men of high intellect, or exquisite skill have been for ages scrutinizing and searching every part of the wonderful structure which constitutes physical man, but never yet have they discovered the contrivance or the forces which produce the thinking principle. They have told us how the eye is arranged for seeing; how the arterial and nervous systems, with the heart, are arranged for the circulation of the blood;

how the stomach and affiliated organs perform the offices of digestion, and how all the functions of animal life are provided for and carried on; but never yet have they pointed out the organization by which thought or moral principle is produced. True, they point to the brain as controlling all voluntary action; they tell us that it is a finely constructed galvanic battery, projecting the electric current through the nerve tissues, and that thus the hand, the foot, the lips, the tongue, are brought into use and controlled at pleasure. But, after all, this leaves the great mystery still veiled. What controls the brain? What sets in motion the cunningly devised battery? Where and what is that mysterious power which says to this marvelous mechanism, "Go!" and it goeth; "Stop!" and it stoppeth? In our telegraph offices there are batteries and connected wires extending over continents and under seas—but the battery does not work itself. It needs the skillful fingers directed by an intelligent mind to put it in play, and send abroad the messages. Without this it is dumb and useless.

BODY AND SOUL.

Is the statement that there is an enduring spirit within us, entirely distinct from the corporeal organization, and which the cessation of the heart liberates to a higher mode of existence, any more startling than the statement that in a drop of water, which may tremble and glisten on the tip of the finger, seemingly the most feeble thing in nature, from which the tiniest flower gently nurses its strength while it hangs upon its leaf, which a sunbeam may dissipate, contains within its tiny globe, electric energy enough to charge 800,000 Leyden jars, energy enough to split a cathedral as though it was a toy? And so that, of every cup of water we drink, each atom is a thunder storm? Is the idea of spiritual communication and intercourse by methods far transcending our present powers of sight, speech and hearing, beset with more intrinsic difficulties than the idea of conversing by a wire with a man in St. Louis as quickly as with a man by your side, or of making a thought girdle the globe in a twinkling? And when we say that the spiritual world may be all around us, though our senses take no impression of it, what is there to embarrass the intellect in accepting it, when we know that within the vesture of the air which we cannot grasp, there is the realm of light, the immense ocean of electricity, and the constant currents of magnetism, all of them playing the most wonderful parts in the economy of the world, each of them far more powerful than the ocean, the earth and the rocks—neither of them comprehensible by our minds, while the existence of two of them is not apprehensible by any sense?

REV. THOS. STARR KING.

NATURE AND MAN.

JOHN B. GOUGH.

COME with me to the Yosemite Valley; yonder stands El Capitan—the atmosphere so clear, it seems as though you might strike it with a stone. Approach nearer; how it looms up; how it grows and widens; how grand! See yonder those shrubs in the crevice—shrubs? They are trees, a hundred feet in height, three feet and more in diameter. Do you see that bend in the face of the rock? That is a fissure, 75 feet wide. Nearer yet, still nearer. It seems as if you might touch it now with your finger. Stand still under the shadow of El Capitan. A plumb line from the summit falls fifty feet from the base. Now look up, up, up, 3,600 feet—two-thirds of a mile—right up. How grand and sublime! Your lips quiver, your nerves thrill, your eyes fill with tears, and you understand in some degree your own littleness. "The inhabitants of the earth are but as grasshoppers." How small I am! I could not climb up fifty feet on the face of that rock, and there it towers above me. Yonder is the great South Dome, rising sheer up 6,000 feet—more than a mile, seamed and seared by the storms of ages, but anchored in the valley beneath. There are the Three Brothers, there the Cathedral rocks and spires, there the Sentinel Dome and the Sentinel Rock. How magnificent! See yonder the wonderful Yosemite Falls leaping through a gorge eighteen feet before it strikes, coming down like skyrockets, exploding as they fall; striking, it leaps 400 feet, and again it leaps 600 feet. More than half a mile the water pours over. What a dash, what a magnificent anthem ascending to the great Creator! Now look around you in every direction, and you feel the littleness of man. Oh! I am but as the dust in the balance, but as the small dust in the balance; but God created man in His own image, and breathed into his nostrils the breath of life, and made him—not gave him—but made him a living soul; therefore I am a man, a living man, but that is a dead rock. I am a living man. The elements shall melt with fervent heat, the world be removed like a cottage, the milky way shall shut its two awful arms and hush its dumb prayer forever, but I shall live, for I am a man with the fire of God in me and a spark of immortality that will never go out. The universe, grand and magnificent and sublime as it is, is but the nursery to man's infant soul, and the child is worth more than the nursery; therefore, I, a living, breathing, thinking, hoping man, with a reason capable of understanding, in some degree, the greatness of the Almighty, a mind capable of eternal development, and a heart capable of loving Him, am worth more than all God's material universe, for I am a man with a destiny before me as high as heaven and as vast as eternity.

MAN REDEEMABLE.

With other ministrations thou, O Nature!
Healest thy wandering and distempered child:
Thou pourest on him thy soft influences,
Thy sunny hues, fair forms, and breathing sweets,—
Thy melodies of woods, and winds, and waters
Till he relent, and can no more endure
To be a jarring and a dissonant thing
Amid this general dance and minstrelsy;
But, bursting into tears, wins back his way,
His angry spirit healed and harmonized
By the benignant touch of love and beauty.
Samuel Taylor Coleridge.

LIFE A JOURNEY.

LIFE is a journey, the end is nearing. It is a race, the goal will soon be reached. It is a voyage, the port will soon be in sight. Time is but a narrow isthmus between two eternities. You are going surely. How many things you have already left behind!—the old home, friends, parents, scenes of childhood and early years. How much of the way you have passed over! You will never return to the place from which you started. You are going on, and on, and away from all your early years. It is a startling thought, that our business will soon be left behind; that our work will be done, and that we shall leave this stage of being—leave it forever—our homes and cares, and all the interests that engage us here, and never more come back. It is an amazing thought that we, if we are Christians, shall soon be in heaven. Think of it! Time and all its opportunities passed forever! The suns and moons and stars all behind us; springs and summers and autumns all gone; the sights and sounds of earth all passed away! Soon—very soon—shall we be in heaven. We shall see God, we shall behold Christ in His glory, we shall look upon the angels. Mothers will be searching for their children, and husbands and wives will find each other; and all hands, parted in Christ, will be clasped again. It is like coming into port after an ocean voyage. The shining shore-line, how it grows on the waiting eye! The joy will be like that with which the Crusaders first saw Jerusalem.

REV. C. L. GOODELL, D. D.

EVOLUTION AND LIFE.

WITHOUT doubt, within certain limits, evolution is law, but it can neither explain the mystery of life nor of conscience. Conscience was created, or else it was in the protoplasm. If in the latter, then I worship protoplasm. But clear-eyed, dispassionate science, studying second causes, cannot thus argue. Christianity, driven out of the door, will come in at the window. I have no fear of a long reign of atheism. In the old effete communities of the East there may linger traces of it, but not in rich, restless, greedy America, where the air is full of oxygen; where the mills of the gods grind fast, as well as fine. What we need is a vivid sense of the personality of God—wise, just and good. Right is what He commands; wrong what He forbids. Man is to be recognized as His offspring, and history a record of the working out of His plan. To be alone with God is to be in the majority, as Mahomet said to one who fled with him and remarked, "We are but two:" "Nay, we are *three*, for GOD is here."

PROF. R. D. HITCHCOCK, D. D.

Why should I wish to linger in the wild,
When Thou art waiting, Father, to receive Thy child?

MATERIAL PROCESSES AND LIFE.

FELIX ADLER.

MR. John Stuart Mill acknowledges that "the evidence is well-nigh complete that all thought and feeling has some action of the bodily organism for its immediate coincident and accompaniment, and that the specific variations, and especially the different degrees of complication of the nervous and cerebral organism, correspond to differences in the development of our mental faculties."

OR VIEWS OF HEAVEN.

The prodigious difficulties in the way of the study of the brain may long retard the progress of the investigator, but for the purpose of our argument we are at liberty to assume whatever is within the limits of possible achievement. We may suppose that physiology will succeed so far that the brain will be accurately and completely mapped out, and that the motion of the atoms upon which the thousand varying modes of thought and feeling depend, will be known and measured. In anticipating such results, we have reached the utmost tenable position of materialism.

But now to our surprise we discover that all of this being allowed, the ultimate question, what is soul, remains still unsolved and as insoluble as ever. The unvarying coincidence of certain modes of soul with certain material processes may be within the range of proof, but what *cannot be proven* is, that these material processes explain the psychic phenomena.

If it is urged that the same difficulty presents itself in the explanation of the most ordinary occurrences, this objection is based upon a misapprehension of the point at issue.

The scientists cannot show why heat should be convertible into motion, but how it is thus transformed is easy to demonstrate, and the exact mechanical equivalent of heat has been calculated. But how certain motions of atoms in the brain should generate, not heat, but consciousness, but thought and love, is past all conception. There are here two different orders of facts, having no common principle to which they could both be reduced. There is an impassable gulf between them which can in nowise be bridged over.

Nor would it avail us to endow the atom itself with the promise and potency of intellect; we should thereby throw back the issue a step further, and disguise the problem whose existence it were better to plainly acknowledge. The broad fact of consciousness therefore remains unexplained and inexplicable as before. Arrived at this limit, science itself pause and refuses to pass further.

ATOMS AND CONSCIOUSNESS.

The eminent physiologist, Dubois Reymond, denies that the connection between certain motions of certain atoms in the brain, and what he calls, the primal, undefinable and undeniable facts of consciousness, is at all conceivable. Professor Tyndall in his address on

"The scope and limits of Scientific Materialism," explains his views with similar precision. "Were our minds so expanded, strengthened and illuminated as to enable us to see and feel the very molecules of the brain; were we capable of following all their motions, all their groupings, all their electric discharges, if such there be; and were we imtimately acquainted with the corresponding states of thought and feeling, we should be as far as ever from the solution of the problem. How are these physical processes connected by and with the facts of conciousness? I do not think the materialist is entitled to say that his molecular groupings and his molecular motions explain everything, in reality they explain nothing. *

* * The problem of body and soul is as insoluble in its modern form as it was in the pre-scientific ages."

FELIX ADLER.

LIFE ONE GREAT RITUAL.

AND as the vesper hymn of Time precedes
The starry matins of Eternity
And daybreak of existence in the Heavens,—
To know this, is to know we shall depart
Into the storm-surrounding calm on high,
The sacred cirque, the all-central infinite
Of that self-blessedness wherein abides
Our GOD, all kind, all loving, all beloved;—
To feel life one great ritual, and its laws
Writ in the vital rubric of the blood,
Flow *in* obedience and flow *out* command,
In sealike circulation; and be here
Accepted as a gift by Him, who gives
An empire as an alms, nor counts it aught,
So long as all His creatures joy in Him,
The great Rejoicer of the Universe,
Whom all the boundless spheres of Being bless.

PHILIP JAMES BAILEY.

THE PERIL OF LIFE.

MRS. SOUTHEY.

Oh, fear not thou to *die!*
Far rather fear to live,—for life
Hath thousand snares by faith to try,
   By peril, pain and strife.
   Brief is the work of death,
But life! the spirit shrinks to see,
How full ere Heaven recalls the breath,
   The cup of woe may be.

Oh, fear not thou to die!
No more, to suffer or to sin;
No snares without thy faith to try,
   No traitor heart within.
   But fear, oh rather fear,
The gay, the light, the changeful scene
The flattering smiles that greet thee here,
   From Heaven thy heart to wean.

Fear lest, in evil hour,
Thy pure and holy hope o'ercome,
By clouds that in the horizon lower,
   Thy spirit feel the gloom
   Which over earth and Heaven
The covering throws of fell despair,
And deems itself the unforgiven,
   Predestined child of care.

Oh, fear not thou to die!
To die, and be that blessed one
Who in the bright and beauteous sky
   May feel his conflict done;—
   May feel that never more
The tear of grief, of shame, shall come
For thousand wanderings from the Power
   Who loved and called him home.

NOT ONE LIFE DESTROYED.

   O, yet we trust that somehow good
      Will be the final goal of ill,
      To pangs of nature, sins of will,
   Defects of doubt and taints of blood;

That nothing walks with aimless feet;
    That not one life shall be destroyed,
    Or cast as rubbish to the void,
When God hath made the pile complete;

That not a worm is cloven in vain,
    That not a moth with vain desire
    Is shrivelled in a fruitless fire,
Or but subserves another's gain.

Behold! we know not any thing;
    I can but trust that good shall fall
    At last,—far off,—at last, to all,
And every winter change to spring.

So runs my dream: but what am I?
    An infant crying in the night:
    An infant crying for the light:
And with no language but a cry.

                         ALFRED TENNYSON.

LIVE AND HELP LIVE.

ALICE CAREY.

MIGHTY in faith and hope, why art thou sad?
Sever the green withes, look up and be glad!
See all around thee, below and above,
The beautiful, beautiful gifts of God's love!

What though our hearts beat with death's sullen waves?
What though the green sod is broken with graves?
The sweet hopes that never shall fade from their bloom,
Make their dim birth-chamber down in the tomb!

Parsee or Christian-man, bondman or free,
Loves and humilities still are for thee;
Some little good every day to achieve,
Some slighted spirit no longer to grieve.

In the tents of the desert, alone on the sea,
On the far-away hills with the starry Chaldee;
Condemned and in prison, dishonored, reviled,
God's arm is around thee, and thou art His child.

Mine be the lip ever truthful and bold;
Mine be the heart never careless nor cold;
A faith humbly trustful, a life free from blame—
All else is unstable as flax in the flame.

And while the soft skies are so starry and blue;
And while the wide earth is so fresh with God's dew,
Though all around me the sad sit and sigh,
I will be glad that I live and must die.

LIFE THE TIME FOR WORK.

WHAT are we set on earth for? Say, to toil;
Nor seek to leave thy tending of the vines
For all the heat o' the day, till it declines,
And death's mild curfew shall from work assoil.
God did anoint thee with His odorous oil
To wrestle, not to reign; and He assigns
All thy tears over, like pure crystallines,
For younger fellow-workers of the soil
To wear for amulets. So others shall
Take patience, labor, to their heart and hand,
From thy hand and thy heart and thy brave cheer,
And God's grace fructify through thee to all.
The least flower, with a brimming cup may stand,
And share its dew-drop with another near.

ELIZABETH BARRETT BROWNING

THE PRESENT LIFE IN VIEW OF THE FUTURE.

OH, if we are not bitterly deceived—
If this familiar spirit that communes
With yours this hour—that has the power to search
All things but its own compass—*is* a spark
Struck from the burning essence of its God—
If, as we dream, in every radiant star
We see a shining gate through which the soul,
In its degree of being, will ascend—
If, when these weary organs drop away,
We shall forget their uses and commune
With angels and each other, as the stars
Mingle their light, in silence and in love—
What is this fleshy fetter of a day
That we should bind it with immortal flowers!
How do we ever gaze upon the sky,
And watch the lark soar up till he is lost,
And turn to our poor perishing dreams away,
Without one tear for our imprisoned wings!

N. P WILLIS.

LONGEVITY OF STUDIOUS AND BUSY MEN.

CHARLES ELAM, M. D. M. R. C. P.

TISSOT states that Gorgias, the rhetorician, lived to the age of one hundred and eight years, "without discontinuing his studies, and without any infirmity." Isocrates wrote his "Pan-Athenæai" when he was ninety-four, and lived to ninety-eight. The above writer also mentions the case of "one of the greatest physicians in Europe, who, although he had studied very hard all his lifetime, and is now almost seventy, wrote me word not long since that he still studied generally fourteen hours every day, and yet enjoyed the most perfect health."

Epimenides, the seventh of the "wise men," lived, it is supposed, to the age of one hundred and fifty-four. Herodicus, a very distinguished physician and philosopher, the master of Hippocrates, lived to the age of one hundred. Hippocrates himself, whose genuine writings alone would be sufficient to testify to a life of arduous study, lived to the age of ninety-nine. Galen wrote, it is said, three hundred volumes; what now remains of his works occupy, in the edition of 1858, five folio volumes. He lived to near one hundred years. Lewis Cornaro wrote seven or eight hours daily for a considerable period of his life, and lived to the age of one hundred, in spite of a feeble constitution originally.

Theophrastus wrote two hundred distinct treatises, and lived to the age of one hundred and seven. Zeno, the founder of the Stoic school, lived to the age of ninety-eight years; and, in the full possession of his faculties, then committed suicide, having received, as he supposed, a warning by a wound of the thumb that it was time for him to depart. Democritus was so devoted to study and meditation that he put out his eyes, it is said, that external objects might not distract his attention. He died aged one hundred and nine years. Sophocles died aged ninety one. Xenophon, Diogenes, and Carneades each lived to eighty-eight years. Euripedes died aged eighty-five; Polybius, eighty-one; Juvenal, above eighty; Pythagoras, eighty; Quintillian, eighty; Chrysippus died of laughter, at eighty. The poet Pindar died aged eighty; Plato, aged eighty-one. Socrates, 'in the full possession of his faculties, was judicially murdered at seventy-one. Anaxagoras, to whom we have before alluded, died at seventy-two. Aristotle died at sixty-three. Thucydides was eighty.

It would be difficult to select twenty-five names which exerted a much greater influence upon literature, philosophy and history than these in old times. Many of them are known to have been most voluminous writers, many of them most profound thinkers. These were not the days of hand-books and vade-mecums; those who wanted information or mental cultivation had to work for it. Yet the average age of these twenty-five men is exactly ninety years. It is much to be questioned whether the united ages of twenty-five of the most distinguished farmers that the world has ever produced would amount to two thousand two hundred and fifty years. The list might easily be enlarged greatly by such men as Seneca and Pliny, who came to untimely deaths by accident or tyranny, and who promised to live as long as the oldest, in the course of nature.

Yet these old writers, commentators, and others were apparently a hardy race,—they were generally long-lived. Beza, lived in the perfect enjoyment of his faculties up to the age of eighty-six. The learned Richard Bentley died at eighty-one. Neander was seventy-eight; Scaliger, sixty-nine; Heyne, eighty-four; Parr, eighty; Pighius, eighty-four; Vossius, seventy-three; Hobbes, ninety-one,—at death.

Dr. Madden, the able author of the "Infirmities of Genius," has constructed some most instructive tables relative to the longevity of men distinguished for their intellectual pursuits. He says that each list contains twenty names, in which no other attention has been given to the selection than that which eminence suggested, without any regard to the ages of those who presented themselves to notice."

An analysis of the tables gives the following averages of life for the various classes:—

	Aggregate years.	Average.
Twenty natural philosophers	1504	75
Twenty moral philosphers	1417	70
Twenty sculptors and painters	1412	70
Twenty authors on law, &c.	1394	60
Twenty medical authors	1368	68
Twenty authors on revealed religion	1350	67
Twenty philologists	1323	66
Twenty musical composers	1284	64
Twenty novelists and miscellaneous authors	1257	62½
Twenty dramatists	1249	62
Twenty authors on natural religion	1245	62
Twenty poets	1144	57

OR VIEWS OF HEAVEN.

This list does not by any means give too high an average of life for literary characters. Many of the oldest are omitted from the calculation, because, though equally laborious, their eminence was not quite so great; and, again, many are inserted because eminent, who died young, obviously not from causes connected with mental application. This is particularly illustrated among the poets by the cases of Byron and Burns, whose deaths certainly were not justly to be attributed to the nature of their mental habits. Amongst artists, also, Fuseli (eighty-four), Nollekens (eighty-six), Kneller (seventy-five), and Albert Durer (eighty-seven); are not mentioned. M. Lordat, in his "Mental Dynamics," gives many remarkable instances of intellectual pursuits being carried on to an extremely advanced age— "for instance, M. des Quersonnieres, one hundred and sixteen years of age, now residing in Paris, an accomplished poet, remarkable for his powers of conversation, and full of vivacity." He mentions also another poet, M. Leroy, aged one hundred years. Fontenelle, considered the most universal genius that Europe has produced, for forty-two years Secretary to the Academy of Sciences in Paris, lived with unimpaired faculties to the age of one hundred years. Father Sirmond, called by Naude "an inexhaustible treasury of ecclesiastical lore," lived to the age of ninety-three. Hutton, the learned geologist and cosmogonist, died at ninety-two.

We will now give a table of distinguished men, with their ages independent of classification or chronology,—such names as are sufficiently known to the world to preclude the necessity of giving an account of their labors:—

	Age.		Age.
Bacon (Roger)	78	Herschel	84
Buffon	81	Laplace	77
Copernicus	70	Linnæus	72
Galileo	78	Metastasio	84
Lowenhoeck	91	Milton	66
Newton	84	Bacon (Lord)	65
Whiston	95	Hobbes	91
Young	84	Locke	72
Ferguson (Adam)	92	Stewart (D.)	75
Kant	80	Voltaire	84
Reid (T.)	86	Cumberland	80
Goethe	82	Southern (Thomas)	86
Crebillon	89	Coke (Lord)	85
Goldoni	85	Wilmot	83
Bentham	85	Rabelais	70
Mansfield	88	Harvey	81
Le Sage	80	Heberden	92
Wesley (John)	88	Michael Angelo	96

	Age.		Age.
Hoffman	83	Handel	75
Pinel	84	Haydn	77
Claude	82	Ruysch	93
Titian	96	Winslow	91
Franklin	85	Morgagni	89
Halley	86	Cardan	76
Rollin	80	Fleury (Cardinal)	90
Waller	82	Anquetil	84
Chalmers	83	Swift	78
South (Dr.)	83	Watts (Dr.)	74
Johnson (Dr.)	75	Watt (James)	83
Cherubini	82	Erasmus	69

This list is taken entirely at random, and might be almost indefinitely enlarged; but these illustrations suffice.

LONG LIFE AND HARD STUDY

Devotion to intellectual pursuits and to studies, even of the most severe and unremitting character, is not incompatible with extreme longevity, terminated by a serene and unclouded sunset. Dr. Johnson composed his "Dictionary" in seven years! And during that time he wrote also the Prologue to the opening of Drury Lane Theatre; the "Vanity of Human Wishes;" the tragedy of "Irene;" and the "Rambler;"—an almost incomprehensible effort of mind. He lived to the age of seventy-five. When Fontenelle's brilliant career terminated, and he was asked if he felt pain, he replied, "I only feel a difficulty of existing."

EXCITEMENT AND SHORT LIFE.

THE deadliest foe to man's longevity is an unnatural and unreasonable excitement. Every man is born with a certain stock of vitality, which cannot be increased, but which may be husbanded or expended as rapidly as he deems best. Within certain limits he has a choice, to live fast or slow, to live abstemiously or intensely, to draw his little amount of life over a single space, or condense it into a narrow one; but when his stock is exhausted, he has no more. He who lives abstemiously, who avoids all stimulants, takes light exercise, never overtasks himself, feeds his mind and heart on no exciting material, has no debilitating pleasure, lets nothing ruffle his temper, keeps his "accounts with God and man squared up," is sure, barring accidents, to spin out his life to the longest limit, which it is possible to attain; while he who lives intensely, who feeds on high-seasoned food, whether material or mental, fatigues his body or brain by hard labor, exposes himself to inflammatory diseases, seeks continual excitement, gives loose reign to his passion, frets at every trouble, and enjoys little repose, is burning the candle at both ends, and is sure to shorten his days

THE BLESSINGS OF A SHORT LIFE,

REV. T. DE WITT TALMAGE, D. D.

E all spend much time in panegyric of longevity. We consider it a great thing to live to be an octogenarian. If any one dies in youth we say, "What a pity!" Dr. Muhlenbergh in old age, said that the hymn written by him in early life by his own hand, no more expressed his sentiment when it said:

" I would not live alway."

If one be pleasantly circumstanced he never wants to go. William Cullen Bryant, the great poet, at eighty-two years of age standing in my house in a festal group, reading "Thanatopsis" without spectacles, was just as anxious to live as when at eighteen years of age he wrote that immortal threnody. Cato feared at eighty years of age that he would not live to learn Greek. Monaldesco at a hundred and fifteen years, writing the history of his time, feared a collapse. Theophrastus writing a book at ninety years of age was anxious to live to complete it. Thurlow Weed at about eighty-six years of age found life as great a desirability as when he snuffed out his first politician. Albert Barnes so well prepared for the next world at seventy said he would rather stay here. So it is all the way down. I suppose that the last time that Methuseleh was out of doors in a storm he was afraid of getting his feet wet lest it shorten his days.

Indeed, I sometime ago preached a sermon on the blessings of longevity, but in this, the last day of 1882, and when many are filled with sadness at the thought that another chapter of their life is closing, and that they have three hundred and sixyt-five days less to live, I propose to preach to you about *the blessings of an abbreviated earthly existence.*

If I were an agnostic I would say a man is blessed in proportion to the number of years he can stay on *terra firma,* because after that he falls off the docks, and if he is ever picked out of the depths it is only to be set up in some morgue of the universe to see if any body will claim him. If I thought God made man only to last forty or fifty or a hundred years, and then he was to go into annihilation, I would say his chief business ought to be to keep alive and even in good weather to be very cautious, and to carry an umbrella and take overshoes, and life preservers, and bronze armor, and weapons of defence lest he fall off into nothingness and obliteration.

But, my friends, you are not agnostics. You believe in immortality and the eternal residence of the righteous in heaven, and therefore I remark that an abbreviated earthly existence is to be desired, and is a blessing because it makes ones life-work very compact.

BUILDING UP LIFE.

TINIEST insects build up loftiest mountains. Broad bands of solid rock, which undergird the earth, have been welded by the patient, constant toil of invisible creatures, working on through the ages, unhasting, unresting, fulfilling their Maker's will. On the shores of primeval oceans, watched only by the patient stars, these silent workmen have been building for us the structure of the world. And thus the obscure work of unknown nameless ages appears at last in the sunlight, the adorned and noble theatre of that life of man, which, of all that is done in this universe, is fullest before God of interest and hope. It is thus, too, in life. The quiet moments build the years. The labors of the obscure and unremembered hours edify that palace of the soul, in which it is to abide, and fabricate the organ whereby it is to work and express itself through eternity.

J. B. Brown.

LIFE—NEW AND OLD.

THERE have been human hearts, constituted just like ours, for six thousand years. The same stars rise and set upon this globe that rose upon the plains of Shinar or along the Egyptian Nile; and the same sorrows rise and set in every age. All that sickness can do, all that disappointment can effect, all that blighted love, disappointed ambition, thwarted hope, ever did, they do still. Not a tear is wrung from eyes now, that, for the same reason, has not been wept over and over again in long succession since the hour that the fated pair stepped from paradise, and gave their posterity to a world of sorrow and suffering. The head learns new things; but the heart forevermore practices old experiences. Therefore our life is but a new form of the way men have lived from the beginning.

H. W. BEECHER.

LIFE AND DEATH.

LIFE makes the soul dependent on the dust,
Death gives her wings to mount above the spheres.
Through chinks, styled organs, dim life peeps at light,
Death bursts th' involving cloud, and all is day;
All eye, all ear, the disembodied power.
Death has *feigned* evils, Nature shall not feel.
Life, ill substantial, Wisdom cannot shun.
Is not the mighty mind,—that son of Heaven—
By tyrant *Life*, dethroned, imprisoned, pained?
By *Death* enlarged, ennobled, deified?
Death but entombs the body; Life the soul!....
Death is the crown of life. ....
Death wounds to cure: we fall, we rise, we reign!
Spring from our fetters, fasten in the skies.
Where blooming Eden withers in our sight,
Death gives us more than was in Eden lost.
This king of terrors is the prince of peace.
When shall I die to vanity, pain, death?
When shall I *die?*—When shall I live forever?

EDWARD YOUNG.

LIFE A RIVER.

PLINY compares life to a river. The river, small and clear in its origin, gushes forth from rocks, falls into deep glens, and wantons and meanders through a wild and picturesque country; nourishing only the uncultivated tree or flower by its dew or spray. In this, in its state of infancy and youth, it may be compared to the human mind, in which fancy, and strength of imagination, are predominant: it is more beautiful than useful. When the different rills or torrents join, and descend into the plain, it becomes slow and stately in its motions, and able to bear upon its bosom the stately barge. In this mature state, it is deep, strong, and useful. As it flows on towards the sea, it loses its force and its motion, and at last, as it were, becomes lost and mingled with the mighty abyss of waters.

SIR HUMPHRY DAVY.

LIFE'S DISCIPLINE A TRAINING FOR HEAVEN.

SIR HUMPHRY DAVY.

ALL speaks of change: the renovated forms
   Of long-forgotten things arise again.
The light of suns, the breath of angry storms,
   The everlasting motions of the main,—
These are but engines of the Eternal will,
   The One Intelligence, whose potent sway
Has ever acted, and is acting still,
   Whilst stars, and worlds, and systems all obey;
Without Whose power, the whole of mortal things
   Were dull, inert, an unharmonious band,
Silent as are the harp's untuned strings
   Without the touches of the poet's hand.
A sacred spark, created by His breath,
   The immortal mind of man His image bears;
A spirit living 'midst the forms of death,
   Oppressed, but not subdued, by mortal cares;
A germ, preparing in the winter's frost
   To rise, and bud, and blossom in the spring;
An unfledged eagle by the tempest tossed,
   Unconscious of his future strength of wing;
The child of trial, to mortality
   And all its changeful influences given,
On the green earth decreed to move and die,
   And yet, by such a fate, prepared for heaven!

LIFE A STREAM.

LIFE bears us on like the stream of a mighty river. Our boat at first glides down the narrow channel, through the playful murmuring of the little brook and the winding of its grassy borders. The trees shed their blossoms over young heads: the flowers on the brink seem to offer themselves to the young hands. We are happy in hope, and we grasp eagerly at the beauties around us; but the stream hurries on, and still our hands are empty. Our course in youth and manhood is along a wilder and deeper flood, amid objects more striking and magnificent. We are animated at the moving pictures, and enjoyments and industry passing us; we are excited at some short-lived disappointment. The stream bears us on; and our joys and griefs are alike left behind us. We may be shipwrecked; but we cannot be delayed. Whether rough or smooth, the river hastens to its home, till the roar of the ocean is in our ears, and the tossing of the waves is beneath our feet, and the land lessens from our eyes, and the floods are lifted up around us; and we take our leave of earth and its inhabitants until, of our future voyage, there is no witness save the Infinite and Eternal.

BISHOP HEBER.

LIFE IS PASSING.

THIS world is turning on its axis once in four and twenty hours; and, besides that, it is moving round the sun in the three hundred and sixty-five days of the year. So that we are all moving; we are flitting along through space. And as we are travelling through space, so we are moving through time at an incalculable rate. Oh! what an idea it is could we grasp it! We are all being carried along as if by a giant angel, with broad outstretched wings; which he flaps to the blast, and, flying before the lightning, makes us ride on the wind. The whole multitude of us are hurrying along,—whither, remains to be decided by the test of our faith and the grace of God; but certain it is, we are all travelling. Your pulses each moment beat the funeral marches to the tomb. You are chained to the chariot of rolling time. There is no bridling the steeds, or leaping from the chariot; you must be constantly in motion.

SPURGEON.

THE PASTOR'S COLLEGE (SPURGEON'S), LONDON.

JOHN WESLEY'S OLD AGE.

SAID the happy old man, when at the age of seventy-seven, "I do not remember to have felt lowness of spirits for one quarter of an hour since I was born." Of course, it is presumed he means that causeless depression which is usually the result of indolence. At the age of eighty-six he writes: "Saturday, March 21st, I had a day of rest, only preaching morning and evening."

It is wonderful to think that at nearly ninety years of age he could continue to make any effort to preach, but he did so, and he continued as a tower of strength to the companies he had formed and called together. But he outlived most of his early contemporaries, friends and foes. He stood in the pulpit of St. Giles', in London; he had preached there fifty years before, prior to his departure for America. "Are they not passed as a watch in the night?" he writes. Old families that used to entertain him had passed away. "Their houses," says he, "know neither me nor them any more." His later letters show that fervid sentiment for woman known only to loftiest minds and hearts; this again is entwined with beautiful simple regards for children. When he ascended the pulpit of Rathby Church, where he was often allowed to preach, a child sat in his way on the stairs, he took it in his arms and kissed it, and placed it tenderly on the same spot. Crabb Robinson heard him at Colchester; he was then eighty-seven; on each side of him stood a minister supporting him; his feeble voice was barely audible. Robinson, then a boy, destined to enter into his ninety-second year, says: "It formed a picture never to be forgotten." He goes on to say: "It went to the heart, and I never saw anything like it in after life." Three days after he preached at Lowestoft, and there he had another distinguished hearer, the poet Crabbe. Here, also, he was supported into the pulpit by a minister on either side; but what really touched the poet naturally and deeply was Wesley's adaptation and appropriation of some lines of Anacreon. The poet speaks of his reverent appearance, his cheerful air, and the beautiful cadence with which he repeated the lines:—

"Oft am I by women told,
Poor Anacreon, thou growest old;
See, thine hairs are falling all,

> Whether I grow old or no,
> By these signs I do not know;
> By this I need not be told,
> 'Tis *time* to *live* if I grow old."

THE SOONER WE GO THE BETTER.

REV. T. DE WITT TALMAGE, D. D.

WHAT fools we all are to prefer the circumference to the centre. What a dreadful thing it would be if we should be suddenly ushered from this wintry world into the Maytime orchards of heaven, and if our pauperism of sin and sorrow should be suddenly broken up by a presentation of an emperor's castle surrounded by parks with springing fountains, and paths up and down which angels of God walk two and two.

We are all like persons standing on the *cold steps of the national picture gallery* in London, under umbrella in the rain, afraid to go in amid the Turners and the Titians, and the Raphaels. I come to them and say: "Why don't you go inside the gallery?" "Oh," they say, "we don't know whether we can get in." I say: "Don't you see the door is open?" "Yes," they say, "but we have been so long on these cold steps, we are so attached to them we don't like to leave." "But," I say, "it is so much brighter and more beautiful in the gallery, you had better go in." "No," they say, "we know exactly how it is out here, but we don't know exactly how it is inside."

So we stick to this world as though we preferred cold drizzle to warm habitation, discord to cantata, sack-cloth to royal purple—as though we preferred a piano with four or five of the keys out of tune to an instrument fully attuned—as though earth and heaven had exchanged apparel, and earth had taken on bridal array and heaven had gone into deep mourning, all its waters stagnant, all its harps broken, all chalices cracked at the dry wells, all the lawns sloping to the river ploughed with graves of dead angels under the furrow. Oh, I want to break up my own infatuation and I want to break up your infatuation with this world. I tell you, if we are ready, and if our work is done, the sooner we go the better, and if there are blessings in longevity I want you to know right well there are also blessings in an abbreviated earthly existence.

> "The rougher the way, the shorter the stay;
> The tempests that rise, shall gloriously
> Hurry our souls to the skies."

BREVITY OF LIFE.

FRANCIS QUARLES.

BEHOLD!
How short a span
Was long enough of old
To measure out the life of man!
In those well-tempered days his time was then
Survey'd, cast up, and found but threescore years and ten.
ALAS!
And what is that?
They come, and slide, and pass,
Before my pen can tell thee what.
The posts of time are swift, which, having run
Their sev'n short stages o'er, their short-liv'd task is done.
OUR DAYS
Begun, we lend
To sleep, to antic plays
And toys, until the first stage end:
Twelve waning moons, twice five times told, we give
To unrecovered loss—we rather breathe than live.
HOW VAIN,
How wretched is
Poor man that doth remain
A slave to such a state as this!
His days are short, at longest; few, at most;
They are but bad, at best; yet lavished out or lost.
THEY BE
The secret springs,
That make our minutes flee
On wheels more swift than eagle's wings.
Our life's a clock, and every gasp of breath
Breathes forth a warning grief, till time shall strike a death.
HOW SOON
Our new-born light
Attains to full-aged noon!
And this, how soon to gray-haired night!
We spring, we bud, we blossom, and we blast,
Ere we can count our days, our days they flee so fast.
THEY END
When scarce begun,
And ere we apprehend
That we begin to live, our life is done.
Man! count thy days; and if they fly too fast
For thy dull thoughts to count, count every day thy last.

FAREWELL LIFE.

Farewell, Life! My senses swim,
And the world is growing dim:
Thronging shadows crowd the light,
Like the advent of the night;

Colder, colder, colder still,
Upward starts a vapor chill;
Strong the earthly odor grows,—
I smell the mould above the rose!

Welcome Life! The Spirit strives!
Strength returns, and hope revives;
Cloudy fears and shapes forlorn
Fly like shadows at the morn,—
O'er the earth there comes a bloom;
Sunny light for sullen gloom,
Warm perfume for vapor cold,—
I smell the rose above the mould!

Thomas Hood.

TO LIVE IS CHRIST.

Death in a sense is the gate of life eternal, but it is in life, this life, that graces must be wrought and fashioned that shall prepare the soul for the enjoyment of eternal life. Paul preaches, with all his heart and soul, the infinite preciousness of life. The Christian has the consciousness that in this life is the very work and presence of Christ. By leaving our work here before the time, we leave His work undone. By turning our backs in impatience on this mortal scene, we turn them on Him who is in these very struggles and sufferings. Every step forward in the cause of good is a step nearer to the life of Christ. Life is the state in which Christ makes Himself known to us and through which we must make ourselves known to Him. He sanctified and glorified every stage of it. And at every place and in every company He was the same Divine Master and Friend. Think then how much we have to do for Christ, and like Christ in whatever is left to us of life, to rise above ourselves, to lose ourselves in the thought of this great work that God has placed before us. For the sake of doing this, the apostle would consent to live, would prefer life with all its sorrows to death with all its gain. Death to us may be perfectly desirable, but life to us should be perfectly beautiful.

Dean Stanley.

LIFE IS FOR CHARACTER, AND CHARACTER FOR IMMORTALITY.

CARDINAL J. H. NEWMAN.

WHAT is our life for? There can be but one answer. This world is a training-school for character; as a pleasure-garden or a workshop it is a failure. Its flowers fade, its beauties pall, its work is never done, and is often broken off in the midst, or at the very beginning. There must be some better vindication of the Creator. It is this: The world is a school-house for man, for the whole of man. He has numerous faculties and powers; none can be left out. He has body, intellect, sensibilities, will. Are these all of man? Has he no conscience, no religious aspiration, no "longing after immortality?" Philosophy must include all the facts. Any view of life which debars from the fullest culture any part of our complex nature is essentially defective, and any view which omits the highest part is practically false.

This last indictment will be found to stand against the scheme of culture drawn out in the eloquent words of Mr. Huxley: "That man, I think, has had a liberal education who has been so trained in youth that his body is the ready servant of his will, and does with ease and pleasure all the work that as a mechanism it is capable of; whose intellect is a clear, cold, logic engine, with all its parts of equal strength and in smooth working order—ready, like a steam-engine, to be turned to any kind of work, and spin the gossamers as well as forge the anchors of the mind; whose mind is stored with the great and fundamental truths of Nature, and of the laws of her operations; one who, no stunted ascetic, is full of life and fire, but whose passions are trained to come to heel by a vigorous will, the servant of a tender conscience; who has learned to love all beauty, whether of nature or art, to hate all vileness, and to respect others as himself." Lovely picture of a culture radically defective; and in this defective form absolutely impossible, for lack of the divine element. No man ever yet trained "a vigorous will, the servant of a tender conscience," and learned "to hate all vileness and to respect others as himself," save under the searching eye of God, and by the transforming energy and abiding inspiration of the Holy Ghost.

There is painful proof that many professing Christians have no better notions of the possibilities of noble culture which every day affords than are indicated in our quotation from Mr. Huxley. They prize not the moments as gold dust, and are often laboriously occupied in "killing time." A competent authority declares the end of life to be to "seek for glory, honor, and immortality:" the glory of a true, symmetrical, godly character; the honor such a character is sure to win, and the immortality to which it leads.

>   Thou art my King—
>   My King henceforth alone;
>   And I, Thy Servant, Lord, am all Thine own.
>   Give me Thy strength; oh! let Thy dwelling be
>   In this poor heart that pants, my Lord, for Thee!
>   Gerhard Tersteegen.

METAPHORS OF LIFE.

> A flower that does with opening morn arise,
> And, flourishing the day, at evening dies;
> A winged eastern blast, just skimming o'er
> The ocean's brow, and sinking on the shore;
> A fire, whose flames through crackling stubble fly;
> A meteor shooting through the summer sky;
> A bowl adown the bending mountain rolled;
> A bubble breaking, and a fable told;
> A noon-tide shadow, and a midnight dream;
> Are emblems which, with semblance apt, proclaim
> Our earthly course; but O my soul! so fast
> Must life run out and death forever last?
>   Prior.

DEATH.

DEATH ON THE PALE HORSE.

THE DEATH-DAY BETTER THAN THE BIRTH-DAY.

REV. C. H. SPURGEON.

THE believer's death-day—the time of triumph and victory, is better than his birth-day. Birth is the beginning of a journey; death is the ending of the weary march to our Father's house above. Again, *about the birthday hangs an uncertainty.* Children are blessings, but we cannot tell what will become of them when they grow up and come under the influence of evil—they may be useful and honorable, or dissolute and degraded. But everything is certain about the saint's death-day. When a child is born we know he is born to sorrow, but when a saint dies, we know he is done with sorrow and pain. Write, therefore, the death-date above the life-date on the headstone.

The believer's death-day is better than all his happy days. What are his happy days? *The day of his coming of age*—he is a man, and an estate may be coming to him. This is a day of great festivity—all around may be called to rejoice with him. But on the death-day of a believer, he comes of age and enters upon his heavenly estate. What a jubilee that will be. *The day of his marriage* Who does not rejoice, what cold heart does not beat with joy on that day? But on the death-day we shall move fully into the joy of our Lord, into that blessed marriage union which is established between Him and us, into that guest chamber where the feast will be spread, and we shall await the Marriage Supper of the Lamb. *Day of gain.* When some sudden windfall enlarges their capital, or multiplies the profit. But there is no gain like that of departure to the Father from a world of trouble to a land of triumph. *A day of honor*—when promoted in office, or receiving the applause of men. But what a day of honor to be carried by angels into Abraham's bosom—heirs of God, joint heirs with Christ. *Days of health and happy days.* But what health can equal the perfect wholeness of a spirit upon whom the Physician has displayed his utmost skill—clean, recovered, and where the inhabitants shall no more say, "I am sick." *Happy days of social friendship*, when hearts warm with hallowed intercourse with a friend, or in the midst of one's family. But no day of social enjoyment can equal the day of death. What troops of blessed ones shall meet us! What priceless friends over yonder! What family greetings there will be! Oh, the bliss of meeting with the Lord! Those who are truly related to us in the bonds of everlasting life shall be there. Natural kinship has ended, spiritual relationship lasts and survives.

It is better than his holy days. *The day of conversion.* Never to be forgotten when the heart began to beat with spiritual life, and the hand grasped the Lord, and the eyes saw His beauty. But what will it be to see Him face to face? *The Sabbath day.* Precious and dear are the Lord's days—sweet rests of love—blessed days. But death gives us an eternal Sabbath, "where congregations ne'er break up." *Communion days.* How sweet to sit at the Lord's table with His memorial in hand, and to think of what He has done, is doing, and has promised. What is that to communing with Him in Paradise. Bless the Lord for every one of the happy days—but heaven's days will be better. There we shall know each other better—more delight, in magnifying the name of Jesus. Our company shall be better—perfect company, and we shall then be at *home*

It is better than the whole of his days put together. All his days here are dying days. Death is the end of dying. Life is conflict—death is victory. Life is full of sorrow, death ends that. Life is longing, death possessing.

THE EVENING OF DEATH.

REV. T. DE WITT TALMAGE.

I have heard it said that we ought to live as though each moment were to be our last. I do not believe that theory. As far as preparation is concerned, we ought always to be ready; but we cannot always be thinking of death, for we have duties in life that demand our attention. When a man is selling goods, it is his business to think of the bargain he is making. When a man is pleading in the courts it is his duty to think of the interests of his clients. When a clerk is adding up accounts it is his duty to keep his mind upon the column of figures. He who fills up his life with thoughts of death is far from being the highest style of Christian. I knew a man who used often to say at night, "I wish I might die before morning!" He is now an infidel.

But there are times when we can and ought to give ourselves to the contemplation of that solemn moment when to the soul time ends and eternity begins. We must go through that one pass. There is no roundabout way, no by path, no circuitous route. Die we must; and it will be to us a shameful occurrence or a time of admirable behavior. Our friends may stretch out their hands to keep us back, but no imploration on their part can hinder us. They might offer us large retainers, but death would not take the fee. The breath will fail and the eyes will close and the heart will stop. You may hang the couch with gorgeous tapestry, but what does death care for bed curtains? You may hang the room with the finest works of art, but what does death care for pictures? You may fill the house with the wailings of widowhood and orphanage; does death mind weeping?

This ought not to be a depressing theme. Who wants to live here forever? The world has always treated me well, and every day I feel less and less like scolding and complaining. But yet I would not want to make this my eternal residence. I love to watch the clouds and to bathe my soul in the blue sea of heaven; but I expect, when the firmament is rolled away as a scroll to see a new heaven, grander, higher and more glorious. You ought to be willing to exchange your body that has headaches and sideaches and weaknesses innumerable, that limps with the stone-bruises or festers

DEATH AND ITS WARNINGS.

D. L. MOODY.

HERE is a legend that I read some time ago of a man who made a covenant with Death; and the covenant was this: that Death should not come on him unawares,—that Death was to give warning of his approach. Well, years rolled on, and at last, Death stood before his victim. The old man blanched and faltered out: "Why, Death, you have not been true to your promise, you have not kept your covenant. You promised not to come unannounced. You never gave any warning." "How, how!" came the answer, "every one of those gray hairs is a warning; every one of your teeth is a warning; your eyes growing dim are a warning; your natural power and vigor abated—that is a warning. Aha! I've warned you—I've warned you continually." And Death would not delay, but swept his victim into eternity.

That is a legend; but how many the past year have heard these warning voices? Death has come very near to many of us. What warnings have come to us all. The preacher's call to repentance, how again and again they have rung in our ears. We may have one or two more calls yet, this year, in the next few hours, but I doubt it. Then how many of us in the last twelve months have gone to the bedside of some loved friend, and kneeling in silent anguish unable to help, have whispered a promise to meet that dying one in heaven? Oh, why delay any longer! Before these few lingering hours have gone, and the year rolls away into eternity, I beg of you, see to it that you prepare to make that promise good. Some of you have kissed the marble brow of a dead parent this year, and the farewell look of those eyes has been, "Make ready to meet thy God." In a few years you will follow, and there may be a reunion in heaven. Are you ready, dear friends?

When visiting the body of my brother just before he was put in the grave, I picked up his Bible, of the size of this in my hand, and there was just one passage of scripture marked. I looked it up and found it read: "Whatsoever thy hand findeth to do, do it with thy might." As I read it that night the hand that wrote it was silent in death. It was written in 1876. Little did he think when he wrote it that in that same year he would be silent in the grave. Little did he think that the autumn wind and the winter snow would go roaring over his grave. Thank God it was a year of jubilee to him. That year he found salvation; it was a precious year to his soul. That year he met his God. How often have I thanked God for that brother's triumphant death! It seems as though I could not live to think he had gone down to the grave unprepared to meet his God,—gone without God and hope. Dear friends, dear unsaved friends,—I appeal to you that you will now accept Christ. Seize the closing hours of this year; let not this year die till the great question is decided. I plead with you once more to come to the Lord Jesus. Oh, hear these blessed words of Christ as I shout them again in your hearing: "Therefore be ye also ready."

DEATH IS YOURS.

REV. JOHN CAIRD, D. D.

DEATH comes at Christ's command to call the believer to Himself; and grim and ghastly though be the look of the messenger, surely that may well be forgotten in the sweetness of the message he brings. Death comes to set the spirit free; and rude though be the hand that knocks off the fetters, and painful though be the process of liberation, what need the prisoner care for that, when it is to freedom, life, home, he is about to be emancipated? Death strikes the hour of the soul's everlasting espousals, and though the sound may be a harsh one, what matters that? To common ears it may seem a death-knell, to the ear of faith it is a bridal peal. "Now," may the fainting passing soul reflect, "now my Lord is coming, I go to meet Him—to be with Jesus—to dwell with Him in everlasting light and love—to be severed from Him no more forever. O, Death, lead thou me on!" Or, if frail nature should faint and fail in that awful hour, surely this may be its strong consolation, the thought that even in the article of dissolution, He to whom the soul belongs is near and close beside it, to sustain the fortitude of His servant, and shield him in the last alarms

"The night falls dark upon my spirit; I tremble to go forth into that awful mystery and gloom; help, Lord, for my spirit faileth,"—is this the cry of its passing anguish? "Fear not," will be the sweet response that falls upon the inner ear—"Fear not, I am with thee; the night is far spent, the day is at hand; a little moment, and the shadows shall flee away for ever!" "O, Death!" may not the dying saint, rising into the magnanimity of this glorious faith, exclaim—"O, Death, I fear thee not: I am not thine, but thou art mine! Thanks be to God that giveth me the victory through Jesus Christ my Lord!"

DEATH IS LIFE.

THEN familiarize your mind with the inevitable event of death. Think of it, as life! Gloomy though the portal seems, death is the gate of life to a good and pious man. Think of it therefore, not as death, but as glory—going to heaven and to your father. Regard it in the same light as the good man who said when I expressed my sorrow to see him sinking into the grave, "I am going home." If you think of it as death, then let it be as the death of sin; the death of pain; the death of fear; the death of care; the death of Death. Regard its pangs and struggles as the battle that goes before victory; its troubles as the swell of the sea on heaven's happy shore; and yon gloomy passage as the cypress-shaded avenue that shall conduct your steps to heaven. It is life through Christ, and life in Christ; life most blissful, and life evermore, How much happier and holier we should be if we could look on death in that light. I have heard people say, that we should think each morning that we may be dead before night; and each night that we may be dead before morning! True: yet how much better to think every morning, I may be in heaven before night; and every night that the head is laid on the pillow, and the eyes are closed for sleep, to think, next time I open them it may be to look on Jesus, and the land where there is no night, nor morning; nor sunset, nor cloud; nor grave nor grief; nor sin, nor death, nor sorrow; nor toil, nor trouble; where "they rest from their labors, and their works do follow them."

Rev. Dr. Guthrie.

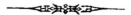

DEATH AN ANGEL OF LIGHT.

ARE we then immortal? Oh! then, we are "blessed" indeed! Death is not the frightful monster which he is so constantly represented to be; he is an angel of light and mercy, veiling his resplendent glories under the shadowy drapery of the tomb, lest the saints should become so much enamored with his loveliness, as to hasten at once to leave this erring, darkened world, to dwell in his radiant dominion, and thus deprive the earth of the salt which has so long preserved it from destruction. His exit, through the frowning portals of the grave, is but to prevent those who are "in the Lord," from crowding, with hasty, willing steps, the pathway to his mysterious dwelling place, so delightful and glorious, as soon as the gloomy exterior is passed! Can it be, that this body, soon to become inanimate, and waste to dust, can, and will, revive and live? that the eye, though dimmed with the film of death, will rebrighten, and sparkle with looks of recognition and love? That this lifeless body, once so loved, and embraced with the fondest affection and delight, but now so loathsome that it is looked upon with horror, and we bear it from our sight, and conceal it from view in the dark earth, will come forth more perfect and glorious than ever? Yea, saith the Spirit; from henceforth, "Blessed are the dead which die in the Lord;" for "It is sown in dishonor, it is raised in glory; it is sown in weakness, it is raised in power. For this corruptible must put on incorruption, and this mortal must put on immortality." Then shall death be swallowed up in victory. Oh! are they not "blessed" who die only to live forever, in a state so infinitely above the most perfect condition of humanity, that it is "not worthy to be compared with the glory which shall be revealed in us."

Rev. SIDNEY DYER, D. D.

WHAT IS DEATH?

"What is the soul? The seminal principle from the loins of destiny,
This world is the womb: the body, its enveloping membrane:
The bitterness of dissolution, dame Fortune's pangs of childbirth.
What is death? To be born again, an angel of eternity."

BUZURGI. (*The Persian Poet*.)

RIGHT AND WRONG VIEWS OF DEATH.

PROF. A. P. PEABODY, D. D.

WE employ with regard to death a great deal of pagan imagery, which can hardly fail to let low and unworthy ideas into our minds. We talk of the *blighting* of early promise, of the *premature* death of the young and the beautiful. We too often speak of the pure and the good that have gone from us, as if they were objects of pity. We regret for them the brief pleasures, the withering joys of the passing day. And then our thoughts revert, oftener than a high Christian culture should permit, to the sad accompaniments of dissolution and the last lonely home of the frail tenement of clay, even as the caterpillar might look upon the torn covering of the chrysalis as all that remained of his fellow-worm, ignorant that the rent and forsaken tabernacle marked the higher birth of its tenant. But our faith tells us that to those to whom it was Christ to live, it is gain to die. Let our thoughts, then, linger not about the grave, but seek our kindred in the nearer presence of their Father and their Saviour, in the home where every holy wish is met and every pure desire fulfilled, where suffering and sorrow are no more, and life clothes itself in eternal youth and unfading beauty. What would our brief joys be to those to whom all the avenues of divine wisdom are free, the riches of infinite love unfolded, and a boundless sphere of duty and of happiness laid open? In the language of Moore:

> How happy
> The holy spirits who wander there,
> 'Mid flowers that shall never fade or fall!
> Though mine were the gardens of earth and sea,
> Though the stars themselves had flowers for me,
> One blossom of heaven outblooms them all.
> Go, wing thy flight from star to star,
> From world to luminous world, as far
> As the universe spreads its flaming wall;
> Take all the pleasures of all the spheres,
> And multiply each through endless years,
> One minute of heaven is worth them all.

THE DEAD ARE THE LIVING.

I HAVE seen one die—the delight of his friends, the pride of his kindred, the hope of his country: but he died! How beautiful was that offering upon the altar of death! The fire of genius kindled in his eye; the generous affections of youth mantled in his cheek; his foot was upon the threshold of life; his studies, his preparations for honored and useful life, were completed; his breast was filled with a thousand glowing, and noble, and never yet expressed aspirations; but he died! He died; while another, of a nature dull, coarse and unrefined, of habits low, base, and brutish, of a promise that had nothing in it but shame and misery—such an one, I say was suffered to encumber the earth. Could this be, if there were no other sphere for the gifted, the aspiring, and the approved, to act in? Can we believe that the energy just trained for action, the embryo thought just bursting into expression, the deep and earnest passion of a noble nature, just swelling into the expansion of every beautiful virtue, should never manifest its power, should never speak, should never unfold itself? Can we believe that all this should die; while meanness, corruption, sensuality, and every deformed and dishonored power should live? No, ye goodly and glorious ones! ye godlike in youthful virtue!—ye die not in vain: ye teach, ye assure us, that ye are gone to some world of nobler life and action.

I have seen one die; she was beautiful; and beautiful were the ministries of life that were given her to fulfill. Angelic loveliness enrobed her; and a grace as if it were caught from heaven, breathed in every tone, hallowed every affection, shone in every action—invested, as a halo, her whole existence, and made it a light and blessing, a charm and a vision of gladness, to all around her: but she died! Friendship, and love, parental fondness, and infant weakness, stretched out their hand to save her; but they could not save her: and she died! What! did all that loveliness die? Is there no land of the blessed and the lovely ones, for such to live in? Forbid it, reason, religion!—bereaved affection, and undying love! forbid the thought! It cannot be that such die in God's counsel, who live even in frail human memory, forever!

REV. ORVILLE DEWEY, D. D.

DEATH THE DESTROYER AND RESTORER.

THERE is proclaimed one mightier than death or hell. He is the Prince of Life and Lord of Glory He, in bringing rescue tasted of death, yea not only met the common lot, but bore on himself the common and concentrated guilt of our race. Doing this he tore the sting from death and to them that believe, He is become the author of life, everlasting life.

To them that receive Christ, the war though fierce has lost its main terror and is stripped of its perils, mortality loses its ghastliness and puts on hopefulness and promise. The grave is like the wet, cold March day, behind whose gloom lie the treasures of bursting spring and the glories of refulgent summer. The light afflictions are but for a moment. Death to the saint changes many of its offices. If pain walks at his side, He is also the queller of strife and the calmer of care. No more throbs or sighs, but rest. He is in one sense the Destroyer, but in another the Restorer. He brings back, through Christ's victorious grave, the lost innocence and peace of Eden. He divides the nearest ties, but also re-unites to those who sleep in Jesus. He is the curse of the law, but through the blessed one, who magnified and satisfied the law, he becomes to the believer in Jesus, the end of sin, the gate of Paradise, and the recompense of a new, a better and an unending life.

REV. W. R. WILLIAMS, D. D.

DEATH DOES NOT END ALL.

IN another and perhaps more philosophical view of the case, no adequate, logical reason could be given for human existence, if this life ended all. Man stood at the apex of a pyramid. Below him were the various forms of life, animal and vegetable, and the inanimate kingdom. Everything in the world had an object, an end. There was a reason in its existence, and it subserved some end. The inanimate world—the dull, cold rock and metal—served a purpose in furnishing the essentials for animal and vegetable life. The vegetable world supported the animal world, and each higher form of life subsisted on a lower form, the end of whose existence was thus attained until man was reached. But what was the end of man's life if it ended here? He was a philosophical failure, a cosmic anti-climax. If this life, however, was but a state of preparation for a future existence, no violence was done to this grand law which seemed to pervade all forms of matter, animate and inanimate.

Rev. H. M. Scudder, D. D.

DESTRUCTION OF THE ASSYRIANS.

BYRON.

The Assyrian came down like the wolf on the fold,
And his cohorts were gleaming in purple and gold;
And the sheen of their spears was like stars on the sea,
When the blue wave rolls nightly on deep Galilee.

Like the leaves of the forest when summer is green,
That host with their banners at sunset were seen;
Like the leaves of the forest when autumn hath blown,
That host on the morrow lay withered and strown.

For the angel of death spread his wings on the blast,
And breathed on the face of the foe as he passed,
And the eyes of the sleepers waxed deadly and chill,
And their hearts but once heaved, and for ever grew still.

And there lay the steed with his nostril all wide,
But through it there rolled not the breath of his pride;
And the foam of his gasping lay white on the turf,
And cold as the spray of the rock-beaten surf.

And there lay the rider, distorted and pale,
With the dew on his brow and the rust on his mail;
And the tents were all silent, the banners alone,
The lances unlifted, the trumpet unblown,

And the widows of Ashur are loud in their wail,
And the idols are broken in the temple of Baal;
And the might of the Gentile, unsmote by the sword,
Hath melted like snow in the glance of the Lord.

THE DESTRUCTION OF THE ASSYRIANS.

THE VOICES OF THE DEAD.

THE world is filled with the voices of the dead. They speak not from the public records of the great world only, but from the private history of our own experience. They speak to us in a thousand remembrances, in a thousand incidents, events, associations. They speak to us, not only from their silent graves, but from the throng of life. Though they are invisible, yet life is filled with their presence. They are with us, by the silent fireside and in the secluded chamber: they are with us in the paths of society, and in the crowded assembly of men. They speak to us from the lonely way-side; and they speak to us, from the venerable walls that echo to the steps of a multitude, and to the voice of prayer. Go where we will, the dead are with us. We live, we converse, with those, who once lived and conversed, with us. Their well remembered tone mingles with the whispering breezes, with the sound of the falling leaf, with the jubilee shout of the spring-time. The earth is filled with their shadowy train.

But there are more substantial expressions of the presence of the dead with the living. The earth is filled with labors, the works, of the dead. Almost all the literature in the world, the discoveries of science, the glories of art, the ever-during temples, the dwelling-places of generations, the comforts and improvements of life, the languages, the maxims, the opinions, of the living, the very frame-work of society, the institutions of nations, the fabrics of empires—all are the works of the dead; by these, they who are dead yet speak. Life—busy, eager, craving, importunate, absorbing life—yet what is its sphere, compared with the empire of death! What, in other words, is the sphere of visible, compared with the mighty empire of invisible life! They live—they live indeed, whom we call dead. They live in our thoughts; they live in our blessings; they live in our life; "death hath no power over them."

REV. ORVILLE DEWEY, D. D.

When the pure soul is from the body flown,
No more shall night's alternate reign be known;
The sun no more shall rolling light bestow,
But from th' Almighty streams of glory flow.
Oh, may some nobler thought my soul employ
Than empty, transient, sublunary joy!
The stars shall drop, the sun shall lose his flame,
But Thou, O, God! for ever shine the same.

JOHN GRAY.

THE SPIRIT SURVIVES IN ITS COMPLETENESS

REV. CANON H. P. LIDDON, D. D.

MY brethren, observe, that man's spirit cannot be resolved like his body into form and material, the former perishing while the latter survives. Man's spirit either exists in its completeness, or it ceases to exist. The bodily form of William the Conqueror has long dissolved into dust. The material atoms which made up the body of William the Conqueror during his lifetime exist somewhere now beneath the pavement of the great church at Caen; but if the memory and the conscience and the will of the Conqueror have perished, then his spirit has ceased to be. There is no substratum below or beyond these which could perpetuate existence; there is nothing spiritual to survive them, for the soul of man— your soul and mine—knows itself to be an indivisible whole— something which cannot be broken into parts, and enter into unison with other souls—with other minds. Each of us is himself. Each can become no other. My memory, my affections, my way of thinking and feeling are all my own; they are not transferable. If they perish they perish all together. There are no atoms to survive them which can be worked into another spiritual existence; and thus the extinction of an animal or a vegetable is only the extinction of that particular combination of matter—not of the matter itself; but the extinction of a soul, if the thing were possible, would be the total extinction of all that made it to be what it ever was. In the physical world, destruction and death are only changes. In the spiritual world, the only possible analogous process would mean annihilation. And, therefore, it is a reasonable and a very strong presumption that spirit is not, in fact, placed at this enormous disadvantage when compared with matter, and that, if matter survives the dissolution of organic forms, much more must spirit survive the dissolution of the material forms with which it has been for a while associated.

He lay within the light of God,
Like a babe upon the breast;
Where the wicked cease from troubling,
And the weary at rest.

DEATH OVERCOME.

Where faith in Jesus raises a dying man above the sufferings of nature, and a sinful man above the terrors of guilt, illuminating the closing scene with the hopes and very light of approaching glory, this close of life is the grandest of sunsets. Nowhere, does religion look so magnificent as amid such scenes. And never does she seem so triumphant as when, with her fingers closing the filmy eyes, she contemplates the peaceful corpse; and bending down to take one fond kiss of pallid lips, or marble brow, rises, and raises her hands to heaven, exclaims, Blessed are the dead! The battle done; the victory won; rest, warrior! workman! pilgrim!—rest! "Blessed are the dead which die in the Lord; for they rest from their labors, and their works do follow them."

Rev. Dr. Guthrie.

It is not death at all; it is life. Some one said to a person dying: "Well, you are in the land of the living yet." "No," said he, "I am in the land of the dying yet, but I am going to the land of the living; they live there and never die." This is the land of sin and death and tears, but up yonder they never die. It is perpetual life; it is unceasing.

D. L. Moody.

DEATH AND IMMORTALITY.

The dreadful night darksomnesse
  Had overspread the light,
And sluggish sleep with drowsinesse
  Had overprest our might:
A glass wherein you may behold
  Each storm that stops our breath,
One bed, the grave, our clothes like mould
  And sleep like dreadful death.

Yet as this deadly night did last
  But for a little space,
And heavenly day, now night is past,
  Doth show his pleasant face;
So must we hope to see God's face
  At last in heaven on high,
When we have changed this mortal place
  For immortality.

George Gascoigne.

CONTRASTS IN DEATH.

BUT "Death robs us of all things," exclaims the sordid worldling. "To die is gain!" responds the expectant believer.—"Death is an eternal sleep," affirms the boasting atheist. "The dead in Christ shall awake, and come forth, incorruptible, immortal, and glorified," replies the confiding Christian.—"Death is the King of Terrors," tremblingly exclaims the unprepared traveller to the grave. "Oh! death, where is thy sting? Oh! grave, where is thy victory?" shouts the trusting disciple of the cross.—"All that I have will I give for my life!" groans the dying lover of this world. "I would not live always," responds the emancipated follower of the Prince of Life.

> "Away with death, away,
> With all his sluggish sleep and chilling damp,
> Imperious to the day,
> Where nature sinks into insanity;
> How can the soul desire
> Such hateful nothingness to crave,
> And yield with joy the vital fire,
> To moulder in the grave!"

Thus shrieks the shrinking voluptuary.

> "Who, who would live alway away from his God,
> Away from yon heaven, that blissful abode,
> Where rivers of pleasure flow o'er the bright plains,
> And the noontide of glory eternally reigns?"

Thus sings the enraptured saint.

REV. SIDNEY DYER, D. D.

OUR BURIAL PLACES SACRED.

How we linger around the cold remains of a friend till absolutely driven from it! How we care for it, as for some precious gem not always to be trodden in the dust! How reverently we commit it to the keeping of its mother earth; bidding it good night as if in attendance on the councils of royalty!

How sacred is the spot where he lies! How often do we retire not alone to weep but to hold sweet communion with the departed, and say, "We shall meet again."

THE REV. ALEXANDER MCCLELLAND, D. D.

TOWARD EVENING.

You are almost through with the abuse and backbiting of enemies. They will call you no more by evil names. Your good deeds will not longer be misinterpreted or your honor filched. The troubles of earth will end in the felicities of heaven! Toward evening! The bereavements of earth will soon be lifted. You will not much longer stand pouring your grief in the tomb like Rachel weeping for her children or David mourning for Absalom. Broken hearts bound up. Wounds healed. Tears wiped away. Sorrows terminated. No more sounding of the dead march! Toward evening. Death will come sweet as slumber to the eyelids of the baby, as full rations to a starving soldier, as evening hour to the exhausted workman. The sky will take on its sunset glow, every cloud a fire-psalm, every lake a glassy mirror; the forests transfigured; delicate mists climbing in the air. Your friends will announce it; your pulses will beat it; your joys will ring it; your lips will whisper it: "Toward evening."

TALMAGE.

DEATH THE GATE OF LIFE.

Oh! death!—dark hour to hopeless unbelief! hour to which, in that creed of despair, no hour shall succeed! being's last hour! to whose appalling darkness, even the shadows of an avenging retribution were brightness and relief—death! what art thou to the Christian's assurance? Great hour of answer to life's prayer—great hour that shall break asunder the bond of life's mystery—hour of release from life's burden—hour of reunion with the loved and lost—what mighty hopes, hasten to their fulfilment in thee! What longings, what aspirations,—breathed in the still night, beneath the silent stars —what dread emotions of curiosity—what deep meditations of joy—what hallowed imaginings of never experienced purity and bliss—what possibilities shadowing forth unspeakable realities to the soul, all verge their consummation in thee! Oh! death! the Christian's death! what art thou but the gate of life, the portal of heaven, the threshold of eternity!

REV. ORVILLE DEWEY, D. D.

TWO FUNERALS.

There are two funerals for every Christian; one the funeral of the body and the other the soul—rather it is the marriage of the soul; for angels stand ready to carry it to the Saviour. The angels, imitating husbandmen, as they near the gates of heaven may shout "Harvest Home." There is a holiday whenever a saint enters—and there is praise to God,

> "While life, or thought, or being lasts
> Or immortality endures."

Spurgeon.

DEATH OF THE GOOD MAN.

Sure the last end
Of the good man is peace! How calm his exit!
Night dews fall not more gently to the ground,
Nor weary worn-out winds expire so soft.
Behold him in the evening-tide of life—
A life well spent—whose early care it was
His riper years should not upbraid his green:
By unpreceived degrees he wears away;
Yet, like the sun, seems larger at his setting.
High in his faith and hopes, look how he reaches
After the prize in view! and, like a bird
That's hamper'd, struggles hard to get away;
While the glad gates of sight are wide expanded
To let new glories in, the first fair fruits
Of the last-coming harvest. Then, Oh, then!
Each earth-born joy grows vile, or disappears,
Shrunk to a thing of nought. Oh, how he longs
To have his passport sign'd, and be dismiss'd!
'Tis done, and now he's happy! The glad soul
Has not a wish uncrown'd! E'en the lag flesh
Rests, too, in hope of meeting once again
Its better half, never to sunder more.
Nor shall it hope in vain: the time draws on
When not a single spot of burial earth,
Whether on land or in the spacious sea,
But must give back its long-committed dust
Inviolate.

Robert Blair.

DEATH PANGS, BIRTH PANGS.

O a child of God, what are its pains but the pangs of birth; its battle, but the struggle that precedes the victory; its tossings but the swell and surf that beats on the shores of eternal life; its grave but a bed of peaceful rest, where the bodies of saints sleep out the night that shall fly away for ever before the glories of a resurrection morn. I know a churchyard where this is strikingly set forth in the rude sculpturing of a burial stone. Beneath an angel figure, that, with outstretched wings and trumpet at the mouth, blows the resurrection, there lies a naked skull. Beneath the angel, and beside this emblem of mortality, two forms stand; one is the tenant of the grave below, the other it is impossible to mistake, it is the skeleton figure of the King of Terrors. His dart lies on the ground broken in two, and the hand that has dropped it is stretched out over the skull, and held in the grasp of the other figure. Enemies reconciled, the man bravely shakes hands with death, and his whole bearing show that they are become sworn friends. As if he had just heard Jesus announcing, I am the resurrection and the life, you seem to hear him saying, O, death, where is thy sting, O, grave, where is thy victory? The sting of death is sin, and the strength of sin is the law; but thanks be to God who giveth me the victory through my Lord Jesus Christ.

Rev. Dr. Guthrie.

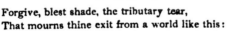

Forgive, blest shade, the tributary tear,
That mourns thine exit from a world like this:
Forgive the wish that would have kept thee here,
And stayed thy progress to the realms of bliss.
    When my dying hour must be,
    Be not absent then from me:
    In that dreadful hour I pray,
    Jesus, come without delay,
        See and set me free.
    When Thou biddest me depart,
    Whom I cleave to with my heart,
    Lover of my soul be near,
    With Thy saving cross appear,
       'Show Thyself to me.

Bernard, of Clairvaux.

WE LOVE TO VISIT OUR CEMETERIES.

AND Death is an event we do not attempt to shut out of view. Here, our city has its cemeteries, which, by their taste and beauty, rather attract than repel a visit. There, where hoary, trees fling their shadow on graves, stands the rural church within whose humble walls the living worship in closest neighborhood with the dead; a type of heaven, the approach to that sanctuary is by a path which passes through the realms of death. When death occurs among us, friends and neighbors are invited to the funeral; and in broad day the sad procession, following the nodding hearse, wends slowly along our most public streets. The spot that holds our dead we sometimes visit, and always regard as a sort of sacred ground; there a monument is raised to record their virtues; or a willow, with its weeping branches flung over the grave, expresses our grief; or a pine or a laurel, standing there in evergreen beauty when frosty blasts have stripped the woods; symbolises the hopes of the living, and the immortality of death; our hands plants some sweet flowers, which though they shed their blossoms as our hopes were shed, and hide their heads awhile beneath the turf, spring up again to remind us how the dear ones who there sleep in Jesus are awaiting the resurrection of the just.

REV. DR. GUTHRIE.

JESUS THE PRECIOUS NAME IN DEATH.

WHAT if the sun of life is about to set? Jesus is the day-spring from on high; the perpetual morning of every ransomed spirit. What if the darkness comes? Jesus is the light of the world and of heaven What though this earthly house does crumble? Jesus has prepared a house of many mansions. Jesus is the anchor that always holds. Jesus is the light that is never eclipsed. Jesus is the fountain that is never exhausted. Jesus is the evening star, hung up amid the gloom of the gathering night.

TALMAGE.

THE DEATH OF DEATH.

Our Lord himself shrank from death; he cast himself at his Father's feet, to cry in an agony, If it be possible let this cup pass from me. And who, unless some unhappy wretch, courts death, wishes to die, to lie down among those naked skulls, and the grim unsocial tenants of the grave? Faith herself turns away from the thought. Standing on the edge of the grave, she turns her eye upward; and, leaving the poor body to worms and dust, she wings her flight heavenward, follows the spirit to the realms of bliss, and loves to think of the dead as living; as not dead; as standing before the Lamb with crowns of glory, and bending on us looks of love and kindness from their celestial seats. Yes; death needs all the comforts that religion can summon to our aid.

Nor has Christ left His people comfortless. By His life, and death, and resurrection, He has fulfilled the high expectations of prophets; nor, bold as it is, is the language too lofty which Hosea puts into his mouth, O, death, I will be thy plagues; O, grave, I will be thy destruction. The death of Death, the life of the grave and greatest of all its tenants, he has conquered the conqueror of kings; he has broken the prison, he has bound the jailer, he has seized the keys, and he comes in the fullness of time to set all his imprisoned people free. They are prisoners of hope. He will bring back his banished. He has entered into glory as their forerunner, or, as "the first-born from the dead."

Rev. Dr. Guthrie.

―――O―――

Fuerbach, a German author of extraordinary acumen and audacity has said: "Only before death, but not in death, is death death. Death is so unreal a being that he only is when he is not, and is not when he is." This—paradoxical and puzzling as it may appear—is susceptible of quite lucid interpretation and defence. For death is, in its naked significance, the state of not-being. Of course, then, it has no existence save in the conceptions of the living. We compare a dead person with what he was when living, and instinctively personify the difference as death. Death, strictly analyzed, is only this abstract conceit or metaphysical nonentity. Death, therefore, being but a conception in the mind of a living person, when that person dies death ceases to be at all. And thus the realization of death is the death of death. He annihilates himself, dying with the dart he drives. Having in his manner disposed of the personality or entity of death, it remains as an effect, an event, a state. Accordingly, the question next arises: What is death when considered in this its true aspect?

W. R. ALGER.

THE DEATH OF A GOOD MAN.

AND when you see the body of a saint, if he has served God with all his might, how sweet it is to look upon him—ah, and to look upon his coffin too, or upon his tomb in after years! Go into Bunhill-fields, and stand by the memorial of John Bunyan and you will say: "Ah! there lies the head that contained the brain which thought out that wondrous dream of the Pilgrim's Progress from the City of Destruction to the better land. There lie the fingers that wrote those wondrous lines which depict the story of him who came at last to the land of Beulah, and waded through the flood, and entered into the celestial city. And there are the eyelids which he once spoke of, when he said: "If I lie in prison until the moss grows on my eyelids, I will never make a promise to withhold from preaching." And there is that bold eye that penetrated the judge, when he said: "If you will let me out of prison to-day, I will preach again to-morrow, by the help of God." And there lies that loving hand that was ever ready to receive into communion all them that loved the Lord Jesus Christ: I love the hand that wrote the book, "Water Baptism no Bar to Christian Communion." I love him for that sake alone, and if he had written nothing else but that, I would say: "John Bunyan, be honored for ever."

SPURGEON.

Let me grow by sun and shower,
  Every moment water me;
Make me really 'hour by hour
  More and more conformed to Thee,
That Thy loving eye may trace,
  Day by day, my growth in grace.

H. R. HAVERGAL.

A STINGLESS DEATH.

REV. J. OSWALD DYKES, D. D.

The Christian's is a stingless death. Death to such a one is an angel of peace. He comes to loose the prison-bands of clay and set them free to go home to their Father's house. Theirs is the gain, ours is the loss, yet not all, for we must not forget that Christ's gospel has a power of transmuting present bereavement into gain. Bereavement is often turned for those who live into a blessing. God did two kindnesses at one stroke when He bereft you of your beloved; one kindness to him; another kindness to you. To him, the perfecting of character and bestowal of bliss; to you, ripening of character and preparation for bliss.

By such sweet solaces of sorrow as these, Christ leads us forward to the hope of a yet future and still grander consolation, when we shall be reunited in a holy place and forever. It was a prediction of this which Jesus gave that day at Nain by the resurrection of the dead son and his reunion to his mother. The resurrection of Christ Himself is that which guarantees the ultimate unpeopling of every tomb, including that "vast and wandering grave," the sea. His risen body presents the type of every reconstructed Christian body. His glorified life is the source and pledge of their life in glory. For this recall from death by the archangel's voice to Christ's own deathless and transfigured immortality, as for the deepest, grandest and last of our consolations, Christ bids us hope. Now we are sad and weary for we dwell apart; but Jesus has compassion on us as he had upon the widow, and he tenderly encourages us to be patient, and to wait, because with such hopes as these He leads us, greatly longing, forward to a day, when He shall give back our lost beloved to our eternal embrace, and us also to theirs, the glorified to the glorified, to be for ever one. Then He shall wipe all tears from our eyes, and say, otherwise and more effectually than He did at Nain, "Weep not."

DEATH HAS LOST ITS TERROR.

To the Christian this present life is simply a pilgrimage to a better country and to a city whose builder and maker is God. Every day he moves his tent nearer to his true home. His citizenship is in heaven, his thoughts, his hopes, his aspirations, are heavenly. This unworldliness or heavenly-mindedness, far from disqualifying him for the duties of earth, makes him more faithful and conscientious in his calling; for he remembers that he must render an account for every word and deed at a bar of God's judgment! Yea, in proportion as he is heavenly-minded and follows the example of his Lord and Saviour, he brings heaven down to earth and lifts earth up to heaven, and infuses the purity of and happiness of heaven into his heart and home. Faith unites us to Christ, who is life itself in its truest, fullest conception; life in God, life eternal. United with Christ, we live indeed, shedding round about us the rays of His purity, goodness, love and peace. Death has lost its terror; it is but a short slumber from which we shall awake in His likeness and enjoy what eye has not seen, nor ear heard, nor even entered the imagination of man. 'Because I live, ye shall live also."

Rev. Philip Schaff, D. D.

DEATH THE FIAT OF GOD.

The grass, has at best, a vanishing form, ready, almost before maturity, to be resolved into its elements—to sink back into the earth from which it sprang. "The breath of the Lord has blown upon it." Death does not come to men, animals or herbs simply in consequence of the chemical solvents which they contain, but because the Being who gave them life, freely withdraws that which he gave. Death is always the fiat of God, arresting the course of life. This truth of revelation is not at variance with the chemistry of animal life. Whatever else human life is, or may imply, it is soon over. It fades away suddenly like the grass. The world may have made great progress during the centuries, but the frontiers of life do not change with the generations of men. We are born and die just as our rudest ancestors. Every one of us shall die. "The grass withereth, the flower passeth." It is not a bit of sentiment, but a solid law, true at this moment and always true.

Rev. Canon H. P. Liddon, D. D.

THE DEAD AND THE LIVING.

WHAT a pleasant thought that when be come to die the people will show us respect, that they will gather around our bier and religiously lay our remains away in the earth for the angels to watch over till the morning of the resurrection. Perhaps a tear will be dropped on our coffin or our grave, and appreciative words will be spoken. But would it not be as well if honors were not entirely posthumous; if a part of the love and affection that gather around the bier of the dead would encircle the home of the living?

Kind words spoken in the ears of a living man, woman or child, are worth a great deal more than the most complimentary utterances over the coffin of the dead. The time to carry flowers is when they can be looked upon and handled, when their fragrance can be inhaled and their beauty enjoyed; when the attention bestowed will warm the heart and awaken more. Love poured out at family altars, in the social circle, amid the struggles and conflicts of life, may lift up the fallen, cheer the fainting heart, convert sorrow into joy, causing many a flower to spring up and bloom along the rugged pathways of this world. Were this done, there would be smiles instead of tears, rosy cheeks, where now there are dull and haggard ones, light in the place of darkness, and a terrestial paradise, perhaps, in the raging, warring elements of an earthly pandemonium.

Of gold, and gems, and jewels rare,
  Earth hides a countless store,
If we may trust the sages
  Deep read in nature's lore;
And many a pearl lies buried
  In ocean's shining caves,
But sacred treasures sleep within
  Our pleasant hill of graves.

THE REV. W. AUGUSTUS MUHLENBURG, D. D.

I WOULD NOT LIVE ALWAY.

WILLIAM AUGUSTUS MUHLENBERG.

I would not live alway—live alway below!
Oh, no, I'll not linger when bidden to go:
The days of our pilgrimage granted us here
Are enough for life's woes, full enough for its cheer:
Would I shrink from the path which the prophets of God,
Apostles, and martyrs, so joyfully trod?
Like a spirit unblest, o'er the earth would I roam,
While brethren and friends are all hastening home?

I would not live alway—I ask not to stay
Where storm after storm rises dark o'er the way;
Where seeking for rest we but hover around,
Like the patriarch's bird, and no resting is found;
Where Hope, when she paints her gay bow in the air,
Leaves its brilliance to fade in the night of despair,
And Joy's fleeting angel ne'er sheds a glad ray,
Save the gleam of the plumage that bears him away.

I would not live alway—thus fettered by sin,
Temptation without and corruption within;
In a moment of strength if I sever the chain,
Scarce the victory is mine, ere I'm captive again;
E'en the rapture of pardon is mingled with fears,
And the cup of thanksgiving with penitent tears:
The festival trump calls for jubilant songs,
But my spirit her own *miserere* prolongs.

I would not live alway—no, welcome the tomb!
Since Jesus hath lain there, I dread not its gloom;
Where he deigned to sleep, I'll too bow my head,
All peaceful to slumber on that hallowed bed.
Then the glorious daybreak, to follow that night,
The orient gleam of the angels of light,
With their clarion call for the sleepers to rise
And chant forth their matins, away to the skies.

Who, who would live alway—away from his God,
Away from yon heaven, that blissful abode
Where the rivers of pleasure flow o'er the bright plains,
And the noontide of glory eternally reigns;
Where the saints of all ages in harmony meet,
Their Saviour and brethren transported to greet,
While the songs of salvation exultingly roll,
And the smile of the Lord is the feast of the soul!

That heavenly music! what is it I hear?
The notes of the harpers ring sweet in mine ear!
And see, soft unfolding those portals of gold,
The King all arrayed in his beauty behold!
Oh, give me, oh, give me the wings of a dove,
To adore him, be near him, enrapt with his love;
I but wait for the summons, I list for the word—
Alleluia—Amen—evermore with the Lord.

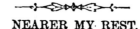

NEARER MY REST.

MARIAN LONGFELLOW.

NEARER my rest with each succeeding day
That bears me still mine own allotted task!
Nearer my rest! the clouds roll swift away,
And nought remains, O, Lord, for me to ask.

If I but bear unflinchingly life's pain,
And humbly lay it at thy feet divine,
Then shall I see each loss a hidden gain,
And thy sweet mercy through the darkness shine!

Nearer my rest! the long, long weary hours
Had well-nigh gained the victory o'er my soul;
Thy mercy, falling soft like summer showers,
Upheld me, fainting near the victor's goal.

Nearer my rest, and as I journey on,
Grant me, dear Lord (my angel-guides to be,
To keep and help me ere that rest be won),
Patience, and Faith, and blessed Purity!

Patience,—that I may never sink dismayed,
However dark and drear may seem the road;
Patience,—though doubt, though every cross that's laid
Upon my heart,—nor sink beneath the load.

Faith,—that e'en though to mortal eyes be hidden
The reason *why* this life be oft opprest,
I only do, with childlike trust, as bidden,
And leave to Thee, confidingly, the rest!

And Purity,—O, Godlike attribute!
Be thou my standard, shield, and armor bright;
Without thee no tree beareth worthy fruit,—
These three, O Lord! to lead me through the night!

NO FEAR OF DEATH.

It is only for Christ to say, "Peace, be still," and all is well. He comes to dwell within us, He comes to give comfort, to be a joy. Hence, it is said, "Christ in you is the hope of glory." He is with me, the joy of my soul. When I come to die He will take me to Himself.

I was struck very much by the remark which Father Tasker made to me the other day. Many of you know him. He told me of his experience when sick. Some one asked him "what he thought of death." He said he scarcely thought of it. He just said to himself, "Jesus is the only one who has any right to me; the devil has no right to me; I don't know where to go or who ought to take me if Jesus don't, and so I left myself in the hands of Jesus and felt all at peace." If Christ dwells in our hearts there is that unison. If He loves me so much as to come and dwell within me here is safe ground for the future

> "This I do find
> We two are so joined;
> He'll not live in glory
> And leave me behind."

Bishop M. Simpson, D. D.

THE RIGHT VIEW OF DEATH.

I received sometime ago a letter from a friend in London, and I thought, as I read it, I would take it and read it to other people and see if I could not get them to look upon death as this friend does. He lost a loved mother. In England it is a very common thing to send out cards in memory of the departed ones, and they put upon them great borders of black—sometimes a quarter of an inch of black border—but this friend has gone and put on gold; he did not put on black at all; she had gone to the golden city, and so he just put on a golden border; and I think it a good deal better than black. I think when our friends die, instead of putting a great black border on their memorials to make them look dark, it would be better for us to put on gold.

D. L. Moody.

DEATH ACCORDING TO PHILO.

MAN'S bodily form is made from the ground, the soul from no created thing, but from the Father of all; so that, man was mortal as to his body, he was immortal as to his mind. Complete virtue is the tree of immortal life. "Vices and crimes, rushing in through the gate of sensual pleasure, change a happy and immortal life to a wretched and mortal one." Referring to the garden of Eden, he says: "The death threatened for eating the fruit was not natural, the separation of soul and body, but penal, the sinking of the soul in the body. Death is twofold, one of man, one of the soul. The death of man is the separation of the soul from the body; the death of the soul is the corruption of virtue and the assumption of vice. To me, death with the pious is preferable to life with the impious. For those so dying, deathless life delivers; but those so living, eternal death seizes."

PHILO, QUOTED BY ALGER.

THE SOUL DOES NOT SLEEP.

I CANNOT agree with some people, that Paul has been sleeping in the grave, and is still there, after the storms of eighteen hundred years. I cannot believe that he who loved the Master, who had such a burning zeal for Him, has been separated from Him in an unconscious state, "Father, I will that they also, whom Thou hast given me, be with me where I am; that they may behold my glory, which Thou hast given me." This is Christ's prayer.

D. L. MOODY.

In the third watch, alert and brave;
  O, joy, the King to see;
To mark His anxious, scanning look,
  Light up, beholding me!
The long watch past; the sobbing fight
  Ended; the victory won;
And, O, for *me*, His words of praise;
  "*Servant of God, well done!*"

UNKNOWN.

WE SHALL REACH THE HAVEN.

As life advances, it does indeed seem to be as a vessel going to pieces, as though we were on the broken fragments of a ship, or in a solitary skiff on the waste of waters; but so long as our existence lasts we must not give up the duty of cheerfulness and hope.

> The sense that kept us back in youth
>   From all intemperate gladness,
> That same good instinct now forbids
>   Unprofitable sadness.

He who has guided us through the day may guide us through the night also. The pillar of darkness often turns into a pillar of fire. Let us hold on though the land be miles away; let us hold on till the morning break. That speck on the distant horizon may be the vessel for which we must shape our course. Forwards, not backwards, must we steer—forwards and forwards, till the speck becomes a mast, and the mast becomes a friendly ship. Have patience and perseverance; believe that there is still a future before us; and we shall at last reach the haven where we would be

DEAN STANLEY.

THE SOUL DEPARTING.

> Father, when thy child is dying,
> On the bed of anguish lying,
> Then, my every want suppling,
>   To me thy love display!
>
> Ere my soul her bonds hath broken,
> Grant some bright and cheering token,
> That for me the words are spoken,
>   "Thy sins are washed away!"
>
> When the lips are dumb that blessed me.
> And withdrawn the hand that pierced me,
> Then let sweeter sounds arrest me,
>   To call my soul away!
>
> Guide me to that world of spirits,
> Where through thine atoning merits,
> E'en thy weakest child inherits,
>   The joys which ne'er decay.

CHARLOTTE ELLIOT.

THE HISTORIC DEAD.

WE can think of no sublimer spectacle within the limits of flesh and blood than that furnished by a great and pure mind, strengthened and adorned by the accumulated knowledge of ages, thrilled with the inspiration of its task, eager for its work, exposing error, finding and defending truth, pleading the cause of justice and right, lifting human thought above its usual level, hastening forward the grand march of society, working by night and by day to illumine and bless mankind, and then through the open gates of eternity ascending to the skies. Such men as Chalmers, Edwards, Butler, Wesley, Luther, Calvin, and a host of others, illustrate the dignity and glory of human nature, developed by culture, stimulated by high motives, and consecrated to the interests of eternal truth. The world has much occasion to thank God for their existence. In living one life they live forever in the results thereof. Posterity feels their moral presence when their personal presence is with archangels. They are incarnated in the world's history. What they did while living, lasts when they are singing in Heaven. The bare possibility of achieving such a life ought to stir every mind with the ardors of the most intense enthusiasm. To make a good impression upon the world—an impression that shall not only endure, but descend along the current of ages with expanding and increasing power, attaching to itself new and auxiliary causes of greatness—is an object which any being may well covet, whether man or angel. A life which attains this object is a grand success. The actor therein has, as he deserves, a place among the HISTORIC DEAD.

REV. SAMUEL T. SPEAR, D. D.

DEATH A TRANSITION.

I THINK you will see clearly, from what I have said, that this earthly life, when seen hereafter from heaven, will seem like an hour past long ago, and dimly remembered; that long, laborious, full of joys and sorrows as it is, it will then have dwindled down to a mere point, hardly visible to the far reaching ken of the disembodied spirit. But the spirit itself soars onward. And thus death is neither an end nor a beginning. It is a transition, not from one existence to another, but from one state of existence to another. No link is broken in the chain of being; any more than in passing from infancy to manhood, from manhood to old age. There are seasons of reverie and deep abstraction, which seems to me analagous to death. The soul gradually loses its consciousness of what is passing around it; and takes no longer cognizance of objects which are near. It seems for the moment to have dissolved its connection with the body. It has passed, as it were, into another state of being. It lives in another world. It has flown over lands and seas; and holds communion with those it loves in the distant regions of the earth, and the more distant heaven. It sees familiar faces, and hears beloved voices, which to the bodily senses are no longer visible and audible. And this likewise is death; save that, when we die, the soul returns no more to the dwelling it has left.

LONGFELLOW.

IF WE COULD ALL DIE TOGETHER.

DURING the past year, how many of my flock have been touched, how many have gone out of this church? You could not keep them, Oh! *if we could all die together!* If we could keep all the sheep and lambs of the family-fold together, until some bright spring day, the birds a-chant, the waters a-glitter, and then we could altogether hear the voice of the Good Shepherd, and, hand in hand, pass through the flood. But no, no, no. It is one by one. It may be in the midnight or spring—it may be alone and suddenly. Death is a bitter, crushing, tremendous curse. I play three tunes on the Gospel harp of comfort. "Weeping may endure for a night, but joy cometh in the morning." That is one. "All things work together for good to those who love God." That is the second. "And the Lamb, which is in the midst of the throne, shall lead them to living fountains of water, and God shall wipe away all tears from their eyes." That is the third.

REV. T. DE WITT TALMAGE, D. D.

THE DEAD ARE OURS STILL.

WHAT we need is to banish all haze from our conceptions of the reality of that state, so that we can think of it heartily and talk about it to each other with clear eye and open brow, as we would talk of some great university or gorgeous landscape of a foreign land. Thus only can we have any comfort when our dearest are transferred hence. What is so inspiring, what aspect of our humanity is so lofty and divine, as when a Christian mother, over the hallowed clay of a little one, can say with assured faith: "This was only the earthly image of an innocence, a wonder, and a love that have been withdrawn into the deeps of eternal life, into that world of truth and essences and peace that is near me in my prayers. Its dawning faculties, which I loved so to watch and guide, are more precious to God than to me, and he has lifted them to a state of being where a purer light and more delightful splendors than the earthly sun sheds or shines upon, surround its unfettered spirit. It is mine still through my faith in God, and my assurance of the supremacy of spirit over clay." That is the way to think of the future world,—not in weak fancy, but in a conviction that our powers of thought, feeling, and worship are our real substance here.

THOMAS STARR KING.

DEATH BINDS US TOGETHER.

EVEN death itself makes life more lovely; It binds us more closely together while Here. Dr. Thomas Browne has argued that death is one of the necessary conditions of human happiness, and supports his argument with great force and eloquence. But when death comes into a household, we do not philosophize—we only feel. The eyes that are full of tears do not see; though in course of time they come to see more clearly and brightly than those that have never known sorrow.

SAMUEL SMILES.

VICTOR OVER DEATH.

BUT this dwelling among Christian dead is not altogether fearful. These walks are toward heaven. The light of the glory beyond falls on these saintly faces. The upturned gaze pierces the heavens. It sees them in bright array, washed, calm, jubilant. It sees, and longs to be there. What is earth to that sight, song, service, society? Concord Cemetery, Forest Hills, Mt. Auburn, Harmony Grove, suddenly soften their wintery aspect to spring-like beauty. The sweet fields beyond sweeten this bank of the river. Like the grand entrance to palatial grounds, they become fascinating above themselves. They allure to brighter worlds, and grow brighter in the allurement.

"Precious in the sight of the Lord is the death of his saints." Heaven is no cheap and paltry place. Its inhabitants are no weak and worthless populace. It is the Lord's garden; they are the Lord's friends. "Henceforth," He says to them, "I call ye not servants, but friends, brothers, sisters, joint heirs. My beloved, beloved forever."

Cling then to Christ, when you walk among the graves. Rejoice, when those you bear thither are His elect, whom He shall call from the four ends of heaven. Strengthen yourselves with His divine terror and truth. Recognize the awfulness of death, that you may be its only possible Victor. Accept the fact in all its horror, and the triumph in all its glory eternal.

BISHOP GILBERT HAVEN.

DEATH A DIVINE MESSAGE.

IT matters little at what point in the perspective of the future the separation enforced by death is thought to cease. Faith and Love are careless time-keepers; they have a wide and liberal eye for distance and duration; and while they can whisper to each other the words: "Meet again," they can watch and toil with wondrous patience,— with spirit fresh and true, and, amid its most grevious loneliness, unbereft of one good sympathy. And since the Grave can bury no affections now, but only the mortal and familiar shape of their object; death has changed its whole aspect and relation to us; and we may regard it, not with passionate hate, but with quiet reverence. It is a divine message from above, not an invasion from the abyss beneath; not the fiendish hand of darkness thrust up to clutch our gladness enviously away, but a rainbow gleam that descends through tears, without which we should not know the various beauties that are woven into the pure light of life.

REV. JAMES MARTINEAU.

ASLEEP IN JESUS.

REV. THEODORE L. CUYLER, D. D.

THEN go to sleep, poor, old, hard-worked body, the apostle seems to say, and Jesus will wake thee up in good time, and thou shalt be "made like to the body of His glory, according to the working whereby He subdues all things unto Himself."

Let us not be charged with pushing this Scripture simile too far, when we hint that it illustrates the different feelings with which different persons regard the act of dying. When we are *sleepy* we covet the pillow and the couch. Even so do we see aged servants of God, who have finished up their life-work, and many a suffering invalid, racked with incurable pains, who honestly long to die. They are sleepy for the rest of the grave and the home beyond it. *For* Christ here, *with* Christ yonder, is the highest instinct of the Christian heart. The noble missionary, Judson, phrased it happily when he said: "I am not tired of my work, neither am I tired of the world; yet, when Christ calls me home, I shall go with the gladness of a boy bounding away from school." He wanted to toil for souls until he proved *sleepy*, and then he wanted to lay his body down to rest and to escape into glory.

A dying bed is only the spot where the material frame falls asleep. Then we take up the slumbering form, and gently bear it to its narrow bed in Mother Earth. Our very word "cemetery" describes this thought. It is derived from the Greek word *koimeterion*, which signifies a sleeping-place. It is a mingled and promiscuous sleeping-place; but the Master "knoweth them that are His." They who sleep in Him shall awake to be for ever with the Lord.

The early Christians were wise in their generation when they carved on the tomb of the martyrs " *In Jesu Christo obdormivit,*"—In Jesus Christ he fell asleep.

The fragrance of this heavenly line perfumes the very air around the believer's resting-place. Giving to the Latin word its true pronunciation, there is sweet melody, as well as Heaven-sent truth, in this song of the sleepers:

> "Oh! precious tale of triumph this!
> And martyr-blood shed to achieve it,
> Of suffering past—of present bliss,
>   'IN JESU CHRISTO OBDORMIVIT.'"
>
> "Of cherished dead be mine the trust,
> Thrice-blessed solace to believe it,
> That I can utter o'er their dust,
>   'IN JESU CHRISTO OBDORMIVIT.'
>
> "Now to my loved one's grave I bring
> My immortelle and interweave it
> With God's own golden lettering,
>   'IN JESU CHRISTO OBDORMIVIT.'"

FILL UP THE RANKS.

REV. JOHN CUMMING, D. D.

BUT the ranks of our congregation have been thinned by translations to the skies. Fill up the ranks. Many soldiers are now listening to me. You know that when a comrade falls the rest must close up, and those to whom the battle is bequeathed must act with the greater energy. We are surrounded by a great cloud of witnesses. You will not think me superstitious when I say that the spirit of our departed brother may be the spectator of those that are left behind, and if so, if one wave of bliss can rise from so poor a place to so rich a heritage—it will be to hear that you have taken up with greater zeal and greater energy the good work in which our brethren, who have gone before, have been so usefully employed. I have read in the stories of my country—and I for one hope its ancient traditions will never be forgotten—that one day, in a great battle, the chief of one of the powerful clans of the Highlands, fell back and lay on his side. The blood ebbed from him, and his clansmen thought he was killed, and they began to fall back disheartened—and you know that, be it a regiment or a fire brigade, let the chief fall, how faint are all hearts, how feeble are all arms—raising himself, with the blood ebbing from him, upon his elbow on the green turf where he had fallen, as his countrymen always fall, with his back to the field and his feet to the foe, he said: "Macdonald, I'm not dead, but I'm watching how my children fight." My dear friends, the great captain of the brigade is not dead, but is watching us, his children, and seeing how they walk worthy of those "who by faith have inherited the promise."

INTO THY HANDS I COMMEND MY SPIRIT.

TAKE my spirit, Lord, and see, as thou art wont, that it has no more to bear than it can bear. Am I going to die? Thou knowest, if only from the cry of thy Son, how terrible that it is; and if it comes not to me in so terrible a shape as that in which it came to him, think how poor to bear I am beside him. I do not know what the struggle means; for, of the thousands who pass through it every day, not one enlightens his neighbor left behind; but shall I not long with agony for one breath of thy air, and not receive it? shall I not be torn asunder with dying? —I will question no more; Father, into thy hands I commend my spirit. For it is thy business, not mine, Thou wilt know every shade of my suffering; thou wilt care for me with thy perfect fatherhood; for that makes my sonship, and inwarps and infolds it. As a child I could bear great pain when my father was leaning over me, or had his arm about me; how much nearer my soul cannot thy hands come! —yea, with a comfort, Father of me, that I have never yet even imagined; for how shall my imagination overtake thy swift heart? I care not for the pain, so long as my spirit is strong, and into thy hand I commend that spirit. If thy love, which is better than life, receive it, then surely thy tenderness will make it great.

GEO. MACDONALD.

MOZART'S REQUIEM.

RUFUS DAWES.

The tongue of the vigilant clock tolled one,
    In a deep and hollow tone;
The shrouded moon looked out upon
A cold, dank region; more cheerless and dun,
    By her lurid light that shone.

Mozart now rose from a restless bed,
    And his heart was sick with care;
Though long had he wooingly sought to wed
Sweet Sleep, 'twas in vain, for the coy maid fled,
    Though he followed her everywhere.

He knelt to the God of his worship then,
    And breathed a fervent prayer,
'Twas balm to his soul, and he rose again
With a strengthened spirit, but started when
    He marked a stranger there.

He was tall, the stranger who gazed on him,
    Wrapped high in a sable shroud;
His cheek was pale, and his eye was dim,
And the melodist trembled in every limb,
    The while his heart beat loud.

" Mozart, there is one whose errand I bear,
    Who cannot be known to thee;
He grieves for a friend, and would have thee prepare
A requiem, blending a mournful air
    With the sweetest melody."

" I'll furnish the requiem then," he cried,
    " When this moon has waned away."
The stranger bowed, yet no word replied,
But fled like the shade on a mountain's side,
    When the sunlight hides its ray.

Mozart grew pale when the vision fled,
    And his heart beat high with fear:
He knew 'twas a messenger sent from the dead,
To warn him, that soon he must make his bed
    In the dark, chill sepulchre.

He knew that the days of his life were told,
    And his breast grew faint within;
The blood through his bosom crept slowly and cold,
And his lamp of life could barely hold
    The flame that was flickering.

Yet he went to his task with cheerful zeal,
  While his days and nights were one;
He spoke not, he moved not, but only to kneel
With the holy prayer, "O God, I feel
  'Tis best thy will be done."

He gazed on his loved one, who cherished him well,
  And weepingly hung over him:
"This music will chime with my funeral knell,
And my spirit shall float, at the passing bell,
  On the notes of this requiem.'

The cold moon waned: on that cheerless day
  The stranger appeared once more;
Mozart had finished his requiem lay,
But e'er the last notes had died away,
  His spirit had gone before.

BURIAL OF MOSES.

[*"And He buried him in the valley of the land of Moab, over against Bethpeor but no man knoweth of his sepulchre unto this day."—Deut. 34: 6.*]

By Nebo's lonely mountain,
  On this side Jordan's wave,
In a vale in the land of Moab,
  There lies a lonely grave.
And no man dug that sepulchre,
  And no man saw it e'er;
For the angels of God upturned the sod
  And laid the dead man there.

That was the grandest funeral
  That ever passed on earth;
But no man heard the tramplings
  Or saw the train go forth.
Noiselessly as the daylight
  Comes when the night is done,
And the crimson streak on ocean's cheek
  Grows into the great sun,—

Noiselessly as the spring-time
  Her crown of verdure weaves:
And all the trees on all the hills
  Open their thousand leaves,—
So, without sound of music,
  Or voice of them that wept,
Silently down from the mountain crown
  The great procession swept.

Perchance the bald old eagle
  On gray Bethpeor's height,
Out of his rocky eyrie

Looked out on the wondrous sight
Perchance the lion stalking
Still shuns that hallowed spot,
For beast and bird have seen or heard
That which man knoweth not.

But when the warrior dieth,
His comrades in the war
With arms reversed and muffled drum
Follow the funeral car.
They show the banners taken,
They tell his battles won,
And after him lead his masterless steed
While peals the minute gun.

Amid the noblest of the land
Men lay the sage to rest,
And give the bard an honored place
With costly marble dressed.
In the great minster transept,
Where lights like glories fall,
And the choir sings and the organ rings
Along the emblazoned wall.

This was the bravest warrior
That ever buckled sword;
This the most gifted poet
That ever breathed a word;
And never earth's philosopher
Traced with his golden pen,
On the deathless page truths half so sage
As he wrote down for men.

And had he not high honor?
The hillside for his pall;
To lie in state while angels wait
With stars for tapers tall;
And the dark rock pines, like tossing plumes,
Over his bier to wave;
And God's own hand, in that lonely land,
To lay him in his grave;

In that deep grave without a name;
Whence his uncoffined clay
Shall break again—most wondrous thought,
Before the judgment day,
And stand with glory wrapped around,
On the hills he never trod,
And speak of the strife that won our life
With the incarnate Son of God.

O lonely tomb in Moab's land,
O dark Bethpeor's hill,
Speak to these curious hearts of ours,
And teach them to be still.
God hath His mysteries of grace—
Ways that we cannot tell;
He hides them deep like the secret sleep
Of him He loved so well.

ON THE DEATH OF A MOTHER.

AT length, then, the tenderest of mothers is gone!
  Her smiles, her love accents, can glad thee no more;
That once cheerful chamber is silent and lone,
  And for thee all a child's precious duties are o'er.

Her welcome at morning, her blessing at night,
  No longer the crown of thy comforts can be;
And the friend seen and loved since thine eyes first saw light
  Thou canst ne'er see again! thou art orphan'd like me.

Oh, change! from which nature must shrink overpower'd,
  Till faith shall the anguish remove and condemn;
For the change to those blest ones who "die in the Lord,"
  Though to us it brings sorrow, gives glory to them.
AMELIA OPIE.

THE DYING MOTHER.

I DO remember, and will ne'er forget
The dying eye! That eye alone was bright,
And brighter grew as nearer death approached:
As I have seen the gentle little flower
Look fairest in the silver beam which fell
Reflected from the thunder-cloud, that soon
Came down, and o'er the desert scattered far
And wide its loveliness. She made a sign
To bring her babe—'twas brought, and by her placed:
She looked upon its face, that neither smiled
Nor wept, nor knew who gazed upon't; and laid
Her hand upon its little breast, and sought
For it with look that seemed to penetrate
The heavens, unutterable blessings, such
As God to dying parents only granted
For infants left behind them in the world.
"God, keep my child!" we heard her say, and heard
No more. The Angel of the Covenant
Was come, and, faithful to His promise, stood
Prepared to walk with her through death's dark vale.
And now her eyes grew bright, and brighter still,
Too bright for ours to look upon, suffused
With many tears, and closed without a cloud.
They set, as sets the morning star, which goes
Not down behind the darkened west, nor hides
Obscured among the tempests of the sky,
But melts away into the light of heaven.
ROBERT POLLOK.

DEATH OF GARFIELD.

WE have no Westminster Abbey in which to bury kings, but we have a great national heart in which we enshrine those who have suffered for our land. Into that great shrine of the national heart we will carry our beloved President, and lay him down beside Adams, and Lincoln, and Washington, and the other mighty men who loved God and toiled for the betterment of the race. Then we will sound forth, partly in requiem and partly in grand march of triumph, the *words which Garfield employed* after another famous assasination: "The Lord reigneth. Though clouds and darkness are round about Him, righteousness and judgment are the habitation of His throne." *God save the President! God save the Nation!*

TALMAGE.

MAN'S MORTALITY.

LIKE as the damask rose you see,
Or like the blossom on the tree,
Or like the dainty flower of May,
Or like the morning to the day,
Or like the sun, or like the shade,
Or like the gourd which Jonah had.
E'en such is man; whose thread is spun,
Drawn out, and cut, and so is done.
The rose withers, the blossom blasteth;
The flower fades, the morning hasteth;
The sun sets, the shadow flies;
The gourd consumes, and man—he dies!

Like to the grass that's newly sprung,
Or like a tale that's new begun,
Or like the bird that's here to-day,
Or like the pearl'd dew of May,
Or like an hour, or like a span,
Or like the singing of a swan.
E'en such is man; who lives by breath,
Is here, now there, in life and death.
The grass withers, the tale is ended;
The bird is flown, the dew's ascended,
The hour is short, the span not long:
The swan's near death—man's life is done.

SIMON WASTELL.

THY WILL BE DONE.

THOUGH dark and heavy sorrow
   Doth cast on thee its spell,
And gloomy seems the morrow,
   Remember " all is well;"
Though grief doth hover o'er thee,
   And dark clouds haunt thy sun,
Keep this sweet prayer before thee:
" Father, Thy will be done."

Though when life's bark seems freighted
   With happiness for thee,
And with bright hopes elated,
   Thy heart with joy may be,
Affliction's dark clouds lower,
   And Grief thy heart doth stun,
Then pray, in that sad hour:
" Father, Thy will be done."

And when earth's sorrows round thee,
   Have fallen thick and fast;
When ties which long have bound thee
   So fondly to the past,
All sundered are, yet alway
   Whate'er to thee may come,
Submissive and resigned, pray:
" Father, Thy will be done."

Whatever in life's pathway
   May come of good or ill,
Confiding, thy fond heart may
   Bend to thy Father's will;
And when sadly thou dost grieve,
   When all seems dark, yet one
Comfort's left for thee, to breathe
" Father, Thy will be done."

When death strikes down the innocent and young,
For every fragile form from which he lets
    The parting spirit free,
    A hundred virtues rise,
In shapes of mercy, charity, and love,
    To walk the world and bless it.
    Of every tear,
That sorrowing mortals shed on such green graves,
Some good is born, some gentler nature comes.

                                                   DICKENS.

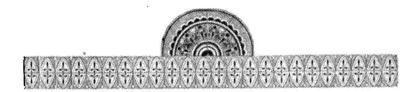

THE DYING

DEATH OF THE WIDOW'S DAUGHTER.

GLIMPSES OF THE FUTURE BY THE DYING.

THE DYING SEEING DEPARTED FRIENDS.

REV. T. DEWITT TALMAGE, D. D.

THERE is one more reason why I am disposed to accept this doctrine of future recognition; that is, so many in their last hour on earth have confirmed this theory. I speak not of persons who have been delirious in their last moment and knew not what they were about, but of persons who died in calmness and placidity, and who were not naturally superstitious. Often the glories of heaven have struck the dying pillow, and the departing man has said he saw and heard those who had gone away from him. How often it is in the dying moments parents see their departed children and children see their departed parents. I came down to the banks of the Mohawk River. It was evening, and I wanted to go over the river, and so I waved my hat and shouted, and after awhile I saw some one waving on the opposite bank, and I heard him shout, and the boat came across, and I got in and was transported. And so I suppose it will be in the evening of our life. We will come down to the river of death and give a signal to our friends on the other shore, and they will give a signal back to us, and the boat comes and our departed kindred are the oarsmen, the fires of the setting day tingling the top of the paddles.

Oh, have you ever sat by such a deathbed? In that hour you hear the departing soul cry. "Hark! look!" You hearkened and looked. A little child, pining away because of the death of its mother, getting weaker and weaker every day, was taken into the room where hung the picture of her mother. She seemed to enjoy looking at it, and then she was taken away, and after awhile died. In the last moment that wan and wasted little one lifted her hands, while her face lighted up with the glory of the next world, and cried out "Mother!" You tell me she did not see her mother? She did. So in my first settlement at Belleville a plain man said to me, "What do you think I heard last night? I was in the room where one of my neighbors was dying. He was a good man, and he said he heard the angels of God singing before the throne. I haven't much poetry about me, but I listened and I heard them too." Said I, "I have no doubt of it." Why, we are to be taken up to heaven at last by ministering spirits. Who are they to be? Souls that went up from Madras, or Antioch, or Jerusalem? Oh, no, our glorified kindred are going to troop around us.

VISIONS OF A DYING YOUTH.

This young man about half-past ten was evidently sinking; but he was still able gently to wave his hand, bidding those around him Farewell; and he added with a smile—"Death! where is thy sting? grave! where is thy victory?" After a little time he spoke once more, to beg all about him would be perfectly still: "Don't speak, don't speak," he feebly uttered, "I am enjoying deep and blessed communion with God." For above half an hour perfect silence was maintained, during which he seemed wrapt in meditation, a smile frequently playing about his face. About the end of that time, his head gradually fell back, his eye brightened, and as if his ear caught the harmonies of the invisible world, he exclaimed in a calm and loud voice, expressive of admiration—"Beautiful! beautiful!" A few moments more, and then as if the veil had been withdrawn, which hides from mortal eye the radiancy of the upper world, he added—'Glory! glory!" And with these words dying on his lips, he fell back upon his pillow, and his purified spirit took its flight to heaven.

This is a description of FACT. It is A FACT, whether Christianity be true or not. It was THE GOSPEL, that sustained and blessed him. And we ask for any system to come forward—any system of belief or any system of no belief—and let us see anything like that in their triumphs and in their results.

"Let me die the death of the righteous; and let my last end be like his!"

REV. THOMAS BINNEY, D. D.

ONLY A LITTLE BROOK.

A SIMPLE but very touching incident has been related in connection with the last moments of a beautiful little girl in Bath, who died at the age of nine. A little while before she died, as the sorrowing friends stood around her, watching the last movings of her gentle breath, the last faint fluttering of the little pulse, they became aware from broken words, that she shrank with natural dread from the unknown way that was opening before her. She had come to the borders of the mysterious river which separates us from the dim hereafter, and her timid feet seemed to hesitate and fear to stem the flood. But after a time her tears subsided, she grew calm, and ceased to talk about the long, dark way, till at the very last she brightened suddenly, a smile of confidence and courage lighted up her sweet face, "Oh, it is only a little brook!" she cried, and so passed over to the heavenly shore.

BISHOP FALLOWS.

THE DYING CHILD AND HER DEPARTED MOTHER.

A LITTLE girl, in a family of my acquaintance, a lovely and precious child, lost her mother at an age too early to fix the loved features in remembrance. She was beautiful; and as the bud of her heart unfolded, it seemed as if won by that mother's prayers to turn instinctively heavenward. The sweet, conscientious, and prayer-loving child, was the idol of the bereaved family. But she faded away early. She would lie upon the lap of the friend who took a mother's kind care of her, and, winding one wasted arm about her neck, would say, 'Now tell me about my mamma!' And when the oft-told tale had been repeated, she would ask softly, 'Take me into the parlor; I want to see my mamma!' The request was never refused; and the affectionate sick child would lie for hours, gazing on her mother's portrait. But

"Pale and wan she grew, and weakly—
Bearing all her pains so meekly,
That to them she still grew dearer
As the trial-hour grew nearer."

"That hour came at last, and the weeping neighbors assembled to see the child die. The dew of death was already on the flower, as its life-sun was going down. The little chest heaved faintly—spasmodically.

"'Do you know me darling?' sobbed close in her ear, the voice that was dearest; but it awoke no answer; All at once a brightness as if from the upper world, burst over the child's colorless countenance. The eyelids flashed open, and the lips parted; the wan, curdling hands flew up, in the little one's last impulsive effort, as she looked piercingly into the far above. "'Mother!' she cried, with surprise and transport in her tone—and passed with that breath to her mother's bosom.

"Said a distinguished divine, who stood by that bed of joyous death, 'If I had never believed in the ministration of departed ones before, I could not doubt it now.'

"'Peace I leave with you,' said the wisest spirit that ever passed from earth to heaven. Let us be at 'peace' amid the spirit-mysteries and questionings on which his eye soon shed the light of Eternity."

REV. H. HARBAUGH.

I loved them so,
That when the Elder Shepherd of the fold
Came, covered with the storm, and pale and cold,
And begged for one of my sweet lambs to hold.
I bade Him go.

He claimed the pet—
A little fondling thing, that to my breast
Clung always, either in quiet or unrest—
I thought of all my lambs I loved him best,
And yet—and yet—

I laid him down
In those white, shrouded arms, with bitter tears;
For some voice told me that, in after years,
He should know naught of passion, grief or fears,
As I had known.

DR. LOWELL MASON.

THAT sweet singer and musical composer, who has done so much for popular American church music, Dr. Lowell Mason, died but a short time since, at an advanced age. Long years ago he had buried his first-born, a lovely boy, named Daniel. About his dying bed friends gathered to watch the ebbing out of life. He had taken his final farewell of the loved ones he was leaving behind. The spirit was still hovering on the confines of the body. Suddenly he opened his eyes. He looked upward with an earnest, intent look. "Daniel, may I come?" he said. And then with a smile of recognition, he added: "Let me come!" And he went. Father and son were once more together.

Bishop Fallows.

BISHOP D. W. CLARK.

In my library is an ably-written book, called "Man all Immortal." It was the production of a valued friend of my earlier Christian ministry, Bishop D. W. Clark. In the full vigor of his intellect, he received the warning that his days on earth were numbered. I took his place, and preached the sermon at the last ministerial gathering he attended. With an unclouded mind he came to the river's brink. He said to his family and friends: "Our separation will not be a complete one. I feel that I shall often be with you, but God in His tenderness and loving kindness will permit me to suggest beautiful thoughts to you, and lead your minds heavenward. This idea is very present with me." A few hours before his departure, as if realizing even now, the society of heaven, he said: "Tireless company! Tireless song! The song of the angels is a glorious song! It thrills my ears even now! I am going to join the angels song!"

Bishop Fallows.

REV. ALFRED COOKMAN.

BISHOP FALLOWS.

AMONG the passengers of the ill-fated *President* was Rev. Alfred Cookman, whose eloquence matched that of Summerfield, and whose piety was akin to that of Fenelon. His son Alfred, upon whom the father's mantle fell, trod in the footsteps of that honored sire for thirty years, and then entered into rest. It was my great privilege to meet with the wife of him who, though in a watery grave, had gone where "there shall be no more sea," and the mother of him who had just gone home "sweeping through the gates into the city, washed in the blood of the Lamb," and with the newly-bereaved widow. Together we talked of the departed, but we talked as Christians.

A few hours before Alfred died, he called his wife to his bedside, and informed her that he had seen a glorious vision. There was no delirium. He was calm and rational. He said he had not been asleep; he knew he was awake, although it seemed to him like a dream. The father, who had left him while he was quite young; the brother who had preceded him to the better land, and the child, for whom the angels had come sometime before, friends in the Chritstian ministry, and others, had appeared to him, and bade him "welcome to the skies."

THE DYING DAUPHIN.

THE little son of Maria Antoinette, nine years of age, was fastened in a cell, and had his "food thrust through a hole in the upper part of the door. Brought out after a year's confinement, during which period that door never once opened, he was brought out to die. 'O,' said he, 'the music, the music, how fine!' 'Where?' 'Why, up there, up there!' And again he repeated the exclamation, 'O, the music, how fine! I wish my sister could hear it!' 'Music? Where?' again asked his attendants. 'Up there!' said the dying dauphin. 'O how fine! I hear *my mother's voice* among them.' And with these words, he went to join her, whom at that time he did not know to be dead."

REV. J. H. POTTS, D. D.

GOD'S ACRE.

DAUGHTER OF REV. T. A. GOODWIN, D. D.

A FRIEND of mine, the Rev. Dr. T. A. Goodwin, who has given a deeply interesting work to the church and the world on "The Mode of Man's Mortality," which I have read and used with great pleasure, although not agreeing with all he has written, gives a personal incident. In the room where his book was written, a daughter, just entering the maturity of womanhood, was called to die. After taking an affectionate farewell of the family she reached out her hand, cold in death, as if to embrace some one unseen by the rest. With a smile of recognition, she began to call by name departed members of the family and others of her acquaintance, who had died, adding, after some minutes of such greetings, "Here we are, an unbroken family in heaven. washed in the blood of the Lamb. Washed, washed, washed!" And in a few minutes she was in heaven.

BISHOP FALLOWS.

THE PEAK IN DARIEN.

FRANCES POWER COBBE.

IN almost every family or circle, a question will elicit recollections of death-bed scenes, wherein, with singular recurrence, appears one very significant incident—namely, that the dying person, precisely at the moment of death, and when the power of speech was lost, or nearly lost, seemed to see something; or rather, to speak more exactly, to become conscious of something present (for actual sight is out of question)—of a very striking kind, which remained invisible to and unperceived by the assistants. Again and again this incident is repeated. It is described almost in the same words by persons who have never heard of similar occurrences, and who suppose their own experience to be unique, and have raised no theory upon it, but merely consider it to be "strange," "curious," "affecting," and nothing more. It is invariably explained, that the dying person is lying quietly, when suddenly, in the very act of expiring, he looks up—sometimes starts up in bed—and gazes on (what appears to be) vacancy, with an expression of astonishment, sometimes developing instantly into joys and sometimes cut short in the first emotion of solemn wonder and awe. If the dying man were to see some utterly-unexpected but instantly-recognized vision, causing him a great surprise, or rapturous joy, his face could not better reveal the fact. The very instant this phenomenon occurs, Death is actually taking place, and the eyes glaze even while they gaze at the unknown sight. If a breath or two still heave the chest, it is obvious that the soul has already departed.

A few narrations of such observations, chosen from a great number which have been communicated to the writer, will serve to show more exactly the point which it is desired should be established by a larger concurrence of testimony. The following are given in the words of a friend on whose accuracy every reliance may be placed:

"I have heard numberless instances of dying persons showing unmistakably by their gestures, and sometimes by their words, that they saw in the moment of dissolution what could not be seen by those around them. On three occasions facts of this nature came distinctly within my own knowledge, and I will therefore limit myself to a detail of that which I can give on my own authority although the circumstances were not so striking as many others known to me, which I believe to be equally true.

"I was watching one night beside a poor man dying of consumption; his case was hopeless, but there was no appearance of the end being very near; he was in full possession of his senses, able to talk with a strong voice and not in the least drowsy. He had slept through the day and was so wakeful that I had been conversing with him on ordinary subjects to while away the long hours. Suddenly, while we were thus talking quietly together, he became silent, and fixed his eyes on one particular spot in the room, which was entirely vacant, even of furniture; at the same time a look of the greatest delight changed the whole expression of his face, and after a moment of what seemed to be intense scrutiny of some object invisible to me, he said to me in a joyous tone, "There is Jim." Jim was a little son whom he had lost the year before, and whom I had known well, but the dying man had a son still living, named John, for whom we had sent, and I concluded it was of John he was speaking, and that he thought he heard him arriving; so I answered,

" 'No. John has not been able to come.'

"The man turned to me impatiently and said, 'I do not mean

John, I know he is not here, it is Jim, my little lame Jim; surely you remember him?'

" 'Yes,' I said, 'I remember dear little Jim who died last year quite well.'

" 'Don't you see him then? There he is,' said the man, pointing to the vacant space on which his eyes were fixed; and when I did not answer, he repeated almost fretfully, 'Don't you see him standing there?'

" I answered that I could not see him, though I felt perfectly convinced that something was visible to the sick man, which I could not perceive. When I gave him this answer he seemed quite amazed and turned round to look at me with a glance almost of indignation As his eyes met mine, I saw that a film seemed to pass over them, the light of intelligence died away, he gave a gentle sigh and expired. He did not live five minutes from the time he first said, 'There is Jim,' although there had been no sign of approaching death previous to that moment.

" The second case was that of a boy about fourteen years of age, dying also of decline. He was a refined, highly educated child, who throughout his long illness had looked forward with much hope and longing to the unknown life to which he believed he was hastening. On a bright summer morning it became evident that he had reached his last hour. He lost the power of speech, chiefly from weakness, but he was perfectly sensible, and made his wishes known to us by his intelligent looks. He was sitting propped up in bed, and had been looking rather sadly at the bright sunshine playing on the trees outside his open window for some time. He had turned away from this scene, however, and was facing the end of the room, where there was nothing whatever but a closed door, when all in a moment the whole expression of his face changed to one of the most wondering rapture, which made his half-closed eyes open to their utmost extent while his lips parted with a smile of perfect ecstasy; it was impossible to doubt that some glorious sight was visible to him, and from the movement of his eyes it was plain that it was not one but many objects on which he gazed, for his look passed slowly from end to end of what seemed to be the vacant wall before him, going back and forward with ever-increasing delight manifested in his whole aspect. His mother then asked him if what he saw was some wonderful sight beyond the confines of this world, to give her a token that it was so, by pressing her hand. He at once took her hand, and pressed it meaningly; giving thereby an intelligent affirmative to her question, though unable to speak. As he did so a change passed over his face, his eyes closed, and in a few minutes he was gone.

"The third case, which is that of my own brother, was very similar to this last. He was an elderly man, dying of a painful disease, but one which never for a moment obscured his faculties. Although it was known to be incurable, he had been told that he might live some months, when somewhat suddenly the summons came on a dark January morning. It had been seen in the course of the night that he was sinking, but for some time he had been perfectly silent and motionless, apparently in a state of stupor; his eyes closed and breathing scarcely perceptible. As the tardy dawn of the winter morning revealed the rigid features of the countenance from which life and intelligence seemed to have quite departed, those who watched him felt uncertain whether he still lived; but suddenly, while they bent over him to ascertain the truth, he opened his eyes wide, and gazed eagerly upward with such an unmistakable expression of wonder and joy, that a thrill of awe passed through all who witnessed it. His whole face grew bright with a strange gladness, while the eloquent eyes seemed literally to shine as if reflecting some light on which they gazed; he remained in this attitude of delighted surprise for some minutes, then in a moment the eyelids fell, the head drooped forward, and, with one long breath, the spirit departed."

A different kind of case to those above narrated by my friend was that of a young girl known to me, who had passed through the miserable experiences of a sinful life at Aldershot, and then had tried to drown herself in the river Avon, near Clifton. She was in some way saved from suicide, and placed for a time in a penitentiary; but her health was found to be hopelessly ruined, and she was sent to die in the quaint old workhouse of St. Peter's at Bristol. For many months she lay in the infirmary literally perishing piecemeal of disease, but exhibiting patience and sweetness of disposition quite wonderful to witness. She was only eighteen, poor young creature! when all her little round of error and pain had been run; and her innocent, pretty face might have been that of a child. She never used any sort of cant (so common among women who have been in Refuges), but had apparently somehow got hold of a very living and real religion, which gave her comfort and courage, and inspired her with the beautiful spirit with which she bore her frightful sufferings. On the wall opposite her bed I had hung by chance a print of the "Lost Sheep," and Mary S———, looking at it one day, said to me, "That is just what I was, and what happened to me; but I am being brought safe home now." For a long time before her death, her weakness was such that she was quite incapable of lifting herself up in bed, or of supporting herself when lifted, and she, of course, continued to lie with her head on the pillow while life gradually and painfully ebbed away, and she seemingly became nearly unconscious. In this state she had been left one Saturday night by the nurse in attendance. Early at dawn next morning—an Easter morning, as it chanced—the poor old women who occupied the other beds in the ward were startled from their sleep by seeing Mary S——— suddenly spring up to a sitting posture in her bed, with her arms outstretched and her face raised, as if in a perfect rapture of joy and welcome. The next instant the body of the poor girl fell back a corpse. Her death had taken place in that moment of mysterious ecstasy.

A totally different case again was told me by the daughter of a man of high intellectual distinction, well-known in the world of letters. When dying peacefully, as became the close of a profoundly religious life, he was observed by his daughter suddenly to look up as if at some spectacle invisible to those around, with an expression of solemn surprise and awe, very characteristic, it is said, of his habitual frame of mind. At that instant, and before the look had time to falter or change, the shadow of death passed over his face, and the end had come.

In yet another case I am told that at the last moment so bright a light seemed suddenly to shine from the face of the dying man, that the clergyman and another friend who were attending him actually turned simultaneously to the window to seek for the cause.

Another incident of a very striking character was described as having occurred in a family, united very closely by affection. A dying lady, exhibiting the aspect of joyful surprise to which we have so often referred, spoke of seeing, one after another, three of her brothers long since dead, and then apparently recognized last of all a fourth brother, who was believed by the bystanders to be still living in India. The coupling of his name with that of his dead brothers excited such awe and horror in the mind of one of the persons present, that she rushed from the room. In due course of time letters were received announcing the death of the brother in India, which had occurred some time before his dying sister seemed to recognize him.

Again, in another case one who had lost his only son some years previously, and who had never recovered the afflicting event exclaimed suddenly when dying, with the air of a man making a most rapturous discovery, "I see him! I see him!"

Not to multiply such anecdotes too far—anecdotes which certainly possess a uniformity pointing to some similar cause, whether that cause be physiological or psychical—I will now conclude with one authenticated by a near relative of the persons concerned. A late colonial Bishop was commonly called by his sisters "Charlie," and his eldest sister bore the pet name of "Liz." They had both been dead for some years, when their younger sister, Mrs. W———, also died, but before her death appeared to behold them both. While lying still and apparently unconscious, she suddenly opened her eyes and looked earnestly across the room as if she saw some one entering. Presently, as if overjoyed, she exclaimed, "O Charlie!" and then, after a moment's pause, with a new start of delight, as if he had been joined by some one else, she went on, "And Liz!" and then added, "How beautiful you are!" After seeming to gaze at the two beloved forms for a few minutes, she fell back on her pillow and died.

An instance in many respects especially noteworthy,—of a similar *impression* of the presence of the dead conveyed through another sense besides sight, is recorded in Caroline Fox's charming "Journals," Vol. II, p. 247. She notes under date September 5th, 1856, as follows:—

"M. A. Schimmelpennick is gone. She said just before her death, 'Oh, I hear such beautiful voices, and the children's are loudest.'"

Can any old Italian picture of the ascending Madonna, with the cloud of cherub heads forming a glory of welcome around her as she enters the higher world, be more significant than this actual fact—so simply told—of a saintly woman in dying hearing *"beautiful voices, and the children's the loudest ?"* Of course, like all the rest it may have been only a physiolgical phenomenon, a purely subjective impression: but it is at least remarkable that a second sense should thus be under the same glamour,—and that again, we have to confront, in the case of *hearing* as of *sight*, the anomaly of the (real or supposed) presence of the beautiful and the delightful, instead of the terrible and the frightful, while Nature is in the pangs of dissolution. Does the brain, then, unlike every unknown instrument, give forth its sweetest music as its chords are breaking?

THE REVELATIONS TO THE DYING.

BISHOP D. W. CLARK, D. D.

Is there not a large class of facts which have a most distinct and impressive bearing upon the relation that exists between the present and the eternal world and the revelations that may be made to the soul while in its transition state? Said a dying Sunday-school scholar from my flock, while in the very article of death, but with perceptive and reasoning powers still unimpaired, "The angels have come." The pious Blumhardt exclaimed, "Light breaks in! Hallelujah!" and expired. Dr. McLain said, "I can now contemplate clearly the grand scene to which I am going." Sargent, the biographer of Martin, with his countenance kindled into a holy fervor, and his eye beaming with unearthly lustre, fixed his gaze as upon a definite object, and exclaimed, "That bright light!" and when asked what light, answered, "The light of the Sun of righteousness." The Lady Elizabeth Hastings, a little before she expired, cried out, with a beaming countenance and enraptured voice, "Lord, what is it that I see?" and Olympia Morata, an exile for her faith, as she sank in death, exclaimed, "I distinctly behold a place filled with ineffable light!" Dr. Bateman, a distinguished physician and philosopher, died exclaiming, "What glory! the angels are waiting for me!" In the midst of delirium, Bishop Wilson was transported with the vision of angels. Not unfrequently the mind is filled with the most striking conceptions of the presence of departed friends. Most touching is the story of Carnaval, who was long known as a lunatic wandering about the streets of Paris. His reason had been unsettled by the early death of the object of his tender and most devoted affections. He could never be made to comprehend that she was dead; but spent his life in the vain search for the lost object of his love. In most affecting terms he would mourn her absence, and chide her long delay. Thus life wore away; and when its ebbing tide was almost exhausted, starting as from a long and unbroken revery, the countenance of the dying man was overspread with sudden joy, and stretching forth his arms, as if he would clasp some object before him, he uttered the name of his long-lost love, and exclaiming, "Ah, there thou art at last!" expired. The aged Hannah More, in her dying agony, stretching out her arms as though she would grasp some object, uttered the name of a much-loved deceased sister, cried, "Joy!" and then sank down into the arms of death.

"Then, then I rose; then first, humanity
Triumphant pass'd the crystal ports of light,
Stupendous guest, and seized eternal youth."

YOUNG.

HEAVEN—NOT FAR AWAY.

OH, heaven is nearer than mortals think,
  When they look with trembling dread,
At the misty future that stretches on,
  From the silent home of the dead.

The eye that shuts in a dying hour,
  Will open the next in bliss,
The welcome will sound in the heavenly world
  Ere the farewell is hushed in this.

We pass from the clasp of mourning friends,
  To the arms of the loved and lost;
And those smiling faces will greet us there,
  Which on earth we have valued most.

Yet oft in the hours of holy thought,
  To the thirsting soul is given,
That power to pierce through the mist of sense,
  To the beauteous scenes of heaven.

I know when the silver cord is loosed,
  When the vail is rent away,
Not long and dark shall the passage be,
  To the realm of endless day.

THE LAST QUIET RESTING PLACE.

Dying Experiences and Testimonies.

THE DYING HUSBAND.

LEIGH HUNT.

SCENE.—*A female sitting by a bedside, anxiously looking at the face of her husband, just dead. The soul within the dead body soliloquizes.*

WHAT change is this! What joy! What depth of rest!
What suddenness of withdrawal from all pain
Into all bliss! into a balm so perfect
I do not even smile! I tried but now,
With that breath's end, to speak to the dear face
That watches me—and lo! all in an instant,
Instead of toil, and a weak, weltering tear,
I am all peace, all happiness, all power,
Laid on some throne in space.—Great God! I am dead!

[*A pause.*] Dear God! Thy love is perfect; Thy truth unknown.
[*Another.*] And He,—and they,—How simple and strange! How
 beautiful!
But I may whisper it not,—even to thought,
Lest strong imagination, hearing it,
Speak, and the world be shattered.
[*Soul again pauses.*] O balm! O bliss! O saturating smile
Unvanishing! O doubt ended! certainty
Begun! O will, faultless, yet all indulged,
Encouraged to be wilful;—to delay
Even its wings for heaven;—and thus to rest
Here, here, ev'n here,—'twixt heaven and earth awhile,
A bed in the morn of endless happiness.
I feel warm drops falling upon my face;
—My wife! my love!—'tis for the best thou canst not
Know how I know thee weeping, and how fond
A kiss meets thine in these unowning lips.

Ah, truly was my love what thou didst hope it,
And more; and so was thine—I read it all—
And our small feuds were but impatiences
At seeing the dear truth all understood.
Poor sweet! thou blamest now thyself, and heapest
Memory on memory of imagined wrong,
As I should have done too,—as all who love,
And yet I cannot pity thee:—so well
I know the end, and how thou'lt smile hereafter.
She speaks my name at last, as though she feared
The terrible, familiar sound; and sinks
In sobs upon my bosom. Hold me fast,
Hold me fast, sweet, and from the extreme grow calm,—
Be cruelly unmoved, and yet how loving!

How wrong was I to quarrel with poor James!
And how dear Francis mistook *me!* That pride,
How without ground it was! Those arguments
Which I supposed so final, O how foolish!
Yet gentlest Death will not permit rebuke,
Ev'n of one's self. They'll know all, as I know,
When they lie thus.
                    Colder I grow, and happier,
Warmness and sense are drawing to a point,
Ere they depart;—myself quitting myself.
The soul gathers its wings upon the edge
Of the new world, yet how assuredly!
Oh! how in balm I change! actively willed,
Yet passive, quiet; and feeling opposites mingle
In exquisitest peace!—Those fleshy clothes,
Which late I thought *myself*, lie more and more
Apart from this warm, sweet retreating *me*,
Who am as a hand, withdrawing from a glove.

So lay my mother, so my father; so
My children: yet I pitied them. I wept,
And fancied them in their graves, and called them "poor!"

O graves! O tears! O knowledge, will, and time,
And fear, and hope! what pretty terms of earth
Were ye! yet how I love ye as of earth
The planet's household words; and how postpone,
Till out of these dear arms, th' immeasurable
Tongue of the all-possessing smile eternal!
Ah, not excluding these, nor aught that's past,
Nor aught that's present, nor that yet's to come,
Well waited for. I would not stir a finger
Out of this rest, to re-assure all anguish;

Such warrant hath it; such divine conjuncture;
Such a charm binds it with the needs of bliss.

That was my eldest boy's—that kiss. And that
The baby with its little unweening mouth;
And those—and those—Dear hearts—they have all come
And think me dead—me, who so now I'm living,
The vitalest creature in this fleshy room.
I part, and with my spirit's eye full opened
Will look upon them.
[*Spirit parts from the body, and breathes upon their eyes.*]

                Patient be those tears,
Fresh heart-dews, standing on these dear clay-moulds.
I quit ye but
To meet again, and will revisit soon
In many a dream, and many a gentle sigh.

SIR ISAAC NEWTON.

HE eminent Dr. Doddridge writes concerning the great philosopher. "According to the best information," "whether public or private, I could ever obtain, his firm faith in the Divine Revelation discovered itself in the most genuine fruits of substantial virtue and piety, and consequently gives us the justest reason to conclude, that he is now rejoicing in the happy effects of it, infinitely more than all the applause which his philosophical works have procured him, though they have commanded a fame lasting as the world."

"Leaving the old, both worlds at once they view,
Who stand upon the threshold of the new."
                                              WALLER.

Threescore and ten, by common calculation,
The years of man amount to—but we'll say
He turns forescore; yet in my estimation,
In all those years he has not lived a day,
                                      J. R. PLANCHE.

MOSES. (BY MICHAEL ANGELO.)

DR. GUTHRIE.

THAT grand and eloquent old Scotchman, Dr. Guthrie, whose sermons so full of rich illustrations have been the comfort of hundreds of thousands, said just before his death: "They tell me I am old. It is not so. I am as young to-day as ever I was. It is true these knees are becoming feeble, and these limbs are somewhat palsied, and these eyes are growing dim; but these eyes are not I, myself, these limbs are not myself. This body is only the house in which I now live. But it will soon be taken down, and then I will appear in another and a better house."

BISHOP FALLOWS.

REV. EDWARD PAYSON, D. D.

Dr. Payson wrote to a friend just before dying "I might date this letter from the land of Beulah, of which I have been some weeks a happy inhabitant. The celestial city is in full view. Its glories beam upon me; its odors are wafted to me; its sounds strike my ear, and its spirit is breathed into my heart. Nothing separates *me* from it but the river of death, which now appears but an insignificant rill which may be crossed at a single step."

Rev. Dr. Olin, President of the Wesleyan University at Middletown, Conn., a giant in frame, and a giant in intellect, whose name is a household word in the Methodist Church, retired from his deeply loved classes, to linger a few months and die. During the early part of his sickness, while he was yet able to walk the room, a sweet young child, two years of age, sickened and sank rapidly. One day it beckoned to its father to take it up. He took it out of its crib, and carried it for a little while, then with failing strength he put it in the crib again. Just as he was doing so, the baby said: "Papa, kiss baby!" He did so tenderly. Then it said: "God take baby!,' and in a few moments the struggle was over. In a few weeks the father followed. He said to his wife: "I am about to die. In a few days you will lay this body in the grave. Do not say you have buried your husband. Your husband will be in heaven."

BISHOP FALLOWS.

REV. PROF. HENRY B. SMITH, D. D.

WHEN Professor Henry B. Smith was almost gone—beyond the power of recognizing by sight his most familiar friends—the Rev. Dr. Goodwin, a close associate from boyhood, came on from Philadelphia to New York to bid the departing sufferer a last good-bye, but was not recognized as he came to the bedside. "Do you not know me, Henry?" he asked. "Yes: I know the finest thread of that intonation and respond to it," was the immediate and distinct reply. That dying faintness cannot be the end of such a spirit's being. Friendships like this, made perfect in Christ, must live and strengthen forever. Nor will souls so attuned to each other find any barrier to reunion in whatever may be the new and strange conditions of the future life. They will find their other selves as naturally as "kindred drops which mingle into one." The wife of Baron Bunsen writes of her dying husband: "In that night I beheld the last full brilliance of eye and smile, when he repeated his solemn farewell, believing death to be at hand: 'Love, love—we have loved each other; love cannot cease; love is eternal; the love of God is eternal; live in the love of God and Christ; those who live in the love of God shall find each other again, though we know not how; we cannot be parted long, we shall meet again.'"

———o———

WHEN John Holland died, it was about five or six in the evening, the shadow of night was gathering around, and it was growing darker and darker. When near the last moment he looked up, and said to the family: "What is this? What is this strange light in the room? Have they lighted the candles, Martha?" "No," she said. He replied: "Then it must be heaven. Welcome, heaven."

TALMAGE.

———o———

MR. MOODY relates the following incident: During the late war a young man lay on a cot, and they heard him say, "Here, and some one went to his cot and wanted to know what he wanted, and he said, "Hark! hush! don't you hear them?" "Hear who?" was asked. "They are calling the roll of heaven," he said, and pretty soon he answered, "Here!"—and he was gone.

FOLDING THE LAMBS IN HIS BOSOM.

THE Savior folds a lamb in His bosom. The little child filled all the house with her music, and her toys are scattered all up and down the stairs just as she left them. What if the hand that plucked four o'clocks out of the meadow is still? It will wave in the eternal triumph. What if the voice that made music in the home is still? It will sing the eternal hosanna. Put a white rose in one hand, and a red rose in the other hand, and a wreath of orange blossoms on the brow; the white flower for the victory, the red flower for the Savior's sacrifice, the orange blossoms for her marriage day. Anything ghastly about that? Oh, no. The sun went down and the flower shut. The wheat threshed out of the straw. "Dear Lord, give me sleep," said a dying boy, the son of one of my elders, "dear Lord, give me sleep," And he closed his eyes and awoke in glory. Henry W. Longfellow writing a letter of condolence to those parents, said: "Those last words were beautifully poetic." And Mr. Longfellow knew what is poetic. "Dear Lord give me sleep."

"'Twas not in cruelty, not in wrath
That the reaper came that day;
'Twas an angel that visited the earth
And took the flower away."

So it may be with us when our work is all done. "Dear Lord give me sleep."

TALMAGE.

BRING THE CHILDREN HOME.

A MOTHER died in one of our Eastern cities a few years ago, and she had a large family of children. She died of consumption, and the children were brought in to her when she was dying. As the oldest one was brought in she gave it her last message and her dying blessing; and as the next one was brought in she put her hand upon its head and gave it her blessing; and then the next one was brought in, and the next, until at last they brought in the little infant. She took it to her bosom and pressed it to her loving heart, and her friends saw that it was hastening her end; that she was excited, and as they went to take the little child from her she said: "My husband, I charge you to bring all these children home with you." And so God charges us as parents to bring our children home with us; not only to have our own names written in heaven, but those of our children also.

D. L. MOODY.

GOING TO JESUS.

AN eminent Christian worker in New York, told me a story that affected me very much.

A father had a son who had been sick some time, but he did not consider him dangerous; until one day he came home to dinner and found his wife weeping, and he asked, "What is the trouble?"

"There has been a great change in our boy since morning," the mother said, "and I am afraid that he is dying; I wish you to go in and see him, and, if you think he is, I wish you to tell him so, for I cannot bear to tell him."

The father went in and sat down by the bedside, and he placed his hand upon his forehead, and he could feel the cold, damp sweat of death, and knew its cold, icy hand was feeling for the chords of life, and that his boy was soon to be taken away, and he said to him:

"My son, do you know you are dying?"

The little fellow looked up at him and said:

"No; am I? Is this death that I feel stealing over me, father?"

"Yes, my son, you are dying."

"Will I live the day out?"

"No; you may die at any moment."

He looked up to his father and he said; "Well, I will be with Jesus to-night, won't I, father?"

And the father answered: "Yes my boy, you will spend to-night with the Savior," and the father turned away to conceal the tears, that the little boy might not see him weep; but he saw the tears, and he said:

"Father, don't you weep for me; when I get to heaven I will go straight to Jesus and tell Him that ever since I can remember, you have tried to lead me to Him."

D. L. MOODY.

DAVID SWING.

WHITEFIELD'S DEATH.

REV. ABEL STEVENS, D. D.

SAID Sir John Herschel, "I could see Sirius announcing himself," as he swept the heavens with his telescope, in search of Sirius, "till the great star rushed in and filled the whole field of vision with a sea of light." The time came for Whitefield to die. The man had been immortal till his work was done. His path had been bright, and it grew brighter to the end, like that of the just.

"You had better be in bed, Mr. Whitefield," said his host, the day he preached his last sermon.

"True," said the dying evangelist, and clasping his hands, cried: "I am weary in, not of, thy work, Lord Jesus."

He preached his last sermon at Newburyport, pale and dying; he herein uttered one of the most pathetic sentences which ever came to his lips:

"I go to my everlasting rest. My sun has risen, shone, and is setting—nay, it is about to rise and shine forever. I have not lived in vain. And though I could live to preach Christ a thousand years I die to be with Him—which is far better."

The shaft was levelled. That day he said: "I am dying!" He ran to the window; lavender drops were offered, but all help was vain; his work was done. The doctor said, "He is a dead man." And so he was; and died in silence. Christ required no dying testimony from one whose life had been a constant testimony.

So passed away on September 30th, 1770, one of the greatest spirits that ever inhabited a human tabernacle. The world has ever been an innumerable gainer by his life. He had preached eighty thousand sermons, and they had but two key-notes: 1. Man is guilty, he must be pardoned. 2. Man is immortal, he must be happy or wretched forever. Weeping filled Newburyport, flags floated at half-mast, and the ships fired minute-guns.

"Mortals cried, a man is dead;
Angels sang, a child is born."

Rev. Daniel Rodgers, remembering in his prayer that Whitefield had been his spiritual father, burst into tears, and cried: "My father! my father! the chariot of Israel, and the horsemen thereof."

Coke sleeps in his grand sea-grave, with the everlasting music of the billows for his dirge; Robert Newton sleeps at Easingwold; Richard Watson, and John and Charles Wesley slumber in a London graveyard; and George Whitefield's dust rests in its Transatlantic abode till

"That illustrious morn shall come,"

when the "dead in Christ shall rise," and they will meet in glory, to die no more. Meantime, earth holds no mightier dust. Blessed be God that ever they lived, and left their influence to mould humanity

GRATEFUL TESTIMONY.

A missionary visited a converted native, in the South Sea Islands, who was in a dying condition, and before his departure, addressed him as follows: "I am going; but you are to remain a little longer. when I get to heaven, I shall first of all praise and thank Jesus for having saved a poor creature like me, and then I'll tell him about you for it was you who first told me the way to heaven. And then I'll look about and see where the door is through which the spirits go up; and if I find such a place, that will be where I will sit and wait for you. And when you come, oh! what a happy day that will be! And after our joyful meeting, I'll take you by the hand and lead you to Jesus, and say to him: 'Jesus! Jesus! this is the man—this is the man I told you about. This is the man whom you sent to tell me about your own love—this is the man!'"

REV. DR. TURNER.

WHAT MESSAGE TO JESUS.

A LITTLE boy on his dying couch. He had a father who was irreligious. Just before he died he said: "Father, I am going to heaven, what shall I tell Jesus is the reason why you won't love him?" The father burst into tears; but before he could give an answer the dear Sunday-school boy had fallen asleep in Christ. Subsequently the reproof, operating upon that father's heart, led him to repentance and to Christ, and he has since joined his son in the happy land.

FELICIA HEMANS.

On her deathbed, Mrs. Hemans dictated to her brother "The Sabbath Sonnet." He wrote for her:

> "*I* may not tread
> With them those pathways—to the feverish bed
> Of sickness bound; yet, O my God! I bless
> Thy mercy, that with Sabbath peace hath fill'd
> My chasten'd heart, and all its throbbings still'd
> In one deep calm of lowliest thankfulness."

In a peaceful and gentle slumber, this sweet singer fell asleep in Jesus.

Her own beautiful lines were inscribed as her epitaph.

> "Calm, on the bosom of thy God,
>   Fair spirit, rest thee now:
> E'en whilst with us thy footsteps trod,
>   His seal was on thy brow.
>
> "Dust, to its narrow cell beneath;
>   Soul, to its place on high:
> They who have seen thy look in death,
>   No more need fear to die."

JOHN LOCKE.

Just before his death Locke wrote as follows to his friend Anthony Collins. "May you live long and happy in the enjoyment of health, freedom, content, and all those blessings which Providence has bestowed on you, and to which your virtue entitles you! You loved me living, and will preserve my memory when I am dead. All the use to be made of it is, that this life is a scene of vanity, which soon passes away, and affords no solid satisfaction but in the consciousness of doing well, and in the hope of another life. This is what I can say upon experience, and what you will find to be true when you come to make up the account. Adieu."

> "I will tell thee even more,
> Ten thousand years from now; if but with thee
> I too reach heaven, and with new language there,
> When an eternity of bliss has gone,
> Bless God for new eternities to be."
>
> COXE.

THE MOTHER AND HER DYING BOY.

BOY.

My mother, my mother! O, let me depart!
Your tears and your pleadings are swords to my heart
I hear gentle voices, that chide my delay;
I see lovely visions, that woo me away.
My prison is broken, my trials are o'er!
O, mother, my mother, detain me no more.

MOTHER.

And will you, then, leave us, my brightest, my best;
And will you run nestling no more to my breast?
The summer is coming to sky and to bower;
The tree that you planted will soon be in flower;
You loved the soft season of song and of bloom;
O, shall it return, and find you in your tomb?

BOY.

Yes, mother, I loved in the sunshine to play,
And talk with the birds and the blossoms all day
But sweeter the songs of the spirits on high,
And brighter the glories around God in the sky.
I see them, I hear them, they pull at my heart;
My mother, my mother, O, let me depart.

MOTHER.

O, do not desert us. Our hearts will be drear,
Our home will be lonely, when you are not here;
Your brother will sigh 'mid his playthings, and say,
I wonder dear William so long can delay.
That foot, like the wild wind,—that glance like a star,—
O, what will this world be when they are afar?

BOY.

This world, dearest mother. O, live not for this.
No, press on with me to the fulness of bliss.
And trust me, whatever bright fields I may roam,
My heart will not wander from you and from home,
Believe me still near you, on pinions of love;
Expect me to hail you, when soaring above.

MOTHER.

Well, go, my beloved; the conflict is o'er;
My pleas are all selfish,—I urge them no more.
Why claim your bright spirit down here to the clod,
So thirsting for freedom, so ripe for its God?
Farewell, then, farewell, till we meet at the throne,
Where love fears no parting, and tears are unknown.

BOY.

O, glory, O, glory, what music, what light.
What wonders break in on my heart, on my sight?
I come, blessed spirits. I hear you from high.
O, frail, faithless nature, can this be to die?
So near, what, so near to my Savior and King?
O, help me, ye angels, His glories to sing.

SIR WALTER RALEIGH.

THIS illustrious Englishman wrote to his wife from the tower of London, just before his execution. "Time and death call me away. The everlasting God, powerful, infinite, and and inscrutable God Almighty, who is goodness itself, the true light and life, keep you and yours, and have mercy on me, and forgive my persecutors and false accusers, and send us to meet in his glorious kingdom! My dear wife, farewell! bless my boy; pray for me; and may my true God hold you both in his arms!

"Yours that was, but not now mine own.

WALTER RALEIGH.

"Ah, yes! the hour has come
When thou must hasten home
Pure soul, to Him who calls;
The God who gave thee breath
Walks by the side of death,
And naught that step appals."

LANDOR.

"'Tis immortality,—'tis that alone,
Amidst life's pains, abasements, emptiness,
The soul can comfort, elevate, and fill."

YOUNG.

"When life's close knot, by writ from Destiny,
Disease shall cut, or age untie;
When, after some delays—some dying strife—
The soul stands shiv'ring on the ridge of life;
With what a dreadful curiosity
Doth she launch out into the sea of vast eternity."

JOHN NORRIS, 1690.

JOSEPH ADDISON.

ADDISON when dying sent for Lord Warwick, a youth nearly related to him, and finely accomplished, but irregular in conduct and principle, on whom his pious instructions and example had not produced the desired effect.

Lord Warwick came: but life now glimmering in the sockets the dying friend was silent. After a decent and proper pause the youth said, "Dear sir, you sent for me, I believe, and hope you have some commands: I shall hold them most dear."

May the reader not only feel the reply, but retain its impression! Forcibly grasping the youth's hand, Addison softly said, "See in what peace a Christian can die!"

> "Death is the crown of life!
> It wounds to cure; we fall, we rise, we reign!
> Spring from our fetters, fasten in the skies,
> Where blooming Eden withers in our sight,
> Death gives us more than was in Eden lost;
> This king of terrors is the prince of peace."
>
> YOUNG.

SIR MATHEW HALE.

THIS eminent Judge continued to enjoy the free use of his reason and senses to the last moment of life. This he had often and earnestly prayed for during his last sickness. When his voice was so sunk that he could not be heard, his friend perceived, by the almost constant lifting up of his eyes and hands, that he was still aspiring toward the blessed state, of which he was now to be speedily possessed. He had no struggles, nor seemed to be in any pang in his last moments. He breathed out his righteous and pious soul in peace.

> The last end
> Of the good man is peace. How calm his exit!
> Night-dews fall not more gently to the ground,
> Nor weary worn-out winds expire so soft.
>
> BLAIR.

JOSEPH ADDISON.

JOHN WESLEY.

A LITTLE after, a person coming in, he strove to speak but could not! Finding they could not understand him, he paused a little, and then, with all the remaining strength he had, cried out, "*The best of all is, God is with us;*" and, soon after, lifting up his dying arm in token of victory, and raising his feeble voice with a holy triumph, not to be expressed, he again repeated the heart-reviving words, "*The best of all is, God is with us.*" Most of the night following, he could only utter,

"I'll praise—I'll praise."

He wished to give utterance to that noble verse he had so often sung:

"I'll praise my Maker while I've breath,
And when my voice is lost in death,
Praise shall employ my nobler powers:
My days of praise shall ne'er be past,
While life, and thought, and being last,
Or immortality endures!"

But in Eternity only could he further continue praise to God and to the Lamb, forever and ever.

"With lifted eyes,
An aspect luminous, as with the light
Of heaven's op'ning gate, he strove to join
His voice with theirs, and breathe out all he felt;
But in the effort, feeble nature sank
Exhausted; and, while every voice was hush'd,
His flutt'ring spirit, struggling to get free,
Rose like a sky-lark singing up to heaven."

WILCOX.

ISAAC WATTS, D. D.

WHEN Dr. Watts was almost worn out, and broken down by his infirmities, he said, in conversation with a friend, "I remember an aged minister used to observe, that 'the most learned and knowing Christians, when they come to die, have only the same plain promises of the Gospel for their support as the common and unlearned;' and so I find it. It is the plain promises of the Gospel that are my support; and, I bless God, they are plain promises, that do not require much labor and pains to understand them.'

> "Is that his deathbed where the Christian lies?
> No! 'tis not his. 'Tis death itself there dies."
>
> COLERIDGE.

REV. JOHN FLETCHER.

MRS. FLETCHER says: "As night drew on, I perceived him dying very fast. His fingers could hardly make the sign, which he scarcely ever forgot; and his speech seemed quite gone. I said, My dear creature, I ask not for myself; I know thy soul; but for the sake of others, if Jesus be very present with thee lift up thy right hand. Immediately he did so. If the prospect of glory sweetly open before thee, repeat the sign. He instantly raised it again, and in half a minute a second time. He then threw it up, as if he would reach the top of the bed. After this his hands moved no more."

> "Life's labor done, as sinks the clay,—
> Light from its load the spirit flies,
> While heaven and earth combine to say,—
> How blest the righteous when he dies!"
>
> BARBAULD.

SIR THOMAS FOWELL BUXTON.

BEFORE dying, this true statesman, with great energy of voice and manner said:—"O God, O God, can it be that there is good reason to believe that such an one as I shall be remembered amongst the just? Is thy mercy able to contain even me? From my heart I give the most earnest thanksgivings for this and for all thy mercies."

> "Now safe arrives the heav'nly mariner;
> The batt'ring storm, the hurricane of life,
> All dies away in one eternal calm.
> With joy Divine, full glowing in his breast,
> He gains—he gains the port of everlasting rest."

REV. CHARLES SIMEON.

"As his end drew near, he broke out, 'It is said,' "O death, where is thy sting?"' Then, looking at us as we stood round his bed, he asked, in his own peculiarly impressive manner, 'Do you see any sting here?'

"We answered, 'No, indeed, it is all taken away.'

"He then said, 'Does not this prove that my principles were not founded on fancies or enthusiasm, but that there is a reality in them? and I find them sufficient to support me in death.'

"Thus departed a laborious servant of Christ, entering into rest at the very moment that the bell of St. Mary's was tolling for the university sermon which he himself was to have preached, November 13, 1836."

> " How sweet the hour of closing day,
>   When all is peaceful and serene;
> And when the sun, with cloudless ray,
>   Sheds mellow lustre o'er the scene:
> Such is the Christian's parting hour,
>   So peacefully he sinks to rest;
> When faith, endued from heaven with power,
>   Sustains and cheers his languid breast."

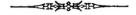

REV. CHARLES WESLEY.

While Charles Wesley remained in a state of extreme feebleness, having been silent and quiet for some time, he called Mrs. Wesley to him, and requested her to write the following lines at his dictation:

> In age and feebleness extreme,
> Who shall a sinful world redeem?
> Jesus, my only hope thou art,
> Strength of my failing flesh and heart·
> O could I catch a smile from Thee,
> And drop into eternity!

For fifty years Christ, as the Redeemer of men, had been the subject of his effective ministry, and of his loftiest songs; and he may be said to have died with a hymn to Christ upon his lips.

> " He taught us how to live; and O! too high
> A price for knowledge, taught us how to die!"

CHARLOTTE ELIZABETH.

BEFORE death, the eyes of this gifted authoress brightened; her husband was leaning over her, and throwing her arm around his neck, and pressing his lips to hers, she exclaimed, with emphasis, "I love you!"

All thought that these were her last words; but it soon became evident that she was gathering her remaining strength for a last effort; and then, with death in every look and tone, gasping between each word, but with a loud, clear, distinct voice, she uttered these words, 'Tell them,' naming some dear Jewish friends,—'tell them that Jesus *is* the Messiah; and tell——;'— her hand had forgotten its cunning; her tongue was cleaving to the roof of her mouth; but Charlotte Elizabeth had not forgotten Jerusalem. Her breathings grew fainter and fainter; she was slightly convulsed, and at twenty minutes past two she entered into everlasting rest. The inscription she wished written on her tombstone was, "LOOKING UNTO JESUS."

> "Yet, Jesus, Jesus! there I'll cling,
> I'll crowd beneath his sheltering wing;
> I'll clasp the cross, and holding there,
> Even me --O bliss!—his wrath may share."
>
> HENRY KIRKE WHITE

MATTHEW HENRY.

THE last words of this distinguished commentator were:—"You have been used to take notice of the sayings of dying men: this is mine—That a life spent in the service of God, and communion with Him, is the most comfortable and pleasant life that any one can live in the present world."

> "The chamber where the Christian meets his fate.
> Is privileged beyond the common walk
> Of virtuous life, quite on the verge of heaven;
> You see the man, you see his hold on heaven
> Heaven waits not the last moment, owns her friends
> On this side death, and points them out to man—
> A lecture silent, but of sovereign power,
> To vice confusion, and to virtue peace."
>
> YOUNG.

THE VANITY OF LIFE.

> Why all this toil for triumphs of an hour!
> What though we wade in wealth or soar in fame!
> Earth's highest station ends in "Here he lies;"
> And "Dust to dust" concludes her noblest song.
>
> Edward Young.

BISHOP McILVAINE.

The Episcopal Clergyman who was with Bishop McIlvaine at his death gives an account of the closing scenes of this honored prelate's life. He says the bishop asked that three hymns should be read to him,—"Just as I am, without one plea," "Rock of Ages, cleft for me," and "Jesus lover of my soul." He said to his friend, "Pray with me." He asked the bishop if he should read from the prayer book. "No. Make the prayer yourself," after which he said, "The Lord is letting me down gently into the grave. This is falling asleep." In a few minutes he was gone.

JOHN FOSTER.

As John Foster approached the close of life, and felt his strength gradually stealing away, he remarked on his increasing weakness, and added, "But I can pray, and that is a glorious thing!" Truly a glorious thing; more glorious than an atheist or pantheist can ever pretend to. To look up to an omnipotent Father, to speak to him, to love him, to stretch upward as an infant from the cradle, that he may lift his child in his everlasting arms to the resting-place of his own bosom; this is the portion of the dying Christian. He was overheard thus speaking with himself: "O death, where is thy sting? O grave, where is thy victory? Thanks be to God, who giveth us the victory through our Lord Jesus Christ." The eye of the terror-crowned was upon him, and thus he defied him.

BISHOP GILBERT HAVEN, D. D.

THE MARTYRS.

MARTYRED HEROES.

PATRIOTS have toil'd, and in their country's cause
Bled nobly; and their deeds, as they deserve,
Receive proud recompense. We give in charge
Their names to the sweet lyre; th' historic muse,
Proud of the treasure, marches with it down
To latest time; and sculpture, in her turn,
Gives bond in stone and ever-during brass
To guard them, and to' immortalize her trust.
But fairer wreaths are due, though never paid,
To those, who, posted at the shrine of Truth.
Have fallen in her defence. *   *   *   *
*   *   *   *   *   Their blood is shed
In confirmation of the noblest claim—
Our claim to feed upon immortal truth,
To walk with God, to be divinely free,
To soar and to anticipate the skies!
Yet few remember them. They lived unknown,
Till persecution dragg'd them into fame,
And chased them up to heaven. Their ashes flew—
No marble tells us whither. With their names
No bard embalms and sanctifies his song!
And history, so warm on meaner themes,
Is cold on this. She execrates indeed
The tyranny that doom'd them to the fire,
But gives the glorious sufferers little praise.
WILLIAM COWPER.

THE REV. ARTHUR PENRYHN STANLEY, D. D.
(Late Dean of Westminster.)

BISHOPS RIDLEY AND LATIMER.

WHEN they came to the stake, Dr. Ridley embraced Latimer fervently and bid him be of good heart. He then knelt by the stake, and after earnestly praying together, they had a short private conversation. Dr. Smith then preached a short sermon against the martyrs, who would have answered him, but were prevented by Dr. Marshal, the vice-chancellor. Dr. Ridley then took off his gown and tippet, and gave it to his brother-in-law, Mr Shipside. He gave away also many trifles to his weeping friends, and the populace were anxious to get even a fragment of his garments. Bishop Latimer gave nothing; and from the poverty of his garb, was soon stripped to his shroud, and stood venerable and erect, fearless of death. Dr. Ridley being unclothed to his shirt, the smith placed an iron chain about their waists, and Dr. Ridley bid him fasten it securely; his brother having tied a bag of gunpowder about his neck, gave some also to Mr. Latimer. A lighted fagot was now laid at Dr. Ridley's feet, which caused Mr. Latimer to say, "Be of good cheer, Ridley, and play the man. We shall this day, by God's grace, light up such a candle in England as, I trust, will never be put out." When Dr. Ridley saw the flame approaching him, he exclaimed, "Into thy hands, O Lord, I commend my spirit!" and repeated often, "Lord, receive my spirit." Bishop Latimer, too, ceased not to say, "O Father of heaven, receive my soul"

> "Instructive heroes! tell us whence
> Your noble scorn of flesh and sense!
> You part from all we prize so dear,
> Nor drop one soft reluctant tear;
> Death's black and stormy gulf you brave,
> And ride exultingly on the wave;
> Deem thrones but trifles all--no more--
> Nor send one wishful look to shore."

> "Death's subtle seed within,
> (Sly, treach'rous miner!) working in the dark,
> Smiled at thy well concerted scheme, and beckon'd
> The worm to riot on that rose so red,
> Unfaded ere it fell, one moment's prey."

YOUNG.

JOHN HUSS.

WHEN the chain was put about John Huss at the stake, he said, with a smiling countenance, "My Lord Jesus Christ was bound with a harder chain than this for my sake, and why then should I be ashamed of this rusty one?"

When the fagots were piled up to his very neck, the Duke of Bavaria was so officious as to desire him to abjure, "No," said Huss, "I never preached any doctrine of an evil tendency and what I taught with my lips I now seal with my blood." He then said to the executioner, "You are now going to burn a goose, (Huss signifying goose in the Bohemian language,) but in a century you will have a swan, whom you can neither roast nor boil." True prophecy! Martin Luther came about a hundred years after, and had a swan for his arms.

> "One army of the living God,
>   To his command we bow;
> Part of the host have cross'd the flood,
>   And part are crossing now."
>
> C. WESLEY.

JEROME OF PRAGUE.

IN going to the place of execution Jerome sung several hymns, and when he came to the spot, which was the same where Huss had been burnt, he knelt down, and prayed fervently. He embraced the stake with great cheerfulness, and when they went behind him to set fire to the fagots, he said, "Come here, and kindle it before my eyes: for if I had been afraid of it, I had not come to this place." The fire being kindled, he sung a hymn, but was soon interrupted by the flames and the last words he was heard to say were these: "This soul in flames I offer, Christ, to thee."

> "Through nature's wreck, through vanquish'd agonies,
>   (Like stars struggling through the midnight gloom,)
> What gleams of joy! What more than human peace!"
>
> YOUNG.

LAWRENCE SAUNDERS.

WHEN Mr. Saunders was come nigh to the place of execution, the officer appointed to see the execution done, said to him that he was one of them who marred the Queen's realm, but if he would recant, there was pardon for him. "Not I," replied the holy martyr, "but such as you have injured the realm. The blessed Gospel of Christ is what I hold; that do I believe, that have I taught, and that will I never revoke!" Mr. Saunders then slowly moved towards the fire, sank to the earth and prayed; he then rose up, embraced the stake, and frequently said, "Welcome, thou cross of Christ! Welcome everlasting life!" Fire was then put to the fagots; and he was overwhelmed by the dreadful flames, and sweetly slept in the Lord Jesus.

> "Though unseen by human eye,
> My Redeemer's hand is nigh;
> He has poured salvation's light
> Far within the vale of night."
>
> KLOPSTOCK.

REV. GEORGE WISHART.

As soon as he arrived at the stake, the executioner put a rope round his neck, and a chain about his middle; upon which he fell on his knees, and thus exclaimed:—

"O thou Savior of the world, have mercy upon me! Father of heaven, I commend my spirit into thy holy hands."

After this he prayed for his accusers, saying, "I beseech thee, Father of heaven, forgive them that have, from ignorance, or an evil mind, forged lies of me: I forgive them with all my heart. I beseech Christ to forgive those who ignorantly condemned me."

> "Though to-night the seed be sown in gloom,
> Amid darkness, and tears, and sorrow,
> It shall spring from the tomb, in immortal bloom,
> On the bright and glorious morrow.
> The tears that we shed o'er holy dust,
> Are the tribute of human sadness;
> But the grave holds in trust the remains of the just,
> Till the day of eternal gladness."

DR. ROWLAND TAYLOR.

THEY bound Dr. Taylor with the chains, and having set up the fagots, one Warwick, cruelly cast a fagot at him, which struck him on his head, and cut his face, so that the blood ran down. Then said Dr. Taylor, "O friend, I have harm enough; what needed that?"

Sir John Shelton standing by, as Dr. Taylor was speaking, and saying the Psalm Miserere in English, struck him on the lips: "You knave," said he, "speak Latin; I will make thee." At last they kindled the fire; and Dr. Taylor, holding up both his hands, called upon God, and said, "Merciful Father of heaven, for Jesus Christ my Savior's sake, receive my soul into thy hands!" So he stood still without either crying or moving, with his hands folded together, till Soyce with a halberd struck him on the head till his brains fell out, and the corpse fell down into the fire.

> "What nothing earthly gives, or can destroy,
> The soul's calm sunshine, and the heartfelt joy,
> Is virtue's prize."

LORD VISCOUNT WINCESLAUS.

APPROACHING the block, he stroked his long gray beard, and said, "Venerable hairs, the greater honor now attends ye—a crown of martyrdom is your portion." Then laying down his head, it was severed from his body at one stroke, and placed upon a pole in a conspicuous part of the city.

> "O that, without a lingering groan,
> I may the welcome word receive;
> My body with my charge lay down,
> And cease at once to work and live."

> "Life is a dream—a bright, but fleeting dream—
> I can but love; but then my soul awakes,
> And from the mist of earthliness, a gleam
> Of heavenly light, of truth immortal, breaks."
>
> FANNY FORRESTER.

ARCHBISHOP CRANMER.

A CHAIN was provided to bind Cranmer to the stake: and after it had tightly encircled him, fire was put to the fuel, and the flames began soon to ascend. Then was the glorious sentiment of the martyr made manifest; then it was, that, stretching out his right hand, he held it unshirkingly in the fire till it was burned to a cinder, even before his body was injured, frequently exclaiming, "This hand—this unworthy right hand!" Apparently insensible of pain, with a countenance of venerable resignation, and eyes directed to Him for whose cause he suffered, he continued, like St. Stephen, to say, "Lord Jesus, receive my spirit!" till the fury of the flames terminated his powers of utterance and existence.

"Farewell, conflicting hopes and fears,
Where light and shade alternate dwell;
How bright the unchanging morn appears!
Farewell, inconstant world, farewell!"

And when the closing scenes prevail,
When wealth, state, pleasure, all shall fail;
All that a foolish world admires,
Or passion craves, or pride inspires;
At that important hour of need
JESUS shall prove a friend indeed.
His hand shall smooth thy dying bed,
His arm sustain thy drooping head;
And when the painful struggle 's o'er,
And that vain thing, the world, no more,
He'll bear his humble friend away,
To rapture and eternal day.
Come, then, be his in every part,
Nor give him less than all your heart."

COTTON.

"The soul uneasy, and confined from home,
Rests and expatiates in a world to come."

POLYCARP.

THE pro-consul urged Polycarp. "Swear, and I will release thee; reproach Christ." The venerable bishop calmly replied: "Eighty and six years have I served him, and he hath never wronged me; and how can I blaspheme my God and King who hath saved me!" "But I have wild beasts," said the pro-consul, "and I will expose you to them unless you repent." "Call them," said the martyr. "I will tame your spirit by fire," said the Roman. "You threaten me," said Polycarp, "with the fire which burns only for a moment, but are yourself ignorant of the fire of eternal punishment, reserved for the ungodly." The pro-consul, finding it impossible to shake his steadfastness, adjudged him to the flames. But in their midst he sung praises to God, and exclaimed." "Oh Father of thy beloved and blessed Son, Jesus Christ! O God of all principalities and of all creation! I bless thee, that thou hast counted me worthy of this day and this hour, to receive my portion in the number of the martyrs—in the cup of Christ."

"Trust thou in Him who overcame the grave;
Who holds in captive ward
The powers of death. Heed not the monster grim,
Nor fear to go through death to him."

CONDER.

"His spirit, with a bound,
Burst its encumb'ring clay;
His tent, at sunrise, on the ground,
A blacken'd ruin lay."

MONTGOMERY.

"An angel's arm can't snatch me from the grave·
Legions of angels can't confine me there!"

YOUNG.

"The weary springs of life stand still at last."

The Death of Children.

THE BROOKLYN TABERNACLE (T. DeWITT TALMAGE, PASTOR).

THE DEATH OF CHILDREN.

THE CHILD IS DEAD.

REV. S. IRENÆUS PRIME, D. D.

THE child is dead. You may put away its playthings. Put them where they will be safe. I would not like to have them broken or lost; and you need not lend them to other children when they come to see us. It would pain me to see them in other hands, much as I love to see children happy with their toys.

Its clothes you may lay aside; I shall often look them over, and each of the colors that he wore will remind me of him as he looked when he was here. I shall weep often when I think of him; but there is a luxury in thinking of the one that is gone, which I would not part with for the world. I think of my child now, a child always, though an angel among angels.

The child is dead. The eye has lost its lustre. The hand is still and cold. Its little heart is not beating now. How pale it looks! Yet the very form is dear to me. Every lock of its hair, every feature of the face, is a treasure that I shall prize the more as the months of my sorrow come and go.

THE BLOSSOM TRANSPLANTED.

TELL us if Christianity does not throw a pleasing radiance around an infant's tomb? And should any parent who hears us, feel softened by the remembrance of the light that twinkled a few short months under his roof, and at the end of its little period expired, we cannot think that we venture too far when we say, that he is only to persevere in the faith, and in the following of the Gospel, and that very light will again shine upon him in heaven. The blossom which withered here upon its stalk, has been transplanted there to a place of endurance; and it will there gladden that eye which now weeps out the agony of an affliction which has been sorely wounded; and in the name of Him who, if on earth, would have wept along with them, do we bid all believers present, to sorrow, not even as others which have no hope, but to take comfort in the hope of that country where there is no sorrow, and no separation.

Dr. Thomas Chalmers.

LITTLE BESSIE.

A. D. F. RANDOLPH.

Hug me closer, closer, mother,
    Put your arms around me tight,
I am cold and tired, mother,
    And I feel so strange to-night;
Something hurts me, here, dear mother,
    Like a stone upon my breast;
Oh, I wonder, wonder, mother,
    Why it is I cannot rest!

All the day while you were working,
    As I lay upon my bed,
I was trying to be patient,
    And to think of what you said;
How the kind and blessed Jesus
    Loves his lambs to watch and keep,
And I wish he'd come, and take me
    In his arms, that I might sleep.

Just before the lamp was lighted,
　　Just before the children came;
While the room was very quiet,
　　I heard some one call my name:
But I could not see the Savior,
　　Though I strained my eyes to see

And I wondered if He saw me—
　　Would He speak to such as me?
In a moment I was looking
　　On a world so bright and fair,
Which was full of little children—
　　And they seemed so happy there.

They were singing—oh! how sweetly!
　　Sweeter songs I never heard!
They were singing sweeter, mother,
　　Than the sweetest singing bird.
And while I my breath was holding,
　　One so bright upon me smiled:
And I knew it must be Jesus,
　　When He said, "Come here, my child"

"Come up here, my little Bessie,
　　Come up here, and live with me,
Where the children never suffer,
　　But are happier than you see!"
Then I thought of all you'd told me,
　　Of that bright and happy land;
I was going when you called me,
　　When you came and kissed my hand.

And at first I felt so sorry
　　You had called me; I would go,—
Oh! to sleep and never suffer!—
　　Mother, don't be crying so!
Hug me closer, closer, mother,
　　Put your arms about me tight;
Oh! how much I love you, mother,
　　But I feel so strange to-night!

* * * * * * *

And the mother pressed her closer
　　To her over-burdened breast,
On the heart so near to breaking
　　Lay the heart so near its rest.
At the solemn hour of midnight,
　　In the darkness, calm, and deep,
Lying on her mother's bosom,
　　Little Bessie fell asleep.

CAN I WISH IT BACK?

COULD I wish that this young inhabitant of heaven should be degraded to earth again? Or would it thank me for that wish? Would it say that it was the part of a wise parent, to call it down from a sphere of such exalted services and pleasures, to our low lives here upon earth? Let me rather be thankful for the pleasing hope, that though God loves my child too well to permit it to return to me, he will ere long bring me to it. And then that endeared paternal affection which would have been a cord to tie me to earth, and have added new pangs to my removal from it, will be as a golden chain to draw me upward, and add one farther charm and joy even to paradise itself. And oh, great joy! to view the change, and to compare that dear idea, so fondly laid up, so often reviewed, with the now glorious original, in the improvement of the upper world.

PHILIP DODDRIDGE, D. D.

ONE YEAR AGO.

MRS. H. B. STOWE.

One year ago,—a ringing voice,
  A clear blue eye,
And clustering curls of sunny hair,
  Too fair to die.

Only a year,—no voice, no smile,
  No glance of eye,
No clustering curls of golden hair,
  Fair but to die!

One year ago,—what loves, what schemes
  Far into life!
What joyous hopes, what high resolves,
  What generous strife!

The silent picture on the wall,
   The burial stone,
Of all that beauty, life, and joy,
   Remain alone!

One year,—one year,—one little year,—
   And so much gone!
And yet the even flow of life
   Moves calmly on.

The grave grows green, the flowers bloom fair,
   Above that head;
No sorrowing tint of leaf or spray
   Says he is dead.

No pause or hush of merry birds
   That sing above
Tells us how coldly sleeps below
   The form we love.

What hast thou been this year, beloved?
   What hast thou seen?
What visions fair, what glorious life,
   Where thou hast been?

The veil! the veil! so thin, so strong!
   'Twixt us and thee;
The mystic veil! when shall it fall,
   That we may see?

Not dead, not sleeping, not even gone;
   But present still,
And waiting for the coming hour
   Of God's sweet will.

Lord of the living and the dead,
   Our Savior dear!
We lay in silence at thy feet
   This sad, sad year!

Isle of the ev'ning skies, cloud-vision'd land,
   Wherein the good meet in the' heavenly fold,
And drink of endless joys at God's right hand.
                                 WILLIAMS.

DEATH OF A CHILD.

Wherefore should I make my moan,
  Now the darling child is dead?
He to rest is early gone,
  He to paradise is fled!
I shall go to him, but he
  Never shall return to me.

God forbids his longer stay,
  God recalls the precious loan!
He hath taken him away,
  From my bosom to his own.
Surely what he wills is best;
  Happy in his will I rest.

Faith cries out, "It is the Lord!
  Let him do what seems him good,
Be thy holy name adored;
  Take the gift a while bestowed;
Take the child no longer mine;
  Thine he is, for ever thine!"

CHARLES WESLEY.

THE ANGELS OF GRIEF.

With silence only as their benediction,
  God's angels come,
Where in the shadow of a great affliction
  The soul sits dumb.

Yet would we say, what every heart approveth,
  Our Father's will,
Calling to him the dear ones whom he loveth,
  Is mercy still.

Not upon us or ours the solemn angel
  Hath evil wrought;
The funeral anthem is a glad evangel,
  The good die not.

God calls our loved ones, but we lose not wholly
  What he has given;
They live on earth in thought and deed as truly
  As in his heaven.

J. G. WHITTIER.

THE KING HATH SENT FOR THE CHILDREN

THE King of kings hath sent for our children to confer a kingdom on them. They are gone from a dark vale of sin and shame; they are gone into the land of light, and life, and love: there they serve the Lord day and night in his temple having all tears wiped from their eyes; and from thence methinks I hear them crying aloud unto us, 'As well as you love us we would not be with you again: weep not for us, but for yourselves, and count not yourselves at home till you come to be, as we are, for ever with the Lord.'

COTTON MATHER.

THE GOOD SHEPHERD.

WHEN on my ear your loss was knelled,
    And tender sympathy upburst,
A little rill from memory swelled,
    Which one had soothed my bitter thirst.

And I was fain to bear to you
    Some portion of its mild relief,
That it might be as healing dew,
    To steal some fever from your grief.

After our child's untroubled breath
    Up to the Father took its way,
And on our home the shade of death,
    Like a long twilight haunting lay;

And friends came round with us to weep,
    Her little spirit's swift remove,
This story of the Alpine sheep
    Was told to us by one we love:

"They in the valley's sheltering care
    Soon crop the meadow's tender prime,
And when the sod grows brown and bare,
    The Shepherd strives to make them clin)

"To airy shelves of pastures green,
  That hang along the mountain's side,
Where grass and flowers together lean,
  And down through mists the sunbeams slide.

" But naught can tempt the timid things
  The steep and rugged path to try,
Though sweet the Shepherd calls and sings,
  And seared below the pastures lie,

" Till in his arms the lambs he takes,
  Along the dizzy verge to go;
Then, heedless of the rifts and breaks,
  They follow on o'er rock and snow.

" And in those pastures lifted fair,
  More dewy soft than lowland mead,
The shepherd drops his tender care,
  And sheep and lambs together feed."

This parable, by nature breathed,
  Blew on me as the south wind free
O'er frozen brooks, that float, unsheathed
  From icy thraldom, to the sea.

A blissful vision through the night
  Would all my happy senses sway,
Of the Good Shepherd on the height,
  Or climbing up the stony way,

Holding our little lamb asleep;
  And like the burden of the sea
Sounded that voice along the deep,
  Saying, " Arise and follow me."

MARIA W. LOWELL.

REGRET BUT NOT MURMUR.

WE are forbidden to murmur, but we are not forbidden to *regret*; and whom we loved tenderly while living, we may still pursue with an affectionate remembrance, without having any occasion to charge ourselves with rebellion against the sovereignty that appointed a separation.

WILLIAM COWPER.

" Why should we dwell on that which lies beneath,
  When living light hath touch'd the brow of death?"

HEMANS.

THE SHEPHERD CARRYING THE LAMBS BEFORE.

WHEN the good Shepherd would draw his wandering sheep away from danger, and gather them safely into his fold, he has no more effective mode, than to take the little lambs up in his arms. Then the sheep will follow him. So He wins our worthless hearts. He takes our lambs away. He allures to brighter worlds, by removing our brightest objects of affection here. Where our treasures are there will our hearts be also. He cuts the ties which bind us down, that our affections may be free to aspire upward to things above. How near the gate of heaven seems, when we know that our children have just passed through it! And how precious the Savior seems, when we feel that our lambs are in his bosom! The ties which bound our hearts to earth, will henceforth bind them to heaven. Who would not follow the good Shepherd to that house of many mansions, where he has been gathering these children of our love? Where is the Christian parent, who has the precious, and unspeakable honor, of a child ascended to God, who has not thereby been made to drink in more of the beauty and power of the gospel? And when the image of that sainted one has been obliterated here by lapse of time, from all other hearts, how will it still linger, like the fragrance of crushed flowers, around his own! and though years may pass, and distance intervene, he will still love to breathe forth the tenderest sympathies of the soul in memory of the infant's dying couch and lowly tomb.

Rev. Leroy J. Halsey.

"The harp of heaven
Had lacked its least, but not its meanest string,
Had children not been taught to play upon it,
And sing from feelings all their own, what men
Nor angels can conceive of creatures born
Under the curse, yet from the curse redeemed,
And placed at once beyond the power to fall,—
Safety which men nor angels ever knew,
Till ranks of these, and all of those had fallen."

Rev. D. Shauffler.

OVER THE RIVER.

MRS. N. A. W. PRIEST.

Over the river they beckon to me—
  Loved ones who've crossed to the further side;
The gleam of their snowy robes I see,
  But their voices are drowned in the rushing tide
There's one with ringlets of sunny gold,
  And eyes the reflection of heaven's own hue;
He crossed in the twilight, gray and cold,
  And the pale mist hid him from mortal view.
We saw not the angels who met him there;
  The gates of the city we could not see;
Over the river, over the river,
  My brother stands waiting to welcome me!

Over the river, the boatman pale
  Carried another—the household pet.
Her brown curls waved in the gentle gale—
  Darling Minnie! I see her yet.
She crossed on her bosom her dimpled hands,
  And fearlessly entered the phantom bark;
We watched it glide from the silver sands,
  And all our sunshine grew strangely dark.
We know she is safe on the further side
  Where all the ransomed and angels be;
Over the river, the mystic river,
  My childhood's idol is waiting for me.

For none return from those quiet shores,
  Who cross with the boatman cold and pale;
We hear the dip of the golden oars,
  And catch the gleam of the snowy sail,—
And lo! they have passed from our yearning heart;
  They cross the stream, and are gone for aye;
We may not sunder the veil apart,
  That hides from our vision the gates of day.
We only know that their barks no more
  May sail with us o'er life's stormy sea:
Yet somewhere, I know, on the unseen shore,
  They watch, and beckon, and wait for me.

And I sit and think, when the sunset's gold,
  Is flushing river, and hill, and shore,
I shall one day stand by the water cold,
  And list for the sound of the boatman's oar;

I shall watch for a gleam of the flapping sail;
   I shall hear the boat as it gains the strand;
I shall pass from sight, with the boatman pale,
   To the better shore of the spirit land;
I shall know the loved who have gone before,—
   And joyfully sweet will the meeting be,
When over the river, the peaceful river,
   The angel of Death shall carry me.

THE DEATH OF A YOUNG GIRL.

WILLIAM H. BURLEIGH.

She hath gone in the spring-time of life,
   Ere her sky had been dimmed by a cloud,
While her heart with the rapture of love was yet rife,
   And the hopes of her youth were unbowed—
From the lovely, who loved her too well;
   From the heart that had grown to her own;
From the sorrow which late o'er her young spirit fell,
   Like a dream of the night she hath flown;
And the earth hath received to its bosom its trust—
Ashes to ashes, and dust unto dust.

The spring, in its loveliness dressed,
   Will return with its music-winged hours,
And, kissed by the breath of the sweet southwest,
   The buds shall burst out in flowers;
And the flowers her grave-sod above,
   Though the sleeper beneath recks it not,
Shall thickly be strown by the hand of Love,
   To cover with beauty the spot.
Meet emblems are they of the pure one and bright,
Who faded and fell with so early a blight.

Ay, the spring will return--but the blossom
   That bloomed in our presence the sweetest,
By the spoiler is borne from the cherishing bosom,
   The loveliest of all and the fleetest!
The music of stream and of bird
   Shall come back when the winter is o'er;
But the voice that was dearest to us shall be heard

In our desolate chambers no more!
The sunlight of May on the waters shall quiver—
The light of her eye hath departed for ever!

As the bird to its sheltering nest,
  When the storm on the hills is abroad,
So her spirit hath flown from this world of unrest
  To repose on the bosom of GOD!
Where the sorrows of earth never more
  May fling o'er its brightness a stain;
Where in rapture and love it shall ever adore,
  With a gladness unmingled with pain;
And its thirst shall be slacked by the waters which spring,
Like a river of light, from the throne of the KING!

There is weeping on earth for the lost!
  There is bowing in grief to the ground!
But rejoicing and praise mid the sanctified host,
  For a spirit in paradise found!
Though brightness hath passed from the earth,
  Yet a star is new-born in the sky,
And a soul hath gone home to the land of its birth,
  There are pleasures and fulness of joy!
And a new harp is strung, and a new song is given
To the breezes that float o'er the gardens of heaven.

A CHILD'S DEATH.

IN some rude spot where vulgar herbage grows,
  If chance a violet rear its purple head,
The careful gardener moves it ere it blows,
  To thrive and flourish in a nobler bed;
    Such was thy fate, dear child,
      Thy opening such!
Pre-eminence in early bloom was shown;
    For earth, too good, perhaps;
      And loved too much—
Heaven saw, and early marked thee for its own.

R. B. SHERIDAN.

"The eternal flow of things,
Like a bright river of the fields of heaven,
Shall journey onward in eternal peace."

BRYANT.

THE LITTLE CHILD AND THE FERRYMAN.

D. L. MOODY.

THE story is told of a father who had his little daughter out late in the evening. The night was dark, and they had passed through a thick woods to the brink of a river. Far away on the opposite shore a light twinkled here and there in the few scattered houses, and farther off still, blazed the bright lamps of the great city to which they were going. The little child was weary and sleepy, and the father held her in his arms while he waited for the ferryman, who was at the other side. At length they saw a little light; nearer and nearer came the sound of the oars, and soon they were safe in the boat.

"Father," said the little girl.

"Well, my child?"

"It's very dark, and I can't see the shore; where are we going?"

"The ferryman knows the way, little one; we will soon be over."

"O, I wish we were there, father!"

Soon in her home, loving arms welcomed her, and her fears and her tremor were gone. Some months pass by, and this same little child stands on the brink of a river that is darker and deeper, more terrible still. It is the River of Death. The same loving father stands near her, distressed that his child must cross this river and he not be able to go with her. For days and for nights he and her mother have been watching over her, leaving her bedside only long enough for their meals, and to pray for the life of their precious one. For hours she has been slumbering, and it seems as if her spirit must pass away without her waking again, but just before the morning watch she suddenly awakes with the eye bright, the reason unclouded, and every faculty alive. A sweet smile is playing upon her face.

"Father," she says, "I have come again to the river side, and am again waiting for the ferryman to come and take me across."

"Does it seem as dark and cold as when you went over the other river, my child?"

"Oh no! There is no darkness here. The river is covered with floating silver. The boat coming towards me seems made of solid light, and I am not afraid of the ferryman."

"Can you see over the river, my darling?"

"Oh yes, there is a great and beautiful city there, all filled with light; and I hear music such as the angels make!"

"Do you see any one on the other side?"

"Why yes, yes, I see the most beautiful form; and He beckons me now to come. Oh, ferryman, make haste! I know who it is! It is Jesus; my own blessed Jesus. I shall be caught in his arms. I shall rest on his bosom—I come—I COME."

And thus she crossed over the river of Death, made like a silver stream by the presence of the blessed Redeemer.

PASSING UNDER THE ROD.

I SAW the young mother in tenderness bend
    O'er the couch of her slumbering boy,
And she kissed the soft lips as they murmured her name,
    While the dreamer lay smiling in joy.
O sweet as the rose-bud encircled with dew,
    When its fragrance is flung on the air,
So fresh and so bright to that mother he seemed,
    As he lay in his innocence there.
But I saw when she gazed on the same lovely form,
    Pale as marble, and silent, and cold,
But paler and colder her beautiful boy,
    And the tale of her sorrow was told!
But the Healer was there who had stricken her heart,
    And taken her treasure away;
To allure her to heaven he has placed it on high,
    And the mourner will sweetly obey:
There had whispered a voice—'twas the voice of her God,
    "I love thee—I love thee—*pass under the rod!*"

MRS. MARY S. B. DANA.

"My home, henceforth, is in the skies;
    Earth, sea, and sun, adieu;
All heaven's unfolded to my eyes,
    I have no sight for you."

THE CHEERFUL GIVER.

"What shall I render Thee! Father Supreme,
For thy rich gifts, and *this* the best of all?"
Said a young mother, as she fondly watched
    Her sleeping babe.
          There was an answering voice
    That night in dreams.
      "Thou hast a little bud
Wrapt in thy breast, and fed with dews
Of love; give me that bud, 'twill be
A flower in heaven."
But there was silence, yea, a hush so deep,
Breathless and terror-stricken,
        That the lip
Blanched in its trance—
          "Thou has a little harp
    How sweetly would it swell the
    Angels' songs! Give me that harp."
There burst a shuddering sob
As if the bosom, by some hidden sword,
Was cleft in twain.
Morn came, a blight had found
The crimson velvet of the unfolding bud;
The harp-string rang a thrilling strain,
And broke,
    And that young mother lay upon
The earth in childless agony.
        Again the voice
    That stirred her vision—
        "He who asked of thee
Loveth a cheerful giver."
      So she raised
Her gushing eye, and ere the tear-drop
Dried upon its fringes, smiled—
      Doubt not that smile,
  Like Abraham's faith,
      "Was counted righteousness."
                  Mrs. L. H. Sigourney.

"O glorious hour! O blest abode!
I shall be near, and like my God;
And flesh and sin no more control
The sacred pleasures of my soul."

THE BUDS OPENING IN HEAVEN.

HEAVEN is greatly made up of little children, sweet buds that have never blown, or which death has plucked from a mother's bosom to lay on his own cold breast, just when they were expanding, flower-like, from the sheath, and opening their engaging beauties in the budding time and spring of life. 'Of such is the kingdom of heaven.' How sweet these words by the cradle of a dying infant! They fall like balm drops on our bleeding heart, when we watch the ebbing of that young life, as wave after wave breaks feebler, and the sinking breath gets lower and lower, till with a gentle sigh, and a passing quiver of the lip, our child now leaves its body, lying like an angel asleep, and ascends to the beatitudes of heaven and the bosom of God. Indeed it may be, that God does with his heavenly garden, as we do with our gardens. He may chiefly stock it from nurseries, and select for transplanting what is yet in its young and tender age—flowers before they have bloomed, and trees ere they begin to bear. REV. DR. GUTHRIE.

> " 'Tis sweet to die! The flowers of earthly love,
> (Fair, frail spring blossoms) early droop and die;
> But all their fragrance is exhaled above,
> Upon our spirits evermore to lie.
>
> FANNY FORRESTER.

INFANT CHOIRS IN HEAVEN.

IT seems to me we need infant choirs in heaven to make up full concert to the angelic symphony. Who will sing like unto them of the manger, and the swaddling clothes, and of the Lord of all, drawing nourishment from the bosom of mortal mothers! True, these are themes of infinite interest, and the delight and wonder of angels. But oh! they are too tender for the archangel's powerful trump— too tender for the thundering notes of cherubim and seraphim. We must have infant choirs in heaven.

A MOTHER'S LAMENT.

JAMES MONTGOMERY.

I LOVED thee, daughter of my heart;
  My child, I loved thee dearly;
And though we only met to part,
  —How sweetly! how severely!—
Nor life nor death can sever
My soul from thine for ever.

Thy days, my little one, were few;
  An angel's morning visit,
That came and vanished with the dew;
  'Twas here, 'tis gone, where is it?
Yet did'st thou leave behind thee
A clue for love to find thee.

The eye, the lip, the cheek, the brow,
  The hands stretched forth in gladness,
All life, joy, rapture, beauty now;
  Then dashed with infant sadness;
Till, brightening by transition,
Returned the fairy vision:—

Where are they now?—those smiles, those tears,
  Thy mother's darling treasure?
She sees them still, and still she hears
  Thy tones of pain or pleasure.
To her quick pulse revealing
Unutterable feeling.

Hushed in a moment on her breast,
  Life, at the well-spring drinking;
Then cradled on her lap to rest
  In rosy slumber sinking,
Thy dreams—no thought can guess them;
And mine—no tongue express them.

For then this waking eye could see,
  In many a vain vagary,
The things that never were to be,
  Imaginations airy;
Fond hopes that mothers cherish,
Like still-born babes to perish.

Mine perished on thy early bier;
  No,—changed to forms more glorious,
They flourish in a higher sphere,
  O'er time and death victorious;
Yet would these arms have chained thee,
And long from heaven detained thee.

Sarah! my last, my youngest love,
  The crown of every other!
Though thou art born in heaven above,
  I am thine only mother,
Nor will affection let me
Believe thou canst forget me.

Then, thou in heaven and I on earth,—
  May this one hope delight us,
That thou wilt hail my second birth,
  When death shall reunite us,
Where worlds no more can sever
Parent and child for ever.

THE CHILDREN COMING AND GOING.

Trailing clouds of glory, do they come
From heaven, which is their home.

His heart grows young again with them; her soul is softened by their infantile caresses; his life is checked in its tendency and they lead him to his Father and theirs. Nature's priesthood, these little children, in their innocence and simplicity, are evermore bringing back the hearts of fathers and mothers into a more simple and childlike trust in joy. Coming to us, they bring the keys of the kingdom of heaven. Going from us they unlock those sacred doors; and we in our bereavement, find our hearts drawn up after them to God. The heavens into which they have gone remain open; and the fragrance and melody of that upper world comes down to us here, and never leaves us again.

JAMES FREEMAN CLARKE.

There sorrow ends, for life and death have ceased;
How should lamps flicker when their oil is spent?

LIGHT OF ASIA.

CALLING HIS CHILDREN HOME.

God often calls these children home. This is the bitter cup he gives us to drink. He knows our soul's disease. He is the wisest and best of physicians, never selects the "wrong bottle," and never gives one drop too much of the correct medicine. He does all things well. His children must trust their Father. He chastens for our profit that we may be partakers of his holiness.

God sees that some one in the family has need of his spiritual skill—from indulged sin, from weakening of the graces, and he gives a cup of bitter disappointment—the gourd that was so grateful and refreshing withers. Patient submission, humble acquiescence, and unfaltering trust and hope are the lessons God would teach and what the soul's disease requires. If the cup had not been drunk the blessings would have been lost; if the child had not died, the idol would have been enthroned.

God's cups may be bitter, and you may be long in draining them, at the bottom lies a precious blessing. Rich graces lie there. For this reason the "trial" of faith is precious. So Abraham and Job and all God's children have found it.

Be not surprised when God mixes such a bitter cup for you as the death of a child. You need that medicine. The best tonic medicines are bitter. They have a merciful purpose, It is your Father's cup. Drink it, unhesitatingly, uncomplainingly, and with the spirit of that Beloved Son, who said, "Not my will but thine be done."

Rev. T. L. Cuyler, D. D.

ONLY SLEEPING.

John, is but gone an hour or two sooner to bed, as children are used to do, and we are undressing to follow. And the more we put off the love of the present world, and all things superfluous beforehand, we shall have the less to do when we lie down.

Archbishop Leighton,

There spring the healing streams
Quenching all thirst! there bloom the immortal flowers.
Light of Asia.

THE PRESENT, PAST AND FUTURE.

IT is a noble faculty of our nature which enables us to connect our thoughts, our sympathies, and our happiness, with what is distant in place or time; and, looking before and after, to hold communion at once with our ancestors and our posterity. Human and mortal although we are, we are nevertheless not mere insulated beings, without relation to the past or the future. Neither the point of time, nor the spot of earth, in which we physically live, bounds our rational and intellectual enjoyments. We live in the past by a knowledge of its history; and in the future by hope and anticipation.

As it is not a vain and false, but an exalted and religious imagination, which leads us to raise our thoughts from the orb, which, amid this universe of worlds, the Creator has given us to inhabit, and to send them with something of the feeling which nature prompts, and teaches to be proper among children of the same Eternal Parent, to the contemplation of the myriads of fellow-beings, with which His goodness has peopled the infinite space—so neither is it false or vain to consider ourselves as interested and connected with our whole race, through all time; allied to our ancestors; allied to our posterity; closely compacted on all sides with others; ourselves being but links in the great chain of being, which begins with the origin of our race, runs onward through its successive generations, binding together the past, the present and the future, and terminating at last with the consummation of all things earthly, at the throne of God.

DANIEL WEBSTER.

<blockquote>
Babes thither caught from womb and breast,
Claim right to sing above the rest;
Because they found the happy shore,
They neither saw nor sought before.
</blockquote>

ERSKINE.

GRANDFATHER'S PET.

CHAMBER'S JOURNAL.

THIS is the room where she slept
  Only a year ago—
Quietly and carefully swept,
  Blinds and curtains like snow;
There, by the bed, in the dusky gloom,
  She would kneel with her tiny clasped hands and pray,
Here's the little white rose of a room,
  With the fragrance fled away.

Nelly, grandfather's pet,
  With her wise little face—
I seem to hear her yet
  Singing about the place;
But the crowds roll on and the streets are drear,
  And the world seems hard with a bitter doom,
As Nelly is singing elsewhere, and here
  Is the little white rose of a room.

Why, if she stood just there,
  As she used to do,
With her long, light-yellow hair,
  And her eyes of blue—
If she stood, I say, at the edge of the bed,
  And ran to my side with a living touch,
Though I know she is quiet, and buried and dead,
  I should not wonder much:

For she was so young, you know—
  Only seven years old,
And she loved me and loved me so,
  Though I was gray and old;
And her face was so wise and sweet to see,
  And it still looked like living when she lay dead,
And she used to plead for mother and me
  By the side of that very bed.

I wonder, now, if she
  Knows I am standing here,
Feeling, wherever she be,
  We hold the place so dear.
It cannot be that she sleeps so sound,

Still in her little night-gown dress,
To hear my heavy footstep round
In the room where she used to rest.

I have held hard fortune's strings,
 And battled in doubt and strife,
And never thought much of things
 Beyond this human life;
But I cannot think that my darling died
 Like great strong men, with their prayers untrue—
Nay! rather she sits at God's own side,
 And sings as she used to do!

DEATH OF AN INFANT.

With what unknown delight the mother smiled,
 When this frail treasure in her arms she pressed!
Her prayer was heard—she clasped a living child:
 But how the gift transcends the poor request!
A child was all she asked, with many a vow!
Mother—behold the child an angel now!

Now in her father's house she finds a place,
 Or, if to earth she takes a transient flight,
'Tis to fulfill the purpose of his grace:
 To guide thy footsteps to the world of light;—
A ministering spirit sent to thee,
That where she is, there thou may'st also be.

GONE BEFORE.

There's a beautiful face in the silent air,
 Which follows me ever and near,
With smiling eyes and amber hair,
With voiceless lips, yet with breath of prayer
 That I feel, but cannot hear.

The dimpled hand and ringlet of gold,
 Lie low in a marble sleep;
I stretch my arms for the clasp of old,
But the empty air was strangely cold,
 And so my vigil alone I keep.

There's a sinless brow with a radiant crown
 And a cross laid down in the dust;

There's a smile where never a shadow comes now,
And tears no more from those dear eyes flow,
  So sweet in their innocent trust.

Ah, well! and summer is coming again,
  Singing her same old song;
But oh! it sounds like a sob of pain,
As it floats in the sunshine and the rain,
  O'er hearts of the world's great throng.

There's a beautiful region above the skies,
  And I long to reach its shore,
For I know I shall find my treasure there,
The laughing eyes and amber hair
  Of the loved one gone before.
                              PHRENOLOGICAL JOURNAL.

DEATH OF AN INFANT.

DEATH found strange beauty on that polished brow,
And dashed it out.—
          There was a tint of rose
On cheek and lip.—He touched the veins with ice,
And the rose faded.—
          Forth from those blue eyes
There spake a wishful tenderness, a doubt
Whether to grieve or sleep, which innocence
Alone may wear. With ruthless haste he bound
The silken fringes of those curtaining lids
For ever.—
          There had been a murmuring sound,
With which the babe would claim its mother's ear,
Charming her even to tears. The spoiler set
His seal of silence.—
          But there beamed a smile
So fixed, so holy, from that cherub brow,
Death gazed—and left it there.
                He dared not steal
The signet ring of Heaven.
                              MRS. L. H. SIGOURNEY.

      "Death is an equal doom
  To good and bad, the common inn of rest;
  But after death the trial is to come,
    When best shall be to them who lived best."
                              SPENSER.

LOW SHE LIES.

MRS. NORTON.

LOW she lies, who blest our eyes
   Through many a sunny day;
She may not smile, she will not rise,—
   The life has past away!
Yet there is a world of light beyond,
   Where we neither die nor sleep;
She is there, of whom our souls were fond,
   Then, wherefore do we weep?

The heart is cold, whose thoughts were told
   In each glance of her glad bright eye;
And she lies pale, who was so bright,
   She scarce seemed made to die.
Yet we know that her soul is happy now,
   Where the saints their calm watch keep;
That angels are crowning that fair young brow,
   Then, wherefore do we weep?

Her laughing voice made all rejoice,
   Who caught the happy sound;
There was a gladness in her very step,
   As it lightly touched the ground.
The echoes of voice and step are gone,
   There is silence still and deep;
Yet we know that she sings by God's bright throne,
   Then, wherefore do we weep?

The cheek's pale tinge, the lid's dark fringe,
   That lies like a shadow there,
Were beautiful in the eyes of all,
   And her glossy golden hair,
But though that lid may never wake
   From its dark and dreamless sleep;
She is gone where young hearts do not break,
   Then, wherefore do we weep?

That world of light with joy is bright,
   This is a world of woe;
Shall we grieve that her soul has taken flight
   Because we dwell below?

We will bury her under the mossy sod,
   And one long bright tress we'll keep;
We have only given her back to God,
   Then, wherefore do we weep?

ON THE DEATH OF MY SON.

My little one, my fair one, are then thy troubles o'er,
And has thy slight and feeble bark arrived at Canaan's shore?
Hast thou at length a haven reached, where thou canst anchor fast
And heed no more the pelting storm, the billow or the blast?

My little one, my fair one, though brief thy course has been,
Few days of sunshine cheered thee on, few smiling coasts were seen;
It seemed as o'er thy shallop frail the raven flapped his wing,
And scared the bright and halcyon tribes, which might thine advent sing.

My little one, my fair one, thy couch is empty now,
Where oft I wiped the dews away, which gathered on thy brow;
No more amidst the sleepless night I smooth thy pillow fair,
'Tis smooth indeed, but rest no more thy small pale features there.

My little one, my fair one, thy tiny carriage waits,
But waits in vain to bear thy form through yon inviting gates;
Where bloom the flowers as erst they did, when thou couldst cull their sweets,
But roams in vain thy father's eye, no answering glance it meets.

My little one, my fair one, thy lips were early trained
To lisp that gracious Savior's name, who all thy guilt sustained:
Nor would I weep because my Lord has snatched my gourd away,
To blossom bright, and ripen fair, in realms of endless day.

My little one, my fair one, thou canst not come to me,
But nearer draws the numbered hour, when I shall go to thee,
And thou, perchance, with seraph smile, and golden harp in hand,
May'st come the first to welcome me, to our Emmanuel's land!

                                      RICHARD HUIE, M. D.

"Life-embark'd, out at sea, 'mid the wave-tumbling roar
The poor ship of my body went down to the floor;
But I broke, at the bottom of death, through a door
And, from sinking, began forever to soar."

THE HOME BEYOND

LUCY.

REV. HORATIUS BONAR, D. D.

ALL night long we watched the ebbing life,
   As if its flight to stay;
Till as the dawn was coming up,
   Our last hope passed away.

She was the music of our home,
   A day that knew no night,
The fragrance of our garden bower,
   A thing all smiles and light.

Above the couch we bent and prayed,
   In the half-lighted room;
As the bright hues of infant life
   Sank slowly into gloom.

Each flutter of the pulse we marked,
   Each quiver of the eye;
To the dear lips our ear we laid,
   To catch the last low sigh.

We stroked the little sinking cheeks,
   The forehead pale and fair;
We kissed the small, round, ruby mouth
   For Lucy still was there.

We fondly smoothed the scattered curls,
   Of her rich golden hair;
We held the gentle palm in ours,
   For Lucy still was there.

At last the fluttering pulse stood still,
   The death-frost through her clay
Stole slowly; and, as morn came up,
   Our sweet flower passed away.

The form remained; but there was now
   No soul our love to share;
No warm responding lip to kiss;
   For Lucy was not there.

Farewell, with weeping hearts we said,
   Child of our love and care!

And then we ceased to kiss those lips,
    For Lucy was not there.

But years are moving quickly past,
    And time will soon be o'er;
Death shall be swallowed up in life
    On the immortal shore.

Then shall we clasp that hand once more,
    And smooth that golden hair;
Then shall we kiss those lips again,
    When Lucy shall be there.

THE DEATH ANGEL.

WITHIN her downy cradle there lay a little child,
And a group of hovering angels unseen upon her smiled;
A strife arose among them, a loving, holy strife,
Which should shed the richest blessing o'er the new-born life.

One breathed upon her features, and the babe in beauty grew,
With a cheek like morning's blushes, and an eye of azure hue;
Till every one who saw her, was thankful for the sight
Of a face so sweet and radiant with ever fresh delight.

Another gave her accents, and a voice as musical
As a spring bird's joyous carol, or a rippling streamlet's fall;
Till all who heard her laughing, or her words of childish grace,
Loved as much to listen to her, as to look upon her face.

Another brought from heaven a clear and gentle mind,
And within the lovely casket the precious gem enshrined;
Till all who knew her wondered, that God should be so good,
As to bless with such a spirit our desert world and rude.
                                               GEORGE W. BETHUNE, D. D.

    "How speeds, from in the river's thought,
        The spirit of the leaf that falls,
    Its heaven in that calm bosom wrought,
        As mine among yon crimson walls!
    From the dry bough it spins, to greet
        Its shadow on the placid river:
    So might I my companions meet,
        Nor roam the countless worlds forever!"

THE HOME BEYOND

THE REAPER AND THE FLOWERS.

HENRY W. LONGFELLOW.

THERE is a Reaper whose name is Death,
   And with his sickle keen,
He reaps the bearded grain at a breath,
   And the flowers that grow between.

"Shall I have naught that is fair?" said he,
   "Have naught but the bearded grain?
Though the breath of these flowers is sweet to me,
   I will give them all back again."

He gazed at the flowers with tearful eyes;
   He kissed their drooping leaves;
It was for the Lord of paradise
   He bound them in his sheaves.

"My Lord hath need of these flowerets gay,"
   The reaper said, and smiled;
"Dear tokens of the earth are they,
   Where *he* was once a child.

"They shall all bloom in fields of light,
   Transplanted by my care,
And saints upon their garments white,
   These sacred blossoms wear."

And the mother gave in tears and pain
   The flowers she most did love;
She knew she should find them all again
   In the fields of light above.

Oh, not in cruelty, not in wrath,
   The reaper came that day;
'Twas an angel visited the green earth,
   And took the flowers away!

"If yonder stars be fill'd with forms of breathing clay like ours,
   Perchance the space which spreads between is for a spirit's powers."

BEAR THEM TO THEIR REST.

REV. GEORGE W. BETHUNE, D. D.

Yes! bear them to their rest;
The rosy babe tired with the glare of day,
The prattler fallen asleep even in his play;
　　Clasp them to thy soft breast,
　　　　O Night,
Bless them in dreams with a deep-hushed delight!

　　　Yet must they wake again;
Wake soon to all the bitterness of life,
The pang of sorrow, the temptation strife,
　　Aye, to the conscience-pain.
　　　　O night,
Canst thou not take with them a longer flight?

　　　Canst thou not bear them far,
Ev'n now all innocent, before they know
The taint of sin, its consequence of woe,
　　The world's distracting jar,
　　　　O Night,
To some eternal, holier, happier height?

　　　Canst thou not bear them up,
Through star-lit skies, far from this planet dim
And sorrowful, ev'n while they sleep, to Him,
　　Who drank for us the cup,
　　　　O Night,
The cup of wrath for souls in faith contrite?

　　　To him, for them who slept
A babe all lowly on his mother's knee,
And, from that hour to cross-crowned Calvary,
　　In all our sorrows wept,
　　　　O Night,
That on our souls might dawn heaven's cheering light?

　　　Go lay their little heads
Close to that human breast, with love Divine
Deep beating; while his arms immortal twine
　　Around them as he sheds,
　　　　O Night,
On them a brother's grace of God's own boundless might.

　　　Let them, immortal, wake
Among the deathless flowers of Paradise,

Where angels' songs of welcome with surprise
 This their last sleep may break,
  O Night,
And to celestial joys their kindred souls invite.

  There can come no sorrow;
The brow shall know no shade, the eye no tears;
For ever young through heaven's eternal years
 In one unfading morrow,
  O Night,
Nor sin, nor age, nor pain, their cherub beauty blight.

  Would we could sleep as they
So stainless and so calm; at rest with thee,
And only wake in immortality.
 Bear us with them away,
  O Night,
To that eternal, holier, happier height.

"OF SUCH IS THE KINGDOM."

I DEARLY love a little child,
 And Jesus loved young children too;
He ever sweetly on them smiled,
 And placed them with his chosen few.
When, cradled on its mother's breast,
 A babe was brought to Jesus' feet,
He laid his hand upon its head,
 And blessed it with a promise sweet.

"Forbid them not!" the Savior said,
 "Oh! suffer them to come to me!
Of such my heavenly kingdom is—
 Like them may all my followers be!"
Young children are the gems of earth.
 The brightest jewels mothers have;
They sparkle on the throbbing breast,
 But brighter shine beyond the grave.

MRS. MARY S. B. DANA.

O Thou, whose infant feet were found
 Within thy Father's shrine,
Whose years, with changeless virtue crowned,
 Were all alike divine.

REGINALD HEBER.

CHRIST RECEIVES CHILDREN INTO HEAVEN.

If He who has the keys of death and of the unseen world sees fit to remove those dear creatures from us in their early days, let the remembrance of the story of Christ taking them up in his arms and blessing them comfort us, and teach us to hope that he who so graciously received these children has not forgotten ours; but that they are sweetly fallen asleep in Him, and will be the everlasting objects of his care and love: 'for of such is the kingdom of heaven.'

Rev. Dr. Doddridge.

> "We miss them when the board is spread,
> We miss them when the prayer is said;
> Upon our dreams their dying eyes
> In still and mournful fondness lies.

Newman.

The kingdom of heavenly glory is greatly constituted of such as die in infancy. Infants are as capable of regeneration as grown persons; and there is abundant ground to conclude that all those who have not lived to commit actual transgressions, though they share in the effects of the first Adam's offense, will also share in the blessings of the second Adam's gracious covenant, without their personal faith and obedience, but not without the regenerating influence of the Spirit.

Rev. Dr. Scott,

> "These birds of paradise but long to flee
> Back to their native mansion."

Prophecy of Dante.

There are flowers for thee, sweet one, which never shall die,
Unfed by a tear, and unfanned by a sigh;
There's a heritage promised thee fadeless above,
Whose title is grace, and whose riches are love,
And a crown of rejoicing to circle thy brow;
Then who'll be so portioned, my baby, as thou?

THE CHILD IS WITH GOD.

HENRY WARD BEECHER.

WHEN our children that are so dear to us are plucked out of our arms, and carried away, we feel, for the time being, that we have lost them, because our body does not triumph; but are they taken from inward man? Are they taken from that which is to be saved—the spiritual man? Are they taken from memory? Are they taken from love? Are they taken from the scope and reach of the imagination, which in its sanctified form, is only another name for faith? Do we not sometimes dwell with them more intimately than we did when they were with us on earth? The care of them is no longer ours, that love-burden we bear no longer, since they are with the angels of God and with God; and we shed tears over what seems to be our loss; but do they not hover in the air over our heads? And to-day could the room hold them all?

As you recollect, the background of the Sistine Madonna, at Dresden (in some respects the most wonderful picture of maternal love which exists in the world), for a long time was merely dark; and an artist, in making some repairs, discovered a cherub's face in the grime of that dark background; and being led to suspect that the picture had been overlaid by time and neglect, commenced cleansing it; and as he went on, cherub after cherub appeared, until it was found that the Madonna was on a background made up wholly of little heavenly cherubs.

Now, by nature motherhood stands against a dark background, but that background being cleaned by the touch of God, and by the cleansing hand of faith, we see that the whole heaven is full of little cherub faces, And to-day it is not this little child alone that we look at, which we see only in the outward guise; we look upon a background of children innumerable, each one as sweet to its mother's heart as this child has been to its mother's heart, each one as dear to the clasping arms of its father as this child has been to the clasping arms of his father; and it is in good company. It is with God. You have given it back to Him who lent it to you.

DON'T PRAY TO KEEP ME MOTHER DEAR.

WILLIAM C. RICHARDS

I SAW a little maiden come,
 A-sudden, to that river,
At whose dark brink bold lips close dumb,
 And stout hearts quail and shiver—
 The marge of Death's cold river.

Down to the stream the little maid
 Was led by white-robed angels;
Around her golden harps they played,
 And sung those sweet evangels
 Sung only by the angels.

Five days upon the brink she lay
 Of that apalling river;
And death shot arrows every day,
 From his insatiate quiver,
 At her bedside, the river.

Oh! but I stood amazed to hear
 Her wan lips sweetly saying,
"Don't pray to keep me, mother dear,
 I must not here be staying;"
 Such words of wonder, saying:

Mother, I do not fear to die,
 My sins are all forgiven;
And shining angels hovering nigh,
 Will bear my soul to heaven,
 Through God's dear Lamb forgiven."

And then, from her fond mother's breast,
 She plunged into that river;
Her fluttering pulses sunk to rest,
 Her heart was still for ever,
 Her soul beyond the river.

Now when my children wait to hear,
 Some tender, touching story,
I tell them how, without a fear,
 She died, and went to glory;
 And tears flow with the story.

TEARS FOR THE DEPARTED CHILDREN.

ARE we stoics that we can see our cradle rifled of the bright eyes and sweet lips? Must we stand unmoved and see the gardens of our earthly delight uprooted? Will Jesus, who wept himself, be angry with us if we weep over the grave that swallows what we loved best? Oh, no. We must weep. You shall not drive back the tears that scald the heart. Thank God for the strange and mysterious relief that comes in tears. Since I last stood here the waves have gone over us. Have you lost a child? Then you understand the grief. Have you not lost one? You cannot understand it. I would not dare trust myself very far in this reference or allusion. I only make reference to it that I may thank you for your deep, wide, magnificent sympathy. First of all, God helped us; next you. And when, last Sabbath afternoon, we were riding to Greenwood, I said, 'I cannot understand this composure which I feel, and this strange peace;' and it was suggested then and there, 'There's a vast multitude of people praying for us!' That solved it. I thank you. God bless you in your persons and your homes. I gave that one to God in holy baptism just after his birth, and God has only taken that which was His own. I stand here to-day to testify of the comforting grace of God.

TALMAGE.

SAY NOT 'TWERE A KEENER BLOW.

Oh! say not 'twere a keener blow,
  To lose a child of riper years;
You cannot feel a mother's woe,
  You cannot dry a mother's tears;
The girl who rears a sickly plant,
  Or cherishes a wounded dove,
Will love them most while most they want
  The watchfulness of love!

Time *must* have changed that fair young brow!
  Time *might* have changed that spotless heart!
Years *might* have taught deceit, but now
  In love's confiding dawn we part!

OR VIEWS OF HEAVEN.

Ere pain or grief had wrought decay,
 My babe is cradled in the tomb;
Like some fair blossom torn away
 Before its perfect bloom.

With thoughts of peril and of storm,
 We see a bark first touch the wave;
But distant seems the whirlwind's form
 As' distant—as an infant's grave!
Though all is calm, that beauteous ship
 Must bear the whirlwind's rudest breath;
Though all is calm, that infant's lip
 Must meet the kiss of death!

T. H. BAYLY.

LAMBS SAFELY FOLDED.

DRY your tears, bereaved parents, or turn them into floods of joy. The voice that called them away, was His who said: They belong to my kingdom. The hand that took them from you was His, who once laid His benediction on the infant's head. He has set them in the midst of his admiring disciples above. They are now the darling little ones of their Heavenly Father's house. The angels who watched over their cradle beds, are now rejoicing over their immortal beauty, as lambs safely folded where the spoiler can never come. Heed them not, who would bid you doubt; point them to the recorded censure of the Master, displeased at so unmerciful an unbelief. "Of such is the kingdom of heaven." "Out of the mouth of" your "babe," Christ's "praise" is "perfected" in the temple on high !

REV. DR. BETHUNE.

May he find a Savior's breast
That when life's weary journey's o'er,
He may—to wake in sin no more—
 Sleep there,
 Free from care,
As on his mother's breast.

JOHN S. B. MONSELL.

ONE LINK GONE

TAKE the pillows from the cradle
    Where the little sufferer lay;
Draw the curtain, close the shutters,
    Shut out every beam of day.

Spread the pall upon the table,
    Place the lifeless body there;
Back from off the marble features
    Lay the auburn curls with care.

With its little blue-veined fingers
    Crossed upon its sinless breast,
Free from care, and pain, and anguish,
    Let the infant cherub rest.

Smooth its little shroud about it;
    Pick the toys from off the floor;
They, with all their sparkling beauty
    Ne'er can charm their owner more.

Take the little shoes and stockings
    From the doting mother's sight;
Pattering feet no more will need them,
    Walking in the fields of light.

Parents, faint and worn with watching
    Through the long, dark night of grief,
Dry your tears and soothe your sighing—
    Gain a respite of relief.

Mother, care is no more needed
    To allay the rising moan,
And though you perchance may leave it,
    It can never be alone.

Angels bright will watch beside it
    In its quiet, holy slumber
Till the morning, then awake it
    To a place among their number

Thus a golden link is broken
    In the chain of earthly bliss,
Thus the distance shorter making
    'Twixt the brighter world and this.

UNKNOWN.

THE DEATH OF THE FIRST-BORN CHILD.

BLACKWOOD'S MAGAZINE.

THOU weepest, childless mother!
  Ay, weep—'twill ease thine heart;
He was thy first-born son,
Thy first, thy only one—
  'Tis hard from him to part!

" 'Tis hard to lay thy darling
  Deep in the damp, cold earth—
His empty crib to see,
His silent nursery,
  Once vocal with his mirth.

" To meet again in slumber
  His small mouth's rosy kiss;
Then waking with a start,
By thine own throbbing heart,
  His twining arms to miss!

" To feel, half conscious why,
  A dull, heart sinking weight;
Till mem'ry on thy soul
Flashes the painful whole,
  That thou art desolate!

" And there to lie and weep,
  And think the live-long night,
Feeding thine own address,
With accurate greediness,
  Of every past delight.

" Of all his winning ways,
  His pretty, playful smiles;
His joy at sight of thee,
His tricks, his mimicry,
  And all his little wiles.

" Oh! these are recollections
  Round mothers hearts that cling,
That mingle with the tears
And smiles of after years,
  With oft awakening.

"But thou wilt then, fond mother!
    In after years look back,
(Time brings such wondrous easing),
With sadness not unpleasing,
    Even on that gloomy track.

"Thoul't say, 'My first-born blessing,
    It almost broke my heart
When thou wert forced to go,
And yet, for *thee* I know
    'Twas better to depart.

"God took thee in His mercy,
    A lamb, untasked, untried;
HE fought the fight for thee,
HE won the victory,
    And thou art sanctified

"'I look around and see
    The evil ways of men,
And oh! beloved child!
I'm *more* than "reconciled"
    To thy departure then,

"'The little hands that clasped me,
    The innocent lips that prest,
Would they have been as pure
Till now, as when of yore
    I lulled them on my breast?

"'Now (like a dew-drop shrined
    Within a crystal stone),
Thou'rt safe in Heaven my dove!
Safe with the *Source* of LOVE—
    The EVERLASTING ONE!

"'And when the hour arrives,
    From flesh that sets me free,
Thy spirit may await,
The first at Heaven's gate,
    To meet and welcome me!'"

BABY'S SHOES

Oh! those little, those little blue shoes!
Those shoes that no little feet use;
    Oh! the price were high
    That those shoes would buy,
Those little blue unused shoes!

For they hold the small shape of feet
That no more their mother's eyes meet;
    That by God's good will,
    Years since grew still,
And ceased from their totter so sweet.

And oh! since that baby slept,
So hushed, how the mother has kept,
    With a tearful pleasure,
    That little dear treasure,
And over them thought and wept!

For they mind her for evermore
Of a patter along the floor;
    And blue eyes she sees
    Look up from her knees,
With the look that in life they wore.

As they lie before her there,
There babbles from chair to chair
    A little sweet face
    That's a gleam in the place,
With its little gold curls of hair.

Then, oh! wonder not that her heart
From all else would rather part
    Than those tiny blue shoes
    That no little feet use,
And whose sight makes such fond tears start.

                    Wm. C. Bennett.

Sleep, sleep then, my infant, sleep softly the while
    I'll sing to thee, sweet one! and watch for thy smile,
For that answering smile, love, which oft as I trace
With its soft light of gladness plays over thy face,
    I'll hail as a dream, sent thee down from the blest,
    And think that my babe's gentle spirit hath rest.

                    John S. B Monsell.

WHICH SHALL GO?

THE mother sat with her children three,
   The Angel of Death drew near:
"I come for one of thy babes," quoth he,—
"Of the little band, say, which shall it be?
I will not choose, but leave it for thee
   To give me the one least dear."

The mother started, with movement wild,
   And drew them all close to her heart:
The Angel reached forth and touched the child
Whose placid features, whene'er she smiled,
Reflected the mother's beauty mild;
   "With this one," said he, "canst thou part?"

"With this one? O God! She is our first-born,—
   As well take my life away!
I never lived till that blessed morn
When she, as a bud, on my breast was worn;
Without her the world would be all forlorn,—
   Spare this one, kind Death, I pray!"

The Angel drew backwards, then touched again;
   This time 'twas a noble boy:
"Will it cause thee, to part with him, less pain?"
"Hold, touch him not!" she cried, "refrain
He's an only son—if we had but twain—
   Oh, spare us our pride and our joy!"

Once more the angel stood waiting there;
   Then he gently laid his hand
On the shining head of a babe, so fair,
That even Death pitied and touched with care;
While the mother prayed, "Merciful Heaven, forbear!
   'Tis the pet of our little band!"

"Then *which?*" said the Angel; "for God calls one."
   The mother bowed down her head;
Love's troubled fount was in tears o'errun—
A murmur—a struggle—and Grace had won,
"Not my will," she said, "but thine be done!"
   The pet lamb of the fold lay dead.

MRS. ELIZABETH C. SINCERE.

HEAVEN IS FULL OF CHILDREN.

I THINK it, at least, highly probable, that where our Lord says, 'Suffer little children to come unto Me, and forbid them not for of such is the kingdom of heaven,' He does not only intimate the necessity of our becoming like little children in simplicity, as a qualification, without which (as he expressly declares in other places) we cannot enter into his kingdom, but informs us of a fact, that the number of infants, who are effectually redeemed unto God by *His* blood, so greatly exceeds the aggregate of adult believers, that, comparatively speaking, *His* kingdom may be said to consist of little children. As if the full import of what HE had said to his disciples was, think not that little children are beneath my notice; think not that I am a stranger to little children; suffer them to come to me, and forbid them not. I have often been in their society; I love their society; the world from which I came, and to which I go, is full of little children.

> "Flowers that once had loved to linger
>   In the world of human love,
> Touch'd by death's decaying finger
>   For better life above!
> O! ye stars! ye rays of glory!
>   Gem-lights in the glittering dome!
> Could ye not relate a story
>   Of the spirits gather'd home?"

THE DEATH OF A CHILD.

YES, thou art fled, and saints a welcome sing;
Thine infant spirit soars on angel wing;
Our dark affection might have hoped thy stay,—
The voice of God has called the child away.
Like Samuel early in the temple found—
Sweet rose of Sharon, plant of holy ground,
Oh, more than Samuel blessed, to thee is given,
The God he served on earth to serve in heaven.

CUNNINGHAM.

MY CHILD.

JOHN PIERPONT.

O, I cannot make him dead!
His fair sunshiny head
Is ever bounding round my study chair,
   Yet, when my eyes, now dim
   With tears, I turn to him,
The vision vanishes—he is not there.

   I walk my parlor floor,
   And through the open door,
I hear a foot-fall on the chamber-stair;
   I'm stepping toward the hall,
   To give the boy a call,
And then bethink me that—he is not there!

   I tread the crowded street;
   A satcheled lad I meet,
With the same beaming eyes and colored hair;
   And as he's running by,
   Follow him with my eye,
Scarcely believing that—he is not there!

   I know his face is hid
   Under the coffin-lid:
Closed are his eyes, cold is his forehead fair;
   My hand that marble felt;
   O'er it in prayer I knelt;
Yet my heart whispers that—he is not there!

   I cannot make him dead!
   When passing by the bed
So long watched over with parental care,
   My spirit and my eye
   Seek it inquiringly,
Before the thought comes that—he is not there!

   When at the cool gray break
   Of day, from sleep I wake,
With my first breathing of the morning air,
   My soul goes up with joy,
   To Him who gave my boy,
Then comes the sad thought that—he is not there!

When at the day's calm close,
Before we seek repose,
I'm with his mother offering up our prayer,
Or evening anthems tuning,
In spirit I'm communing
With our boy's spirit, though—he is not there!

Not there!—Where, then, is he?
The form I used to see
Was but the raiment that he used to wear!
The grave, that now doth press
Upon that cast-off dress,
Is but his wardrobe locked: he is not there!

He lives!—in all the past
He lives; nor, to the last,
Of seeing him again will I despair.
In dreams I see him now,
And, on his angel-brow,
I see it written: "Thou shalt see me there!"

Yes, we all live to God!
Father, thy chastening rod
So help us, thine afflicted ones, to bear,
That in the spirit-land,
Meeting at thy right hand,
'Twill be our heaven to find that—Thou art there!

WOULD YOU CALL HIM BACK.

AS if an angel had lost his way, and for a few days had wandered among the sons of men, till his companions suddenly discovered him in this wilderness, and caught him, and bore him off to his native residence among the blessed; so the child is taken kindly in the morning of its wanderings, and gathered among the holy and brought home to his Father's house. How pure his spirit now; how happy he is now!

"Apostles, martyrs, prophets, there
Around my Savior stand,"

and among them I behold the infant forms of those whose little graves were wet with the tears of parental love. I hear their infant voices in the song. Do you see in the midst of that bright and blessed throng the child you mourn? I ask not now if you would call him back again. I fear you would! But I ask you, "*What would tempt him back again?*" Bring out the playthings that he loved on earth, the toys that filled his childish heart with gladness and pleased him on the nursery floor; the paradise that was ever bright when he smiled within it; hold them up, and ask him to throw away his harp, and leave the side of his new found friends, and the bosom of his Savior; and would he come, to be a boy again, to live and laugh, and love again, to sicken, suffer, die, and *perhaps* be lost I think he would stay. I think I would shut the door if I saw him coming.

Rev. S. I. Prime, D. D.

BE RECONCILED IN THE DEATH OF A CHILD.

I HOPE you are both well reconciled to the death of your child. Indeed I cannot be sorry for the death of infants, How many storms do they escape! Nor can I doubt, in my private judgment, that they are included in the election of grace. Perhaps those who die in infancy, are the exceeding great multitudes of all people, nations, and languages mentioned in Revelation vii. 9, in distinction from the visible body of professing believers, who were marked on their foreheads, and openly known to be the Lord's. Rev. John Newton.

> But thou, the mother of so sweet a child,
> Thy false imagined loss cease to lament,
> And wisely strive to curb thy sorrows wild;
> Think what a present thou to God hast sent,
> And render him with patience what he lent.
>
> Milton.

EDMUND SPENSER.

IMMORTALITY.

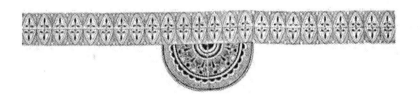

THE RAISING OF JAIRUS' DAUGHTER.

IMMORTALITY.

RT. REV. SAMUEL FALLOWS, D. D.

WITHOUT any attempt at an exhaustive presentation of the all-important subject of Immortality, I may be able to give, in brief, an outline of the arguments by which the doctrine is supported. Although they will not be arguments amounting to demonstration, they will afford the highest probability to every thoughtful Christian mind, that if a man die, he shall live again.

I shall avoid, as far as possible, a dry, metaphysical treatment of the question, and avail myself more of the logic of the heart, than of the understanding.

We are met on the threshold of our theme with the fact, that among all the nations of the earth the idea of Immortality has been held. This is a signal proof that the idea is true. It does not affect the validity of the position taken, that the ideas of these various nations were incorrect as regards the nature of the future state. The clearing up of all doubts, the dispelling of all mists, depends upon revelation. The function of God's revealed truth is not to discover new and fundamental ideas to the universal intelligence of man. It is to clarify them of all error in their application, to bring them out into fullness and prominence; to make them nutritive and determinative in the moral and spiritual life.

While holding to the transmigration of the soul, the ancient Hindoos believed in its essential immortality. It was taught by them, "as a man throweth away his old garment and putteth on new, so the soul, having quitted its old mortal frames, entereth into others which are new. The weapon divideth it not. The water corrupteth it not. The wind drieth it not away. It is indivisible, inconsumable, incorruptible."

Herodotus says of the Egyptians: "They were the first of mankind who had defended the immortality of the soul."

Lord Bolingbroke, free-thinker though he was, declares that 'the doctrine of the immortality of the soul, and a future state of rewards and punishments, began to be taught before we have any light into antiquity. And when we begin to have any, we find it established that it was strongly inculcated from time immemorial." Volney admits that all the earliest nations taught that the soul survived the body, and was immortal.

It has been the belief of earlier and later peoples. The nations of Northern Europe, the fierce, restless hordes who forced the gates of the Eternal City and crushed the Roman power, believed that the slothful and cowardly, at death, went into dark caves underground, full of noisesome creatures, and there they groveled in endless stench and misery. But those who died in battle, went immediately to the vast palace of Odin, their god of war, where they were entertained in perpetual feasts and mirth.

Among civilized and uncivilized nations, on continents and islands, in every quarter of the globe, the belief in immortality has been entertained. Whence came the idea? Some of the deniers of the soul's inherent immortality have attempted to answer the question. Philosophers and statesmen, they allege, "practicing a pious fraud" upon the people, foisted it upon them. It was found necessary to bring in the idea of a future life, to hold the masses in subjection; to secure their allegiance to the State, and uphold the dignity of philosophy. Plato is represented as quoting a Pythagorean philosopher, who taught that, "as we sometimes cure the body with unwholesome remedies, when such as are most wholesome have no effect, so we restrain those minds by false relations which will not be persuaded by the truth." In like manner, it is claimed, the philosophers and statesmen reasoned, and so invented the idea of immortality to compass their ends.

We have only one question to ask. *What* philosopher, or *what* statesman invented it? When his name is ascertained, we may entertain such an unfounded assertion. He will be found closely akin to the one who invented the love of the beautiful, the sentiment of harmony, the love of children, the fact of conscience, and the idea of God. If the historical argument for immortal existence were pressed no further than the admitted position that it is congenial to the universal mind of man, a strong presumption would be created in favor of the doctrine. But it goes much further, and proves that the idea of continued being is *native* to the human soul. The consent of all nations, is the grandest affirmation possible of what the consciousness of man teaches.

The philosopher, the statesman, and the priest may have played upon the credulity of the people, and held them fast in dire superstitious bondage; but it was through a perversion of the instincts and principles God had implanted in the constitution of man himself.

II. I may adduce the metaphysical and moral argument.

In the Kensington Museum, in England, I saw some of the sketches from the master hand of Turner. Rough and rude they were, but yet such only as his hand could draw. Over against them were the finished pictures, with all their faithfulness of detail, accuracy of expression, and magnificence of execution.

The best human life here, with its marvelousness of inventive powers, its royal reach of reason, its sublime daring of genius, its amplitude of affection, its deeds of goodness, is but an imperfect sketch; and yet a sketch that the hand of God only could draw. It is but the alphabet out of which the stately, glowing, and immortal epic of a Paradise regained shall spring from a Paradise Lost. It is but the wail of a new-born child compared with the symphonies of angels.

No clearer truth does the open book of Nature unfold to the wise and reverent reader, than the existence of a plan in the development of the animal kingdom.

No St. Peter's or St. Paul's can more clearly indicate the idea of Michael Angelo or Sir Christopher Wren, than the *four* great types on which organic life is built, the *idea* of the Great Architect of the universe.

This plan, in its four-fold manifestations, implies predetermination, and involves consummation. Every organ, however rudimentary at any particular stage of the unfolding, becomes a function somewhere on the line of development. It is sure to be employed down in the scale of existence. Some animals have fingers, which are never used. They are given them by the Being who unvaryingly adheres to His plan. They are there, because when man, the lord and head of the kingdom, comes to the throne, bringing forward and *completing* all the lower and preceding types, he *must* and does possess five fingers on each hand, of varying length and strength. Those rough and rigid protuberances, in the structure of his inferior relations, prophesied the free, facile and flexible use of the most perfect instruments for carrying out the thought of the brain and the love of the heart. If there be no immortal life, all the prophecies of Nature fail—suddenly and unaccountably fail.

In the splendid make and mechanism of the body, compared with which the most cunning piece of man's workmanship is a bungling performance, every promise has been redeemed, and every prophecy fulfilled. It is correlated to the world about it. Light has been made for the eye, sound for the ear, food for the palate. Nay, in the very constitution of the mind, axioms have been given to the reason, truth to the intellect, and beauty to the æsthetic taste. Still further the conscience has asked for light and cleansing, and they have been given; the soul has cried out for God, for the living God, and "the invisible appeared in sight, and God was seen by mortal eye."

We have the instinctive fear of death—the unutterable dread of annihilation—the passionate longing for continued existence. We have powers capable of endless progression; faculties which find no appropriate sphere on earth, which are caged and confined, as the panting bird, aspiring after liberty, beats its breast against the restraining bars.

We *feel*, we *know* our kinship with the skies. This world *now* can not bound our intellect; burning worlds and burnt-out worlds, swinging in their brilliant and gloomy orbits, throw up no barriers against the swift feet of our soaring imaginations. Beyond the uttermost limits of creation, we send our thoughts, our adoring love; beyond prostrate cherubim and seraphim, above the very throne itself, to Him that sitteth upon the throne, God over all, blessed for evermore.

This light of intellect to be quenched in oblivion's waters! These powers to be stamped out by annihilation! These longings to be unsatisfied, these hopes to be mocked! O, what a superb farce is this!

The God of Nature is the father of the immortal soul. The brute attains its ends. Man would be a little lower than the brute, if he did not attain his. There is no annihilation of a single *substance* in Nature, though the *form* may be endlessly changed. There is no annihilation of spirit. The body may wax and wane. "I call it *mine*, not me." Connected with it, I yet know, that from it, "I am distinct. as is the swimmer from the flood.', My thought, emotion, and will are not acids and phosphates. Our essential instincts are not a supreme forgery. Our faith in the God of Nature, and man, is not in vain.

> " 'Tis the Divinity that stirs within us,
> 'Tis heaven itself that points out an hereafter
> And intimates eternity to man."

In the same line of thought is the revelation of God to man, through Jesus Christ our Lord, who taught us to say, in the most perfect form of words, at the beginning of his universal prayer, "Our Father who art in heaven." In that sublime and comforting teaching, Father, and heaven, and man are brought together in vital relationship.

Edward Everett, in his just and glowing eulogy of Daniel Webster, mentions the following incident: " I happened one bright starry night to be walking with Daniel Webster, at a late hour, from the Capitol at Washington, after a skirmishing debate, in which he had been speaking at no great length, but with much earnestness and warmth, on the subject of the Constitution as forming a united government. The planet Jupiter, shining with unusual brilliancy, was in full view. He paused, as we descended Capitol Hill, and unconsciously pursuing the train of thought which he had been enforcing in the Senate, pointed to the planet, and said: 'Night unto night showeth knowledge;' take away the independent force, emanating from the hand of the Supreme, which impels that planet onward, and it would plunge in hideous ruin from those skies into the sun; take away the central attraction of the sun, and the attendant planet would shoot madly from its sphere; urged and restrained by the balanced forces, it wheels its eternal circles through the heavens." The underlying thought in that majestic mind, was this: These several States must be bound by supreme law to the one central government; "broad based upon the people's will;" not clashing in endless confusion, but moving on in harmony, progressiveness and light.

But a still grander thought does the illustration illumine and glorify.

We lift up our eyes and our hearts to that Supreme One whose hand "guideth Arcturus with his sons, bindeth the sweet influences of the Pleiades, and looseth the bands of Orion," and it is the hand of "Our Father in Heaven."

There is the point of man's original departure.

> "Not in entire forgetfulness,
> Not in utter nakedness,
> But trailing clouds of glory, do we come
> From God who is our home."

You never can think of the Christian's God without thinking of the Christian's *home*. You never can take that endearing name of "Father" upon your lips, and leave out the Father's house in which are many mansions. The two are forever united. Try to cut loose from God, you swing away from the heaven in which he dwells. Try to shut out from your vision that heaven, and you send the "sun of the soul" under an eclipse. If there is a *real* God, there is a *real* heaven.

You can not sail upon the ocean, out of sight of land, without calling upon the heaven and its orbs of light to aid you. You must rectify your compass and your course by its central sun. You can not sail life's sea without life's heaven. Your compass of philosophy, history, of political economy, of statesmanship, of civilization must have the rectification of the skies, or you never can reach the heaven of humanity's hopes.

Break away from the Heaven-Father, and you are plunged in the blackness of darkness, and the horrors of chaotic ruin. You have read that poem on Darkness, by one of the most gifted but sadly erring writers this earth has ever held. It was

"A dream which was not all a dream.

> The bright sun was extinguished, and the stars
> Did wander darkling in the eternal space
> Rayless and pathless, and the icy earth
> Swung blind and blackening in the moonless air."

You know the rest. The prayer for light; the watch-fires of thrones, and palaces, and huts; the burning cities, the blazing homes, the crackling trunks of forest fires; the crouching of the freezing multitudes before their ineffectual flames; the looking up with mad, disquiet awe on the dull sky, the pall of a past world; the cursing, the gnashing of teeth, the howling of despair in the dust; the shrieking of the wild birds and the flapping of their useless wings; the wildest brutes becoming tame and tremulous; the crawling vipers, hissing, but stingless; the glut of war, the gorging with blood; the death of love; the pang of famine the dropping dead; the last two who survived—enemies, "scraping with their cold, skeleton hands the feeble ashes;" the gaze of each upon the other; their shriek, and death from mutual hideousness!

> "The world was void, the waves were dead,
> The tides were in their grave;
> The winds were withered in the stagnant air,
> And the clouds perished; *darkness* had no need of aid
> From them, she was the universe!"

Extinguish those greater and lesser lights of God and immortality from our sky, and you make the poet's dream a fearful reality on our earth.

In that awful winter, which shall bring icy death to man's religious nature, and to his instincts, and aspirations for the life to come, all else that we hold dear below, government, home, social order, civilization, faith, hope, love, shall perish with eternal frost. And the horrors of the vision of atheism, seen by the philosophic Jean Paul, shall be added to those of the poet Byron: "Raising his eyes toward the heavenly vault, he beheld a deep, black, bottomless void! Eternity resting on chaos, was slowly devouring itself!"

The end of the life of that greatest of American statesmen, foremost of American lawyers, and most commanding of American orators, whose language I have quoted from Mr. Everett, came in the course of time. Too feeble to hold his pen, he said in a whisper to Mr. Curtis, his biographer, "I had intended to prepare a work for the press, to bear my testimony to Christianity; but it is now too late. Still, I would like to bear witness to the Gospel, before I die. Writing materials were brought, and he dictated: "Lord, I believe; help thou my unbelief. Philosophical objections have often shaken my reason with regard to Christianity, especially the objections drawn from the magnitude of the universe contrasted with the littleness of this planet; but my *heart* has always assured me, and reassured me, that the Gospel of Jesus Christ is a divine reality;" and these words are carved on the marble that rests over his sacred dust at Marshfield. But, as that brilliant orb was going down behind the western hills, he asked, as if still intently anxious to preserve his consciousness to the last, and to watch for the moment and act of his departure, so as to comprehend it, "whether he were alive, or not." On being assured he was, he said, as if assenting to what had been told him, because he, himself, perceived it was true, "*I still live!*"—his last words. The sunset had come; but it was a sunrise to know no more setting. His earnest soul repeated, I think, the last words he spoke on earth as his first in heaven—*I still live.*

HOPE BEYOND THE GRAVE.

'IS night, and the landscape is lovely no more;
   I mourn; but, ye woodlands, I mourn not for you,
For morn is approaching your charms to restore,
   Perfumed with fresh fragrance, and glittering with dew.
Nor yet for the ravage of winter I mourn;
   Kind nature the embryo blossom will save.
But when shall spring visit the mouldering urn?
Oh! when shall it dawn on the night of the grave?

'Twas thus, by the glare of false science betrayed,
   That leads to bewilder, and dazzles to blind,
My thoughts wont to roam, from shade onward to shade,
   Destruction before me, and sorrow behind.
"Oh, pity, great Father of Light!" then I cried,
   "Thy creature, who fain would not wander from Thee!
Lo! humbled in dust, I relinquish my pride:
   From doubt and from darkness Thou only canst free."

And darkness and doubt are now flying away;
  No longer I roam in conjecture forlorn:
So breaks on the traveller, faint and astray,
  The bright and the balmy effulgence of morn.
See Truth, Love, and Mercy, in triumph descending,
  And Nature all glowing in Eden's first bloom.
On the cold cheek of Death smiles and roses are blending,
  And Beauty immortal awakes from the tomb.

JAMES BEATTIE, LL. D.

THE DYNASTY OF THE FUTURE.

THE dynasty of the future is to have glorified man for its inhabitant; but it is to be the dynasty—"the kingdom"—not of glorified man in the image of God, but of God, himself in the form of man. In the doctrine of the two conjoined natures, human and Divine, and in the further doctrine that the terminal dynasty is to be peculiarly the dynasty of Him in whom the natures are united, we find that required progression beyond which progress cannot go. We find the point of elevation never to be exceeded, meetly coincident with the final period never to be terminated—the infinite in height harmoniously associated with the eternal in duration. Creation and the Creator meet at one point, and in one person. The long ascending line from dead matter to man has been a progress Godwards.

HUGH MILLER.

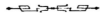

THE UPWARD TENDENCIES OF THE SOUL.

From the birth
Of mortal man, the sovereign Maker said,
That not in humble nor in brief delight,
Not in the fading echoes of Renown,
Power's purple robes, nor Pleasure's flowery lay
The soul should find enjoyment; but from these
Turning disdainful to an equal good,
Through all the ascent of things enlarge her view,
Till every bound at length should disappear,
And infinite perfection close the scene.

AKENSIDE.

THE HOPE OF IMMORTALITY.

PROF. DAVID SWING.

SUCH worshipers of the new are all made by the creative genius of our era, that in order to appreciate the old you must ask your imagination to picture them as coming up before you for the first time. With what tears of joy would you hail the hope of immortality had that hope just come into the world! If dust had been the assumed end of man, what discovery of science or art would compare in sublimity with the sudden assurance of a second and blessed life? Such an expectation dwarfs all the common hopes of this world. A Prince yearly approaching a throne, a gifted mind gathering up the honors of learning or power, a citizen drawing near a fabulous fortune, are all small scenes or outlooks compared with that of a humble child steadily moving toward an endless and painless being. When you remember how you all love life and feel sad over the fact that the grave is before you, you may well be amazed at the height and depth of the doctrine of a second existence that shall be in all ways higher and sweeter than this. The slowness with which this notion came to man has hidden its vastness. Its age is a witness for its truth, but is against its grandeur as a thought. It is modified by its antiquity as mountains are made treeless and cold by intervening miles. Their verdure, and cascades, and song of birds are all toned away from the senses by their distance. They are spoken of as "gray," or "hazy," or "blue." One simple attribute thus remains out of a marvelous richness and variety. From many old doctrines has the multitude moved away until ideas are seen in some one dead color—ideas vast as God and beautiful as Paradise.

When love once fears that it may cease, it has already ceased. It is all the same to our hearts, whether the beloved one fades away or only his love.

JEAN PAUL.

INSURANCE AND THE FUTURE LIFE.

REV. T. DE WITT TALMAGE, D. D.

THE scientific Hitchcocks and Sillimans and Mitchells of the world have united with the sacred writers in making us believe that there is coming a conflagration to sweep across this earth, compared with which, that of Chicago in 1871, and that of Boston in 1872, and that of New York in 1835 were a mere nothing. Brooklyn on fire! New York on fire! Charleston on fire! San Francisco on fire! Canton on fire! St. Petersburg on fire! Paris on fire! London on fire! The Andes on fire! The Appenines on fire! The Himalayas on fire! What will be peculiar about the day will be that the water with which we put out great fires will itself take flame, and the Mississippi, and the Ohio, and the St. Lawrence, and Lake Erie, and the Atlantic and Pacific Oceans, and tumbling Niagara shall with red tongues lick the heavens. The geological heats of the centre of the world will burn out toward the circumference, and the heats of the outside will burn down from the circumference to the centre, and this world will become a living coal—the living coal afterward whitening into ashes, the ashes scattered by the breath of the last hurricane, and all that will be left of this glorious planet will be the flakes of ashes fallen on other worlds. O! on that day will you be fire-proof, or will you be a total loss? Will you be rescued or will you be consumed? When this great cathedral of the world, with its pillars of rock, and its pinnacles of mountain, and its cellars of golden mine, and its upholstery of morning cloud, and its baptismal font of the sea, shall blaze, will you get out on the fire-escape of the Lord's deliverance? O! on that day for which all other days were made, may it be found that these Life Insurance men had a paid-up policy, and these Fire Insurance men had given them instead of the *debris* of a consumed worldly estate, a house not made with hands, eternal in the heavens!

THE DESIRE FOR CONTINUED EXISTENCE.

REV. CANON H. P. LIDDON, D. D.

MAN'S spirit lives more in the past, more in the future, than in the present, exactly in the degree in which man makes the most of himself. Man, as a spirit, reaches back into the past, reviews it, lives it over again in memory, turns it to account in the way of experience. Man, as a spirit, reaches forward into future time—gazes wistfully at its uncertainties, maps it out—so far as he can, provides for it—at least, conditionally, disposes of it. Man, as a spirit, rises out of—rises above—the successive sensations which make up to an animal its whole present life. Man understands what it is to exist. He understands his relation to other beings, and to nature. He sees something—something at any rate—of the unique grandeur of his being among the existences around him. And thus he desires to exist beyond the present into the future which he anticipates—to exist into a very distant future if he may. The more his spirit makes of itself—the more it makes of its powers and its resources—the more earnestly does it desire prolonged existence. And thus the best heathens had the clearest presentiment of a life beyond the grave. These men of high thoughts and noble resolves could not understand that because material bodies were perishing around them, therefore conscience, reason, will, the common endowments of human kind, must or could be extinguished too. These men longed to exist—aye, after death, that they might continue to make progress in all such good as they had begun in this life, in their high thoughts, and their excellent resolves; and with these longings they believed that they would thus exist, after all, when this life was over. The longing, itself, you see, was a sort of proof that this object was real. How else was the existence of the longing to be satisfactorily explained? If all enterprise in thought and in virtue was to be abruptly broken off by the shock of death, at any rate in this longing, and in the power of self-measurement out of which it grew, the spirit of man discovered its radical unlikeness to the lower forms of life around it. It became familiar with the idea of a prolonged existence, under other conditions, beyond the grave.

THE GREAT HEREAFTER.

NOW sweet to think while struggling
   The goal of life to win,
That just beyond the shining shore
   The better years begin.

When through the nameless ages
   I cast my longing eyes,
Before me, like a boundless sea
   The Great Hereafter lies.

Along the brimming bosom
   Perpetual summer smiles
And gathers, like a golden robe
   Around the emerald isles.

And in the blue, long distance,
   By lulling breezes fanned,
I seem to see the flowering groves
   Of fair old Beulah's land.

And far beyond the islands,
   That gem the waves serene,
The image of the golden shore
   Of holy Heaven is seen.

And to the Great Hereftear
   Afore-time, dim, and dark,
I freely now, and gladly give,
   Of life, the wandering bark.

Then in the far-off haven,
   When shadowy seas are passed,
By angel hands, her quivering sails
   Shall all be furled at last.

                                      CLARK.

LITTLE CONCERN FOR THE FUTURE.

THOUGHTS of the future should give us very little concern. I think this way: If Christ loved me six thousand years ago so as to offer to die for me, and during all that six thousand years to keep me in mind, and four thousand years after that did come and die for my sins, and since then to watch over and keep me, that Jesus that loved me and gave Himself for me, and who now comes to take possession of that heart, will not give me up when I get old and sick and die. Is that the way a mother does? The sicklier and feebler the child is the more she clings to it. The Lord Jesus loves with more than a mother's love.

BISHOP M. SIMPSON.

THE IMMORTAL LIFE.

The insect bursting from its tomb-like bed—
  The grain that in a thousand grains revives—
The trees that seem in wintry torpor dead—
  Yet each new year renewing their green lives;
All teach, without the added aid of Faith,
That life still triumphs o'er apparent death!

But dies the insect when the summer dies;
  The grain hath perished, though the plant remain;
In death, at last, the oak of ages lies;
  Here Reason halts, nor further can attain,
For Reason argues but from what she sees,
Nor traces to their goal these mysteries.

But Faith the dark hiatus can supply—
  Teaching, eternal progress still shall reign;
Telling (as these things aid her to espy)
  In higher worlds that higher laws obtain;
Pointing, with radiant finger raised on high,
From life that still revives, to life that cannot die.

THE IDEA OF MAN'S IMMORTALITY DIVINELY IMPRESSED.

ALL nations, are, in a manner, agreed that there is an immortality to be expected, as well as a Deity to be worshiped; though ignorance of circumstances makes religion vary even to monstrosity, in many parts of the world. But both Religion and the belief of the Reward of it, which is a blessed state after death, being so generally acknowledged by all the inhabitants of the earth; it is a plain argument that it is true, according to the Light of Nature. And not only because they believe so, but because they do so seriously desire it, or are so horribly afraid of it if they offend much against their consciences: which properties would not be in man so universally, if there were no objects in Nature answering to these Faculties. I therefore demand, and I desire to be answered without prejudice or any restraint laid upon our Natural Faculties. To what purpose is this indelible Image or Idea of God, in us, if there be no such thing as God existent in the world? Or who sealed so deep an impression of that character upon our minds?

HENRY MOORE.

IMMORTALITY AND DEATH.

FAITH builds a bridge across the gulf of Death,
To break the shock blind Nature cannot shun,
And lands Thought smoothly on the farther shore.
Death's terror is the mountain Faith removes,
That mountain-barrier between men and peace.
'Tis Faith disarms Destruction, and absolves
From every clam'rous charge the guiltless tomb.

* * * * *

The chamber where the good man meets his fate
Is privileged beyond the common walk
Of virtuous life, quite in the verge of heaven.
Fly, ye profane! if not, draw near with awe,
Receive the blessing, and adore the chance
That threw in this Bethesda your disease;

If unrestored by this, despair your cure;
For here resistless demonstration dwells.
A death-bed's a detector of the heart;
Here tired Dissimulation drops her mask,
Through life's grimace that mistress of the scene;
Here real and apparent are the same.

    *   *   *   *   *

What gleams of joy! what more than human peace!
Where the frail mortal? the poor abject worm?
No, not in death the mortal to be found.
His conduct is a legacy for all,
Richer than Mammon's for his single heir.
His comforters he comforts; great in ruin,
With unreluctant grandeur gives, not yields,
His soul sublime, and closes with his fate.
How our hearts burnt within us at the scene.
Whence this brave bound o'er limits fix'd to man?
His God sustains him in his final hour!

EDWARD YOUNG.

THE STRAIN OF IMMORTALITY.

"STRANGE," said a gifted metaphysician once, "that the barrel-organ, man, should terminate every tune with the strain of immortality!" Not strange, but divinely natural. It is the tentative prelude to the thrilling music of our eternal bliss written in the score of destiny. When at night we gaze far out into immensity, along the shining vistas of God's abode and are almost crushed by the overwhelming prospects that sweep upon our vision, do not some premonitions of own unfathomed greatness also stir within us? Yes: "the sense of Existence, the ideas of Right and Duty, awful intuitions of God and immortality,— these, the grand facts and substance of the spirit, are independent and indestructible."

W. R. ALGER.

MORAL LIFE BEYOND EARTH.

SOMETIMES like to fancy things about the stars. May there not be moral systems as well as physical?—moral wholes or plans; a portion of the plan being carried on in one world, and another in another world, so that, like different pieces of a machine, or like the different stars themselves, the whole must be examined before the plan can be understood. The world may be a moral center; the center being the cross from which moral radii extend throughout the moral universe. Physical space and moral space have no connection. It used to be an old question how many angels could dance on the point of a needle, but it had a glimmer of wisdom, too, for it arose from the feeling that spiritual things have no relation to space.

REV. NORMAN MACLEOD, D. D.

THIS LIFE AN ARGUMENT FOR THE NEXT.

HERE are times when the best life seems a sheer failure to the man who has lived it; his wisdom folly, his genius impotence, his best deed poor and small; when he wonders why he was suffered to be born; when all the sorrows of the world seem poured upon him; when he stands in a populous loneliness, and, though weak, can only lean upon himself. In such hours he feels the insufficiency of this life. It is only his cradle-time—he counts himself just born; all honors, wealth and fame are but baubles in his baby-hand: his deep philosophy but nursery rhymes; yet he feels the immortal fire burning in his heart. Still worse, the consciousness of sin comes over him; he feels that he has insulted himself. All about him seems little: himself little, yet clamoring to be great. Then we feel an immortality; through the garish light of day we see a star or two. The soul within us feels her wings, contending to be borne, impatient for the sky, and wrestles with the earthly worm, that folds us in.

THEODORE PARKER.

DANIEL WEBSTER.

A SECOND LIFE.

THE most of fame goes under the grass with the other wreaths placed upon the coffin. To compose that vast and immortal thing called truth, millions of minds are consumed. There must be elsewhere a compensation for the individual thus rudely torn from life. A second life, a readjustment beyond the tomb, is the only explanation of that destroying angel which moves to and fro in our streets and homes. Society is immortal here, man is immortal hereafter. Earth consumes our great ones and our loved ones, but heaven looks down in pity and receives them to herself. Earth refines man as silver is refined—refines, but does not destroy. After the dross of the body and soul have been consumed the spirit thus whitened begins elsewhere a higher life.

Prof. David Swing.

IMMORTAL FLOWERS.

LET us walk with the Gardener while He points out to us some of His rarer plants. He points to this bed and says, "There rests a precious seed, O how lovely will its blooming be! On earth it was called Bleeding Heart. It grew in great tribulation. But the terminology of the botany of heaven is not known on earth. It has a new name, written on a white stone, which no man knoweth. Tears and afflictions were needed to bring out its rare qualities."

And what lies here in this bed, Gardener? "You would call that in earth's botany, a Heliotrope—the flower that ever turns toward the sun."

"And there lies the Lily of the Valley; and there the Calla, whose roots had to be submerged in water."

"But," we ask, "Gardener, canst Thou care for all these? Will there be no confusion or neglect? Thy flower beds are so many, is there no possibility that some will be overlooked?"

"Oh, no," He answers; "their names are all graven on the palms of My hands, and are written also in the Book of Life."

O blessed truth! What flowers shall spring up from these grassy mounds!

Rev. P. E. Kipp.

I SEEK relief and I find it in the consolatory opinion, that this dreary and wretched life is not the whole of man; that a being, capable of such proficiency in science and virtue, is not like the beasts that perish; that there is a dwelling-place prepared for the spirits of the just; that the ways of God will yet be vindicated to man.

Sir James MacKintosh.

ARGUMENT FOR IMMORTALITY FROM THE HEART-LIFE.

H. W. THOMAS, D. D.

I WANT to advance an argument that I do not remember to have ever seen in any book or to have ever heard. The argument is this: that the same reasons which led to the creation of human beings will demand their continuance. We are not able to say certainly what were the reasons in the Divine mind that led to the creation of man. That creation might have been the outgrowth of the universal love, the outgrowth of a desire to create beings with whom he might hold communion and raise to the realms of his feelings, and ultimately elevate to companionship with himself. Whatever those reasons might have been, we cannot but conceive that what led to the creation of man would in some way seek to perpetuate man's being. It will not do to say that God is a mere model-builder, that He will go on age after age simply experimenting. When he endows humanity with the crown of mind and spirit, when it comes to that point where that which is distinctive in man is given, and love for his fellow-man, belief in his own immortal destiny, and faith in God—in all reason we are bound to the conclusion that the cause which led to our creation will continue to influence the Divine Being to our preservation.

We may offer another argument, not new, drawn from the pleadings of morality, the pleadings of the heart-life. This world is certainly a moral battle-field, where through all the centuries truth has been pitted against error, reason against passion, justice against injustice. The whole history of mankind shows that the battle has been a tedious one. The lines have wavered, and at no time has the final result been certain except to the eye of faith. Now I would take my stand by the side of every patriot who ever loved his country, by the side of every martyr who ever died for truth, by the side of every teacher who ever taught, by the side of every minister who ever preached, by the side of every missionary who ever went forth to heathen lands, by the side of those who have wiped away the tear of sorrow, who have tried to lift up the fallen, who have sat by the bedside of the dying and tried to push back the shadows of night—in the name of every one who has ever worked, or thought, or suffered for humanity, do I claim that there must be some future where the results of this great struggle are to be crowned with a compensation beyond what is reached here; a future where the uneven scales of justice in this life may find their balance, where man shall be dealt with according to his merits. Taking our stand by the heart-life, I ask, in the name of reason, is all the longing in human souls to be left out? Is all the affection of this world, that has clung about life as the vine about the ark, to go for naught?

So flits the world's uncertain span!
Nor zeal for God, nor love for man,
Gives mortal monuments a date
Beyond the power of Time and Fate.
The tower's must share the builder's doom;
Ruin is theirs, and his a tomb;
But better boon benignant Heaven
To Faith and Charity has given,
And bids the Christian hope sublime
Transcend the bounds of Fate and Time.
                                    SIR WALTER SCOTT.

THE ARGUMENTS OF PLATO.

PROF. B. F. CROCKER, D. D.

THE soul is immortal, because it is incorporeal. There are two kinds of existences, one compounded, the other simple; one perceptible to sense, the other comprehended by mind alone. The one is visible, the other is invisible. When the soul employs the bodily senses, it wanders and is confused; but when it abstracts itself from the body, it attains to knowledge which is stable, unchangeable, and immortal. The soul, therefore, being uncompounded, incorporeal, invisible, must be indissoluble—that is to say, immortal.

2. The soul is immortal, because it has an independent power of self-motion—that is, it has self-activity and self-determination. No arrangement of matter, no configuration of body, can be conceived as the originator of free and voluntary movement. Now that which cannot move itself, but derives its motion from something else, may cease to move and perish. "But that which is self moved, never ceases to be active, and is also the cause of motion to all other things that are moved." And "whatever is continually active is immortal." This "self-activity," says Plato, "is the very essence and true notion of the soul." Being thus essentially causative, it therefore partakes of the nature of a "principle," and it is the nature of a principle to exclude a contrary. That which is essentially self-active can never cease to be active; that which is the cause of motion and of change, cannot be extinguished by the change called death.

3. The soul is immortal, because it possesses universal, necessary, and absolute ideas, which transcend all material conditions, and bespeak an origin immeasurably above the body. No modifications of matter, however refined, however elaborated, can give the Absolute, the Necessary, the Eternal. But the soul has the ideas of absolute beauty, goodness, perfection, identity, and duration, and it possesses these ideas in virtue of its having a nature which is one, simple, identical, and in some sense eternal. If the soul can conceive an immortality, it cannot be less than immortal. If, by its very nature, "it has hopes that will not be bounded by the grave, and desires and longings that grasp eternity," its nature and its destiny must correspond.

THE IMMORTAL SPIRIT.

This spirit shall return to Him
  That gave its heavenly spark;
Yet think not, Sun, it shall be dim
  When thou thyself art dark!
No! it shall live again and shine
In bliss unknown to beams of thine
  By Him recall'd to breath,
Who captive led captivity,
Who robbed the grave of victory,
  And took the sting from death.

Go, Sun, while mercy holds me up
  On nature's awful waste,
To drink this last and bitter cup
  Of grief that man shall taste—
Go tell the night that hides thy face,
Thou saw'st the last of Adam's race,
  On earth's sepulchral clod,
The dark'ning universe defy
To quench his immortality,
  Or shake his trust in God.

THOMAS CAMPBELL.

IMMORTAL LIGHT.

"Creature all grandeur, son of truth and light,
  Up from the dust! the last great day is bright;
Bright on the holy mountain, round the throne,—
Bright where, in borrowed light, the far stars shone.
Look down! the depths are bright! and hear them cry,
'Light! light!' Look up! 't is rushing down from high!
Regions on regions, far away they shine:
'T is light ineffable, 't is light divine!
'Immortal light, and life forevermore!'
Off through the deeps is heard from shore to shore,
Of rolling worlds,—'Man, wake thee from the sod,—
Wake thee from death,—awake!—and live with God!'"

THE HOME BEYOND
THROUGH A GLASS DARKLY.

REV. HUGH BLAIR, D. D.

WE are strangers in the universe of God. Confined to that spot on which we dwell, we are permitted to know nothing of what is transacting in the regions above and around us. By much labor we acquire a superficial acquaintance with a few sensible objects which we find in our present habitation; but we enter and we depart, under a total ignorance of the nature and laws of the spiritual world. One subject in particular, when our thoughts proceed in this train, must often recur upon the mind with peculiar anxiety; that is, the immortality of the soul, and the future state of man. Exposed as we are at present to such variety of afflictions, and subjected to so much disappointment in all our pursuits of happiness, why, it may be said, has our gracious Creator denied us the consolation of a full discovery of our future existence, if indeed such an existence be prepared for us?

Reason, it is true, suggests many arguments in behalf of immortality; Revelation gives full assurance of it. Yet even that Gospel, which is said to have brought "life and immortality to light," allows us to see only "through a glass darkly." "It doth not yet appear what we shall be." Our knowledge of a future world is very imperfect; our ideas of it are faint and confused. It is not displayed in such a manner as to make an impression suited to the importance of the object. The faith even of the best men is much inferior, both in clearness and in force, to the evidence of sense; and proves on many occasions insufficient to counterbalance the temptations of the present world. Happy moments indeed there sometimes are in the lives of pious men; when, sequestered from worldly cares, and borne up on the wing of divine contemplation, they rise to a near and transporting view of immortal glory. But such efforts of the mind are rare, and cannot be long supported. When the spirit of meditation subsides, this lively sense of a future state decays; and though the general belief of it remains, yet even good men, when they return to the ordinary business and cares of life, seem to rejoin the multitude, and to reassume the same hopes, and fears, and interests, which influence the rest of the world.

CHRIST BRINGS IMMORTALITY TO LIGHT.

PRESIDENT NOAH PORTER, D. D. LL. D.

THOSE who acknowledge no God, but a mysterious force, those who deny to God personality and thought, and affection and sympathy, most reasonably find no evidence in nature for a future life—when they look in her stony and inflexible face, they find all the evidence to be against it. Let such a man awake to the fact that God is, that he lives a personal life, that nature is not so much his hiding-place as it is a garment of his revealing light, that the forces of nature are his instruments and the laws of nature his steadying and eternal thoughts, that man is made after God's image and can interpret his thoughts and commune with his living self, that life is man's school, every arrangement and lesson of which points to a definite end, that the end is not accomplished here—then not only does there spring up in his heart the hope that this life shall be continued another, but this hope becomes almost a certainty. Let now God be seen to break forth from his hiding-place, and to manifest himself in the Christ who conquers death and brings the immortal life to light through his rising and ascension, and the hope that had been reached as a conclusion of assured conviction is shouted forth in the song of triumph—" Blessed be the God and Father of our Lord Jesus Christ, who, according to his abundant mercy, hath begotten us again unto a lively hope by the resurrection of Jesus Christ from the dead, to an inheritance incorruptible, undefiled, and that fadeth not away."

Can we forget departed friends? Ah, no!
Within our hearts their memory buried lies;
The thought that where they are we too shall go,
Will cast a light o'er darkest scenes of woe.

THE HOME BEYOND THE IMMORTAL MIND.

ANNE STEELE.

WHY should this immortal mind
Enslav'd by sense, be thus confined,
   And never, never rise?
Why, thus amused with empty toys,
And soothed with visionary joys,
   Forget her native skies?

The mind was formed to mount sublime
Beyond the narrow bounds of time,
   To everlasting things;
But earthly vapors cloud her sight,
And hang with cold, oppressive weight
   Upon her drooping wings.

The world employs its various snares,
Of hopes and pleasures, pains and cares,
   And chained to earth I lie:
When shall my fettered powers be free,
And leave these seats of vanity,
   And upward learn to fly?

Bright scenes of bliss, unclouded skies,
Invite my soul; oh, could I rise,
   Nor leave a thought below!
I'd bid farewell to anxious care,
And say to every tempting snare,
   Heaven calls and I must go.

Heaven calls,—and can I yet delay?
Can aught on earth engage my stay?
   Ah! wretched lingering heart!
Come, Lord, with strength, and life, and light,
Assist and guide my upward flight,
   And bid the world depart.

I look to recognize again, through the beautiful mask of their perfection,
The dear familiar faces I have somewhile loved on earth;
I long to talk with grateful tongue of storms and perils past,
And praise the mighty Pilot that hath steered us through the rapids.

THE RESURRECTION.

ECCE HOMO.

THE RESURRECTION.

THE RESURRECTION OF CHRIST.

RT. REV. SAMUEL FALLOWS, D. D.

MAKE clear the fact of the resurrection of Christ, it will be a fact that chimes with humanity's unutterable longings, and fits in as the key-stone of the radiant arch of its hopes. Make clear that fact, and then, as the meridian sun brings out in all their boldness the mountains, and in all their beauty, the swarded valleys faintly described in the dim twilight, so will a risen Sun of righteousness bring out these hints, and truths, and ideas, in controlling power over the intellect, and influence over the practical life. Make clear that fact, and one simple-minded Christian believer, full of resurrection power, shall chase a thousand carping rationalists, and two shall put ten thousand to flight. Our faith in God, asks of God—a risen Redeemer.

St. Paul claims, if Christ be not risen, faith in Him is vain. So interwoven with the very life, and teachings, and death of Christ was the truth of His resurrection, that to deny the latter would be to destroy, root and branch, all faith in Him as Teacher and Savior. He had said, "Destroy this temple, and in three days I will raise it again." After the surpassing glory of the transfiguration, he had commanded, "Tell the vision to no man until the Son of man be risen from the dead."

He must either have been unconsciously deceived, and then he would have shown himself a weak, erring man, and no longer entitled to the claim of a teacher sent from God; or he must have been a willful impostor, and thus have sunk in the mire trodden beneath the feet of indignant, deluded men. If Christ be not risen, your faith is vain; your faith in Him as a Savior is vain. Your Christian consciousness is a nullity, and a lie. There has been no atonement. Ye are yet in your sins. Life, death, resurrection, all enter into the redeeming work of Christ. He was "delivered for our offenses, and raised again for our justification." "If thou shalt confess with thy mouth, the Lord Jesus, and believe in thine heart that God raised him from the dead, thou shalt be saved." No resurrection, no salvation.

He asserts of the apostles: "We are found *false* witnesses." We, who were fully competent by reason of our numbers, to be believed, for there were the eleven apostles, the two Marys, Cleopas. the most of the seventy, and five hundred others beside. Nearly all were living, and ready to testify. Fully competent, as to our powers of judgment and varied experience; fully competent, from the opportunities we have enjoyed of knowing the facts to which we bear witness. We have been with the Savior; we have known him intimately; we have treasured up His words. His image is stamped upon our hearts; we beheld His miracles; we knew he was crucified; we went to the tomb, expecting to find the body there; we saw Him alive again; we saw His pierced hands and wounded side; we heard the familiar voice; we received our high commission; we saw Him ascend into glory.

We have gained nothing, from an earthly standpoint, but loss of home, of friends, of reputation, We are made the filth and offscouring of the world. We are made a spectacle unto angels and to men. Stripes, bonds, imprisonment are before us. The headsman's axe glitters in the sun. "To the lions, to the lions!" rings in our ears. Covered with pitch, and set on fire, we shall light the streets of Rome by midnight! If in this life only, we have hope in Christ, we are of all men most miserable.

How the apostle, with jubilant utterance, turns away from the loathsome impossibility he has presented.

"Now is Christ risen from the dead and become the first fruits of them that slept." The irrefutable fact stands forth in all its glorious majesty and infinite sweep of meaning.

The Gospel records must be torn to tatters, and scattered with the rent sybilline leaves, never more to be gathered. The whole colossal fabric of Christianity must have been built upon an abyss. The head and founder of the Church must have been created by the Church. A man must have been the father of his own ancestors, before this fact can be successfully denied.

Christ is risen from the dead. His own words have been justified. Christ is risen from the dead, and God has given the seal and sign manual to his Messianic mission. He has declared Him to be the Son of God, with power. Christ is risen from the dead, and an unsetting sun—the new and unfailing center of attraction—has burst forth in glory from the darkness of the tomb. Christ is risen, and we, too, shall rise. Every charnel house is robbed of its terrors. The sting has been plucked from death, and the grave been robbed of its victory. The darkness has forever passed. *It is morning.*

In that beautiful city of the dead, Greenwood cemetery, where the precious dust of so many loved ones reposes—that city, on its eminence, graced with flowers, fit resurrection—emblems of life and loveliness springing from decay, and melodious with the music of birds—that city, overlooking the city of the living below it, and the river and the sea beyond it, contains here and there a broken pedestal, which speaks of plans unrealized, and expectations unfulfilled; of aspirations unsatisfied, and ends unachieved. But on some of them is a hand pointing upward. A risen Christ is the inspiration of the thought. The upward pointing is the mute and eloquent suggestion, that on the plains of the New Jerusalem, the column of life shall be erected.

A limited sphere here, a boundless amphitheatre there. Seeming failure here, assured success there. Dead hopes here, living realizations there. Bafflings, disappointments here; unimpeded progress there. Home there, rewards there, friends there, Jesus there. Can we doubt the life beyond? "Therefore, my beloved brethren, be ye steadfast, unmovable, always abounding in the work of the Lord, forasmuch as ye know that your labor is not in vain, in the Lord."

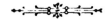

CHRIST IS RISEN.

RT. REV. SAMUEL FALLOWS, D. D.

THE funeral grief of the world was poured out when the crucified Son of God yielded up His life, broken-hearted, for the sins and sorrows of mankind. The night of gloom deepened as hour succeeded hour during the tragic scenes of that awful Good Friday. But the morning has come, bright, resplendent, and glorious. The stone is rolled away; the tomb is empty; the two angels in shining garments announce: "He is not here; He is risen."

No wonder this is the chief of festivals. A risen Christ—what does it mean? The miracles of Christ were the badges of a minister plenipotentiary of the skies. The resurrection showed Him to be the Son of God with power. The sun of Righteousness out of that momentary eclipse has emerged to be clouded no more forever. The winter of doubt and discontent is over and gone, for His coming has made glorious summer in the soul.

Christ is risen, and the pledge of omnipotent love is given, of pardon, peace and purity to the penitent soul. Christ is risen, and comfort comes to every desponding heart. Christ is risen, and the old man sees in it the renewing of perpetual youth. Christ is risen, and death is a discrowned monarch. For the earthly crown is laid down at the feet of the last enemy, but the heavenly one is taken from the hands of death's conqueror.

Christ is risen. And when we are called to send our little children away from the home-fold below, we know that the tender Shepherd waits to fold them to his bosom in the home-fold above. Christ is risen, and the knightly soldier in the thick of the battle, on sentry or on guard, knows his Commander is not dead. In every righteous cause he can draw his sword, and feel the assurance of ultimate victory, for he hears the voice of the Captain of our salvation, who was dead but is alive again forevermore. "Lo! I am with you alway, even unto the end of the world."

> With might of ours can nought be done;
> Soon were our loss effected,

> But for us fights the Valiant One
> Whom God Himself elected.
> Ask ye Who is this?
> Jesus Christ it is,
> Of Sabaoth Lord,
> And there's none other God—
> He holds the field forever.

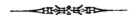

THE RESURRECTION OF CHRIST ATTESTS THE INCARNATION.

AS the incarnation is the central and fundamental miracle of Christianity, so the resurrection of Jesus Christ from the dead is the crowning attestation of the reality of the incarnation. It is the linch-pin to that central wheel of the series. No mere ordinary human soul, of its own unaided power, ever returned into and reanimated the body it forsook at death. But this is just what Jesus of Nazareth promised He *would* do, and what Christianity claims He *did* do. If this claim be good, then Jesus was no ordinary mortal, but He was what He professed to be: He was the Incarnate God. His resurrection proves His claim, and His nature corresponds to His works. Such a resurrection puts the final and absolute seal of genuineness upon all His pretensions, the seal of authority upon all His teachings. All that the Bible records of Him, from Genesis to Revelation, is fulfilled and established: all that He says of Himself is truth and law. The resurrection of Christ is, therefore, the sign-manual of Jehovah to the whole volume of Revelation. It is the key-stone to the entire arch of human redemption and salvation. Not without profoundest reason, therefore, has the whole Christian Church, from the earliest age until now, celebrated Christ's resurrection-day with the sublimest anthems ever born of mortal rapture and of mortal art. Not without reason have sculpture and painting, eloquence and poetry, contended through all ages for the noblest expression of this triumph of the God man over death. The incarnation, like the roots of the mountain, lies vast, profound, obscure, mysterious, at the bottom of our Christian hope. The resurrection stands like that mountain's summit, clear, dazzling, sublime, in the objective light of history.

REV. GEO. LANSING TAYLOR, D. D.

FAITH IN CHRIST'S RESURRECTION.

In the belief of Christ's resurrection, the gifted Baron Bunsen took his solemn and exultant farewell of his deeply-loved wife, saying: "Love, love, we have loved each other; love cannot cease: love is eternal; the love of God is eternal; live in the love of God and Christ; those who live in the love of God must find each other again though we know not how; we cannot be parted; we shall see each other beyond."

Faith in it made the dying soldier-boy say to his commanding officer after the battle was over: "General, I feel as if I was going to the front." It rung out with the voice of transport, in the utterances of that Dutch lad in the Netherlands, who, with his father, was fastened to the stake by the brutal persecutor Titleman: "Look, my father," he said, amid the flames; "all heaven is opening, and I see a hundred thousand angels rejoicing over us! Let us be glad, for we are dying for the truth."

BISHOP FALLOWS.

THE RESURRECTION MORNING.

AND early in the morning, we are told by the Evangelists, these same women started to go to the sepulchre to anoint his body, and found out that he was risen. Why, do you think if they had thought he was going to rise that they would have left that sepulchre? They would have lingered around it: it would have taken more than a hundred Roman soldiers to keep those disciples away from the sepulchre, if they thought he was going to rise. Now, early in the gray of the morning, you could see these women going toward the sepulchre. They had got their spices all ready to anoint that body again, and they were greatly troubled, because they did not know who was going to roll away the stone. And you see them as they draw near to the sepulchre; and the sun has just driven away the darkness of the night, and that beautiful morning is bursting upon the earth, the best morning this world had ever seen. And one says to another, "Who shall roll away the stone?" But a messenger came from yon world of light; he flew faster than the morning light, and arrived first. And he rolled away the stone; and those men that had been sent there by Pilate, to watch and guard that sepulchre, began to tremble, and fell as dead men; they hadn't any power. One angel was enough to roll away that stone; not to let him out, but to let you and I look in to see that the sepulchre was empty, to let the morning light into that sepulchre to light it up that we might know that he had risen, "the first fruits of them that slept." Yes, thank God, he has conquered Death and the grave; and you can shout now, "O grave, where is thy victory!" He went down into the grave and conquered it, and came up out of it; and now he says, "Because I live, ye shall live also."

D. L. MOODY.

A CHANGED BODY.

It has been asked how it could be that the resurrection of bodies which had crumbled into dust and returned again to earth—had reappeared in animal and vegetable life—could be accomplished. This could not be understood by man, who had better leave to God the question of philosophy, satisfied in His power to accomplish the apparent impossibility. But, for the satisfaction of the skeptical, the accomplishments of modern science, with whose aid metals could be apparently destroyed and again reunited in their full bulk and purity, and the gases of the air decomposed and again conjoined together, might be quoted as giving a proof that even man could do that which not so long ago would have been deemed impossible. And surely, if the chemist with his little vial of acid could do these things, the Omniscient and Omnipotent God could reconstruct anybody and everybody that had ever existed.

The doctrine of the resurrection of the body did not necessarily imply the preservation of the identity of the person. It is not to be supposed that the resurrected blind man would be blind, the dwarf a dwarf, and the cripple a cripple. The teachings of Scripture give a more beautiful belief when they make likeness to the Lord Jesus that which would belong to the body which would arise.

Rev. E. P. Goodwin, D. D.

A RISEN CHRIST VICTORIOUS.

BISHOP FALLOWS.

"WHAT a brilliant dream that was of Napoleon's!" He expected to find at St. Jean D'Acre the treasure of the Pasha and arms for 300,000 men. He then intended to raise and arm Syria, already waiting for the movement. He would then advance upon Damascus and Aleppo, recruit from a discontented country, arrive at Constantinople with his vast army, overturn the Sublime Porte, found a splendid Oriental empire, unsurpassed for magnificence, "fix his position with posterity," and come back to Paris, through Vienna, dragging a subjugated Austria in triumph at his chariot wheels." But Waterloo and St. Helena shattered his dream. Death made absolutely impossible what imprisonment made improbable. But arrest, imprisonment, scourging, crucifixion, death, cannot stop the victorious progress of the King, eternal, immortal, invisible. The glorious prediction made centuries before His advent in the world shall yet find its full and final accomplishment. "He shall see of the travail of His soul and be satisfied." "He shall have dominion from sea to sea, and from the rivers to the end of the earth." "Yea, all kings shall fall down before him; All nations shall serve Him."

WE DO NOT WORSHIP A DEAD SAVIOR.

Oh, may God help us to realize what a precious truth we have to preach; that we are not worshiping a dead Savior; that he is a resurrected Savior, and in such a day and hour as we think not he will return. And although we do not know when that will be, there is one thing we do know, and that is that he has promised to come; and that day is not far distant; we haven't but a little while to work. As Christine Evans says: "The songs of these bursting sepulchres, when Christ shall come, will be sweeter than the song of the morning star." We shall come up from the grave, by and by, with a shout. "He is the first fruits;" he has gone into the vale, and will call us by and by. The voice of the Son of God shall wake up the slumbering dead! Jacob will leave his lameness, and Paul will leave his thorn in the flesh; and we shall come up resurrected bodies, and be forever with the Lord. I pity those people who know nothing about the resurrection of Christ, and think Christ does not live, and was merely a man, and perished in the grave of Joseph Arimathea. What hope have they got?

Oh, what gloom and darkness settles down upon this world, if it was not for the glorious day of resurrection. And those that have been sown in dishonor and corruption shall be raised, by and by, in glory and honor; they shall come up out of their graves, and we shall be forever with them. Oh, may this blessed truth take hold of all our hearts, and may we go out from this Tabernacle and spread the news that the Lord has risen. He has gone up on high, and he will bless the sons of men, if they will receive a blessing from him.

D. L. Moody.

"Be worthy of death; and so learn to live
That every incarnation of thy soul
In other realms, and worlds, and firmaments
Shall be more pure and high."

THE AGONY IN THE GARDEN.

RAISED ON THE LAST DAY.

BY. REV. BISHOP JOHN HENRY HOBART, D. D.

WHAT can reason teach us here? She may indeed, by analogy, illustrate and confirm the doctrine of the resurrection when it is revealed; but as an original truth she knew nothing of it. The tomb received in its dark embrace the mouldering body, and there was no light that dawned on the night of the grave. "Blessed then be the God and Father of our Lord Jesus Christ, who hath begotten us to a lively hope by the resurrection of Jesus Christ from the dead" (I Pet. i. 3). "He is the first-fruits of them that slept" (I Cor. xv. 20); and at the great harvest, in the last day, "those who sleep in Jesus will God bring with him" (I Thess. iv. 14). The body, sown in corruption, shall be raised in incorruption—sown in dishonor, it shall be raised in glory—sown in weakness, it shall be raised in power—sown a natural body, it shall be raised a spiritual body.

How is all this to be effected? By that mighty power which raised up Christ from the dead. Here we take our stand—on the omnipotence of God—and defy every attack against the doctrine of the resurrection. We laugh to scorn all attempts to wrest from us our hope, through a supposed impossibility of the resurrection, as puny struggles against the omnipotence of God. Did he not at first construct a human form from the dust of the earth? Did he not breathe into a mass of clay the breath of life? And when he again speaks, shall it not be done? Can he not again bring bone to bone, sinew to its sinew, flesh to its flesh? Fear not, Christian! thy dust may be scattered to the winds of heaven—but thy God is here. It may repose in the lowest abysses of the grave—He is there. It may dwell in the uttermost parts of the sea—even there His hand shall lead thee, His right hand shall hold thee, and bring thee forth, incorruptible and glorious, like unto that body which now receives the homage of the angels around the throne. Thou shalt be raised at the last day. Let us comfort one another with these words.

CHRIST'S RESURRECTION BODY.

I THINK if you would look through your Bibles carefully, you will find that ten different times He appeared to his disciples, not in the spirit, but in the body, in person. I want to get this thing established in all our minds, that Christ has come out of the grave personally, that His body has gone back to heaven, The same body they crucified, the same body they laid in Joseph's sepulchre has come out of the jaws of death and out of the sepulchre; and he has passed through the heavens and gone back on high. We are told He had an interview with Peter, who is alluded to as Simon and as Cephas. We can imagine what took place at that interview, and that Peter's old difficulty was settled. Peter denied Him, but at that interview Christ forgave him. What a Sabbath it must have been for Peter! What a blessed day for that poor backslider! And if there is some backslider here to-day, who will have an interview with the Son of God, he will forgive you this Easter morning, and blot out all your wanderings and all your sins, if you will come back; and it will be a joyful day for you.

D. L. Moody.

CHRIST CONQUERED DEATH FOR US.

CHRIST has not only conquered sin and death in Himself, but in and for some of our kind. These, thus raised, are the evidences of His victory and the pledges of our resurrection. They are the first fruits, with Himself, of them that slept. As Enoch and Elijah are types and assurances of those who will be changed at the last day, so these trophies of Christ are the sure tokens of His victory and type of our own resurrection. With these He ascended up on high, and made an open show of them. If a man die, shall he live again? asks Job. This question is sublimely and satisfactorily answered in the text. Our assurance in Christ, is that we shall have an eternal life of body, soul, and spirit—painless and deathless. He came not to destroy, but that we might have life more abundantly.

Rev. Joseph Wild, D. D.

THE DEAD GLORIFIED THROUGH CHRIST.

REV. DR. GUTHRIE.

AND in Christ, the first-born, I see the grave giving up its dead; from the depths of the sea, from lonely wilderness and crowded churchyard they come, like the dews of the grass, an innumerable multitude. Risen Lord! we rejoice in thy resurrection. We hail it as the harbinger and blessed pledge of our own. The first to come forth, thou art the elder brother of a family, whose countless numbers the patriarch saw in the dust of the desert, whose holy beauty he saw shining in the bright stars of heaven.

The first-born! This spoils the grave of its horrors, changing the tomb into a capacious womb that death is daily filling with the germs of life. The first fruits! This explains why men called the church-yard, as once they did, God's acre. Looking at these grassy mounds in the light of that expression, the eye of faith sees it change into a field sown with the seeds of immortality. Blessed field! What flowers shall spring there! What a harvest shall be gathered there! In the neighboring fields "whatsoever a man soweth, that shall he also reap;" but here how great the difference between what is sown amid mourners' tears, and what shall be reaped amid angels' joys; between the poor body we restore to the earth, and the noble form that shall spring from its ashes. Who saw the rolling waves stand up a rocky wall; who saw the water of Cana flow out rich purple wine; who saw Lazarus's festering corpse, with health glowing on its cheek, and its arms enfolding sisters ready to faint with joy, saw nothing to match the change the grave shall work on these moulder-ing bones. Sown in corruption, they shall rise in incorruption, mortal putting on immortality. How beautiful they shall be! Never more shall hoary time write age on a wrinkled brow. The whole terrible troop of diseases cast with sin into hell, the Saints shall possess un-fading beauty, and enjoy a perpetual youth; a pure soul shall be mated with a worthy partner in a perfect body, and an angel form shall lodge an angel mind. There shall be be no more death, nor sighing, nor sorrow for there shall be no more sin.

PROOF OF CHRIST'S RESURRECTION.

REV. JOHN EADIE, D. D. LL. D.

THE apostle could easily have given them indubitable evidence that Christ had been raised from the dead; as, for example, that His tomb was guarded, and that the sentinels only befooled themselves and those who suborned them, by their contradictory announcement—"His disciples came and stole Him away while we slept." Roman soldiers asleep on special duty, and forward to confess it—asleep on a post which they were warned might be assailed—all of them asleep at the same instant, and when under orders of unusual strictness—asleep, and yet able to tell what happened, what was done, and who did it, too, when their eyes were shut in unanimous slumber—all of them asleep, and yet not one of them awakened by the noise and confusion of the earthquake which preceded the resurrection! Nor had the disciples any motive to do the act imputed to them. They had no idea that their Master should rise again, and all their hopes were buried along with Him. They could, therefore, never dream of such an attempt as stealing His body, it being of no use to them, as they had no romance to base upon its absence; and if they had, the eleven poltroons who "forsook Him and fled" at the sight of the soldiers in the garden, would never have ventured to attack a Roman guard of sixteen men under the bright moonlight of the eastern heavens. Farther, He who had risen appeared to His former friends who could identify Him, and on the spot, too, where He had been put to death. It was not as if one supposed to have risen in Glasgow should be said to have appeared first in Inverness, where he was a comparative stranger. It was not as if it were alleged that one had risen, but that the story was only first heard of a half century after the imagined event. At the time when, and in the place where He had died and been buried, did the Lord appear, when full investigation could be made into all the circumstances, and into the testimony of crowds of living witnesses. But those who should have originated and conducted the inquiry shrank from it under the impression that the result would not be to their satisfaction, and resorted to the miserable refuge of authority, "straitly threatening" the witnesses to say no more on the matter; while they who were "witnesses of these things" had no end to gain, and no worldly advantage to secure; on the contrary, proscription and death resulted from the avowal of their belief in this momentous tenet.

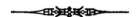

BEHOLD THE PLACE WHERE THEY LAID HIM.

THE angels would have the disciples see the empty sepulchre, as if that sight were enough to convince them of the certainty of Christ's resurrection. So it was. His disciples were too timid to attempt the removal, and his enemies were determined to hold the dead body in their grasp. The sight of the empty place should therefore be sufficient evidence of Christ's resurrection.

Let us also "behold the place," gaze on the consecrated spot and gather in the wonders with which it is haunted. It is the scene of the mightiest prodigy ever known on earth. There the dead stirred itself, the inanimate Being sprung by his own volition into life. Behold, and acknowledge the Divinity of Christ. "Behold the place;" in being emptied, earth and sea may be said to have given up their dead—Christ was the representative of the countless myriads of human kind. Behold the change effected by the Redeemer for his followers—the grave, instead of being the home of all that is hideous and revolting, has an angel for its tenant, rich odors for its perfume. The grave has become a bed and death a sleep to those who put faith in His name. Behold it in your tears and sorrow, not as those who have no hope—in your hopes, that you may look for glorious things from your Forerunner. Behold it, ye who care little for the soul and eternity, and think if Christ can be neglected with impunity—flee to Him as a Saviour before He appears as an Avenger. Patiently inspect the empty sepulchre and learn all its lessons.

REV. CANON H. MELVILLE, D. D.

THE BURIAL OF CHRIST.

THE RESURRECTION BODY.

JOSEPH COOK.

IF you come to the conclusion that there is an invisible, non-atomic, ethereal enswathement, which the soul fills, and through which it flashes more rapidly than electricity any cloud, you must remember that the majestic authority for that statement is simply the axiom that every change must have an adequate cause. This is cool precision; this is exact research on the edge of the tomb. Professor Beale says, in so many words, "that the force which weaves these tissues must be separable from the body;" for it very plainly is not the result of the action of physical agents. Ulrici shows, especially in a magnificent passage on immortality, that all the latest results of physiological research go to show that immortality is probable.

You say that, unless we can prove the existence of something for the substratum of mind, we may be doubtful about the persistency of memory after death; but what if this non-atomic, ethereal body goes out of the physical form at death? In that case, what materialist will be acute enough to show that memory does not go out also? You affirm that, without matter, there can be no activity of mind; and that, although the mind may exist without matter, it cannot express itself. You say that unless certain, I had almost said material, records remain in possession of the soul when it is out of the body, there must be oblivion of all that occurred in this life. But how are you to meet the newest form of science, which gives the soul a non-atomic enswathement as the page on which to write its records? That page is never torn up. The acutest philosophy is now pondering what the possibilities of this non-atomic, ethereal body are, when separated from the fleshy body; and the opinion of Germany is coming to be very emphatic, that all that materialists have said about our memory ending when our physical bodies are dissolved, and about there being no possibility of the activity of the soul in separation from the physical body, is simply lack of education. There is high authority and great unanimity on the propositions I am now defending; and although I do not pledge myself always to defend every one of these theses, yet I must do so in the present state of knowledge and in the name of a gulf. Current of speculation which is twenty-five years old, and has a very victorious aspect as we look backward to the time when the microscope began its revelations.

It becomes clear, therefore, that, even in that state of existence which succeeds death, the soul may have a spiritual body.

The existence of that body preserves the memories acquired during life in the flesh.

If this ethereal, non-atomic enswathement of the soul be interpreted to mean what the Scriptures mean by a spiritual body, there is entire harmony between the latest results of science and the inspired doctrine of the resurrection. . . .

When the Bible speaks of a spiritual body, it does not imply that the soul is material; it does not teach materialism at all; it simply implies that the soul has a glorified enswathement, which will accompany it in the next world. I believe that it is a distinct biblical doctrine, that there is a spiritual body as there is a natural body, and that the former has extraordinary powers.

"WHETHER buried in the earth, or floating in the sea, or consumed by the flames, or enriching the battle-field, or evaporated in the atmosphere,—all, from Adam to the latest-born, shall wend their way to the great arena of the judgment. Every perished bone and every secret particle of dust shall obey the summons and come forth. If one could then look upon the earth, he would see it as one mighty excavated globe, and wonder how such countless generations could have found a dwelling beneath its surface.

REV. GARDNER SPRING, D. D.

HE IS NOT HERE; HE IS RISENN.

CANON F. W. FARRAR, D. D.

"CHRIST is risen." How these words change the whole aspect of human life! Nothing short of this could be our proof and pledge that we also shall rise. We are not left to dim intimations or vague hopes, or faint analogies, but we have a permanent and a firm conviction, a sure and certain hope. Look into the Savior's empty tomb. "He is not here: He is risen, as He said." They that sleep in all those narrow graves shall wake again, shall rise again. Weep not widowed wife, father, orphan boy, Thy dead shall live. They shall come forth from the power of death and Hades. What a mighty victory! What a giant sporting! What a trampling of the last enemy beneath the feet! What a hope, what a change in the thought of life! Bravely and happily let us walk through the dark valley, for out of it is a door of immortality that opens on the gardens of heaven and the streams of life, where the whole soul is flooded by the sense of a newer and grander being, and our tears wiped away by God's own hand. This is the Christian's hope truly, and herein Christ makes us more than conquerors, for we not only triumph over the enemy, but profit by him, wringing out of his curse a blessing, out of his prison a coronation and a home, "It is sown in corruption, it is raised in incorruption." Let us live in love, in humility, in Christ and for Christ. This will make us noble and happy in life, this will strengthen us to smile at death, this will cause us to live all our days in the continual light of these two most marvelous of all Christian truths: the resurrection of the body, and the immortality of the soul.

"So, thou hast immortality in mind?
   Hast grounds that will not let thee doubt it?
The strongest ground herein I find:—
   That we could never do without it!"

HE IS NOT HERE, HE IS RISEN.

THE RESURRECTION MORNING.

DR. TALMAGE.

NUMEROUS scriptural accounts say that the work of gravebreaking will begin with the blast of trumpets and shoutings; whence I take it that the first intimation of the day will be a sound from heaven such as has never before been heard. It may not be so very loud, but it will be penetrating. There are mausoleums so deep that undisturbed silence has slept there ever since the day when the sleepers were left in them. The great noise shall strike through them. Among the corals of the sea, miles deep, where the shipwrecked rest, the sound will strike. No one will mistake it for thunder or the blast of earthly minstrelsy. There will be heard the voice of the uncounted millions of the dead, who come rushing out of the gates of eternity, flying toward the tomb, crying: "Make way! O grave, give us back our body! We gave it to you in corruption; surrender it now in incorruption." Thousands of spirits arising from the field of Waterloo, and from among the rocks of Gettysburg, and from among the passes of South Mountain. A hundred thousand are crowding Greenwood. On this grave three spirits meet, for there were three bodies in that tomb; over that family vault twenty spirits hover, for there were twenty bodies. From New York to Liverpool, at every few miles on the sea route, a group of hundreds of spirits coming down to the water to meet their bodies. See that multitude! that is where the "Central America" sank. And yonder multitude! —that is where the "Pacific" went down. Found at last! That is where the " City of Boston " sank. And yonder the "President" went down. A solitary spirit alights on yonder prairie—that is where a traveler perished in the snow. The whole air is full of spirits: spirits flying north, spirits flying south, spirits flying east, spirits flying west. Crash! goes Westminster Abbey, as all its dead kings, and orators, and poets get up. Strange commingling of spirits searching among the ruins. William Wilberforce, the good; and Queen Elizabeth, the bad. Crash! go the Pyramids, and the monarchs of Egypt rise out of the heart of the desert. Snap! go the iron gates of the modern vaults. The country graveyard will look like a rough-ploughed field as the mounds break open. All the kings of the earth; all the senators; all the great men; all the beggars; all the armies—victors and vanquished; all the ages—barbaric and civilized; all those who were chopped by guillotine, or simmered in the fire, or rotted in dungeons; all the infants of a day; all the octogenarians—all! all! Not one straggler left behind. All! all! And now the air is darkened with the fragments of bodies that are coming together from the opposite corners of the earth. Lost limbs finding their mate—bone to bone, sinew to sinew—until every joint is reconstructed, and every arm finds its socket, and the amputated limb of the surgeon's table shall be set again at the point from which it was severed. A surgeon told me that after the battle of Bull Run he amputated limbs, throwing them out of the window, until the pile reached up to the window-sill. All those fragments will have to take their places. Those who were born blind shall have eyes divinely kindled; those who were lame shall have a limb substituted. In all the hosts of the resurrected not one eye missing; not one foot clogged; not one arm palsied; not one tongue dumb; not one ear deaf.

THE EVENING CLOUD.

A cloud lay cradled near the setting sun,
   A gleam of crimson tinged its braided snow:
Long had I watched the glory moving on
   O'er the still radiance of the lake below.
Tranquil its spirit seem'd, and floated slow,
   Even in its very motion there was rest;
While every breath of eve that chanced to blow
   Wafted the traveller to the beauteous west.
Emblem, methought, of the departed soul!
   To whose white robe the gleam of bliss is given,
And by the breath of mercy made to roll
   Right onwards to the golden gates of heaven,
Where, to the eye of faith, it peaceful lies,
And tells to man its glorious destinies.

                              PROFESSOR WILSON.

THE RESURRECTION ILLUSTRATED.

H. W. THOMAS, D. D.

SO it is that out of these elementary particles human bodies are builded, and out of nature's storehouse God will in some way reinvest the spirit with a material organism. We can well believe that this is possible in the light of what chemistry can do. There are many things which the chemist can do which we would not believe to be possible did we not know them to be facts. I think it is Dr. Brown who quotes from Mr. Hallet the story of a gentleman who was something of a chemist, who had given a faithful servant a silver cup. The servant dropped the cup in a vessel of what he supposed to be pure water, but which in reality was *aqua fortis*. He let it lie there, not thinking it could receive any harm, but, returning some time after, saw the cup gradually dissolving. He was loudly bewailing his loss when he was told that his master could restore the cup for him. He could not believe it. "Do you not see," he said' "that it is dissolving before our sight?" But at last the master was brought to the spot. He called for some salt water, which he poured into the vessel, and told the servant to watch. By and by the silver cup began to gather as a white powder at the bottom. When the deposit was complete the master said to the servant, "Pour off the liquid, gather up this dust, have it melted and run together, then take it to the workman and let him hammer the cup again." You may take gold; you may file it down to a powder, mix it with other metals, throw it into the fire, do what you will with it, and the chemist will bring back with certainty the exact gold.

Thus our bodies are built up by fruits from the tropics, by grain from the prairies. The flesh that roamed the plains as cattle has become part of us. If God can build up human bodies here, can He not find and convert the dust that we put away in the grave, and bring it back to forms of life? In my judgment, God is able to preserve even the particles of the human body and restore them. So far as the power is concerned, it can be done, and will be done, as God may think best.

THE COMING FORTH OF LAZARUS.

CHRIST ROSE BY HIS OWN POWER.

REV. DR. GUTHRIE.

HE rose in the night; no hand at the door, no voice in his ear, no rough touch awaking him. Other watchers than Pilate's soldiers stood by the sepulchre; but these angels whom it well became to keep guard at this dead man's chamber door, beyond opening it, beyond rolling away the stone, beyond looking on with wondering eyes, took no part in the scenes of that eventful morning. The hour sounds; the appointed time arrives. Having slept out his sleep, Jesus stirs; he awakes of his own accord he rises by his own power; and arranging, or leaving attending angels to arrange, the linen clothes, he walks out on the dewy ground, beneath the starry sky, to turn grief into the greatest joy, and hail the breaking of the brightest morn that ever rose on this guilty world. That open empty tomb assures us of a day when ours too shall be as empty. Having raised himself, he has power to raise his people. Panic-stricken soldiers flying the scene, and Mary rising from his blessed feet to hasten to the city, to rush through the streets, to burst in among the disciples, and with a voice of joy to cry, He is risen, He is risen! prove this is no vain brag or boast, "I lay down my life that I might take it again. No man taketh it from me, but I lay it down of myself. I have power to lay it down, and I have power to take it again."

THE MAGI AND THE RESURRECTION.

WE have the unequivocal assertion of Theopompus, in the fourth century before Christ, that the Magi taught the doctrine of a general resurrection. "At the appointed epoch Ahriman shall be subdued," and "men shall live again and shall be immortal." And Diogenes adds, "Eudemus of Rhodes affirms the same things." Aristotle calls Ormuzd Zeus, and Ahriman Haides, the Greek names respectively of the lord of the starry Olympians above, and the monarch of the Stygian ghosts beneath.

W. R. ALGER.

CHRIST'S RETURN TO HEAVEN.

REV. T. DE WITT TALMAGE, D. D.

THE fourth exceptional gala day in heaven, was the day of Christ's resumption of his old place. The psalms and the epistles give us some intimation of the excitement, If we have an intimate friend go away to be gone a year, we accompany him to the wharf, we go out with him to the "Narrows," we enjoin him that he write to us often, and we are impatient for the return. If a sea captain be gone on a whaling voyage for two or three years, it is a long time ; but Christ was absent from home thirty-three years, and that is a long time, whether on earth or in heaven. But the day of his expatriation was over. The day of his return has arrived. Heaven presses out toward the banks to welcome him. All the bright, sailing craft of heaven push out toward the mouth of the harbor, Jesus is coming! See the flotilla rounding in, bringing our king and conqueror. Millions at one instant catch a glimpse of him and cry "Hail! Hail!" The batteries of heaven boom forth their greeting. Jesus disembarks amid the joy and acclamation of all the nations of the saved, Those whose tears he had wiped away, those whose dead he had raised—they crowd around him, they lift him on their shoulders,, they hoist him on that white horse that St. John saw in Apocalyptic vision—all heaven following him on white horses, while at every turn the cry is, "Ride on, Conqueror!" On, under triumphal arches, not such as were lifted for Titus, or Cæsar, or Alexander, but such of amethystine masonry as heaven only can afford. On, by glassy sea. On, by pearly gate. On, by eternal columns. On, covered with the scars of Golgotha. On, until he reaches the palace gate. "Lift up your heads, ye everlasting gates, and let the King of Glory come in!" cry the heralds as they swing their swords of flame to the porters who keep the gates, "Lift up your heads!" They lift. The way is clear. The torn and bleeding feet that went up the heights of Calvary go up the stairs of the eternal throne, and on the forehead once cut with the twisted thorns are placed the garlands into which are woven all the coronals of universal dominion. Down, all heaven, at his feet and worship. Prophets, and martyrs, and apostles,

and confessors—down. Some on your knees and some on your face.
—down. Cherubim and arch-angel—down. All heaven—down.
And he shall reign forever and ever. Hallelujah!

JEWISH RABBIS ON THE RESURRECTION.

WHEN you bury me, put shoes on my feet, and give me a staff in my hand, and lay me on one side, that when the Messiah comes I may be ready.

RABBI JEREKIAH.

RABBI ABBU says, "A day of rain is greater than the resurrection of the dead; because the rain is for all, while the resurrection is only for the just. 'Sodom and Gomorrah shall not rise in the resurrection of the dead.'"

THE patriarchs so vehemently desired to be buried in the land of Israel, because those who are dead in that land shall be the first to revive and shall devour his years, [the years of the Messiah.] But for those just who are interred beyond the holy land, it is to be understood that God will make a passage in the earth, through which they will be rolled until they reach the land of Israel.

RABRICHEBBO.

CAREFULNESS leads us to innocence, innocence to purity, purity to sanctity, sanctity to humility, humility to fear of sins, fear of sins to piety, piety to the holy spirit, the holy spirit to the resurrection of the dead; the resurrection of the dead to the prophet Elias.

RABBI PINCHAS.

THE very nerves and sinews of religion is hope of Immortality. The destruction of such high powers is something which can never, and under no circumstances, even come into question.

GOETHE.

THE ASCENSION OF CHRIST.

THE ASCENSION OF CHRIST.

D. L. MOODY.

THE last interview he had with them was in Jerusalem; and he took the little band of believers out of the city, down through the Eastern Gate, down through the valley of Jehosaphat, over the brook Kedron, past that garden where he sweated drops of blood, past Calvary, over the brow of the hill, and went out past Bethany, where Martha and Mary and Lazarus (the resurrected man) lived; and perhaps right there, under a cluster of little olive trees, he met his disciples for the last time to bid them farewell, and gave them his parting message. Now He says: "I go home; I go back to the throne; (He had been out of the grave forty days); now I ascend to God." And while he was blessing them—for you know he came blessing, the first thing he said on that memorable mountain when he preached that wonderful sermon (there were nine blessings right out of his heart, he could not go on until he got them out): "Blessed are the poor;" "Blessed are the peacemakers;" "Blessed, blessed; and he recited those wondrous things and blessed them. And while he was blessing them he began to ascend; and he rose higher and higher; and his voice grew fainter and fainter, and at last it died away in the clouds; and the clouds received him out of their sight.

I can imagine up in the clouds there was a chariot from the throne, to take him back home; his work was finished; he rides like Elijah in that golden chariot, and sweeps away through the heavens to the throne. Look at Him on his way to that world where all honor him, and all love him! And as he went sweeping upon his way home, he did not forget his little church; he could see them, but they could not see him; and I can see Peter and John looking up, in hopes that there will be a break in the clouds so that they may see him once more. And while they stand there, gazing up into heaven, you can see tears trickling down their cheeks, their hearts have almost gone out of their body; and he looks back and sees them; and he says to two of the angels who were conveying him home, "Go back, and tell those men that I will come back again." I don't know but they were the two, Mary saw in the sepulchre; and they said:

"Ye men of Gallilee, why stand ye gazing up into heaven? This same Jesus which is taken up from you into heaven, shall so come in like manner as ye have seen him go into heaven." Thank God he is coming back! It is only a question of time. And in such a day and hour as we think not, he will rend the heavens and come back. Lift up your hearts, for the time of your redemption draweth near. We don't worship a dead Savior! He has passed through the heavens, gone up on high, led captivity captive and taken his seat at the right hand of God.

Paul saw him, and Stephen saw him, standing at the right hand of God. He is there, my friends. Thanks be to God, he is not here. They laid him in Joseph's sepulchre; he is risen and up yonder.

WEAVING OF EASTER FLOWERS.

BISHOP FALLOWS.

It is eminently fit that these beautiful flowers, touching the springs of joy and educating the sense of beauty, arranged with such appropriateness by loving and reverent hands, should be about us to-day, filling the chancel and the church with their grateful fragrance. Flowers, the symbols of the fresh, unconsciousness loveliness of children, bloom in field, or garden, or home, or sanctuary with new attractiveness because the Christ-child has been in the world. Symbols of the purity, the sweetness, the gentleness of mature lives, and of the consummate flowering of heroic self-sacrifice, they speak in their mute eloquence with added power to the heart, because He, the perfect man, lived the life which regenerates and died the death which redeems. But a still richer glory is hidden in the inner meaning of these Easter flowers. They are the symbols of the immortality of the true, the beautiful, the good. They have the bloom and the odor of the Eden of love. We place Easter flowers in wreaths and anchors and crosses and crowns above the still forms of our sainted dead, knowing that as they sleep in Jesus, they shall also live and reign with Him forevermore.

Heaven.

THE LAND WHICH IS AFAR OFF.

THE SPLENDOR OF HEAVEN.

REV. F. W. FABER, D. D.

OH, what is this splendor that beams on me now,
   This beautiful sunrise that dawns on my soul,
While faint and far off land and sea lie below,
   And under my feet the huge golden clouds roll?

To what mighty king doth this city belong,
   With its rich jeweled shrines, and its gardens of flowers.
With its breath of sweet incense, its measures of song.
   And the light that is gilding its numberless towers?

See! forth from the gates, like a bridal array,
   Come the princes of heaven, how bravely they shine!
'Tis to welcome the stranger, to show me the way,
   And to tell me that all I see round me is mine

There are millions of saints in their ranks and degrees,
   And each with a beauty and crown of his own;
And there, far outnumbering the sands of the seas,
   The nine rings of angels encircle the throne.

And oh, if the exiles of earth could but win
   One sight of the beauty of Jesus above,

From that hour they would cease to be able to sin,
  And earth would be heaven; for heaven is love.

But words may not tell of the vision of peace,
  With its worshipful seeming, its marvelous fires;
Where the soul is at large, where its sorrows all cease,
  And the gift has outbidden its boldest desires.

No sickness is here, no bleak, bitter cold,
  No hunger, debt, prison, or weariful toil;
No robbers to rifle our treasures of gold,
  No rust to corrupt, and no canker to spoil.

My God! and it was but a short hour ago,
  That I lay on a bed of unbearable pains;
All was cheerless around me, all weeping and woe;
  Now the wailing is changed to angelical strains.

Because I served Thee, were life's pleasures all gone?
  Was it gloom, pain, or blood, that won heaven for me?
Oh no! one enjoyment alone could life boast,
  And that, dearest Lord! was my service of Thee.

I had hardly to give; 'twas enough to receive,
  Only not to impede the sweet grace from above;
And, this first hour in heaven, I can hardly believe
  In so great a reward for so little a love.

CHRIST IS IN HEAVEN.

HEAVEN would not be all that we love unless Christ was there. I would be unhappy, when I got to heaven, if I could not find him there who redeemed me, who died for me, who bought me with his own blood. Some one asked a Christian man once, what he expected to do when he got to heaven? He said he expected to spend the first thousand years in looking at Jesus Christ, and after that he would look for Peter, and then for James, and for John; and all the time he could conceive of would be joyfully filled with looking upon these great persons. But oh, it seems to me that one look at Jesus Christ will more than reward us for all that we have ever done for him down here; for all the sacrifices we can possibly make for him, just to see him; and not only that, but we shall become like him when we once have seen him, because we shall be like the Master himself. Jesus, the Savior of the world, will be there. We shall see him face to face.

D. L. Moody.

REMINISCENCES OF THE PAST IN HEAVEN,

The reminiscences of the past will be sources of profit and gladness. After a success we look back with joy upon the trials over which we triumphed. After having made a perilous ocean voyage the remembrance brings gladness. Youth and childhood, with their victories and defeats, joys and sorrows, who would wish obliterated from their memories? Man will never be grateful for sin, but will gladly remember that through the grace of God he triumphed over it. The very blackness of the sin will add glory to his victory. It is the rain dropping from the clouds and catching the rays of light which give hues to the rainbow; so the tears and sorrows of the present life, catching the light from that new heaven and new earth, will add beauty and gladness to the experiences of that day.

Rev. R. S. Storrs, D. D.

HEAVEN, A PLACE PREPARED BY CHRIST.

REV. HOWARD CROSBY, D. D.

THERE is order in God's universe. There are first and second and third; there are cause and effect. There was a reason why the Messiah appeared not immediately after sin appeared, but 4,000 years later; and there is a reason why his second coming is delayed. There is no delay like man's delay—from weakness. The necessary preparations are going on for the glorious consummation. Christ's work has not ceased. His glory is his grace, and he guides all things in his providence for the full development of that grace. We know nothing of the detailed character of the work he is performing in heaven. We only know he is *preparing a place* for his own, that he is in the presence of God *for us*, and that he ever lives *to make intercession for us*. Something has to be done in the other world before we can go there. We cannot imagine how or in what respect the place is prepared, because we can have no conception of the contents of the other world. All we can know is, that preparation is being made, and that Christ is making it.

We are accustomed to say that space and time are conditions only of our finite and composite natures. Whether this be so or not no man can tell. It is a transcendentalism that it is folly to talk about. Time and sense are absolute necessities to our thinking. Every conception of our minds is formed on these as a foundation, and we can have no idea of God himself except as in time and space. Hence we must, whether we will or no, take the word "place" in our text literally. Even if it be not literally a place, we must *think of it* as a place, for we cannot think of it in any other way. Nor did Christ say, simply, "I go to prepare for you."

What a place that must be which Christ prepares! It must be a place where every purified desire of the heart shall have perpetual satisfaction. The inner soul longs for happiness; it is only the outward and changeable sense that would dictate its form. That it is a pure and holy place and that it has Christ in it, is enough. We know the delicious contents of the vessel, if we do not know the shape and color of the vessel.

What a comfort and joy the thought, that Christ is preparing our place. God's consolations are not like men's mere soothers of a troubled mind, but seeds of positive and independent joy. God's grace comes with a set-off that belittles the earthly care and sorrow. If a soldier in the ranks is wounded, it is one thing to apply soothing cataplasms to stay the pain; but it is a grander thing and a better thing for his general to come to him and bestow upon him the title, rank, and insignia of a high officer. "To depart" is "to be with Christ;" this is the *"far better"* of the apostle.

HEAVEN A PLACE.

D. L. MOODY.

I LIKE to locate heaven, and find out all about it I can. I expect to live there through eternity. If I was going to dwell in any place in this country; if I was going to make any place my home, I would want to inquire all about the place, about its climate, about what kind of neighbors I was going to have, about the schools of my children, about everything, in fact, that I could learn concerning it. If any of you who are here were going to emigrate, going off to some other country, and I was going to take that for my subject tonight, why, would not all your ears be open to hear what you could learn about it? Would you then be looking around to see who was sitting next you; and who among your acquaintances were here; and what people were thinking about you? You would all be interested in hearing of this country that I was talking about. You could not think anything about the latest fashion, or about some woman's bonnet. If it is true that we are going to spend eternity in another world, and that God is inviting us to spend it with him, shall we not look and listen, and find out where he is, and who is there, and how we are to get there?

THE ETERNAL LIFE INDESCRIBABLE.

D. L. MOODY.

I HAVE often thought if I could only tell or picture eternal life I would have but one sermon and I would tell it out. I would go to civilized nations and I would go to heathen nations and I would tell it out. But I can't do it. I have tried many a time to describe what it is, but I don't know somehow or another it seems as if my tongue was tied; it seems to me if I could only picture what the gift of God, what eternal life is, that the people would come to God this morning—that men, women and children would flock into the kingdom by hundreds, if I could only picture what it is. There is nothing we value in this world as we do life. A man will go around the world to lengthen out his life a few years. If he has got wealth he will give money by thousands if he can get medical aid. But this is a world that is filled with sorrow and separation. As I look over this audience I see the emblems of mourning all through the congregation. Not a circle that has not been broken—and many a dear circle has been broken since I stood on this platform last. Death is constantly coming in and taking away this one and that one, and in many you see here and there the natural force is becoming abated and they are tending towards the grave. In a little while they know they must go down to the grave. And so we think life is very sweet here; but just think of the life in the world where there is no stooping form, no gray hair, where the natural force never becomes abated, where the eye never grows dim, where the step is firm and moves on and on through the palaces of the King, where perpetual youth stands on your brow forever, a city where death never enters and sin never comes, a city where all is bright and joyful, a city without a night in it, a city without pain, without sorrow, and without death. Think of it! Not only that, but a city where we shall be with the King himself, and be in His presence. Yea, better still, where these vile bodies shall be found like His own glorious body and shall reign with Him forever! That is eternal life. Why, what are your bonds and stocks when you get to looking at eternal life? Why do you want to go on the Board of Trade and make a few thousands or a few millions? What is that? Think of life forever; a life that is as pure as God's life, that floats on and on unceasingly through joys that last forever. The wages of sin is death, but the gift of God is eternal life. You may have it this morning. Come, friends, will you seek him? If you will take my advice you will not go out of this house this morning without seeking eternal life—without making up your mind that you will seek it.

ZION OUR HOME.

Zion is our home;
Jerusalem, the city of our God.
O happy home! O happy children here!
O blissful mansions of our Father's house!
O walks surpassing Eden for delight!
Here are the harvests reap'd once sown in tears.
Here is the rest by ministry enhanced;
Here is the banquet of the wine of heaven
Riches of glory incorruptible,
Crowns, amaranthine crowns of victory,
The voice of harpers harping on their harps,
The anthems of the holy cherubim,
The crystal river of the Spirit's joy,
The bridal palace of the Prince of Peace,
The Holiest of Holies—God is here.
E. H. BICKERSTETH.

"There shall we see His face,
  And never, never sin;
There from the rivers of His grace,
  Drink endless pleasures in."

THE REV. THEODORE L. CUYLER, D. D.

HEAVEN INDESCRIBABLE.

BISHOP BASCOM, D. D.

BUT in describing the heavenly state—the celestial world of light and life—thought, language and images all fail us. It is a theme too high for conception, too grand for description, too sacred—too ineffably sacred—to admit of comparison. The grandeur of nature and the glory of art, the dreams of fancy and the creations of poetry, all fade in the vision. Admiration no longer hovers over the elysian fields of Virgil. Homer's sparkling rills of nectar, streaming from the gods, woo our thirst no more. The bright Blandusian fountain, and the magnificent vale of far-famed Cashmere, lose their splendor. Even the paradise of Milton, with its trees and its rivers, its fruits and its flowers, its hymns and its harps—a living landscape with its vernal diadem and voiced with melody—dwindles into sterility! And, until we die to share the ripened powers of immortality and heir the thrones of heaven, we can only say, that interminable spring shall bloom upon the scene and chase the winter of affliction by its smiles! We feel how utterly language sinks beneath the majesty of the subject—but let the infirmity be eloquent of its praise; for who can sustain himself when every thought bends and breaks with the burden of its own meaning!

We would, but cannot, tell you of the place to which we go—the home of our Father—the residence of his family—the central abode of final virtue. The august vision makes us tremble as we gaze, and the sublimest reach of human thought can only point, feebly point, to its deep foundations and God built stories—its rainbow coverings and sunlike splendors—walled with adamant and paved with sapphire—crowded with the redeemed, and God in the midst. The high circuit of eternity, the scene of improvement, and the boundless roll of ages—the only key to the evolution of its wonders!

THE FUTURE WILL CLEAR UP MANY MYSTERIES.

REV. THEO. L. CUYLER, D. D.

THE future will clear up many a mystery. A few months ago I went into the house of one of the leading merchants, whose beloved daughter had been brought home dead from being run down in the public street. The first word was, "Tell me now why God took away that girl." Said I, "My brother, I have not come here to interpret God's mysteries. I have come here to lead you closer to God's heart. Be still, and know that He who gave takes away. She already knoweth why she is yonder; wait till God clears away the cloud, and thou wilt find that even this was right and well." Do you not remember how the prophet of old once had his eye touched at Dothan, and he beheld the mountains round about him filled with chariots and horsemen? When you and I work in some great cause of reform, and we have met with defiance and discouragement—why, if God were to open the eyes of our faith, and we could see the battle-field as He does, we would find all round about us a great army of God's promises, assuring us of inevitable victory—nothing to do with chariots and horsemen, but simply to stand our ground and fight out the battle, and trust that he will finally clear away the cloud, and the light of His glory shall shine on the banners of truth borne over the field; for by and by shall come the last great day of revelation, when nothing that is right shall be found to have been vanquished, and nothing that is wrong shall be found to have triumphed.

Jesus, my only hope Thou art!
Strength of my failing flesh and heart;
Oh, could I catch a smile from Thee,
And drop into eternity.

THE MANY MANSIONS.

FABER.

AS one of the many mansions is the destined future Heaven of the redeemed human race, the other numerous mansions must be other heavens, severally allotted to those armies of angels over all of whom, though each army be immediately subjected to its own special commander, the great archangel presides, and is thence congruously revealed as the Captain of the Host of Jehovah.

But the particular mansion allotted to the redeemed human race, is this very planet of ours when the dissolved first earth shall have passed away so far as its present organization is concerned, and shall have been succeeded by a new earth framed out of the present dissipated materials.

Hence, if our future heaven be *one* of the innumerable orbs which are all the handiwork of the Almighty Creator, analogy requires that the *other* heavens should be the other orbs: and thus we have a consistent explanation of the *many* mansions which our Lord declares to be in the House of His Heavenly Father.

FUTURE REVELATIONS.

CANNOT we imagine how the hearts of the saints will be enraptured as they see and comprehend all these wonders in their Lord? The astronomer, as he surveys the vast expanse of heaven through his telescope, has his admiration drawn out as it never could have been if he surveyed it only with the naked eye; and he who examines a flower through a microscope rises from his steady gaze, and strong light, and high magnifying power which has let him into nature's secrets with an enthusiasm which otherwise he never could have felt; but neither telescope or microscope ever admitted any philosophers into such secrets in the natural world as those to which this "I will" (John xvii: 24) of Jesus shall admit His glorified people in the spiritual world.

POWER.

MORAL HEROES IN HEAVEN.

REV. DR. TALMAGE.

My friends, when the battle of life is over, and the resurrection has come, and our bodies rise from the dead, will we have on us any scars showing our bravery for God? Christ will be there all covered with scars. Scars on the brow, scars on the hand, scars on the feet, scars all over the heart, won in the battle of redemption. And all heaven will sob aloud with emotion as they look at those scars. Ignatius will be there, and he will point out the place where the tooth and paw of the lion seized him in the Coliseum, and John Huss will be there, and he will show where the coal first scorched the foot on that day when his spirit took wing of flame from Constance. M'Millan, and Campbell, and Freeman, American missionaries in India, will be there—the men who with their wives and children went down in the awful massacre at Cawnpore, and they will show where the daggers of the Sepoys struck them. The Waldenses will be there, and they will show where their bones were broken on that day when the Piedmontese soldiery pitched them over the rocks. And there will be those there who took care of the sick and who looked after the poor, and they will have evidences of earthly exhaustion. And Christ, with His scarred hand waving over the scarred multitude, will say, "You suffered with Me on earth; now be glorified with Me in heaven." And then the great organs of eternity will take up the chant, and St. John will play: "These are they who came out of great tribulation and had their robes washed and made white in the blood of the Lamb,"

But what will your chagrin and mine be if it shall be told that day on the streets of heaven that on earth we shrank back from all toil and sacrifice and hardship. No scars to show the heavenly soldiery. Not so much as one ridge on the palm of the hand to show that just once in all this battle for God and the truth, we just once grasped the sword so firmly, and struck so hard that the sword and the hand struck together and the hand clave to the sword. O my Lord Jesus, rouse us to Thy service,

"Thy saints in all this glorious war
Shall conquer though they die;

> They see the triumph from afar,
> And seize it with the eye.
>
> "When that illustrious day shall rise,
> And all thy armies shine
> In robes of victory through the skies,
> The glory shall be thine."

WHO ARE IN HEAVEN?

DWELLERS on the Mississippi and Missouri, and in the back woods of Canada and the prairies of the West, are there. Millions from the Andes and the isles of the Pacific, from the mountains of Thibet and the cities of China; from every jungle of India and from every pagoda of Hindostan, the untutored Arab and the uncultivated Druse, and the 'tribes of the weary foot,' the children of Salem are there, * * and Augustine and Luther are there also, and many, we in our uncharitableness, or bigotry, or exclusiveness, or ignorance, excluded from Heaven, will be there also; and our sires and sons and babes and parents will be there, completed circles never again to be broken, and their united voices will give utterance to their deep and enduring gratitude "Unto Him that loved us, and washed us from our sins in His own blood, and that hath made us kings and priests unto God, even the Father; to Him be glory and dominion for ever and ever. Amen."

REV. DR. CUMMING.

ROWLAND HILL said he would be willing to go into heaven if he had to get through the crevices of the door; but he didn't get in that way. When that good man got through his work in Surrey Chapel, a voice in the heavens cried out, "Lift up your heads, ye everlasting gates, and let him come in."

TALMAGE.

FROM GLORY TO GLORY.

H. W. BEECHER.

I DO not expect, the moment I drop this body, to mount up, glowing like a star, into the presence of God, with all the fullness of perfection that I am ever to attain. I expect that through period after period will go on unfolding, that spiritual germ which God has implanted in me. I expect by growth to become really and truly a son of God in those heavenly conditions. I cannot go further in affirming what my state shall be. But I know what happiness is. I know what love is. I know what the devotion of one soul to another is. I know how blessed it is for a person to be lost in one to whom he can look up. I know what it is to have in single hours glimpses of the presence of God. I have had them, that is, as a peasant has some sense of the ocean, who has only seen some inland lake, and cannot, even by a stretch of the imagination, magnify that lake so as to make it the ocean, world-encompassing, and sounding with all the music of its storms. I have had some sight of God; but I know it is like a little lake, as compared with a full vision of the infinite, shoreless, fathomless, measureless ocean of the divine nature. And I shall be amazed, when I see it, that I ever knew anything about it. Yet I shall see it, and not another for me. I shall see God himself. And I shall be satisfied then, for the first time in all my life.

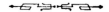

HEAVEN NOT A STRANGE PLACE.

HEAVEN will not be like a strange place, but like a home from which we had been detained; for we shall see, not strangers, but old familiar faces; and faces never by us seen before, will be known instantly by us, by that law of spiritual, subtle recognition by which spirits know each other everywhere, even as they know and are known instantly of God; and heaven will be, in its sights, and sounds, and greetings, a great home gathering to us who enter it.

UNKNOWN.

WHAT MAKES HEAVEN FOR US?

D. L. MOODY.

BUT it won't be the pearly gates; it won't be the jasper walls, and the streets paved with transparent gold, that shall make it heaven for us. These would not satisfy us, If these were all, we would not want to stay there forever. I heard the other day of a child whose mother was very sick; and while she lay very low, one of the neighbors took the child away to stay with her until the mother should be well again. But instead of getting better, the mother died; and they thought they would not take the child home until the funeral was all over; and would never tell her about her mother being dead. So a while afterward they brought the little girl home. First she went into the sitting-room to find her mother; then she went into the parlor, to find her mother there; and she went from one end of the house to the other, and could not find her. At last she said, "Where is my mamma?" And when they told her her mamma was gone, the little thing wanted to go back to the neighbor's house again. Home had lost its attractions to her, since her mother was not there any longer. No; it is not the jasper walls and the pearly gates that are going to make heaven attractive. It is the being with God, We shall be in the presence of the Redeemer; we shall be forever with the Lord.

THEY LOVE US STILL.

They who loved us love us still as we still love, for Christ has made the love of those who are in Him as immortal as themselves; and the re-opening of the interrupted intercourse in the form of re-union will be as welcome and natural as though no weary years of separation had been interspersed.

Blessed love which death cannot kill, which links earth to Heaven, and keeps a spirit in bliss and a man in flesh, still one in indissoluble bonds. Blessed day when it shall give back our lost beloved to our eternal embrace, and as also to theirs, the glorified to the glorified to be forever one.

Rev. J. Oswald Dykes, D. D.

THE BETTER HOME.

REV. DANIEL MOORE, A. M.

AND hallowed as this world is, as the sphere of our probation, the battle-field of victorious saints and the temporary home of God's Son, it is yet to be regarded as our passage to another and better country. "Arise and depart, this is not your rest," for it is marked by vicissitude, disappointment, uncertainty, polluted by wickedness, injustice, impiety. Because your heart troubles you, makes this world a scene of constant disquietude, and draws away from better thoughts and hopes, seek a better country. Let the spirit aspire after a brighter, better home. These patriarchs were persuaded there was such a home. They looked for it, rejoiced in it, lived in anticipation of it, and even had, while here, a blessed foretaste of the country they were seeking.

They looked for a city—its builder was Christ. They looked for a country—its Lord was Christ. They looked for a cleansing from all their pilgrim stains and they found it in Christ. They looked for rest from all their pilgrim toils and they found it in Christ—the tired pilgrim's home, the saint's everlasting rest.

TELEGRAPHING AHEAD TO HEAVEN.

TURN a moment to Paul's epistle to the Philippians, 4th chapter, 3d verse: "And I entreat thee also, true yoke-fellow, help those women which labored with me in the gospel, with Clement, also, and with my other fellow-laborers whose names are in the book of life." Why, it is not only they themselves who know it, but Paul seemed to know their names are there. He sent them greeting, "whose names are in the book of life." My dear friend, is your name there? It seems to me it is a very sweet thought to think we can have our names there and know it; that we can send our names on ahead of us, and know it is written in the book of life.

I had a friend coming back from Europe, some time ago, and she came down with some other Americans from London to Liverpool. On the train down they were talking about the hotel they would stop at. They had got to stay there a day or two before the boat sailed; and so they all concluded to go to the Northwestern Hotel; but when they reached Liverpool, they found that the hotel was completely filled, and had been full for days. Every room was taken, and the party started to go out, but this lady did not go with them; and they asked her, "Why, are you not coming?" "No," said she; "I am going to stay here." "But how? The hotel is full." "Oh," said she, "I have got a room." "How did you get it?" "I telegraphed on a few days ago for one." Yes; she had alone taken pains to telegraph her name on ahead, and had thus secured her room. That is just what God wants you to do. Send your name on ahead. Have your mansion ready for you when you come to die.

D. L. MOODY.

THE GLORIES TO COME.

THE Saxons and the Britons went out to battle. The Saxons were all armed. The Britons had no weapons at all; and yet history tells us the Britons got the victory. Why? They went into battle shouting, three times, "hallelujah!" and at the third shout of "hallelujah" their enemies fled, panic struck; and so the Britons got the victory. And, my friends, if we could only appreciate the glories that are to come, we would be so filled with enthusiasm that no power of earth or hell could stand before us; and at our first shout the opposing forces would begin to tremble, and at our second shout they would begin to fall back, and at our third shout they would be routed forever. There is no power on earth or in hell that could stand before three such volleys of hallelujah.

DR. TALMAGE.

HEAVEN A LOCALITY.

REV. W. H. COOPER, D. D.

I AM at a loss to understand why there should be difficulty in receiving the idea of heaven a locality—a fact of materiality, within the domain of physics, equally positive with the existence of Jupiter or Saturn, Venus or Uranus. The telescope, it is most true, has given wondrous revelations of the magnitude and the magnificence of God's glorious universe; but even that has not been able to reveal the secrets of the milky way, nor to calculate the distances of the nearest of the fixed stars, as the astronomer will tell you. But when we come to think, as is most probably true in fact, that with all the wonders thus laid open to our view—and they are most stupendous—we stand as yet but within the vestibule of God's great temple. Like Newton, we saunter along picking up here and there a pebble from the shore, the great ocean of truth meanwhile lying all unexplored beyond us. I doubt not that, could we but see them, as in prophetic vision, we should behold myriads upon myriads of shining orbs peopling the infinitudes of space, and of which the most accurate of all the sciences has not conceived the most remote idea. Inasmuch, then, as we as yet know nothing in comparison of what yet remains to be revealed to the eye of science, how dare we presume to say that the idea of heaven as a locality is a Utopian figment of the imagination—a mere poetic creation? We have picked up a sand or two from the beach, and say these are all there is of them! We have become slightly acquainted with the wonders of this, our own solar universe, and from *that* premise attempt the impossible feat of proving a negative, predicating the non-existence of any other!

Most assuredly, since God has found place for the worlds we do see, He is of might sufficient to the finding of room in the vast depths of space for the heaven or heavens which at present we do not see?

HEAVEN A HOME CIRCLE.

TALMAGE.

HEAVEN is not a stately, formal place, as I sometimes hear it described, a very frigidity of splendor, where people stand on cold formalities and go around about with heavy crowns of gold on their heads. No, that it is not my idea of heaven. My idea of heaven is more like this.

You are seated in the evening-tide by the fire-place, your whole family there, or nearly all of them there. While you are seated talking and enjoying the evening hour, there is a knock at the door and the door opens, and there comes in a brother that has been long absent. He has been absent, for years you have not seen him, and no sooner do you make up your mind that it is certainly he than you leap up, and the question is who shall give him the first embrace. That is my idea of heaven—a great home circle where they are waiting for us. Oh, will you not know your mothers there? She who always called you by your first name long after others had given you the formal "Mister?" You were never anything but James, or John, or George, or Thomas, or Mary, or Florence to her. Will you not know your child's voice? She of the bright eye, and the ruddy cheek, and the quiet step, who came in from play and flung herself into your lap, a very shower of mirth and beauty? Why, the picture is graven in your soul. It cannot wear out. If that little one should stand on the other side of some heavenly hill and call to you, you would hear her voice above the burst of heaven's great orchestra. Know it! You could not help but know it.

HEAVEN ABOVE US.

Soon after I was converted, an infidel got hold of me one day, and he asked me why I looked up when I prayed. He said that heaven was no more above us than below us, that heaven was everywhere. Well, I was greatly bewildered, and the next time I prayed it did seem as though I was praying into the air. His words had sowed the seed. Since then I have not only become better acquainted with the Bible, but I have come to see that heaven is above us; it is upward. If you will turn to the 17th chapter of Genesis, you will see that it says that God went up from Abraham. In the 3d chapter of John, in the wonderful conversation that Christ had with Nicodemus, he told them that he came down from heaven; and as we read in the 1st chapter of Acts, "They saw him go up into heaven"—not down—"and the clouds received him out of their sight."

D. L. Moody.

NOT WRONG TO SPECULATE ABOUT HEAVEN.

I do not think it is wrong for us to speculate, and think about, and talk about heaven. I was going to meeting once, some time ago, when I was asked by a friend on the way, "What will be the subject of your speech?" I said, "My subject will be heaven." He scowled, and I asked, "Why do you look so?" He said: "I was in hopes you would give us something practical to-night. We cannot know anything about heaven. It is all speculation." Now, all Scripture is given us by the inspiration of God. Some is given for warnings, some for encouragement. If God did not want to think about heaven and talk about it down here, there would not be so much said about heaven in Scripture. There would not be so many promises about it. If we thought more about those mansions God is preparing for us, we would be thinking more of things above, and less of things of this earth.

D. L. Moody.

HEAVEN, GOD'S DWELLING PLACE.

If you will turn to the 8th chapter of 1st Kings, 30th verse, I will show you that God has a dwelling-place. A great many people have gone upon their reason until they have reasoned away God.

They say God is not a person that we can ever see. He is the God of Nature. "And hearken thou to the supplication of thy servant, and of thy people, Israel, when they shall pray towards this place; and hear Thou in heaven, thy dwelling-place, and when Thou hearest, forgive." Some people are trying to find out and wonder how far heaven is away. There is one thing we know about that; it is, that it is not so far away but that God can hear us when we pray. There is not a sigh goes up to him but that he hears it. He hears his children when they cry. God has a throne and a dwelling place in heaven.

D. L. Moody.

WHO ARE FIT FOR HEAVEN.

THE new earth and the new heaven, the state of consummated history, is only for the purified, for those from whom sin is expelled. If any ask, Is that future state for me? the answer is positive, only those over whom sin is losing its power can hope to dwell in that new earth where "God shall wipe away all tears from their eyes." Here is poetry beyond any ever written. It is the triumph of the right, of God. Only those who are ready for an advanced state are profited when the victory is consummated. The emperor only who is ready to lay down his sceptre can profit by a revolution in the interests of the people. It is that master only who is ready to take his slave by the hand as an equal who can profit when emancipation comes. He who resists a change, is crushed when the change takes place. So he only in whom there is now an earnest and continuous endeavor to overthrow sin in the soul will be prepared to profit by the change which will extirpate evil.

Rev. R. S. Stevens, D. D.

WHAT is the heaven our God bestows?
No prophet yet, no angel knows.

John Keble.

AT EVENING TIME IT SHALL BE LIGHT.

THE revolution of years is silently bringing nearer and nearer the evening time of the moral world. God's administration of this world's affairs is approaching a glorious completion. The mystery and darkness that now invest His throne will be dissipated, and his ways shall be justified before the assembled universe. The hands of the clock of time are moving on, slowly and silently, to an hour which shall be universally known and felt, soon as it is reached, as the end of Time. Oh, that last evening time of the world, what pen can adequately picture it? The cloudy day of Providence will end, and in the light of the great white throne of judgment the grandest vindication of His government will be made by Jehovah Himself! The reason and equity of his acts will no longer appear uncertain. A thousand queries, suggested by as many strange things of our present state, will be answered. The prayer of the old reformer, that we offer, now and then as we are brought under darkness, "more light, Lord; more light, more light!" will be granted in a manner that will awe us down into the profoundest attitude of thankfulness.

Then will there be made an adjustment of contrary things. Innocence will be vindicated and rewarded, and guilt exposed and punished. Hypocrisies will be bared to the sight of ten times ten thousand angelic witnesses, and sincerity will lift up its face without a blush. Inequalities of rank and condition will be rectified. Good and evil will be forever separated. Truth and error will dissolve companionship. The right shall be established and the wrong put down. Justice will be administered by One who cannot err. Merit will be recognized and receive its due reward, and mere pretense will be put to shame. Oh! what a clearing away of mists there will be! What startling revelations will be made! And the *finale* of that wonderful scene of the last judgment the voices of ten times ten thousand angels and archangels, joining with the hosts of the saved from earth, shall be heard exclaiming, "Blessing and honor, and power, and glory be unto Him that sitteth upon the throne! Great and marvelous are Thy works, Lord God Almighty, just and true are Thy ways, Thou King of Saints!" REV. W. H. LICKENBACK.

THE CITY OF GOD FOR ME.

REV. R. S. STORRS, D. D.

THERE is a city of God for me. His promises, thick as the fragments of the jasper floor, will all be redeemed. He has prepared for me a city. Kings have reared their cities. Rome sits on her seven hills, and Venice on her lagoon, the Queen of the Adriatic; Naples on her crescent bay, Paris on the Seine, and Vienna on the Blue Danube. But in the city "not made with hands," God has combined all beauty and opulences suited to a spiritual body. There will be song and worship, work and rest. The expectation of it has given a lustre to many a humble life and the death-bed. It is our privilege to walk in the light of this inspiring hope. In all our study and labor, in all our joy and gloom, let this eternal, illuminating truth of the lordship of God and his public presidency over all events interpret every mystery, for "all these come forth from the Lord of hosts, wonderful in counsel and excellent in working."

THERE comes the thought of glory,
  To which our friends are gone;
The far surpassing glory,
  Beyond what earth has known.
Estate of light and gladness,
  Where tears are wiped away;
The joy in blessed fullness
  Of everlasting day.

THE REV. JOHN KEBLE.

JESUS INTERCEDING IN HEAVEN.

REV. WM. ORMISTON, D. D.

CHRIST has not entered into the holy places made with hands which are the figures of the true, but into heaven itself, now to appear in the presence of God for us." Jesus, whom the disciples knew, whom they recognized after His resurrection, and who ascended in their presence, is now, in our nature, in the heavenly sanctuary. In the midst of the throne—that is, between the worshiper and the throne—He is seen as "a lamb, as it had been slain." These words are affectingly mysterious, yet profoundly significant. We learn that after His resurrection, He bore the marks of his crucifixion; and it may be that his human form retains them now, and ever will. His appearance in the presence of God for us was typified by the entrance of the high-priest within the veil, on the great day of atonement, bearing in one hand the blood of sprinkling, and in the other the censer of sweet incense. "For, Christ being come a high-priest of good things to come by a greater and more perfect tabernacle, not made with hands—that is, not of this building, neither by the blood of goats and calves, but by His own blood—He entered in, once, into the holy place, having obtained eternal redemption for us."

CITIZENS OF HEAVEN

AND when now the dignified forms of another world appeared before their raptured vision, when they beheld the pillars of the old covenant in conversation with Jesus—namely, the majestic lawgiver, Moses, and the mighty prophet, Elijah—must they not have felt already as the citizens of another and higher sphere, as members of that blessed assembly of the just who are gathered on the other side, at home with the Lord? In such company it is no wonder that Peter exclaimed in ecstacy: "It is good for us to be here." It seemed to him as if he was greeted with the salutation of the world to come: "Now, therefore, we are no more strangers and foreigners, but fellow citizens with the saints, and of the household of God." (Eph. ii: 19.

CHARLES GEROK, D. D., (*Germany*.)

VIEWS OF HEAVEN CHANGED.

AN EMINENT LIVING DIVINE QUOTED BY MOODY.

When I was a boy, I thought of heaven as a great, shining city, with vast walls and domes and spires, and with nobody in it except white-robed angels, who were strangers to me. By and by my little brother died; and I thought of a great city with walls and domes and spires, and a flock of cold, unknown angels, and one little fellow that I was acquainted with. He was the only one I knew at that time. Then another brother died; and there were two that I knew. Then my acquaintances began to die; and the flock continually grew. But it was not till I had sent one of my little children to his Heavenly Parent—God—that I began to think I had got a little in myself. A second went, a third went; a fourth went; and by that time I had so many acquaintances in heaven, that I did not see any more walls and domes and spires. I began to think of the residents of the celestial city. And now there have so many of my acquaintances gone there, that it sometimes seems to me that I know more in heaven than I do on earth.

THE ARISTOCRACY OF HEAVEN.

The society of heaven will be select. No one who studies Scripture can doubt that. There are a good many kinds of aristocracy in this world, but the aristocracy of heaven will be the aristocracy of holiness. The humblest sinner on earth will be an aristocrat there. It says in the fifty-seventh chapter of Isaiah: For thus saith the High and Lofty One, that inhabiteth eternity, whose name is holy: I will dwell in the high and holy place with him that is of a contrite and humble spirit. Now what could be plainer than that? No one that is not of a contrite and humble spirit will dwell with God in His high holy place.

D. L. Moody.

"Good servant, well done;
Come enter thy home, these mansions above."

THE HEAVENLY CITY.

D. L. MOODY.

HEAVEN is God's habitation, and when Christ came on earth He taught us to pray: "Our Father which art in heaven." This habitation is called "the city of eternal life." Think of a city without a cemetery—they have no dying there. If there could be such a city as that found on this earth what a rush there would be to it! How men would seek to get into that city! You can't find one on the face of this earth. A city without tears—God wipes away all the tears up yonder. This is a time of weeping, but by and by there is a time coming when God shall call us where there will be no tears. A city without pain, a city without sorrow, without sickness, without death. There is no darkness there. The lamb is the light thereof. It needs no sun, it needs no moon. The paradise of Eden was as nothing compared with this one. The tempter came into Eden and triumphed, but in that city nothing that defileth shall ever enter. There will be no tempter there. Think of a place where temptation cannot come. Think of a place where we will be free from sin; where pollution cannot enter, and where the righteous shall reign forever. Think of a city that is not built with hands, where the buildings do not grow old with time; a city whose inhabitants no census has numbered except the Book of Life, which is the heavenly directory. Think of a city through whose streets runs no tide of business, where no nodding hearses creep slowly with their burdens to the tomb; a city without griefs or graves, without sins or sorrows, without marriages or mournings, without births or burials; a city which glories in having Jesus for its king, angels for its guards, and whose citizens are saints!

We believe this is just as much a place and just as much a city as New York is, or London or Paris. We believe in it a good deal more, because earthly cities will pass away, but this city will remain forever. It has foundations whose builder and maker is God. Some of the grandest cities the world has ever known did not have foundations strong enough to last.

THE "OPEN SESAME" TO HEAVEN.

If there is one sound above another that will swing open the eternal gates, it is the name of Jesus. There are a great many passwords and by-words down here, but that will be the countersign up above. Jesus Christ is the "Open Sesame" to heaven. Any one that tries to climb up some other way, is a thief and a robber. But when we get in, what a joy above every other joy we can think of, it will be to see Jesus Himself all the time, and to be with him continually.

Isaiah has given his promise of God to every one that is saved through faith: Thine eyes shall see the King in his beauty; they shall behold the land that is very far off. Some of us may not be able to get around the world. We may not be able to see any of the foreign countries; but every Christian by and by is going to see a land that is very far off. This is our Promised Land. John Milton says of the saints that have gone already:

"They walk with God
High in salvation, and the climes of bliss."

D. L. MOODY.

JESUS IN HEAVEN.

Dr. Dick said that in heaven he expected to study chemistry. Dr. Southey longed to meet Shakespeare and Milton and Dante. Dr. Dick may have his Conic Sections, and Dr. Southey his Shakespeares and Miltons; all I will want will be the company of Jesus and my dear friends on earth, and to know that forever I am safe.

REV. DR. TALMAGE.

"A home in heaven! what a joyful thought
As the poor man toils in his weary lot!"

HEAVEN SOUGHT THROUGH TROUBLE.

REV. T. DE WITT TALMAGE, D. D.

WHAT is the use of an eastern storm when we might have a perpetual nor'-wester? Why, when a family is put together, not have them all stay, or if they must be transplanted to make other homes, then have them all live? the family record telling a story of marriages and births, but of no deaths. Why not have the harvests chase each other without fatiguing toil, and all our homes afflicted? Why the hard pillow, the hard crust, the hard struggle? It is easy enough to explain a smile, or a success, or a congratulation; but, come now, and bring all your dictionaries and all your philosophies and all your religions, and help me this evening to explain a tear. A chemist will tell you that it is made up of salt and lime, and other component parts, but he misses the chief ingredients—the acid of a soured life, the viperan sting of a bitter memory, the fragments of a broken heart. I will tell you what a tear is; it is agony in solution.

Hear me, then, while I discourse to you of the ministry of tears, and of the ending of that ministry when God shall wipe them all away.

If it were not for trouble, this world would be a good enough heaven for me. You and I would be willing to take a lease of this life for a hundred million years, if there were no trouble.

The earth cushioned and upholstered and pillared and chandeliered with such expense, no story of other worlds could enchant us. We would say: "Let well enough alone. If you want to die and have your body disintegrated in the dust, and your soul go out on a celestial adventure, then you can go; but this world is good enough for me." You might as well go to a man who has just entered the Louvre at Paris, and tell him to hasten off to the picture galleries of Venice or Florence. "Why," he would say, "what is the use of my going there? There are Rembrandts and Rubens and Raphaels here that I havon't looked at yet." No man wants to go out of this world, or out of any house until he has a better house.

After a man has had a good deal of trouble, he says, "Well, I am ready to go. If there is a house somewhere whose roof doesn't leak, I would like to live there. If there is an atmosphere somewhere that does not distress the lungs, I would like to breathe it. If there is a society somewhere where there is no tittle-tattle, I would like to live there. If there is a home-circle somewhere where I can find my lost friends, I would like to go there." He used to read the first part of the Bible chiefly, now he reads the last part of the Bible chiefly. Why has he changed Genesis for Revelation? Ah! he used to be anxious chiefly to know how this world was made, and all about its geological construction. Now he is chiefly anxious to know how the next world was made, and how it looks, and who live there, and how they dress. He reads Revelation ten times now where he reads Genesis once. The old story, "In the beginning God created the heavens and the earth," does not thrill him half as much as the other story, "I saw a new heaven and a new earth." The old man's hand trembles as he turns over this apocalyptic leaf, and he has to take out his handkerchief to wipe his spectacles. That book of Revelation is a prospectus now of the country into which he is to soon immigrate; the country in which he has lots already laid out, and avenues opened, and tress planted, and mansions built. The thought of that blessed place comes over me mightily, and I declare that if this house were a great ship, and you all were passengers on board it, and one hand could launch that ship into the glories of heaven, I should be tempted to take the responsibility, and launch you all into glory with one stroke, holding on to the side of the boat until I could get in myself! And yet there are people here to whom this world is brighter than heaven. Well, dear souls, I do not blame you. It is natural. But, after a while, you will be ready to go. It was not until Job had been worn out with bereavements and carbuncles and a pest of a wife that he wanted to see God. It was not until the prodigal got tired of living among the hogs that he wanted to go to his father's house. It is the ministry of trouble to make this world worth less, and heaven worth more.

PROGRESSION IN HEAVEN.

REV. D. M. REID.

THE soul will have a progressive life there. This is its present nature. Begin with it as you find in the infant, and watch it until it attains the power and brilliancy of a Newton's or Shakespeare, and have you not sufficient evidence that it is a progressive entity? It will continue thus.

There will, however, be one striking difference between its progress here and its progress on the higher fields of its endeavors. While here it encounters many things which check it in its outfoldings; hereafter it will be free from such bafflements, be enabled to achieve more rapid advancements, and more brilliant. Here it is tempted to sin; there it will not be, for the centre of temptations is in the material nature, and that is to be discarded. When temptation ceases sin must cease.

The future life may be represented as an inclined plane, on whose radiant surface all souls shall ascend farther and farther as eternity rolls along its immense cycles. Over it will hang the holy, genial, inspiring presence of God: across it float winds freighted with heaven's aromas; into its meandering avenues fall the light of the Infinite Love, and out of its crystal fountains gush waters of rarest sweetness. No tear of grief shall fall on its fadeless flowers, no world of unkindness disturb its placid air, no sighs of suffering blend with its seraphic music, and no discord sweep in the midst of its blessed harmonies.

If I may stand before His throne,
And look upon His face,
What shall I care that oft, alone,
Like Him, I ran my race.

Safe on thy ever blissful plains,
My heart's own treasure gathered there;
Farewell, forever, sins and pains,
Farewell, bereavement, sorrow, care!

C. HUNTINGTON.

THE REV. F. W. FARRAR, D. D.
(CANON OF WESTMINSTER.)

THE SAINTS' VIEWS OF HEAVEN.

THE BEAUTIFUL GATES AJAR.

HANNAH MORE.

THIS noble woman, before her death, said:—"It pleases God to afflict me, not for His pleasure, but to do me good, to make me humble and thankful. Lord, I believe; I do believe with all the power of my weak sinful heart! Lord Jesus, look down upon me from Thy holy habitation, strengthen my faith, and quicken me in my preparation! Support me in that trying hour when I most need it! It is a glorious thing to die!' When one talked to her of her good deeds, she said, 'Talk not so vainly—I utterly cast them from me, and fall low at the foot of the cross.'"

> Since the dear hour that brought me to thy foot,
> And cut up all my follies by the root,
> I never trusted in an arm but thine;
> Nor hoped but in thy righteousness Divine,
> My prayers and alms, imperfect and defiled,
> Were but the feeble efforts of a child;
> Howe'er perform'd, this was their brightest part,
> That they were offerings of a thankful heart;
> I cast them at thy feet, my only plea
> Is, what it was,—dependence upon thee;
> While struggling in the vale of griefs below,
> This never failed, nor shall it fail me now."
>
> COWPER.

HARRIET NEWELL.

THE husband of Harriet Newell says:—"When I told her that she could not live through the day, she replied, 'O joyful news! I long to depart.' Some time after, I asked her, 'How does death appear to you now?' She replied, 'Glorious; truly welcome.' During Sabbath night she seemed to be a little wandering; but the next morning she had her recollection perfectly. As I stood by her, I asked her if she knew me. At first she made no answer. I said to her again, 'My dear Harriet, do you not know who I am?'

"'My dear Mr. Newell, my husband,' was her reply; but in broken accents, and a voice faltering in death."

> "Was this then death?
> O soft, yet sudden change, what shall I call thee?
> No more—no more thy name be 'death. And thou,
> Corruption's dreaded power, how changed to joy?
> Sleep, then, companion of my first existence,
> Seed sown by God to ripen for the harvest."
>
> BULMER'S MESSIAH.

REV. DAVID SIMPSON.

AS the strength of the author of "A Plea for Religion and the Sacred Writings" declined apace, he was soon unfit to see any of his friends but his immediate attendants, who had now given up all hope of his recovery. The violence of the fever acting on his enfeebled system, had left only the ruins of a noble mind. He spoke much of the glories of heaven, and the happiness of separate spirits; of their robes of righteousness, and their palms of victory; then, breathing his ardent wishes for the happiness of all who were present, he added, "Pardon, peace, and everlasting felicity, are desirable things."

> "The soul, reposing on assured relief,
> Feels herself happy amidst all her grief;
> Forgets her labor as she toils along,
> Weeps tears of joy, and bursts into a song."

HENRY MARTYN.

TEN days before his death, in Persia, he said, "O when shall time give place to eternity! When shall appear that new heaven and new earth wherein dwelleth righteousness! There—there shall in no wise enter in anything that defileth: none of that wickedness that has made men worse than wild beasts—none of those corruptions that add still more to the miseries of mortality, shall be seen or heard of any more."

" See the guardian angels nigh
Wait to waft my soul on high!
See the golden gates display'd!
See the crown to grace my head!
See a flood of sacred light,
Which shall yield no more to night!
Transitory world, farewell!
Jesus calls with him to dwell."

RICHARD BAXTER.

HE said to a friend the day before he died, "I have pain, there is no arguing against sense; but I have peace, I have peace." His friend replied, "You are now approaching your long desired home." He answered, "I believe, I believe." As he approached near his end, when asked how he did, his usual reply was, "Almost well." And when, in his own apprehension, death was nearest, his joy was most remarkable. The long wished for hour at length arrived, and in his own expressive language, he became "entirely well."

" Stronger by weakness, wiser men become
As they draw near to their eternal home;
Leaving the old, both worlds at once they view,
Who stand upon the threshold of the new."

WALLER.

REV. WILBUR FISK, D. D.

AT one time, after a fruitless effort to lie down, he said:—"I have always thought I should have a lingering sickness, but an easy death. I would like to have my bed my dying pillow, but my Savior died on the cross." He then repeated the stanza, commencing,

"How bitter that cup,"

and ending,

"Did *Jesus* thus suffer, and shall *I* repine?"

At another time, when nature seemed exhausted and life was fast ebbing out, as he was lifted from the bed to his chair, he sighed forth, "From the chair to the throne!" A friend said:

"You suffer a great deal of distress, sir, from fatigue and exhaustion; but it must be over soon, and how sweet is rest to a weary man! There is a place 'where the wicked cease from troubling, and the weary are at rest.'" He responded distinctly, "Bless God for that!" When he was still further sunk into coma, the same friend coming into the room, said, "I have come to see you again, sir; do you know me?" Pressing his hand, he said in a whisper, "Yes; glorious hope!" After this, when Mrs. Fisk took his hand and inquired if he knew her, he returned the pressure, saying, "Yes, love; yes."

"Like a shadow thrown
Softly and lightly from a passing cloud,
Death fell upon him."
WORDSWORTH.

LORD BACON.

LORD BACON breathed this prayer before death:—"Thy creatures, O Lord, have been my books, but thy holy Scriptures much more. I have sought Thee in the courts, fields, and gardens; but I have found Thee, O God, in thy sanctuary, thy temples."

"O what new life I feel!
Being of beings, how I rise! Not one,
A thousand steps I rise! And yet I feel
Advancing still in glory—I shall soar
Above these thousand steps. Near and more near
(Nor in his works alone, these beauteous worlds)
I shall behold the Eternal face to face."
BULMER'S MESSIAH.

REV. RICHARD WATSON.

"THERE is no rest or satisfaction for the soul but in God—my God. I am permitted to call him *my* God. O God, thou art my God, early will I seek thee: my soul thirsteth for thee, my flesh longeth for thee, in a dry and thirsty land where no water is."

"At another time, in a state of deep feeling, he said, 'When shall my soul leave this tenement of clay, to join in the wide expanse of the skies, and rise to nobler joys and to see God?' In a happy state of mind he burst forth but a short time before he was deprived of the power of connected speech, and exclaimed, 'We shall see strange sights to-day; not different, however, from what we might realize by faith; but it is not the glitter and glare, not the topaz and diamond; no, it is God I want to see; He is all and in all.'"

"The festal morn, my God, is come,
That calls me to thy hallow'd dome."

ZWINGER.

SAMUEL RUTHERFORD.

In Rutherford's last moments he said to the ministers around him, "There is none like Christ. O, dear brethren, pray for Christ, preach for Christ, do all for Christ; feed the flock of God. And O, beware of men-pleasing." Having recovered from a fainting fit, he said, "I feel, I feel, I believe, I joy, I rejoice, I feed on manna; my eyes shall see my Redeemer, and I shall be ever with him. And what would you more? I have been a sinful man; but I stand at the best pass that ever a man did. Christ is mine and I am his. Glory, glory to my Creator and Redeemer forever. Glory shines in Immanuel's land. O for arms to embrace him! O for a well-tuned harp!"

"More I would ask, but all my words are faint,
Celestial Love, what eloquence can paint?
No more by mortal words can be express'd;
But vast eternity shall tell the rest."

MRS. ROWE.

MR. M'LAREN, OF EDINBURGH.

When Mr. M'Laren was dying, Mr. Gustart his associate pastor, paid him a visit, and inquired of him, "What are you now doing, my brother?" The strong and earnest response of the dying minister was, "I'll tell you what I am doing, brother; I am gathering together all my prayers, all my sermons, all my good deeds, all my ill deeds; and I am going to throw them all overboard, and swim to glory on the single plank of free grace."

> "This—only this subdues the fear of death;
> And what is this?—Survey the wondrous cure;
> And at each step, let higher wonder rise!
> Pardon for infinite offence! * * *
> A pardon bought with blood!—with blood divine!"
>
> Young.

REV. S. R. BANGS.

He looked out at the window: "The sun," said he, "is setting, mine is rising." Then, with a look of heavenly delight, he gazed upon his hands, where the blood was already ceasing to circulate. "I go from this bed to a crown," cried he, with his right arm pointing upward; "farewell;" laid his hands upon his breast, gasped and expired.

> "Whence this brave bound o'er limits fixed to man?
> His God sustains him in his final hour!
> We gaze; we weep; mix tears of grief and joy!
> Amazement strikes! devotion bursts to flame!
> Christians adore! and infidels believe!"
>
> Young.

> "And O, when I have safely pass'd
> Through every conflict but the last,
> Still, still unchanging, watch beside
> My bed of death, for Thou hast died."
>
> Grant.

> "A path that must be trod,
> If man would ever pass to God."

JOHN HOWARD.

A LITTLE before the last time of John Howard's leaving England, when a friend expressed his concern at parting with him, from an apprehension that they should never meet again he cheerfully replied: "We shall soon meet in heaven;" and as he rather expected to die of the plague in Egypt, he added: "The way to heaven from Grand Cairo is as near as from London." He said he was perfectly easy as to the event, and made use of the words of Father Paul, who when his physicians told him he had not long to live, said, "It is well; whatever pleases God pleases me."

> " Howard, thy task is done, thy Master calls,
> And summons thee from Cherson's distant walls;—
> 'Come, well-approved, my faithful servant come.
> My minister of good, I've sped the way,
> And shot through dungeon glooms a leading ray;
> I've led thee on through wondering climes,
> To combat human woes and human crimes;
> But 'tis enough,—thy great commission's o'er;
> I prove thy faith, thy love, thy zeal no more.'"
>
> AIKEN.

> " If in that name no deathless spirit dwell,
> If that faint murmur be the last farewell,
> If faith unite the faithful but to part,
> Why is their memory sacred to the heart?"
>
> CAMPBELL.

> "Time is eternity;
> Pregnant with all eternity can give,
> Pregnant with all that makes archangels smile."
>
> YOUNG.

> " That sov'reign Plant, whose scions shoot
> With healing virtue, and immortal fruit,—
> The Tree of Life, beside the stream that laves
> The fields of Paradise with gladdening waves."

STRASBURG CATHEDRAL.

VARIOUS VIEWS OF FUTURE HAPPINESS.

When the ancients applied the term "god" to a human soul departed from the body, it was not used as the moderns prevailingly employ that word. It expressed a great deal less with them than with us. It merely meant to affirm similarity of essence, qualities and residence, but by no means equal dignity and power of attributes between the one and the other. It meant that the soul had gone to the heavenly habitation of the gods and was thenceforth a participant in the heavenly life.

Heraclitus was accustomed to say, "Men are mortal gods; gods are immortal men," Macrobius says, "The soul is not only immortal, but a god." And Cicero declares, "The soul of man is a Divine thing,—as Euripides dares to say, a god." Milton uses language precisely parallel, speaking of those who are "unmindful of the crown true Virtue gives her servants, after their mortal change, among the enthroned gods on sainted seats." Theophilus, Bishop of Antioch in the second century, says that " to become a god means to ascend into heaven."

Virgil, celebrating the death of some person under the fictitious name of Daphnis, exclaims, "Robed in white, he admires the strange court of heaven, and sees the clouds and the stars beneath his feet. He is a god now." Porphyry ascribes to Pythagoras the declaration that the souls of departed men are gathered in the zodiac. Plato earnestly describes a region of brightness and unfading realities above this lower world, among the stars, where the gods live, and whither, he says, the virtuous and wise may ascend, while the corrupt and ignorant must sink into the Tartarean realm.

The Emperor Julian says, in his Letter on the Duties of a Priest, "God will raise from darkness and Tartarus the souls of all of us who worship him sincerely: to the pious, instead of Tartarus he promises Olympus." "It is lawful," writes Plato, "only for the true lover of wisdom to pass into the rank of gods."

In a tragedy of Euripides the following passage occurs, addressed to the bereaved Admetus:—"Let not the tomb of thy wife be looked on as the mound of the ordinary dead. Some wayfarer, as he treads the sloping road, shall say, 'This woman once died for her husband; but now she is a saint in heaven.'" W. R. ALGER.

ENOCH was probably a prophet authorized to announce the reality of another life after this; and he might be removed into it without dying, as an evidence of the truth of his doctrine.

DR. PRIESTLY.

A SIMILITUDE drawn from the resurrection, to foreshadow the restoration of the people of Israel, would never have been employed unless the resurrection itself were believed to be a fact of future occurrence; for no one thinks of confirming what is uncertain by what has no existence. JEROME.

MONEY CANNOT BUY HEAVEN.

LET us recognize the fact, however, that while there is a lawful and profitable use of it, money cannot satisfy a man's soul. It cannot pay our fare across the Jordan of death. It cannot unlock the gate of heaven. Salvation by Christ is the only salvation. Treasures in heaven are the only incorruptible treasures. However fine your apparel, the winds of death will flutter it like rags. A homespun and threadbare coat has sometimes been the shadow of coming robes made white by the blood of the Lamb. Oh, my dear hearers, whatever you lose, though your house go, though all your earthly possessions go—may God Almighty, through the blood of the everlasting covenant, save all your souls! "What is a man profited if he shall gain the whole world, and lose his own soul?"

TALMAGE.

MANY MANSIONS.

WHY has God "broken up the solid material of the universe into innumerable little globes, and swung each of them into the centre of an impassable solitude of space," unless it be to train up in the various spheres separate households for final union as a single diversified family in the boundless spiritual world?

ISAAC TAYLOR.

JOY IN HEAVEN.

D. L. MOODY.

THERE is joy in heaven, we are told, over the conversions that take place on earth. In the 15th chapter of Luke and the 7th verse we read: "I say unto you that likewise joy shall be in heaven over one sinner that repenteth, more than over ninety-and-nine just persons which need no repentance." If there was going to be an election for President of the United States, there would be tremendous excitement—a great commotion. There is probably not a paper from Maine to California that would not have something on nearly every page about the candidate: the whole country would be excited; but I doubt if it would be noticed in heaven; I doubt if they would take any note of it at all, If Queen Victoria should leave her throne, there would be great excitement throughout the nations of the earth; the whole world would be interested in the event; it would be telegraphed around the world; but it would probably be overlooked altogether in heaven. Yet if one little boy or one little girl, one man or one woman should repent of their sins, this day and hour that would be noticed in heaven. They look at things differently up there; things that look very large to us, look very small in heaven; and things that seem very small to us down here, may be very great up yonder. Think of it! By an act of our own, we may cause joy in heaven. The thought seems almost too wonderful to take in. To think that the poorest sinner on earth, by an act of his own, can send a thrill of joy through the hosts of heaven!

The Bible says: "There is joy in the presence of the angels," not that the angels rejoice, but it is "in the presence" of angels. I have studied over that a great deal, and often wondered what it meant. "Joy in the presence of the angels?" Now, it is speculation; it may be true, or it may not; but perhaps the friends who have left the shores of time—they who have gone within the fold—may be looking down upon us; and when they see one they prayed for while on earth repenting and turning to God, it sends a thrill of joy to their very hearts. Even now, some mother who has gone up there may be looking down upon a son or daughter, and if that child should say : "I will meet that mother of mine ; I will repent ; yes, I am going to join you, mother," the news, with the speed of a sunbeam reaches heaven, and that mother may then rejoice, as we read, "In the presence of the angels."

HEAVEN AND ETERNAL LIFE.

REV. WM. MORLEY PUNSHON D. D.

THAT word, *life* is always music—that word, next to the word "God in Christ," has in it the deepest meaning in the world. Let us cross the flood where that life especially is, whose path the Savior is to show, the mansions which he has gone to prepare. Jesus is called, "The true God and eternal life." What is this eternal life, which is held before the believer's eye, and chartered as his privilege ?

This life is conscious ; death cannot for one moment paralyze the soul. Paul said it was "far better to depart." He knew the moment he was released from mortality he should be with Christ There is no moment's interval of slumber for the soul—we do not cease to be. We only change the conditions of our being. There is no human soul, which from the day of Adam until now has ever dwelt in clay ; that is, not *alive to-day!* It is a conscious world into which we are passing.

Again; heaven is not a solitude. It is a peopled city—where there are no strangers, no homeless, no poor, where one does not pass another in the street without greeting, where no one is envious of another's superior minstrelsy or of another's more brilliant crown. They are not only with the Savior, but with the "General Assembly," and with "the spirits of the just made perfect ;" all affections are pure, all enjoy conscious recognition, all abide in perpetual recognition, abide in perpetual reunion, in a home without a discord, without an illness, without a grave.

Take comfort, then ; those from whom you have parted or whom you shall have soon to separate, shall be your companions again, recognized as of old, and loved with a purer love.

The resurrection and the life—what heart is not thrilled with the preciousness of the promise—who does not feel more grateful to the Redeemer, who brings him life ? Enjoyed recompense, recovered friends—there for ever and Jesus with us there !

NEW POWERS IN HEAVEN.

CHRIST's presence with His saints constitutes a pledge that their powers will be adopted to their new condition, and that the loftiest sources of enjoyment will be opened for their participation. These bodily and mental capacities with which man was originally endowed by God, were grievously impaired through the entrance of sin into the world. But in that blessed world, the spirit will be made capable of wondrous discoveries as to the works and ways of God, of enraptured contemplation on the plan of Providence, and out of the riches of His goodness, and the boundless treasures of His love, will have every desire satisfied, and will have fresh sources of delight continually abounding. How decided and full must the happiness of the Saint be, when he has taken possession of the kingdom prepared for him from the beginning of the world, when he "shall be for ever with the Lord."

REV. ANDREW R. BONAR, D. D.

MARTYRS IN HEAVEN.

REV. T. DEWITT TALMAGE.

ERE pass the regiment of Christian *martyrs*. They endured all things for Christ. They were hounded; they were sawn asunder; they were hurled out of life. Here come the eighteen thousand Scotch Covenanters who perished in one persecution. Escaped from the clutches of Claverhouse, and bloody McKenzie, and the horrors of the Grass Market, they ride in the great battalion of Scotch martyrs.

Hugh McKail, and James Renwick, and John Knox, and others whose words are a battle-shout for the church militant—men of high cheek bones, and strong arms, and concentrated spirits. Greyfriars church-yard took some of their bodies, but heaven took all their souls. They went on weary feet through the glens of Scotland in times of persecution, and crawled up the crags on their hands and knees; but now follow the Christ for whom they fought and bled, on white horses of triumph. Ride on ye conquerors! Victors of Dunottar Castle, and Bass Rock: and Rutherglen! Ride on!

Here comes the Regiment of *English Martyrs*. Queen Mary against King Jesus made an even fight. The twenty thousand chariots of God coming down the steep of heaven will ride over any foe. Queen Mary thought that by sword and fire she had driven Protestants down, but she only drove them up. Here they pass: Bishop Hooper, and Rogers, Prebendary of St. Paul's; and Archbishop Cramer, who got his courage back in time to save his soul; and Anne Askew, who, at twenty-five years of age, rather than forsake her God, submitted first to the rack without a groan, and then went with bones so dislocated she must be carried on a chair to the stake, her last words rising through the flames being a prayer for her murderers. O cavalcade of men and women, whom God snatched up from the iron fingers of torture into eternal life! Ride on, thou glorious regiment of English martyrs!

Look at this advancing host of a hundred thousand. Who are they? Look upon the flag, and upon their uniform, and tell us. They are the Protestants who fell on St. Bartholomew's Day in Paris, in Lyons, in Orleans, in Bordeaux, while the king looked out of the window and cried, "Kill! Kill!" Oh, what a night, followed by what a day! Who would think that these on white horses were tossed out of windows, and manacled, and torn, and dragged, and slain, until it seemed that the cause of God had perished, and cities were illuminated with infernal joy, and the cannon of St. Angelo thundered the triumph of hell! Their gashed and bespattered bodies were thrown into the Seine, but their souls went up out of a nation's shriek into the light of God; and now they pass along the boulevards of heaven

" Soldier of God, well done!
Rest be thy loved employ;
And while eternal ages run,
Rest in thy Master's joy."

Ride on ye, mounted troops of St. Bartholomew's Day!

NO NIGHT IN HEAVEN.

REV. R. W. CLARK, D. D.

IS it not a blessed announcement that there is a world in which "there shall be no night;"—no night of crime, deceit, treachery or temptation; no night of sorrow or ignorance; no night of pain, sickness or death. O, tell it to the penitent, who is struggling against the evil habits and depraved inclinations of a wicked heart,—who, on life's fierce battle-field, is striving to win an immortal crown! Tell it to the dying man, who, restless upon his couch, through long, wearisome nights, is trying to learn the lessons of submission, and faith, and moral discipline, which his sufferings are teaching,—who longs for light to break through the dark clouds that are gathering about him! Hasten with the tidings to the bereaved family, and assure them that there is a world where these griefs shall be lifted from their oppressed spirits, and their present afflictions, if rightly improved, shall work out of them "a far more exceeding and eternal weight of glory." For where God is, there can be no night. Where bright, holy angels throng, there can be no sorrow. Where celestial music rolls through the galleries and arches of temples filled with the effulgence of the Deity, there can be no sighing. Where Jesus reigns in his majesty and glory, " all tears shall be wiped away."

No night in heaven! Then no sad partings are experienced there;—no funeral processions move, no death-knell is heard, no graves are opened. Then no mysterious providences will there perplex us, no dark calamities will shake our faith; but we shall walk the golden streets of the eternal city, surrounded with perpetual brightness, breathing an atmosphere of heavenly purity, and free to enter the palaces of our King or climb to heights over which no shadow ever passes.

Henry Kirke White

WORSHIP IN HEAVEN.

REV. RICHARD WATSON.

PART of the felicity of the saints in heaven shall consist in the worship of God.

And who would wish it otherwise? Could we find a man who would exclude from his idea of this place of blessedness, the eternal, ceaseless worship of his God, I would deny to him all claim to a single ennobling thought: that by itself would prove his total want of preparation for the kingdom of God. But it is not so; the tabernacle of God is with men, and to that they shall bring the homage of their hearts, and the tribute of their praises. So in the tabernacle of old; the sin-offerings, the peace-offerings, the thank-offerings, were all brought there; and with a variety of instruments and voices the praises of God were there sung. There, especially, were sung the songs which the sweet psalmist received from the inspiring Spirit; songs, indeed, containing " thoughts that breathe and words that burn," and which to our own day retain all their animation and power. It was this which made David say, " A day in thy courts is better than a thousand. I had rather be a doorkeeper in the house of my God, than dwell in the tents of wickedness." And, when distant from it, he envied even the birds which found shelter in the sanctuary, were covered by its shadow and cheered by its sounds. And have we not felt the inspiration of worship ourselves? Wherever God is devoutly adored, feelings at once the strongest and the richest are called forth, from

> ' The speechless awe which dares not move,
> And all the silent heaven of love,"

to the thanksgivings which break from a heart overcharged with its grateful recollections.

These are the feelings which are to be brightened and perfected in heaven. The worship there shall be ceaseless and eternal; and it is an interesting view of it, that it shall be all praise. No prayer shall be here, for there shall be no sense of want; all is praise, for all is manifestation and light; all is praise, for all is triumph; all is praise, for all is blessedness and enjoyment. Whatever the feeling, praise, eternal praise, is the expression of it, from the breathing whisper of adoring love which flits through the prostrate ranks of the redeemed, to the full chorus of praise, the high, the universal shout of glory, and honor, and blessing, to him that sitteth upon the throne, and to the Lamb forever.

THE SOUL'S POWER IN HEAVEN.

REV. HORACE BUSHNELL, D. D.

WE exist here only in the small, that God may have us in a state of flexibility, and bend or fashion us, at the best advantage, to the model of his own great life and character. And most of us, therefore, have scarcely a conception of the exceeding weight of glory to be comprehended in our existence. If we take, for example, the faculty of memory, how very obvious is it that, as we pass eternally on, we shall have more and more to remember, and finally shall have gathered more into this great storehouse of the soul than is now contained in all the libraries of the world. And there is not one of our faculties that has not, in its volume, a similar power of expansion. Indeed, if it were not so, the memory would finally overflow and drown all our other faculties. and the spirits, instead of being powers, would virtually cease to be anything more than registers of the past.

But we are obliged to take our conclusion by inference. We can see for ourselves that the associations of the mind, which are a great part of its riches, must be increasing in number and variety forever, stimulating thought by multiplying its suggestives, and beautifying thought by weaving into it the colors of sentiment endlessly varied.

The imagination is gathering in its images and kindling its eternal fires in the same manner. Having passed through many trains of worlds, mixing with scenes, societies, orders of intelligence and powers of beatitude—just that which made the apostle in Patmos into a poet by the visions of a single day—it is impossible that every soul should not finally become filled with a glorious and powerful imagery, and be waked to a wonderfully creative energy.

By the supposition it is another incident of this power of endless life, that, passing down the eternal galleries of fact and event, it must be forever having new cognitions and accumulating new premises. By its own contacts it will, at some future time, have touched even whole worlds and felt them through, and made promises of all there is in them. It will know God by experiences correspondingly enlarged, and itself by a consciousness correspondingly illuminated, Having gathered in, at last, such worlds of premises. it is difficult for us now to conceive the vigor into which a soul may come, or the volume it may exhibit, the wonderful depth and scope of its judgments, its rapidity and certainty, and the vastness of its generalizations. It passes over more and more, and that necessarily, from the condition of a creature gathering up premises, into the condition of God, creating out of premises; for if it is not actually set to the creation of worlds, its very thoughts will be a discoursing in world-problems and theories equally vast in their complications.

In the same manner, the executive energy of the will, the volume of the benevolent affections, and all the active powers, will be showing. more and more impressively, what is to be a power of endless life. They that have been swift in doing God's will and fulfilling his mighty errands, will acquire a marvellous address and energy in the use of their powers. They that have taken worlds into their love will have a love correspondingly capacious, whereupon also it will be seen that their will is settled in firmness and raised in majesty according to the vastness of impulse there is in the love behind it. They that have great thoughts, too, will be able to manage great causes, and they that are lubricated eternally in the joys that feed their activity will never tire. What force, then, must be finally developed in what now appears to be the tenuous and fickle impulse, and the merely frictional activity of a human soul?

On this subject the Scriptures indulge in no declamation, but only speak in hints, and start us off by questions, well understanding that the utmost they can do is to waken in us the sense of a future scale of being unimaginable, and beyond the compass of our definite thought. Here they drive us out in the almost cold mathematical question, "What shall it profit a man to gain the whole world and lose his own soul?" Here they show us, in John's vision, Moses and Elijah, as angels, suggesting our future classification among angels, which are sometimes called chariots of God, to indicate their excelling strength and swiftness in careering through his empire to do his will. Here they speak of powers unimaginable as regards the volume of their personality, calling them dominions, thrones, principalities, powers, and appear to set us on a footing with these dim majesties. Here they notify us that it doth not yet appear what we shall be. Here they call us sons of God. Here they bolt upon us, but "I said, Ye are gods;" as if meaning to waken us by a shock! In these and all ways possible, they contrive to start some better perception in us of ourselves, and of the immense significance of the soul; forbidding us always to be the dull mediocrities into which, under the stupor of our unbelief, we are commonly so ready to subside. Oh, if we could tear aside the veil, and see for but one hour what it signifies to be a soul in the power of an endless life, what a revelation would it be!

THE NEW SONG.

YES, we will have a new song. It is the song of Moses and the Lamb. I don't know just who wrote it or how, but it will be a glorious song. I suppose the singing we have here on earth will be nothing compared with the songs of that upper world. Do you know the principal thing we are told we are going to do in heaven is singing, and that is why men ought to sing down here. We ought to begin to sing here so that it won't come strange when we get to heaven. I pity the professed Christian who has not a song in his heart—who never feels like singing. It seems to me if we are truly children of God, we will want to sing about it. And so, when we get there, we can't help shouting out the loud hallelujahs of heaven.

D. L. MOODY.

NO REGRET IN HEAVEN.

BISHOP L. L. HAMLINE.

In heaven there will be no regret for the past any more than for the present. Now we review our lives with disapprobation which uses grief. However we may disapprove, in heaven there can be no grief.

Our past sorrows will not seem too many or too severe. We shall feel that we never suffered a pang too much. Whether it arose from repentance or from providence, whether it was seated in the body or in the soul, we shall feel that every pang came in the right form, at the right time, and in the right measure; that it was neither too light nor too heavy, too early nor too late. Every sigh, and tear, and groan, every deprivation and every persecution, will then be recollected with inconceivable gratification, and will provoke our complacency and gratitude.

Now, if our living is taken away or our honor is tarnished, if our health is impaired, or our friends fade and die. we are ready to exclaim against Providence, or to wither in silent despair. But the saints will remember and review such afflictions with unspeakable satisfaction.

In that blessed world the sins of this life will inflict upon the soul neither remorse nor repentance. Here gracious hearts are filled with godly sorrow at the remembrance of transgression and the remains of carnal appetite. But the hearts of the glorified will not lament. The just made perfect will feel no repentance, and the sanctified and spotless will have no carnal tempers. Now sin provokes in the believers self-reproach and indignation. Such cannot forgive themselves, even when God forgives them. They abhor themselves like Job, and repent as in sack-cloth. Their penitence is not distrustful and death-working, like the sinner's, but still it is penitence; and they are unwilling to part from it all the days of their life. The happiest hours of the best Christians are softened by this penitence. They may have ascended the mount of regeneration, the mount of faith, the mount of love; but on the loftiest summit they shall find no soil barren of repentance, no region so clear and lofty as never to see a cloud, or feel the refreshing moisture of its gently-falling showers. Our earthly graces are moral buds and blossoms. They are most beautiful and fragrant when watered with drops of generous sorrow. When these buds of grace become the ripened fruits of glory, they can endure perpetual sunshine. There they will be garnered in a tearless heaven.

Not even sin in its recollections will afflict the sainted spirit. It had a sting on earth which cannot reach to heaven. The saved will not love sin. They will abhor it most intensely, but it will have no power to inflict pain or unpleasant regret on the redeemed and glorified. Sin purged away by the blood of the Lamb will be as though it had not been. The restitution of the soul to its original innocence and purity will be complete. Consider how much rapture must arise from perfect self-complacency!

Rest, on the bosom of thy God ; young spirit, rest thee now—
None of the sorrows here portrayed, shall fall upon thy brow!
    The vital cup in part, your lips had quaffed,
    But, with it sickened, you repelled the draught—
    Opposed; then turning from the blaze of day,
    You gently breathed your infant soul away.
Oh, mourn not for the dead, in youth who passed away,
Ere peace and joy and bliss have fled, and sin has brought decay.
Better in youth to die, life being fair and bright,
Than when the soul has lost its truth, in age and sorrow's night
Then shed not the tear of grief upon the sable bier,
Her wearied spirit finds a rest, in a more blissful sphere.

"Our home in heaven! Oh, the glorious home,
  And the spirit joined with the bride, says, 'Come.'
  Come, seek His face, and your sins forgiven,
  And rejoice in hope of your home in heaven."

I love to think of heaven, it seems not far away,
Its crystal streams refresh me as I near the closing day;
Its balmy winds are wafted from the heavenly hills above,
And they fold me in an atmosphere of purity and love."

THE HEAVENLY COUNTRY.

O TELL me no more
Of this world's vain store;
The time for these trifles with me now is o'er;
A country I've found
Where true joys abound;
To dwell I'm determined on that happy ground.

The souls that believe,
In paradise live;
And me in that number will Jesus receive.
My soul, don't delay,
He calls thee away,
Rise, follow thy Saviour, and bless the glad day.

No mortal doth know
What He can bestow,
What light, strength, and comfort do after Him go.
So onward I move,
And, but Christ above,
None guesses how wondrous the journey will prove

Great spoils I shall win
From death, hell, and sin;
'Midst outward afflictions shall feel Christ within.
Perhaps for His name,
Poor dust as I am,
Some works I shall finish with glad loving aim.

I still (which is best)
Shall in His dear breast,
As at the beginning, find pardon and rest.
And when I'm to die,
Receive me, I'll cry,
For Jesus has loved me, I cannot tell why.

But this I do find,
We two are so joined,
He'll not live in glory and leave me behind.
Lo! this is the race
I'm running through grace,
Henceforth till admitted to see my Lord's face.

And now I'm in care
My neighbors may share
Those blessings: to seek them will none of you dare?
In bondage, oh why,
And death will you lie,
When one here assures you free grace is so nigh?

SCRIPTURE NAMES OF HEAVEN.

REV. J. E. EDMONSON, A. M.

HEAVEN is called a *house*; which implies the residence of a family, sweetly united by the ties of interest and pure benevolence. Jesus calls it his "Father's house," because his Father dwells there with his family, ever exercising his paternal love and watchful care; and every individual in the family is treated by his heavenly Father as a beloved child. This house was built by God, and is inconceivably glorious; and the family in this house is lovely and happy beyond description. It is a house which will never decay; and a family that will never be separated; a house that cannot be shaken; and a family that cannot be moved. Part of the family has already arrived there; and the other part will soon arrive.

Heaven is called a *city*, on account of its security, high privileges, grandeur, and stability. Abraham, who is called the friend of God, looked for a city which hath foundations, whose builder and maker is God; and it may be said of all good men, "God is not ashamed to be called their God; for he hath prepared for them a city." In this world they are at a considerable distance from that city; but they are on their journey home; and even now they are citizens of the New Jerusalem above.

Here they dwell in tents, and wander up and down; but the Lord leads them "by the right way," that they may "go to a city of habitation." There they will be permanently settled, and enjoy all the privileges of free citizens; nor can they ever be removed by the cross events of this ever-changing world; for all things there are absolutely fixed and unalterable. "Here have we no continuing city, but we seek one to come," which will abide forever. That is the city of the living God. It was built by him; it is governed by him; and it is placed under his immediate protection. Other cities perish; but that is eternal: in other cities death reigns; but the citizens of heaven are immortal.

In allusion to the division of Canaan by lot, and to the settlement of Israel in the land of promise, heaven is called an *inher-*

itance; and it may be said to every holy person in reference to the eternal world, as it was said to Daniel, "Thou shalt rest, and stand in thy lot at the end of thy days." There is an evident allusion to the same thing in the following passage: "Blessed be the God and Father of our Lord Jesus Christ, which according to his abundant mercy hath begotten us again unto a lively hope by the resurrection of Christ from the dead, to an inheritance incorruptible, and undefiled, and that fadeth not away, reserved in heaven for you."

Heaven is called the *holiest*, on account of its transcendent purity, and in allusion to the holy of holies in the temple at Jerusalem. There the Lord dwelt between the cherubim; there was his mercy-seat; and from thence he communed with his people. Psa. xcix, 1; Exod xxv, 22. This was typical of the heavenly world, to which we have now access, in the high duties of prayer and praise; for we have "boldness to enter into the holiest by the blood of Jesus, by a new and living way which he hath consecrated for us, through the veil, that is to say, his flesh," Heb. x, 19, 20. And that must be the holiest place in the universe, where God appears in his transcendent purity, and where the holiest spirits, of every rank and order, appear in his immediate presence.

The heavenly world, where holy spirits reside, is called a kingdom; and the King, whose power is unlimited, is "the Lord God omnipotent." The subjects over whom he reigns are angels and saints; and the law, by which he governs his kingdom, is his own all-perfect will. The universal prayer of the church militant is, "Thy will be done in earth, as it is in heaven." And in heaven they do the will of God in all things, with cheerfulness and with steady perseverance.

Heaven is called a *better country*. It is better than Ur of the Chaldeans, or the land of promise, where Abraham dwelt as a stranger and pilgrim; and yet those countries were famous for the production of every comfort that man could desire as an inhabitant of this lower world. But Abraham and his pious companions looked forward to a better state of things in the world to come. They desired " a better country, that is, a heavenly," where they might enjoy the happiness of the eternal state. And if we carefully examine all the good things that are enjoyed, in the most highly favored countries on earth, the enjoyments of heaven are far better than those of any other. We should be thankful to God for every earthly blessing; but we are allowed to hope for a better place and state in heaven.

Here we are but "strangers and pilgrims," as were all our forefathers; but there we shall have a permanent abode, and shall enjoy eternal blessedness. Here we may look out for a country where the air is salubrious, the land fruitful, the prospects delightful to the eye, the inhabitants peaceful, and the government wise and good; but heaven, where all excellences meet, and are found in the highest state of perfection, is better and more to be desired than the most lovely country on the face of the earth.

The habitations where saints will reside in the heavenly world are called *mansions*. To comfort his disciples, when they were cast down by the prospect of his departure of the world, Jesus said, "In my Father's house are many mansions." The word mansion generally signifies a house; but here are mansions.". It is probable that our blessed Savior had an eye to the retired and peaceful apartments in the temple, where many pious persons dwelt, and were daily employed in the delightful exercises of devotion; and that he pointed out by this emblem the employments and enjoyments of the upper world. But be this as it may, two ideas are included in this figurative representation: first, that the house of his Father is spacious; for there are many mansions: and, secondly, that there will be different degrees of glory; some apartments being vastly superior to those of others. In the heavenly house, there is room for every soul of man. Many have already entered into it; "and yet there is room." But as our Lord prepares the mansions, they will be exactly suited to our circumstances; and those of the lowest order will be unspeakably glorious. And Jesus not only prepares a place for us, but he prepares us for the place. The work of grace in the soul, from its commencement to its highest state of perfection, is a preparation for the mansions of glory; and what an encouraging thought it is, that our glorious mansion in the sky, prepared by Jesus, "shall evermore endure!"

Jerusalem was a great city,—a city where God was adored in his holy sanctuary; and in that view it may be considered as a type of heaven. Hence heaven is called the *New Jerusalem*. "This city as Wesley says is wholly new, belonging not to this world, not to the millennium, but to eternity,"

It will be a glorious city; illuminated by the glory of God and the Lamb; made secure by a wall great and high; twelve gates, with a guardian angel stationed at each gate; four sides with open gates, to receive the worthy from every quarter of the world; the names of the twelve tribes, of Israel written on the twelve gates, and of the twelve apostles on the twelve foundations, to represent the union of the Jewish and the Christian churches; built of the richest materials, and garnished with gold and precious stones, emblems of Eastern wealth and magnificence: its stones resembling those of Aaron's breast-plate, to denote that the URIM AND THUMMIM, the light and perfection of God's oracle, are there; but no temple there, because the whole city is the temple of God and the Lamb,

> "Our business this, our only aim.
> To find the New Jerusalem."

Another name given to heaven is *paradise*. This word literally signifies a garden of pleasure, and particularly the garden of Eden, where God placed the first man in a state of innocence; and the residence of the saints in heaven bears this name, in allusion to the happy place and state of our first parents before their sad apostacy. But our Savior went to the heavenly paradise, when he had given up the ghost and the cross; and the penitent thief, who confessed him before men, was allowed to accompany him to that happy place: for our Lord said to him, "To-day shalt thou be with me in paradise." There is the tree of life; and if we overcome our spiritual enemies, we shall eat of that tree, and live for ever.

The heavenly paradise is a garden of pleasure and delight; a place and state of innocence and pure enjoyment. In allusion to the river which watered the garden of Eden, it is stated, that there is a pure river of the water of life, clear as crystal, proceeding out of the throne of God and the Lamb; a beautiful emblem of that pure and overflowing joy, and of all those hallowed pleasures, which ever flow to all in heaven from the divine throne. On either side of the river is the tree of life, which bears twelve manners of fruits, and yields her fruit every month; denoting the rich variety, the permanency, and the fulness of heavenly pleasures. The leaves of that tree are for the healing of the nations, ever preserving them in a state of life, health, and vigor.

THE COTTAGE IN WHICH MR. SPURGEON PREACHED HIS FIRST SERMON.

NO DEATH IN HEAVEN.

REV. J. EDMONSON A. M.

If there be no death in heaven, it is a legitimate inference, that the inhabitants are ever blooming and ever young. Their life and vigor remain in full force, and cannot be subject to decays. There is no helpless infancy in heaven; no sick-beds; no palsied limbs; no withering old age; no funerals; and no mourners going about the streets. When millions of ages have passed by, speaking after the manner of men, those immortals will be as fresh, as lively, and as strong as they were when they first entered the portals of the celestial city. Their beauty will not fade, their Powers will not suffer any abatement, the eye, will not be dim, the ear will not be dull of hearing, the understanding will not be weakened, the memory will not fail, the affections will not become languid, nor will any quality, either of body or of mind, lose its perfection by the lapse of ages.

There will be a complete deliverance from the fear of death in the regions of immortality. That has been painfully felt by dying mortals in the present life; but it will never be felt again by the saints in glory to all eternity; for how can they fear that which they know, assuredly, will never happen? Here, we calculate years by the revolutions of the heavenly bodies; but there, duration will have no measure and no end. Here we behold the approach of old age in the feebleness of man, and in the wrinkles of his face; but there we shall see no infirmities, or any indications of approaching dissolution.

How absurd it would appear, to ascribe either old age, or any decay of beauty or strength, to the angels of light! and yet it must be allowed, that they have lived thousands of years in the heavenly world. And is it not equally absurd to apply old age, or a want of youthful beauty, to the saints in light? They are ever young, ever vigorous, and ever beautiful. The heavenly bodies, in the solar system, are fine emblems of the unfading beauty and glory of all the hosts above. The sun has shone, with undiminished splendor, for nearly six thousand years; the moon and stars are as bright and as beautiful as they were when God created them; and "they that be wise shall shine as the brightness of the firmament, and they that turn many to righteousness, as the stars for ever and ever."

THE HOME BEYOND THE TRUE HEAVEN.

PAUL E. HAYNE.

The bliss for which our spirits pine,
    That bliss we feel shall yet be given—
Somehow, in some far realm divine,
    Some marvellous state we name a heaven—

Is not the bliss of languorous hours,
    A glory of calm measured range,
But life which feeds our noblest powers
    On wonders of eternal change;

A heaven of action freed from strife,
    With ampler ether for the scope
Of an immeasurable life,
    And an unbaffled, boundless hope;

A heaven wherein all discords cease,
    Self-torment, doubt, distress, turmoil,
The core of whose majestic peace
    Is God-like power of tireless toil—

Toil without tumult, strain, or jar,
    With grandest reach of range indued,
Unchecked by even the farthest star
    That trembles through infinitude,

In which to soar to higher heights
    Through widening ethers stretched abroad,
Till in our onward, upward flights,
    We touch, at last, the feet of God!

Time swallowed in Eternity!
    No future, evermore, no past,
But one unbending Now to be
    A boundless circle round us cast.

BEYOND THE GRAVE.

BISHOP R. S. FOSTER, D. D.

TO my own mind, when I look in the direction of the future, one picture always rises—a picture of ravishing beauty. Its essence, I believe, to be true. Its accidents will be more glorious than all that my imagination puts into it. It is that of a soul forever growing in knowledge, in love, in holy endeavor; that of a vast community of spirits, moving along a pathway of light, of ever-expanding excellence and glory; brightening as they ascend; becoming more and more like the unpicturable pattern of infinite perfection; loving with an ever-deepening love; glowing with an ever-increasing fervor; rejoicing in ever-advancing knowledge; growing in glory and power. They are all immortal. There are no failures or reverses to any of them. Ages fly away; they soar on with tireless wing. Æons and cycles advance toward them and retire behind them; still they soar, and shout, and unfold!

I am one of that immortal host. Death cannot destroy me. I shall live when stars grow dim with age. The advancing and retreating æons shall not fade my immortal youth. Thou, Gabriel, that standest near the throne, bright with a brightness that dazzles my earth-born vision, rich with the experience of uncounted ages, first-born of the sons of God, noblest of the archangelic retinue, far on I shall stand where thou standest now, rich with an equal experience, great with an equal growth; thou wilt have passed on, and, from higher summits, wilt gaze back on a still more glorious progress!

Beyond the grave! As the vision rises how this side dwindles into nothing—a speck—a moment—and its glory and pomp shrink up into the trinkets and baubles that amuse an infant for a day. Only those things, in the glory of this light, which lay hold of immortality seem to have any value. The treasures that consume away or burn up with this perishing world are not treasures. Those only that we carry beyond are worth the saving.

EMPLOYMENTS OF HEAVEN.

REV. ASA MAHAN.

THE reader will recollect certain expressions occurring in the parable of the talents, Matt. xxv., which have an important bearing on this point, and which are repeated so often and in such connections as authorize us to regard them as general principles in the government of God. When he who received five talents came and brought other five talents which he had gained besides them, his Lord said to him: "Well done, thou good and faithful servant, thou hast been faithful over a few things, I will make thee ruler over many things; enter thou into the joy of thy Lord." Thou hast been faithful here on a small scale of trust; I will give thee higher responsibilities and more abundant joy hereafter. I will make thee ruler over many things. Thy trustworthiness shall be amply rewarded. A nobler sphere of labor and of honor is before thee.

Compare with this another passage, Rev. iii. 21: "To him that overcometh will I grant to sit with me on my throne, even as I also overcame, and am sit down with my Father in his throne." The Bible often alludes to the fact that Christ is gloriously exalted on account of his obedience unto death, and his voluntary humiliation for and in the work of human redemption. He fought a glorious fight on earth, and rose to his ineffable reward; he now promises the same reward to all who follow in his footsteps. Amazing, incredible though it be, he speaks of taking them to sit with himself on his own throne of glory! This must mean something; and though it does not yet appear in all points what it does mean, yet none can doubt that it speaks of glory and honor immortal, far too exalted for the comprehension of mortal thought. These are some of the intimations which Scripture gives on this subject.

We said there were also some probabilities as to the future condition of the saints, which are derivable from known facts in Jehovah's kingdom. It is not probable that such mental and moral powers as our Creator has given us will lie inactive through eternity. The most sublime feature in the human mind is its law of unlimited progression. Place it under circumstances favorable for development, and there is no limit to its onward progress. Verily, such minds were made for heaven—made for a sphere where God is to be known—where we come into perfect sympathy with the Infinite Mind, and where both mental and moral powers will be eternally active, and where consequently such attainments as angels make will be our perfect blessedness.

Again, it is not probable that in such a universe as this there can be any lack of ample field for effort. God has not thrown worlds and systems of worlds from his creative hand, peopling universal space with material globes for nothing. Those twinkling points of light have some other object than to excite the wonder or task the science of mortals on earth. We cannot doubt that God has peopled them all with sentient beings, and probably most, if not all, with beings of intelligence. If so, there is ample enough space in this universe of God for eternal study, even though our minds are eternally progressing in capacity, and forever enjoy the mental and moral vigor of an archangel. It is not probable that, launched abroad upon such a universe, there will be any lack of created things, the study of which will forever reveal more and more of God; nor will there be any lack of intelligent beings with whom we may have the sweet intercourse of mind with mind and heart with heart.

Again, it is not probable, considering the cost, so to speak, of the arrangements and provisions for the redemption of the race, that God will suffer the whole scheme to go into oblivion in his kingdom, or to be confined in its influence to an insignificant portion of his universal empire. It cannot be that he will fail to make the most of it for the well-being of the moral universe. Indeed, we are told that "we are a spectacle to angels;" that they sung the birth-day song of human salvation; that they strike a fresh note over every fresh convert; minister to each heir of salvation through his earthly toils and trials; blend their voices in the mighty pæan of universal praise to God and to the Lamb that was slain, forever and forever:—how then can we doubt that they will catch the story of redemption in all its thrilling details from the lips of redeemed saints, and help to bear it far away and away to the remotest provinces of Jehovah's empire. It is not on earth alone that we have missionary work to do. The next great commission will be—Go ye through all this outspreading, far-reaching universe, and preach the glad tidings to every creature. Tell them for their joy what infinite love has done. Tell them how God's own dear Son was given up; came down from his co-equal throne to earth; allied himself to mortal flesh; endured reproach and death from those he would save; tell them the whole story of the cross; lay open the scenes of Calvary, and then disclose the scheme of God's providential agency and of his spiritual agency to turn from sin to holiness a countless people to the praise of his grace; let each saint tell his own story and show how God followed him with mercies, converted him by his power, and then kept him through faith unto salvation; go, you have enough to say; testify to those minds in that far-off world, that they may learn more of their own Maker and Father." Such may be a part of the employments of the heavenly world.

KNOWING BY AND BY.

REV. C. H. FOWLER, L.L. D.

"NOW we know in part, but then shall I know even as also I am known." In another line of thought we know only in part the work and movement of his providence. I cannot tell you why it is that that little child in that home of luxury and comfort, with all the advantages of Christian culture, trained to be a child of God, with all the chances of education, with everything to make its promises for the future large, is smitten and carried away, while that one having an inheritance of shame, degradation and crime, should grow up to make society tremble, and increase the burden and the weight of the world's sin. I cannot tell you why it is, because I see such a small part of it. I do not know why it is that that boy whose heart is fixed on doing God's will, who is determined, if possible, to take hold of men, even at the bottom of society, and lift them up into the light and comfort of God, and into fellowship with him, should be touched in his sight and slip out into the darkness to be a burden to his friends, while that boy who uses his sight only for purposes of evil, who uses his eyes only to plan the destruction of the innocent and unwary, is permitted to live and see his way to destruction. I cannot comprehend it at all; I may find it out by and by, as I understand this way; I shall know by and by something about this. I may find out that we cannot weave a garment and not have the threads touch each other; I may find out that we cannot perpetuate the race without keeping in all the links in the chain. I may find out that God purposed that that boy in the alley should have the largest chance from his start; that, by looking into the face of some Christian man, and by hearing his voice from the pulpit, and the word out of his book, he must have some chance of getting a home yonder. It may all come clear in what I call now "the mystery of my freedom;" but this I do know, that somehow, some time, by and by I shall know.

We cannot see the significance of many things that happen in this life. It was a dark day for you when he took that little lamb out of your arms where it was warm, and put her away in the cold earth. You could not understand it at all; she was so gentle and full of smiles and tenderness; she was unto you all in all. You know how you trembled and quaked when she grew thin; you thought you would never see the sunshine again. When you put her in the silent house, away in the darkness, you did not understand it, and do not understand it to-day. It may be you have carried that little grave these many years; it is a sad fact in your experience, but you shall know by and by. Oh! sometimes it seems a weary, worn way! We go along heavy paths; we carry hard loads and stagger under them; and one after another falls; we see ourselves left alone with nobody in the universe but God. We think it strange; we take a little more hope and gird ourselves for the race. But know this, even though we run in the darkness, we shall see and we shall know even as we are known. Time hacks out our frames; we grow gray, and thin, and wrinkled; we wonder how those who went away when we were young and in the vigor of our early manhood will ever know us, what changes will come over them, and how we shall see them, but we shall know even as we are known.

The less of this brief life, the more of heaven;
The shorter time, the longer immortality.

JOYS OF HEAVEN.

NANCY A. W. PRIEST.

Beyond these chilling winds and gloomy skies,
   Beyond Death's cloudy portal—
There is a land where beauty never dies,
   And love becomes immortal.

A land whose light is never dimmed by shade,
   Whose fields are ever vernal,
Where nothing beautiful can ever fade,
   But blooms for aye eternal.

We may not know how sweet its balmy air,
   How bright and fair its flowers;
We may not hear the songs that echo there,
   Through those enchanted bowers.

The city's shining towers we may not see,
   With our dim earthly vision:
For Death, the silent warder, keeps the key
   That opes those gates elysian.

But sometimes, where adown the western sky
   The fiery sunset lingers,
Its golden gates swing inward noiselessly,
   Unlocked by silent fingers.

And while they stand a moment half ajar,
   Gleams from the inner glory,
Stream lightly through the azure vault afar,
   And half reveal the story.

O land unknown! O land of love divine!
   Father all-wise, eternal,
Guide, guide, these wandering, way-worn feet of mine,
   Unto those pastures vernal.

O glorious land of heavenly light,
Where walked the ransomed, clothed in white,
On hills of myrrh, through pastures green,
No curse, no cloud upon the scene!

NO NIGHT IN HEAVEN.

REV. J. EDMONSON.

IF there be no night in heaven, there cannot be any interruptions either of employments or enjoyments. If the delightful exercises, or the pleasurable. feelings of heaven could be interrupted for a moment, they might come to an end; and if they come to an end, all the promises of God would fail. But that these services and enjoyments may not be interrupted, there is no night, and no sleep. The night is made for sleep, and sleep is fit for the night; but these belong to time, and will not be necessary in eternity. When we are truly happy in God, in the present state of things, we are always ready to say, "O, could I ever live in such a frame as this!" and that which we now desire, in our best moments, will be realized when we are advanced to the glory of heaven.

When our works are holy and useful, we desire to continue in them without interruption; and this desire will be gratified when we mix with immortals in that world where there is no night. God never ceases to work. He has no night; and we shall be like him in his holy temple. Here, our holy Sabbaths end in night; and our public worship is interrupted. We depart from the holy sanctuary of our God, lie down and sleep, and then return to the duties of life; but in heaven, the Sabbath will be one eternal day, and all its delightful exercises will be perpetual. For there will never be a moment, to all eternity, in which the celestial hosts will not be employed in doing the will of Him that sitteth upon the throne.

But what a contrast is found, by those who examine the subject, between our night in this world, and their day in the world above! a contrast which casts a deep shade on earth and earthly things; but which adds fresh lustre to the glory of heaven. Our night, except when favored with the feeble light of the moon and the stars, is a season of darkness; but their light always shines, in all its strength, and in all its beauty. In our night, robbers and murderers carry on their infernal works of darkness; but in heaven, all are pure and holy. Here, wickedness, in all its horrid forms, is committed under the cover of darkness; but there, the wickedness of the wicked is unknown, and the just are established in peace; the volupteous sons of folly pursue unhallowed nocturnal pleasures, when they are covered by the darkness of night; but in the regions of light and day there are no unsanctified pleasures to allure the soul from a pure enjoyment of God.

Here, wearisome nights are appointed to the sons and daughters of affliction, and they often cry out, "O that it were morning!" but there is no affliction of any kind in the eternal day above. The sons of light, in that world, rejoice in the day. They have nothing, either within or without, that they wish to hide; nor do they wish to hide themselves, like Adam and Eve in the Garden of Eden, from the presence of the Lord. The open day suits their character and state. They love to be seen by their God and Father, by all his holy angels, and by all the saints in light. The night may cover guilt and depravity; but they are neither guilty nor depraved.

But in heaven, there are ever-blooming prospects, and delightful assurances of never-ending glory.

But the sweet and lovely prospect of an eternal day awakens in the soul the most lively and ardent desire to mingle with the saints in light. Their sun will never go down; the shades of evening will never fall on them; nor will they have any gloomy fears of darkness or of night. The glory of the Lord shines upon them with undiminished splendor; and they all behold it with unceasing rapture and delight.

O! where shall human grief be stilled
　And joy for pain be given,
Where dwells the sunshine of a love
In which the soul may always rove?
　A sweet voice answered—Heaven.

O, heart, I said, when death shall come
　And all thy cords be riven,
What lies beyond the swelling tide?
The same sweet voice to mine replied
　In loving accents—Heaven.

JESUS IS PRESENT IN HEAVEN.

WHEN Jesus ascended into heaven, he took his seat at the right hand of God, and appeared in his glorified humanity to all the heavenly host; and all his followers, when they enter into the regions of immortality, will behold his glory. This is clearly expressed in the following words:—
"Father, I will that they also, whom thou hast given me, be with me where I am; that they may behold my glory, which thou hast given me," John xvii, 24.

The glorious appearance of our Lord, in the heavenly world, will far exceed our present conceptions. When he appeared to Saul of Tarsus, on his way to Damascus, "a light from heaven, above the brightness of the sun" in his meridian splendor, shone on that persecutor, and on his companions. Acts xxvi, 13. And when he appeared to John in the Isle of Patmos, "his countenance was as the sun shineth in his strength," Rev. i, 16. But how transcendently glorious will be his appearance in heaven, where all is light and perfection, and where every saint will be strengthened to behold his glory!

The Shechinah, or visible symbol of the divine presence, will be seen in the glorified humanity of our Lord. The Jewish writers denominate the cloud of glory which appeared to the Israelites in the wilderness, the *Shechinah*, or the *habitation* of the divine Majesty, meaning *to dwell or inhabit;* but the glorified humanity of our Lord will be the tent or tabernacle in which the glory of his divinity will dwell, and from which he will shine forth. So it was in the days of his flesh, when he dwelt, or tabernacled, among men; for then his glory was seen by his holy apostles. John i, 14. But the splendor of his Godhead will shine in heaven with a lustre that no mortal eye can see, and the "brightness of his glory" will fill all his saints with ineffable delight.

Then we shall behold the Father on his throne, arrayed in robes of light and glory; the Son will appear as the only begotten of the Father, full of grace and truth; and the Holy Ghost will be seen as "seven lamps of fire burning before the throne," to represent his various gifts and graces; for these seven lamps which burn before the throne are the seven spirits of God. Rev. i, 4; iv, 5. Lawman says, "The Holy Spirit, I think, is meant by the seven spirits which are before the throne. Seven, in the language of prophecy, often expresses perfection, and may better be understood of the most perfect Spirit of God, the author of all spiritual blessings, than of seven angels, as a more natural interpretation of the expression in prophecy, as well as much more agreeable to the manner of the gospel blessing, from Father, Son and Holy Ghost."

The appearance of our Lord, in his ineffable glory, will be a source of unutterable joy to all his followers. With what rapture will they behold the once crucified, but now exalted Savior; every one exclaiming, "He loved me, and gave himself for me!" And will they not all unite, and cry aloud with grateful feelings, "Thou wast slain, and hast redeemed us to God by thy blood, out of every kindred, and tongue, and people, and nation?" Rev. v, 9. Thus all heaven will ring with the high praises of the spotless Lamb; and his sacrificial death will be proclaimed in songs of everlasting praise.

The lovely character of Jesus, in all his gracious undertakings, will be clearly seen and gratefully acknowledged; and the wondrous plan of redemption and salvation will be opened to our view in all its vast extent, and in all its depths and heights. Then we shall see the amazing love which brought our Savior from the skies; and that will be finely illustrated by all his mediatorial works. His merciful designs will appear in his humble birth, his holy life, his pure ministry, his mighty miracles, his painful death, his glorious resurrection, and his triumphant ascension into heaven.

>Go, wing thy flight from star to star,
>From world to luminous world, as far
>As the universe spreads its flaming wall;
>Take all the pleasures of all the spheres,
>And multiply each through endless years,
>One minute of heaven is worth them all.

'Tis a blessing to live, but a greater to die;
And the best of the world, is its path to the sky.

NO FEAR IN HEAVEN.

Fear is the parent of many sufferings; and frail man has ten thousand fears. As a sinner he fears the wrath of God, the terrors of death, and the torments of hell; and when he is converted to God he is often afraid of the tempter, the loss of grace, and the loss of heaven; nor is he wholly delivered from tormenting fear until he is made perfect in love. That love may be lost in this world, and tormenting fear may return; but all fear that hath torment will cease forever when we take our seats above. If this were not the case, a dread of future evil would destroy the sweet enjoyments of all the saints and angels before the throne of God; and heaven, with all its glories, would not be viewed as a place of perfect bliss.

We must allow that there will be a filial fear of God our Father in the world of glory; but there cannot be any painful dread of his divine Majesty, or any fear of evil in that holy place. We shall view God as the greatest and the best of beings; and while we stand in awe of his greatness and glory, we shall love him with undivided hearts. We shall not fear the saints in light; for they will be our companions and friends; we shall not fear the holy angels who have been our ministering spirits, and who conducted us to the realms of day; nor shall we fear either evil or danger when we are placed under the immediate protection and care of our Almighty Savior. Thus all our painful and distressing fears forever end in the heavenly world.

Rev. J. Edmonson a. m.

NO SORROW IN HEAVEN.

Sorrow and sighing are at an end in the realms of bliss. "There sighing grief shall weep no more." All pain is removed, every want is abundantly supplied, and suffering is forever banished from the place. There will not be either "sorrow or crying" in the New Jerusalem. Rev. xxi, 4. Every cause of sorrow will be entirely and eternally removed. To instance in a few particulars: there cannot be any sorrow for our own sins, because every saint has been forgiven and cleansed from all unrighteousness; there cannot be any sorrow for the sins of others, for sinners will not be allowed to enter into that place where all are pure and holy; there cannot be any sorrow for the dead, for all the inhabitants are immortal; nor can there be any sorrow from the oppressions of cruel tyrants, for all in heaven are under the influence of pure love.

In that blessed world there are no sufferings from painful reflections on past events; nor any fear or dread of what may happen in futurity. "Weeping may endure for a night, but joy cometh in the morning." This comfortable passage is in part realized in this world; but will have its full accomplishment in the next. For "the ransomed of the Lord shall return, and come to Zion with songs and everlasting joy upon their heads; they shall obtain joy and gladness; and sorrow and sighing shall flee away." These words may be applied, in a lower sense, to the deliverance of the Jews from the invasion of the king of Assyria; to their return from the Babylonish captivity; or to the Christian church under the reign of the Messiah: but they will not be fully realized until the church returns to the heavenly Zion, where there will be an eternal day of joy and gladness. EDMONSON.

PARADISE.

ARCHBISHOP TRENCH.

Oh! Paradise must show more fair
    Than any earthly ground,
And therefore longs my spirit there
    Right quickly to be found.

In Paradise a stream must flow
    Of everlasting love:
Each tear of longing shed below
    Therein a pearl will prove.

In Paradise a breath of balm
    All anguish must allay,
Till every anguish growing calm,
    Even mine shall flee away.

And there the tree of stillest peace
    In verdant spaces grows;

Beneath it one can never cease
  To dream of blest repose.

For every thorn that pierced me here
  The rose will there be found;
With joy, earth's roses brought not near,
  My head will there be crowned.

There all delights will blossom forth,
  That here in bud expire,
And from all mourning weeds of earth
  Be wove a bright attire.

All here I sought in vain pursuit
  Will freely meet me there,
As from green branches golden fruit,
  Fair flowers from garden fair.

My youth, that by me swept amain,
  On swift wing borne away,
And love that suffered me to drain
  Is nectar for a day—

These, never wishing to depart,
  Will me forever bless,
Their darling fold unto the heart,
  And comfort and caress.

And there the Loveliness, whose glance
  From far did on me gleam,
But whose unveiled countenance
  Was only seen in dream,

Will, meeting all my soul's desires,
  Unveil itself to me,
When to the choir of starry lyres
  Shall mine united be.

O, heaven is where no secret dread
  May haunt love's meeting hour;
Where from the past no gloom is shed
  O'er the heart's chosen bower.

HEAVEN OUR HOME.

REV. E. ADKINS, D. D.

THE saints will be blessed with a delightful sense of *home*. Home is the dearest spot on earth, the scene of our purest enjoyments. But oh, how precarious are all its pleasures and endearments in such a world as this! How few, comparatively, are favored whith a genuine home! The greater part of mankind are wanderers, sojourners, tenants at will. And this is the lot of God's dear children as well as others. But even at best an earthly home fails to satisfy the innate longing of the soul. The Creator has placed within us aspirations which conform to a nobler, happier destiny. Those who are "made heirs of God according to the hope of eternal life," are sensible of this, and cheerfully acquiesce in the thought that they have here "no certain dwelling place," nor perfect objects of affection, while they look upward with joyful anticipations to their future heavenly home. And these hopes will not be disappointed when Christ shall take his elect to himself, when they shall receive their inheritance in his everlasting kingdom and dwell in the blest mansions prepared for them. King's palaces are but temporary, comfortless booths compared with the "everlasting habitations" into which they will be received; and the sweetest domestic enjoyments are scarcely a forestate of the blessedness of those heavenly connections and associations amid which they will dwell. There will be no precariousness, or imperfection attendant upon that blissful home. In it the feeble earthly foretaste will be exchanged for complete fruition. The soul's indefinite longing will be satisfied, its ideal realized. Home with God, with loved ones, among kindred spirits loving and beloved, and in the midst of all things lovely—what more could be desired?

> The warmest love on earth is still
> Imperfect when 'tis given;
> But there's a purer clime above,
> Where perfect hearts in perfect love
> Unite; and this is heaven.

HEAVEN A HAPPY PLACE.

REV. J. EDMONSON.

TWO things are found in heaven which cannot fail to make its inhabitants happy: the first is, the absence of all evil; and the second is, the presence of all good. The one prevents sorrow; and the other brings fulness of joy.

There is no natural evil or affliction in the heavenly world. The saints have suffered; but they will not suffer any more. There is no moral evil, or sin, in heaven. The saints were once sinners; but they will not sin any more. Evil examples are not seen in the holiest place; for all are wise and good, There cannot be any temptation to evil there; for the tempter is shut out for ever. Nothing in the vast extent of heaven can excite fear or dread; but everything inspires the soul with hope. There is no folly, and no vice in that happy world; but wisdom and goodness are found in rich abundance, for all are wise and good.

Everlasting goodness will flow, in copious streams, from the fountain of love; and every thing that is good, every thing that is holy, and every thing that can be desired, will be plentifully supplied. There will be no want of anything that is necessary to complete the felicity of God's family. A rich feast of the most delicious intellectual pleasure is already provided; and it will be an eternal feast. The appetite will never clog; but the relishes of holy souls for pure enjoyments will be strong and vigorous; and their supplies will be full, satisfying, and eternal, The absence of evil excludes the possibility of suffering; the presence of all that is good includes every kind of enjoyment; and where these are found, there is perfect felicity. What has the world to equal this? If a man could gain the whole world, and enjoy it without sorrow, his state would be vastly inferior to that of the humblest saint in the paradise of God.

Reflections on past deliverances will afford a considerable portion of happiness to all the saints in the heavenly world. It is highly probable that the guardian angels of their infancy will give them delightful details of many surprising deliverances from danger in that early period of life; and of those deliverances which they experienced when they where but little ones in grace; for then those angels, that behold the face of God, were employed in their protection. Matt. xviii, 10. Holy spirits will recollect with inexpressible joy their deliverance from the guilt and power of sin; and that grace which enabled them to obey the gospel of God their Savior. Once they were tossed on the stormy ocean of life; but now they are in a peaceful haven. They had many conflicts with the world, the flesh, and the devil; but they conquered in the strength of Jesus, and have left the field of battle.

HEAVEN.

REV. GEO. H. HEPWORTH D. D.

Let me speak to you upon that state which is called heaven. The people of every nation seem to have an idea of a future life. No nation has ever existed without it. There are many things about heaven that we cannot think of. They are beyond the scope of human thought. No man can conceive the glories of the future any more than he can perceive the perfume of flowers without the odor. Brutal nations have a brutal heaven; Christian nations have a sentiment of enjoyment in it. The American Indian dreams of a promised land where he and his dog will be united and where his wigwam will never be torn down; where his little ones will play about his homestead forever and where there will be no more sorrow. Even the rude Scandinavian lived in contemplation of a future state, where he would be victorious over his enemies from sunrise to sunset and where he would drink out of the skulls of his vanquished foes. The Indian carries to his heaven his bows and arrows and dog; the Scandinavian carried his enemies and his hatred to his paradise; the Indian cannot conceive of any higher heaven than one vast continent covered by forests, dotted by running rivulets and quiet glistening lakes. The Christian passes from Nazareth to Jerusalem; he dreams of something brighter; his general tone of life has been elevated, his feelings are deeper, sympathies are brighter and purer; a better nature animates the Christian and supplements his future home. We look forward to that other land where we can take complete rest, where there shall be no darkness or sorrow, but eternal light and joy. It is a home for us. How much is implied in the term "home!" Persons who have travelled in Europe can well appreciate it. They get sick and tired, after having travelled from place to place, of the continual change. Many persons during the first week of their sojourn through Paris think it a paradise; in a few weeks more it becomes tedious and they long for their home. They went to Germany and whirled about in railroad cars, until they sickened of perpetual travel. But they entertained a hope; it was for that sweet little homestead in New England, on a hill side or the other home in the city, because they have made that habitation their home so long. Heaven is such a home, and we await here until the King sends word that He requires us to attend in His august presence. That thought is the foundation stone of the Christian religion.

ATTRACTIONS OF HEAVEN

Though earth has fully many a beautiful spot,
As a poet or painter might show,
Yet more lovely and beautiful, holy and bright,
To the hopes of the heart and the spirit's glad sight,
Is the land that no mortal may know.
O! who but must pine in this dark vale of tears,
From its clouds and its shadows to go,
To walk in the light of glory above,
To share in the peace, and the joy, and the love,
Of the land that no mortal may know!
There the crystalline stream, bursting forth from the throne,
Flows on, and forever will flow;
Its waves as they roll are with melody rife,
And its waters are sparkling with beauty and life,
In the land which no mortal may know.
And there, on its margin, with leaves ever green,
With its fruits healing sickness and woe,
The fair tree of life, in its glory and pride,
Is fed by that deep, inexhaustible tide
Of the land which no mortal may know.

BERNARD BARTON.

THERE SHALL BE NO MORE SEA.

NO MORE SEA.

REV. RUFUS W. CLARK D. D.

HOW little, after hearing of a wreck, and of the sad fate of all on board the ship, do we realize that there were sons, fathers and husbands, in that struggling, gasping group,—that those lifeless forms were bound to friends by ties as strong and tender as those that unite us to the dearest objects of our affection! How little do we think of the families in different towns and villages, to whom the announcement of the wreck comes as a thunderbolt,—whose sighs, and tears, and habiliments of mourning, tell where the lightning of affliction has struck!

Is there not a depth and intensity of meaning, to such, in the declaration of St. John, that in the heavenly world there is no more sea,—no more separation from dear friends,—no more nights of weary watchings and deep agony,—no more startling intelligence of the loss of those we love?

The sea is the emblem of all life's trials. Its ceaselessly rolling billows shadow forth the agitations of many hearts. Its roar is the echo of the groans of an afflicted world. Its perils are emblematic of the moral dangers that surround the soul of man. We are all upon the ocean. Every human being has his voyage to make, his dangers to encounter. Many a dark wave lies between us and the haven of rest. We have barks freighted with more precious substances than silver or gold. The merchant may lose his ships. The sea may engulf his property, and leave him a bankrupt. This is a calamity. But greater calamities threaten many voyagers now sailing upon the ocean of life. They are attempting to make the passage without noticing the compass, whose needle points to the throne of God, and with no pilot at the helm. They seldom consult their chart, that marks out the only course by which they can reach the celestial city,—that indicates the rocks and dangers of the way. They heed not the beacon-lights held forth by patriarchs, prophets and apostles. Though the forms of these holy messengers may be seen moving along the shore, with torches in their hands,—though their voices may be heard amid the roar of the waters, warning the careless mariner of the dangers that surround him, pleading with him to escape the wild breakers that have swallowed up thousands of human beings,—yet he heeds them not. Bent upon his pleasures, absorbed by his schemes for transient good, he thinks that it will be time enough to arouse himself, when the peril is more apparent. He sees that his ship is strong. Every timber is sound; every plank is bolted with iron. He looks above, and every mast, spar, sail and rope, is in its place. What need of alarm, when every thing appears so secure? Thus reasons the man in health and prosperity. But suddenly the alarming tidings ring through the cabin, that the ship has struck, and is fast upon the rocks. Now, in the panic of the hour, the voyager runs to his chart; but this cannot help him. He looks at the compass; but it points whither he cannot go. He seizes the helm; but its power is gone. He pleads for deliverance; but there comes from the shore a voice, "Too late."

O! is it not a blessed announcement, that there is a world where no such moral danger will surround the soul,—where no waves of temptation will roll over us, and no sea of sorrow endanger our hopes or our happiness?

In the next place, we are assured, by the declaration before us, that no storms will arise in the home of the blessed.

The sea is emphatically the theatre of storms. Here they rage with their greatest fury, and produce the most marked and terrific results. How frail an object is the stoutest ship, when in the fatal grasp of an ocean tempest! With what speed it is driven before the resistless force of the wind! How easily the billows sport with it, tossing it from wave to wave, as though it were but a feather! The stroke of a single surge makes every timber tremble, and causes the vessel to quiver like an aspen-leaf. I need not describe a storm at sea. Its violence, its awful grandeur and disastrous effects, have oft been told. The piercing, maddened winds; the wild, foaming surges; the lurid lightning, the crashing thunder, the reeling of the ship like a drunken man, the strained and cracking ropes, the bending mast, falling spars, rent and torn sails, the cold mist that fills and darkens the air, the consternation of rapidly-beating hearts, the dread, horrible suspense of the hour,—all these are familiar to the reader. I have read of Christian voyagers who have said that they never knew the full meaning of the apostle's declaration until they had experienced a storm at sea! And not a few, going down into the dark waters, have derived great comfort from the assurance that in the heavenly world there is no more sea. There serene skies, an unclouded atmosphere and perfect peace, forever reign. The saint, instead of gazing upon a wild waste of waters, is surrounded with the splendors of celestial cities. Instead of the roar of midnight tempests, the music from angelic choirs, and from the worshiping multitude around the throne, thrills his soul.

In heaven there is no sea to furnish a burial-place for the dead. Since the beginning of the world, what vast multitudes have been deposited in the seaman's church-yard! Though no tolling bell has called together sympathizing friends, though no green sod has opened to receive them, and no quiet grove invited them to rest beneath its shadows, yet they have had their funeral services. The winds have sung their requiem, the waves have furnished a winding sheet, and coral monuments mark their resting-places. Generation after generation have sunk in the dark waters, and now wait the summons of the last trumpet-peal. Multitudes more will follow them, and go down to sleep beside them.

Mrs. Hemans has beautifully described a wreck and death at sea, in the following touching words:

> All night the booming minute-gun
>   Had pealed along the deep,
> And mournfully the rising sun
>   Looked o'er the tide-worn steep.
> A bark, from India's coral strand,
>   Before the raging blast,
> Had veiled her topsails to the sand,
>   And bowed her noble mast.
>
> The queenly ship! brave hearts had striven
>   And true ones died with her!—
> We saw her mighty cable riven,
>   Like floating gossamer.
> We saw her proud flag struck that morn,
>   A star once o'er the seas,—
> Her anchor gone, her deck uptorn,
>   And sadder things than these.
>
> We saw the strong man still and low,
>   A crushed reed thrown aside;
> Yet, by that rigid lip and brow,
>   Not without strife he died.
> And near him on the sea-weed lay,—
>   Till then we had not wept,—

> But well our gushing hearts might say,
>   That there a *mother* slept!
> For her pale arms a babe had pressed,
>   With such a wreathing grasp,
> Billows had dashed o'er that fond breast,
>   Yet not undone the clasp.
> Her very tresses had been flung
>   To wrap the fair child's form,
> Where still then wet, long streamers hung,
>   All tangled by the storm.
>
> And, beautiful 'midst that wild scene,
>   Gleamed up the boy's dead face,
> Like slumbers trustingly serene,
>   In melancholy grace.
> Deep in her bosom lay his head,
>   With half-shut violet eye;—
> *He* had known little of her dread,
>   Naught of her agony!
>
> O, human love, whose yearning heart,
>   Through all things vainly true,
> So stamps upon thy mortal part
>   Its passionate adieu,
> Surely thou hast another lot,—
>   There is some home for thee,
> Where thou shalt rest, remembering not
>   The moaning of the sea!

Yes, there is a home, far above all ocean tempests,—a home where the death-chill from cold waters will never be experienced!

At the appointed hour, the sea shall give up its dead. Coral tombs, and "the giant caverns of the unfathomed ocean," will resign their charge; and this corruption shall put on incorruption, and this mortal be clothed with immortality. Then may the glorified saints, having reached the haven of peace, cast their anchors within the vail, and feel secure from all danger.

> " O, for a breeze of heavenly love,
>   To waft my soul away
> To the celestial world above,
>   Where pleasures ne'er decay!
>
> From rocks of pride on either hand,
>   From quicksands of despair,
> O, guide me safe to Canaan's land,
>   Through every fatal snare!

> Anchor me in that port above,
>   On that celestial shore,
> Where dashing billows never move,
>   Where tempests never roar!"

THE SHORE OF ETERNITY.

REV. F. W. FABER, D. D.

Alone! to land alone upon that shore,
With no one sight that we have ever seen before;
    Things of a different hue,
    And the sounds all new,
And fragrances so sweet the soul may faint.
Alone! Oh, that first hour of being a saint.

Alone! to land upon that shore,
On which no wavelets lisp, no billows roar,
    Perhaps no shape of ground,
    Perhaps no sight or sound,
No forms of earth our fancies to arrange—
But to begin, alone, that mighty change!

Alone! to land alone upon that shore,
Knowing so well we can return no more;
    No voice or face of friend,
    None with us to attend
Our disembarking on that awful strand,
But to arrive alone in such a land!

Alone! to land upon that shore!
To begin alone to live forevermore,
    To have no one to teach
    The manners or the speech
Of that new life, or put us at our ease;
Oh! that we might die in pairs or companies!

Alone? The God we know is on that shore,
The God of whose attractions we know more
    Than of those who may appear
    Nearest and dearest here;
Oh, is He not the life-long friend we know
More privately than any friend below?

THE HOME BEYOND
THE NEW JERUSALEM.

REV. HORATIUS BONAR, D. D.

Bathed in unfallen sunlight,
　Itself a sun-born gem,
Fair gleams the glorious city,
　The new Jerusalem!
　　City fairest,
　　Splendor rarest,
　　　Let me gaze on thee!

Calm in her queenly glory,
　She sits all joy and light;
Pure in her bridal beauty,
　Her raiment festal-white!
　　Home of gladness,
　　Free from sadness,
　　　Let me dwell in thee!

Shading her golden pavement
　The tree of life is seen,
Its fruit-rich branches waving,
　Celestial evergreen.
　　Tree of wonder,
　　Let me under
　　　Thee forever rest!

Fresh from the throne of Godhead
　Bright in its crystal gleam,
Bursts out the living fountain,
　Swells on the living stream.
　　Blessed river,
　　Let me ever
　　　Feast my eye on thee!

Streams of true life and gladness,
　Springs of all health and peace;
No harps by thee hang silent,
　Nor happy voices cease.
　　Tranquil river,
　　Let me ever
　　　Sit and sing by thee!

River of God, I greet thee,
　Not now afar, but near;
My soul to thy still waters
　Hastes in its thirstings here.
　　Holy river,
　　Let me ever
　　　Drink of only thee!

Recognition of Friends in Heaven.

RECOGNITION OF FRIENDS IN HEAVEN.

SUMMARY OF REASONS FOR RECOGNITION.

BISHOP SAMUEL FALLOWS D. D.

THIS doctrine of future recognition is reasonable, because many of the same means which will enable us to identify ourselves in another life, will also enable us to identify our friends and former acquaintances. The consciousness of our mortality remains and connects us with all the past. The life on earth with its associations must come up before the mind and awake in the heart; and with this must appear our friends with whom we were bound below by social ties and relations.

Second. Memory will continue in another life. "Son, *remember* that thou in thy *life time!*" are the words of Abraham to the rich man.'

Memory cannot exist without recognition. The associations of friendship and love are the deepest seated and most precious of all. In a new country a desire after friends is among the first and strongest emotions of the soul; why should this desire not be gratified in heaven.

Third. The social law so radical and deeply seated in our nature is a further reason for belief in recognition. We are all by nature and in our constitution—physical, intellectual and moral,—united, related and dependent beings.

Our highest earthly happiness springs from our social feelings. The Kingdom of Christ on earth hallows and perfects these. Why should they be ignored or annihilated in the Kingdom of Christ in Heaven.

Fourth. "Death sometimes makes interruptions in the process of things which seem, in the nature of things, to require completion in a future life ; which, however, can only be done by recognition."

Benefits and blessings may have been conferred upon us by persons to whom we have not been able to express our gratitude. They are in the better land, we desire to see them there and thankfully acknowledge the good which has been done to us. The one conferring the benefit, the philanthropist, the minister of Christ, the faithful missionary or Sunday-school worker would be robbed of his just due if the acknowlegement is not made in some way to him.

Fifth. The final judgment necessarily involves details of act of persons inseparably associated with each other, so as to lead naturally to recognition.

All our good deeds are of a social kind—a great many of our good acts are so connected with the acts of others, and their influences are so merged into each other, that even we ourselves cannot trace our own acts in all their consequences. We influence others, and they us. Thus, faithfulness of parents in their family duties—faithfulness on the part of the members of a congregation towards each other, and in the community generally—makes the recollection and recognition of those thus associated absolutely neccessary, in the proceedings of that great day.

Sixth. The doctrine of heavenly recognition is highly reasonable to us, when we consider the ground we have for believing that our knowledge in the future world will be vastly enlarged in a general way, and of course in this respect in particular. If, our knowledge will increase in general, it must also increase in particular; and if our present knowledge will not be destroyed, but merged and included in the higher wisdom of our eternal state, it will most assuredly bear along with it that particular knowledge which is associated with the heavenly recognition of our sainted friends.

Seventh. "The interest which heavenly beings feel in the affairs of saints on earth, furnishes us reasonable ground for the belief in heavenly recognition.

There is no difficulty in believing that, on the part of saints in heaven, an acquaintance with us is kept up. We have lost them for a time, but they have not lost us. As they have gone higher, they have capacities and privileges which we, who are still beneath them, have not; and this may extend to a constant oversight and interest in us. This sense is as natural as any other to the passage, "Then shall I know even as also I am known." We are now known to them; but when we enter the state in which they now are, then shall we know them as they now know us."

ISOLATION AND FUTURE UNION.

We walk alone through all life's various ways,
Through light and darkness, sorrow, joy, and change;
And greeting each to each, through passing days,
    Still we are strange.

We hold our dear ones with a firm, strong grasp;
We hear their voices, look into their eyes;
And yet, betwixt us in that clinging clasp
    A distance lies.

We cannot *know their hearts*, howe'er we may
Mingle thought, aspiration, hope, and prayer;
We cannot reach them, and in vain essay
    To enter there.

Still, in each heart of hearts a hidden deep
Lies, never fathomed by its dearest, best;
With closest care our purest thoughts we keep,
    And tenderest.

But, blessed thought! we shall not always so
In darkness and in sadness walk alone;
There comes a glorious day when we shall know
    As we are known.

SHALL WE KNOW EACH OTHER.

REV. T. DE WITT TALMAGE D. D.

IF we part on earth *will we meet again in the next world?* "Well," says some one, "that seems to be an impossibility. Heaven is so large a place we never could find our kindred there." Going into some city, without having appointed a time and place for meeting, you might wander around for weeks and for months, and perhaps for years, and never see each other; and heaven is vaster than all earthly cities together, and how are you going to find your departed friend in that country? It is so vast a realm. John went up on one mountain of inspiration, and he looked off upon the multitude, and he said, "Thousands of thousands." Then he came upon a greater altitude of inspiration and looked off upon it again, and he said, "Ten thousand times ten thousand." And then he came on a higher mount of inspiration, and looked off again, and he said, "A hundred and forty and four thousand and thousands of thousands." And he came on a still greater height of inspiration, and he looked off again, and exclaimed: *"A great multitude that no man can number."*

Now I ask, how are you going to find your friends in such a throng as that? Is not this idea we have been entertaining after all a falsity? Is this doctrine of *future recognition* of friends in heaven a guess, a myth, a whim, or is it a granite foundation upon which the soul pierced of all ages may build a glorious hope? Intense question? Every heart in this audience throbs right into it. There is in every soul here the tomb of at least one dead.

TREMENDOUS QUESTION!

It makes the lip quiver, and the cheek flush, and the entire nature thrill: Shall we know each other there? I get letters almost every month asking me to discuss this subject. I get a letter in a bold, scholarly hand, on gilt-edged paper, asking me to discuss this question, and I say, "Ah! that is a curious man, and he wants a curious question solved." But I get another letter. It is written with a trembling hand, and on what seems to be a torn-out leaf of a book, and here and there is the mark of a tear; and I say, "Oh, that is a broken heart, and it wants to be comforted."

The object of this sermon is to take this theory out of the region of surmise and speculation into the region of *positive certainty* People say, "It would be very pleasant if that doctrine were true. I hope it may be true. Perhaps it is true. I wish it were true." But I believe that I can prove the doctrine of future recognition as plainly as that there is any heaven at all, and that the kiss of reunion at the celestial gate will be as certain as the dying kiss at the door of the sepulchre.

SHALL WE KNOW EACH OTHER.

Dr. Luther made remarks on the question: "Whether in the future blessed and eternal assembly and church we shall know each other?" And as we anxiously desired to know his opinion, he said: How did Adam do? He had never in his life seen Eve—he lay and slept—yet, when he awoke did not say, "Whence did you come? who are you?" but he said: "This is now bone of my bone, and flesh of my flesh." How did he know that this woman did not spring forth from a stone? He knew it because he was full of the Holy Spirit, and in possession of the true knowledge of God. Into this knowledge and image we will, in the future life, again be renewed in Christ; so that we will know father, mother, and one another, on sight, better than did Adam and Eve." Luther's Conversations.

EXPECTATION OF MEETING FRIENDS.

I must confess, as the experience of my own soul, that the expectation of loving my friends in heaven principally kindles my love to them on earth. If I thought that I should never know them, and consequently never love them after this life is ended, I should in reason number them with temporal things, and love them as such. But I now delight to converse with my pious friends, in a firm persuasion that I shall converse with them for ever; and I take comfort in those of them that are dead or absent, as believing I shall shortly meet them in heaven, and love them with a heavenly love that shall there be perfected. Rev. Richard Baxter.

FRIENDS WILL BE KNOWN IN HEAVEN.

MANY are anxious to know if they will recognize their friends in heaven. In the 8th chapter of Matthew and the 11th verse, we read: And I say unto you, that many shall come from the east and west, and shall sit down with Abraham and Isaac and Jacob, in the kingdom of heaven.

Here we find that Abraham, who lived so many hundreds of years before Christ, had not lost his identity, and Christ tells us that the time is coming when they shall come from the east and west and shall sit down with Abraham and Isaac and Jacob in the kingdom of God. These men had not lost their identity; they were known as Abraham, Isaac and Jacob. And if you will turn to that wonderful scene that took place on the Mount of Transfiguration, you will find that Moses, who had been gone from the earth 1,500 years, was there; Peter, James and John saw him on the Mount of Transfiguration; they saw him as Moses; he had not lost his name. God says over here in Isaiah, "I will not blot your names out of the Lamb's Book of life." We have names in heaven; we are going to bear our names there; we will be known.

Over in the Psalms it says: When I wake in His likeness I shall be satisfied. This is enough. Want is written on every human heart down here, but there we will be satisfied. You may hunt the world from one end to the other, and you will not find a man or woman who is satisfied; but in heaven we will want for nothing.

D. L. MOODY.

CALVIN.

GOD bless you, best and noblest brother; and if God permits you still longer to live, forget not that tie that binds us, which will be just as agreeable to us in heaven as it has been useful to the church on earth.   JOHN CALVIN'S LETTER TO FAREL.

WE LIVE IN HOPE OF SEEING FRIENDS AGAIN.

WE ought not to mourn for those who are delivered from the world by the call of the Lord, since we know they are not lost, but sent before us; that they have taken their leave of us in order to precede us. We may long after *them* as we do for those who have sailed on a distant voyage, but not lament them. We may not here below put on *dark* robes of mourning, when *they* above have already put on *white* robes of glory; we may not give the heathens any just occasion to accuse us of weeping for those as lost and extinct, of whom we say that they live with *God*, and of failing to prove by the witness of our hearts the faith we confess with our lips. We, who live in hope, who believe in God, and trust that Christ had suffered for us and risen again; we, who abide in Christ, who through him and in him rise again—why do we not ourselves wish to depart out of this world?—or why do we lament for the friends who have been *separated* from us, as if they were lost?   CYPRIAN.

THE STRONG IMMORTAL HOPE.

If death my friend and me divide,
Thou dost not, Lord, my sorrows chide,
  Nor frown my tears to see;
Restrained from passionate excess,
Thou bidst me mourn in calm distress,
  For them that rest in thee.

I feel a strong, immortal hope,
Which bears my mournful spirit up
  Beneath its mountain load;
Redeemed from death, and grief, and pain,
I soon shall find my friend again,
  Within the arms of God.

Pass the few fleeting moments more,
And death the blessing shall restore,
  Which death hath snatched away:
For me, thou wilt the summons send,
And give me back my parted friend,
  In that eternal day!

IS MEMORY ANNIHILATED.

IT has been asked, shall we know each other in heaven? Suppose you should not; you may be assured of this, that nothing will be wanting to your happiness. But oh! you say, how would the thought affect me now! There is the babe that was torn from my bosom; how lovely then, but a cherub now! There is the friend, who was as mine own soul, with whom I took sweet counsel, and went to the house of God in company. There is the minister—whose preaching turned my feet into the path of peace—whose words were to me a well of life. There is the beloved mother, on whose knees I first laid my little hands to pray, and whose lips first taught my tongue to pronounce the name of Jesus! And are these removed from us forever? Shall we recognize them no more?—Cease your anxieties. Can memory be annihilated? Did not Peter, James, and John know Moses and Elias? Does not the Savior inform us that the friends, benefactors have made of the mammon of unrighteousness, shall receive them into everlasting habitations? Does not Paul tell the Thessalonians that they are his hope, and joy, and crown, at the coming of our Lord Jesus Christ?

REV. WM. JAY.

RECOGNITION IN HEAVEN.

And the saints now crowned in triumph,
  Like the sun, in radiance glow,
Greet each other in that gladness
  Which the saints alone can know;
Whilst secure they count their battles
  With their subjugated foe.

To their first estate return they,
  Freed from every mortal sore;
And the truth forever present,
  Ever lovely, they adore;
Drawing from that living fountain
  Living sweetness evermore.

PETER DAMIANI.

FRIENDS AND ENEMIES MEET IN HEAVEN.

WHEN we come to heaven we shall meet with all those excellent persons, those brave minds, those innocent and charitable souls, whom we have seen, and heard, and read of in the world. There we shall meet many of our dear relations and intimate friends, and perhaps with many of our enemies, to whom we shall then be perfectly reconciled, nothwithstanding all the warm contests and peevish differences which we had with them in this world, even about matters of religion. For heaven is a state of perfect love and friendship.

Archbishop Tillotson.

OUR DEPARTED FRIENDS ARE IN HEAVEN.

If there is anything that ought to make heaven near to Christians, it is knowing that God and all their loved ones will be there. What is it that makes home so attractive? Is it because we have a beautiful home? Is it because we have beautiful lawns? Is it because we have beautiful trees around that home? Is it because we have beautiful paintings upon the walls inside? Is it because we have beautiful furniture? Is that all that makes home so attractive and so beautiful? Nay, it is the loved ones in it; it is the loved ones there.

I remember after being away from home some time, I went back to see my honored mother, and I thought in going back I would take her by surprise, and steal in unexpectedly upon her, but when I found she had gone away, the old place didn't seem like home at all. I went into one room and then into another, and I went all through the house, but I could not find that loved mother, and I said to some member of the family, "Where is mother?" and they said she had gone away. Well, home had lost its charm to me; it was that mother that made home so sweet to me, and it is the loved ones that are going to make heaven so sweet to all of us.

D. L. Moody.

THE REV. WM. ORMISTON, D. D.

RECOGNITION A TRULY CATHOLIC IDEA.

THAT the saints in glory shall continue to know those whom they have known and loved on earth, seems to me to flow necessarily from the idea of their immortality itself; for this cannot be real, except as it includes personal identity or a continuation of the same consciousness. It is moreover a strictly catholic idea, the sense of which has been actively present to the mind of the church, through all ages, in her doctrine of the "Communion of Saints." This regards not merely Christians on earth, but also the sainted dead; according to the true word of the hymn; "The saints on earth and all the dead, but one communion make." But communion implies a continuity of reciprocal knowledge and affection.

Rev. J. W. Nevin, D. D.

According to the representations contained in the holy scriptures, the saints dwell together in the future world, and form, as it were, a kingdom or state of God. They will there partake of a common felicity.

Dr. George Christian Knapp.

DYING FRIENDS PIONEERS.

Our dying friends come o'er us like a cloud
To damp our brainless ardors; and abate
That glare of life, which often blinds the wise.
Our dying friends are pioneers, to smooth
Our rugged path to death, to break those bars
Of terror and abhorrence, nature throws
'Cross our obstructed way; and thus, to make
Welcome as safe, our port from every storm.

Young.

All is not over with earth's broken tie—
Where, where should sisters love, if not on high?

Mrs. Hemans.

THE FUTURE LIFE.

W. C. BRYANT.

How shall I know thee in the sphere which keeps
    The disembodied spirits of the dead,
When all of thee that time could wither sleeps
    And perishes among the dust we tread?

For I shall feel the sting of ceaseless pain
    If there I meet thy gentle presence not;
Nor hear the voice I love, nor read again
    In thy serenest eye, the tender thought.

Will not thy own meek heart demand me there?
    That heart whose fondest throbs to me were given;
My name on earth was ever in thy prayer,
    Shall it be banished from thy tongue in heaven?

In meadows fanned by heaven's life-breathing wind,
    In the resplendence of that glorious sphere,
And larger movements of the unfettered mind,
    Wilt thou forget the love that joined us here?

A love that lived through all the stormy past,
    And meekly with my harsher nature bore,
And deeper grew, and tenderer to the last,—
    Shall it expire with life, and be no more?

A happier lot than mine, and larger light
    Await thee there; for thou hast bowed thy will
In cheerful homage to the rule of right,
    And lovest all, and renderest good for ill.

For me, the sordid cares in which I dwell,
    Shrink and consume my heart, as heat the scroll;
And wrath has left its scar—that fire of hell
    Has left its frightful scar upon my soul.

Yet though thou wear'st the glory of the sky,
    Wilt thou not keep the same beloved name,
The same fair thoughtful brow, and gentle eye,
    Lovelier in heaven's sweet climate, yet the same?

Shalt thou not teach me, in that calmer home,
    The wisdom that I learned so ill in this—
The wisdom which is love—till I become
    Thy fit companion in the world of bliss?

THE DEPARTED PRESERVE THEIR INTEGRITY.

PROF. A. P. PEABODY, D. D.

WHEN I think of the kindred and friends who may welcome me to heaven, I want to think not of any precise number of angelic beings, alike except in their degrees of attainment, —I would bring them up in their individual forms and features, in those delicate hues and blendings of character, those traits of loveliness to be felt, yet not described, which linger always on our memories. And as their tones of voice still dwell upon our hearts, and their countenances are ever living there, why need we suppose that even these in their individuality have passed away, that is, so far as the soul gave them shape and utterance? The tongue, the face, is indeed forever cold and dead. But in some form or way spirits must be manifest to, and hold converse with, one another. Why, then, may not some likeness to the earthly countenance and voice (at least so far as to produce sameness of impression) survive in whatever form of life the translated spirit may assume, so that, when friends meet friends in heaven, there may be something in their so widely different mode of existence to recall even the looks and tones through which they had known each other here?.

He, with his guide, the farther fields attained,
Where, severed from the rest, the warrior souls remained.
Fidens he met, with Meleager's race,
The pride of armies, and the soldier's grace;
And pale Adrastus, with his ghastly face.
Of Trojan chiefs he viewed a numerous train,
All much lamented, all in battle slain—
Glaucus and Medon, high above the rest
Antenor's sons, and Ceres' sacred priest,
And proud Idæus, Priam's charioteer,
Who shakes his empty reins, and aims his airy spear.
The gladsome ghosts in circling troops attend,
And with unwearied eyes behold their friend;
Delight to hover near, and long to know
What business brought him to the realms below.

VIRGIL.

MORE FRIENDS IN HEAVEN THAN ON EARTH.

THERE is a period of mortal life at which the friends who are gone, begin to bear a large proportion to those who remain, if they do not even outnumber them. The Christian man beholds the heavenly company increase of those who wait for him. He finds himself living more in the past and less in the future time of his earthly life. He loses not his cheerfulness, but he is continually acquiring thoughtfulness. The bonds between heaven and him are multiplying. His faithful eye beholds, and his faithful heart records the lengthening train of the departed. And not only his nearest relatives and most intimate friends are on the register of his spirit, but those whose sweetness and worth he has known from the communion of a few years or months, or even from a few casual meetings, are all added to the list as they put on immortality. Of these he thinks, and with these he converses, with increasing frequency, and with a pleasure which the unbelieving and the doubting cannot experience. As he lives on, the number of his earthly companions is every year decreasing, till perhaps they all go, and then what is there for him but to wait? He will not grieve, but wait and hope. The departed are not a source of sorrow, but now his only solace and joy. In the cheerful words of an old poet, he may say,

> "They all are gone into a world of light,
> And I alone sit lingering here;
> Their very memory is fair and bright,
> And my sad thoughts doth clear."
>
> REV. F. W. P. GREENWOOD, D. D.

IF this (Col. i. 28) be rightly interpreted, then it affords the manifest and necessary inference, that the saints in a future life will meet and be known again to one another; for how, without knowing again his converts, in their new and glorious state, could St. Paul desire or expect to present them at the last day?

ARCHDEACON WILLIAM PALEY, D. D.

JOY OF PASTOR AND PEOPLE IN HEAVEN.

Is it a joy too low for saints in heaven to meet, know and love? What joy on earth is so pure and sweet as to bless others, or to be blest and feel grateful for good received? How much more—how unspeakably more and purer must the joy be, which those feel in heaven, who have labored, prayed and wept together on earth, when they are at last safely landed together in realms of endless bliss!

> Such, Christian pastor, is thy heart's delight,
> To serve thy God, and see thy people share
> His service, led by thee: with them how bright
> The joy to come, let holy Paul declare;
> A joy, a glory, and a crown of light,
> Which kings might envy, and exult to wear!
> REV. H. HARBAUGH, D. D.

BELIEF OF THE HEBREWS.

The Hebrews regarded life as a journey, as a pilgrimage on the face of the earth. The traveller, as they supposed, when he arrived at the end of his journey, which happened when he died, was received into the company of his ancestors, who had gone before him. Opinions of this kind (viz., that life is a journey, that death is the end of that journey, and that, when one dies, he mingles with the hosts who have gone before), are the origin and ground of such phrases as the following: "To be gathered to one's people; to go to one's fathers.' This visiting of the fathers has reference to the immortal part, and is clearly distinguished from the mere burial of the body.

JOHN ARCH.

It is reasonable to believe that the saints shall know that they had such and such a relation to one another when they were on earth. The father shall know that such a one was his child; the husband shall know that such a one was his wife; the spiritual guide shall know that such belonged to his flock; and so all other relations of persons shall be renewed and known in heaven

THE UPWARD PROCESSION.

THUS from Abel to Abraham; from him to Malachi; from Christ to John, and from John till now, what a mighty stream of the Lord's saints have been sweeping onwards and upwards from amongst every kindred and tongue and nation under Heaven! And they will all be there. Oh, what a mighty phalanx of patriarchs and prophets, apostles and evangelists, martyrs and confessors shall we behold, my brethren, when we get to Heaven; and what mighty volumes of praise shall roll upwards from that vast throng, to the throne of God! Timid women who for Christ alone were valiant; strong-minded, noble men, who endured reproach and contumely in the Master's cause, and thought not even their lives dear unto them, if only by their sacrifice they might finish their course acceptably and win their crown, oh, what hosts of these shall we behold! Confessors of whom the world was not worthy! True men and women who endured with patience all that the ingenuity of the wicked, prompted by Satan, could do to their hurt—all the fiery darts that could be hurled against them: those barbed arrows of calumny, detraction and persecution that must bring the quivering flesh away whenever you would extract them!

There shall we see crowds from the poor and despised of earth —those who slept upon wretched pallets, dwelt in miserable hovels who day by day ate the bread of poverty, and by night watered their couch with tears, but whose sins were washed away in the ocean of the Redeemer's blood—their hearts steadfast with God. There we shall see the afflicted and distressed, though no longer sick; the forlorn and the friendless; the despised and the outcast, but not of God—men and women who waded through the waters and forced their way through the fires to reach their crown, or who endured the biting pangs of penury and want, rather than accept the glittering wages, together with the dread retributions of sin.

REV. W. H. COOPER D. D.

'Tis sweet, as year by year we lose
Friends out of sight, to muse
How grows in Paradise our store.

REMEMBRANCE OF THE DEAD.

WE know the spot where lie
   Our sleeping dead—but where
Is that which cannot die—
   The soul? Lord is it there?
The carrier pigeon brings
   A message 'neath his wings,
From India's distant shore,
   Sails pass from place to place,
But from its narrow space,
   The soul returns no more.

The infant at the breast,
   From its mother's bosom torn,
To its icy bed of rest,
   From its little cradle borne!
All that we loved and mourn,
   Bear away part of us,
From the dust murmuring cry—
   Ye who beheld the sky,
Do ye still remember us?

                       LAMARTINE.

Remembrance, faithful to her trust,
Calls thee in beauty from the dust;
Thou comest in the morning light,
Thou 'rt with me through the gloomy night,
In dreams I meet thee as of old;
Then thy soft arms my neck enfold,
And thy sweet voice is in my ear,
In every scene of memory dear.
      I see thee still.

      I see thee still;
Thou art not in the grave confined—
Death cannot chain the immortal mind;
Let earth close o'er its sacred trust,
But goodness dies not in the dust,
Thee, O my daughter! 'tis not thee
Beneath the coffin's lid I see;
Thou to a fairer land art gone,
There, let me hope, my journey done,
      To see thee still.

                       CHARLES SPRAGUE.

MESSAGES TO THE OTHER SIDE.

REV. DR. TALMAGE.

HAVE you any appreciation this evening of the good and glorious times your friends are having in heaven? How different it is when they get news there of a Christian's death from what it is here. It is the difference between embarkation and coming into port. Everything depends upon which side of the river you stand when you hear of a Christian's death. If you stand on this side of the river you mourn that they go. If you stand on the other side of the river, you rejoice that they come. Oh, the difference between a funeral on earth and a jubilee in heaven—between requiem here and triumphal march there—parting here and reunion there. Together! Have you thought of it? They are together. Not one of your departed friends in one land, and another in another land; but together in different rooms of the same house—the house of many mansions. Together! I never appreciated that thought so much as recently, when we laid away in her last slumber my sister Sarah. Standing there in the village cemetery, I looked around and said: "There is father, there is mother, there is grandfather, there is grandmother, there are whole circles of kindred;" and I thought to myself. "Together in the grave—together in glory." I am so impressed with the thought that I do not think it is any fanaticism when some one is going from this world to the next if you make them the bearer of dispatches to your friends who are gone, saying: "Give my love to my parents, give my love to my children, give my love to my old comrades who are in glory, and tell them I am trying to fight the good fight of faith, and I will join them after a while." I believe the message will be delivered; and I believe it will increase the gladness of those who are before the throne. Together are they, all their tears gone. No trouble getting good society for them. All kings, queens, princes, and princesses. In 1751, there was a bill offered in your English Parliament, proposing to change the almanac so that the first of March should come immediately after the 18th of February, But, oh, what a glorious change in the calendar when all the years of your earthly existence are swallowed up in the eternal year of God!

WE SHALL KNOW ONE ANOTHER.

When we come to behold the glorious majesty of God, we shall not only know our Savior Christ, and such as we were acquainted with in this world, but all the elect and chosen people of God, who have been from the beginning of the world. When we are once come into the heavenly Jerusalem, we shall, without doubt, both seek and know all the holy and most blessed company of the patriarchs, prophets, apostles, and martyrs, with all others of the faithful. As we are all members of one body, whereof Jesus Christ is the Head, so shall we know one another, rejoice together, and be glad with one another.

Thos. Becon.

GONE—BUT NOT LOST.

Sweet bud of earth's wilderness, rifled and torn!
Fond eyes have wept o'er thee, fond hearts still will mourn;
The spoiler hath come, with his cold withering breath,
And the loved and the cherished lies silent in death.

He felt not the burden and heat of the day!
He has passed from this earth, and its sorrows, away,
With the dew of the morning yet fresh on his brow:—
Sweet bud of earth's wilderness, where art thou now?

And oh! do you question, with tremulous breath,
Why the joy of your household lies silent in death?
Do you mourn round the place of your perishing dust?
Look onward and upward with holier trust!

Who cometh to meet him, with light on her brow?
What angel form greets him so tenderly now!
'Tis the pure sainted mother, springs onward to bear
The child of her love from this region of care!

Mrs. Ellen Stone.

I am, therefore, more than fully persuaded, that we shall know in heaven our parents and our friends, and generally all the persons whom we have known here below.

Rev. Charles Drelincourt.

NOT LOST, BUT GONE BEFORE.

Friend after friend departs;
  Who hath not lost a friend?
There is no union here of hearts,
  That finds not here an end;
Were this frail world our final rest,
Living or dying none were blest.

Beyond the flight of time,
  Beyond the reign of death,
There surely is some blessed clime,
  Where life is not a breath;
Nor love's affections transient fire,
Whose sparks fly upward and expire.

There is a world above,
  Where parting is unknown;
A long eternity of love,
  Formed for the good alone;
And faith beholds the dying here,
Translated to that glorious sphere.

Thus star by star declines,
  'Till all are passed away,
As morning high, and higher shines,
  To pure and perfect day:
Nor sink those stars in empty night,
But hide themselves in heaven's own light.
                              MONTGOMERY.

WHAT A MEETING IN HEAVEN.

WHAT a meeting on the other shore! If we could see there this morning how our hearts would enlarge. Multitudes around the throne to day. I am charmed with that thought, There's a central figure I am more charmed with—the Man on the Throne. His kingdom shall triumph over all. The time will come when every knee shall bow and every tongue confess.

I think of the men gone before—fathers, mothers, little children—that cloud up yonder. I think I can see them. Oh, there is a cloud of witnesses. I urge on my way, run my race, ever looking to Jesus, who is alone the finisher of faith. Oh, may this audience all follow Jesus and be a part of that grand gathering that shall meet on that other shore!   BISHOP M. SIMPSON, D. D.

WE MOURN NOT WITHOUT HOPE.

Let those mourn without measure, who mourn without hope. The husbandman does not mourn, when he casts his seed into the ground. He expects to receive it again, and more. The same hope have we, respecting our friends who have died in faith. You do not lament over your children or friends, while slumbering on their beds. Consider death as a sleep from which they shall certainly awake. Even a heathen philosopher could say that he enjoyed his friends, expecting to part with them; and parted with them, expecting to see them again. And shall a heathen excel a Christian in bearing affliction with cheerfulness. LAVEL.

I need not say to myself, or my dear friends who are in the Lord, *Quo nunc abilis in loco?* We know where they are, and how employed. There I humbly trust my dear Mary is waiting for me, and in the Lord's own time I hope to join with her and all the redeemed in praising the Lamb, once upon the cross, now upon the throne of glory. REV. JOHN NEWTON.

Very soon they who are separated will be reunited, and there will appear no trace of the separation. They who are about to set out upon a journey, ought not to set themselves far distant from those who have gone to the same country a few days before. Life is like a torrent; the past is but a dream; the present, while we are thinking of it, escapes us, and is precipitated into the same abyss that has swallowed up the past; the future will not be of a different nature; it will pass as rapidly. A few moments, and a few more, and all will be ended; what has appeared long and tedious, will seem short when it is finished. FENELON.

My little one, my fair one, thou canst not come to me,
But nearer draws the numbered hour, when I shall go to thee;
And thou, perchance, with seraph smile, and golden harp in hand,
May'st come the first to welcome me, to our Emanuel's land.
R. HUIE.

HEAVEN A PLACE OF JOY.

How can the place of departed spirits fail to be a place of joy to the Christian? for there he shall meet all those pious relatives and friends whom heaven indulgent gave to him awhile, and heaven mysterious soon resumed again.

Rev. S. S. Schmacker, D. D

Death separates, but it can never disunite those who are bound together in Christ Jesus. To them, death in his power of an endless separation, is abolished. It is no more death, but a sweet departure, a journey from earth to heaven. Our children are still ours. We are still their parents. We are yet one family—one in memory—one in hope—one in spirit. Our children are yet with us, and dwell with us in our sweetest, fondest recollections. We too are yet with them in the bright anticipations of our reunion with them, in the glories of the upper sanctuary. We mingle together indeed no more in sorrow and in pain,

> But we shall join love's buried ones again
> In endless bands, and in eternal peace.

Rev. Thomas Smyth, D. D.

RECOGNITION NOT A FANCY.

It is no dreaming fancy to expect, that in *another* world we shall preserve our identity—shall know and be known even as in this. Let the mourner in Sion continue "patient in well-doing;" "looking for and hasting to the coming of the Lord," when shall begin the reunion of kindred spirits, whom in this world death had separated. Parent to child, sister to brother, husband to wife, friend to friend, shall then be restored—a blessed communion of saints, whom nor sin nor sorrow shall sever more.

Rev. John James, D. D.

WE SHALL KNOW EACH OTHER IN HEAVEN.

THAT it should ever have been doubted whether the inhabitants of the spiritual world recognize each other in that abode, is but an example of the wide influence of unbelief, suggesting the strangest dimness wherever the Scriptures had not spoken in the most explicit words, even though the obvious reason for which the words had not been spoken was, that to speak them was needless. Why should not the departed recognize and be recognized? How can their very nature and being be so utterly changed that they should be able to exist in the same world, to remember, and to be a general assembly, a church, a society, without recognition? If the future life is the sequel, and result, and retribution of the present, how can recognition fail? Not a step can we proceed, not a conception can we form, not a statement of divine revelation can we clearly embrace in our contemplations of the future life, without admitting or involving the necessity of mutual recognition as well as mutual remembrance and affection. Were Moses and Elias unknown to each other? Did the Martyrs below the altar utter the same cry, without knowing the history of their companions, each a stranger amongst strangers? Was Abraham a stranger to Lazarus, or was Lazarus seen and known by the rich man only? Could those who watch for souls render account for them with joy or grief, and yet not know their doom? Could Christian converts be the "glory and joy" of an Apostle at the coming of the Lord if He knew them not? Could the Patriarchs be seen in the kingdom of God by none but those who should be shut out? All proceeds on the supposition of just such knowledge there as here. It is probable, indeed, that the human soul must always clothe itself with form, even in the separate state; and such a form would bear the same impress which had been given to the mortal body. There is no extravagance in the wish of Dr. Randolph to know Cowper above from his picture here, or in the same thought as expressed in the verses of Southey on the portrait of Heber. Rt. Rev. Geo. Burgess D. D.

BELIEF OF MELANCTHON, CRUCIGER, OLEVIANUS, SCALIGER.

MELANCHTON, a few days before his death, told Camerarius that he trusted their friendship should be cultivated and perpetuated in another world. Cruciger, another of the school of the Reformers, spoke, in his last hours, of meeting and recognition. Casper Olevianus, a divine of Heidelberg, who has the honor of sharing with Ursinus the anthorship of the celebrated Heidelberg Catechism—the symbol of all the Reformed churches in all lands and languages where the Reformed faith is held, when his son had been summoned to see him before he should die, sent to him also the message, that "he need not hurry: they should see one another in eternal life." So Joseph Scaliger spoke of "soon meeting and embracing, no longer the subjects of age and infirmity."

Rt. Rev. Geo. Burgess D. D.

THE QUESTION OF RECOGNITION UNNECESSARY.

It has been asked whether, in this blessed abode, the saints will know one another? One should think that the question was unnecessary, as the answer naturally presents itself to every man's mind; and it could only have occurred to some dreaming theologian, who, in his airy speculations, has soared far beyond the sphere of reason and common sense. Who can doubt whether the saints will know one another? What reason can be given why they should not? Would it be any part of their perfection to have all their former ideas obliterated, and to meet as strangers in the other world? Would it give us a more favorable notion of the assembly in heaven, to suppose it to consist of a multitude of unknown individuals, who never hold communication with each other; or by some inexplicable restraint are prevented, amidst an intimate intercourse, from mutual discoveries? Or have they forgotten what they themselves were, so that they cannot reveal it to their associates? What would be gained by this ignorance no man can tell; but we can tell what would be lost by it.

Rev. Dr. Dick.

WE SHALL KNOW EACH OTHER IN GLORY.

REV. J. EDMONSON.

WE know each other in the present world. All human beings have certain distinctive marks by which they are known : and will these be lost in the world to come? Will our knowledge of each other be less perfect, in a world of perfection, than it is in this imperfect state. It cannot be ascertained how we may be known to each other there ; but if we examine the subject on the principles of analogy, we cannot doubt the fact. There is a high probability that we shall then know all whom we have known before, by some resemblance of their former appearance, which they may still retain. There is a general likeness in the countenances of men, accompanied with such amazing variety, that there never were two faces exactly alike, since the world was made ; but when any one is well known by his freinds and acquaintances, it is not an easy matter to forget him. He is remembered when absent; and is not forgotten after he has been removed by death.

And why may we not suppose that the spirits of men, when they are seen by spirits, will be recognised by some identical appearance? Will the peculiarities of their respective forms be so far changed, that they cannot be known to those who knew them in the body, and who conversed with them in the flesh? It has been supposed by physiognomists, that every feature of man arises from some peculiar property in his soul ; and if this be true, that property will appear conspicuously after he has laid aside his body. And after his resurrection, he will still retain that peculiarity in external appearance which he had on earth. And if this reasoning be correct, we shall most assuredly know each other, both before and after the resurrection of the dead.

Is it possible to lose a recollection of our dearest friends in a world of perfection? This implies a contradiction ; and he who attempts to prove it, must affirm that we know our friends in a state of comparative ignorance, but that we shall be for ever unknown to each other when we are perfected in knowledge. Recollections of persons and things, in ages that have passed away, will be one source of eternal blessedness ; and to be deprived of this would cut off that stream of pleasure, which will be enjoyed in the happy junction of all the wise and good of every age and nation.

But if we shall be wholly unacquainted with those pious persons who have lived on earth, our knowledge will be limited within a very narrow circle ; and their society will not afford us that pleasure which we now anticipate. It has always been considered, that a knowledge of men and things is a high attainment ; and shall we be ignorant either of the one or the other, when we live in a world of light and glory? Will all be strangers and unknown to each other in the heavenly society? The idea is extremely absured ; and should be banished from the mind of every intelligent man. The question how we shall know each other is unnecessary, and cannot be resolved ; but if we possess this knowledge in the present world, surely it will be continued in a higher state.

Lazarus was known in heaven. The angels that carried him to the bosom of Abraham knew him well. They had seen him in abject poverty, covered with sores, and shamefully neglected. They saw him in the hour of death ; and they saw him in glory. And if he were known to them, when advanced to the heavenly feast, and clothed with honor, was he not known to others? Abraham knew him, mentioned his former name, and stated his sufferings on earth. He was greatly changed, but still appeared as the identical person who lay at the gate of the rich man. And it is highly probable that a vast concourse of celestial spirits, who witnessed his arrival, knew who he was, and what he had suffered, If this be allowed, it proves a great deal : for if one knew him, why not others also, when they saw him lodged in Abraham's bosom?

Pastors will know their flocks in heaven ; and the flocks will know their pastors. This fact is stated by the apostle Paul, in words that cannot be misunderstood by any impartial reader Thus, he informed the Thessalonian believers of his hope and joy in meeting them at the coming of Jesus : " For what is our hope, or joy, or crown of rejoicing? are not even ye in the presence of our Lord Jesus Christ at his coming? For ye are our glory and joy," 1 Thess. ii, 19, 20. But if ministers cannot know their flocks when Jesus comes how can they joy in them at his appearance? Or how can they be a crown of rejoicing, if they are totally unknown to their pious and holy instructors?

We shall be presented to God, in a state of perfection, by those ministers who have warned us, and taught us in all wisdom. Hence they make this appeal to their converts, "Christ in you the hope of glory; whom we preach, warning every man, and teaching every man, in all wisdom; that we may present every man, perfect in Christ Jesus," Col. i, 28. And will they not know those whom they present to their God and Savior? The steady perseverance of saints inspires a minister with confidence, because he will meet them with joy at the coming of Jesus. "And now, little children, abide in him; that when he shall appear, we may have confidence, and not be ashamed before him at his coming," 1 John ii, 28. And can this be realized if they do not know their flocks?

But if the pastor know his flock, will not the flock know their pastor? And will not their joy be mutual when they meet in the heavenly fold? Will they not then recollect all those refreshing seasons which they enjoyed together, in the green pastures of divine ordinances, while they dwelt on earth? But all this implies a recollection of persons and things in the present world, when we are with Jesus in a state of immortal joy and felicity. With what unknown pleasure shall we behold those teachers who cared for our souls, and who showed us the way of salvation! But all the praise, and all the glory, will be given to God and the Lamb.

We may argue this question from that fellowship of saints which is begun on earth, but perfected in heaven. Can this be carried into effect, if they do not know each other, when they meet in glory? It is affirmed of our present state, that "if we walk in the light, as he is in the light, we have fellowship one with another," 1 John i, 7. And will not this continue, and increase, when we meet in the New Jerusalem? Shall we not know those holy and happy souls with whom we have held sweet communion on earth, and with whom we shall enjoy a delightful union in heaven? With them we have fought and conquered.

Our souls, united by love, have jointly offered up praise and thanksgiving to God; and we have worshiped him together in spirit and in truth in his holy sanctuary. Will all these things, with all our pious conversations, be buried in eternal oblivion, when we stand before the Lord, and worship him in his holy temple on Mount Zion? The idea is extremely absurd. Says Dr. Price: "Is it possible that we should be happy hereafter in the same seats of joy, under the perfect government, and as members of the same heavenly society, and yet remain strangers to one another? Shall we be together with Christ, and yet not with one another? Being in the same happy state with our present virtuous friends and relatives, will they not be accessible to us? And if accessible, shall we not fly to them, and mingle hearts and souls again?"

I SHALL KNOW HIM.

That each, who seems a separate whole,
  Should move his rounds, and, fusing all
  The skirts of self again, should fall
Remerging in the general Soul,

Is faith as vague as all unsweet?
  Eternal form shall still divide
  The eternal soul from all beside,
And I shall know him when we meet.

And we shall sit at endless feast,
  Enjoying each the other's good;
  What vaster dream can hit the mood
Of Love on earth? He seeks at least

Upon the last and sharpest height,
  Before the spirit fades away,
  Some landing-place, to clasp and say,
Farewell! We lose ourselves in light!"

TENNYSON.

Oh, weep not for the dead!
Rather, oh! rather give the tear
To those that darkly linger here,
  When all besides are fled.
Weep for the spirit withering
In its cold, cheerless sorrowing;
Weep for the young and lovely one,
That ruin darkly revels on;
  But never be a tear-drop shed
  For them, the pure enfranchised dead.

UNKNOWN.

HOW SHALL WE KNOW EACH OTHER IN HEAVEN?

REV. J. EDMONSON, D. D.

AND how shall we know those holy persons who lived in former ages, and in distant climes? The answer is easy: Intelligent spirits, who knew them well, will make them known to us in friendly conversations. How did the three disciples of our Lord know Enoch and Elijah, when they appeared with him on the mount? It is probable that they received information from their Master, to whom those departed saints were well known; and in the heavenly world it may be said to us, This is Abraham, that is Job, and that is Daniel. And all those saints, when once made known to us, will be known for ever. If we were to travel to any civilized region of this world, should we not be introduced to the inhabitants of the place, by some friendly person who might know them? And are saints less courteous in the heavenly world than men on earth? In that world of felicity, holy spirits of every rank take pleasure in communicating happiness; and our happiness will be greatly augmented by a knowledge of all the inhabitants of that place, where we shall live to all eternity.

And will not the Lord of all worlds, who has connected our happiness with the sacred ties of friendship, appoint certain spirits to discover to us those holy friends whom we knew before, and with whom we shall live forever? Angels have had charge of every good man on earth, from the beginning of the world, and they know every one by name. And will not those lovely spirits discover the saints to each other? And shall we not receive from extensive information of those good men to whom they ministered in the present world? And the saints of former ages, who are far advanced in knowledge, may be appointed to instruct their younger brethren. The divine Being, who knows all things, employs instruments and agents to instruct men; and why may he not pursue a similar plan, in his wise government of angels and saints, in the world of glory?

We do not pretend to explain how those happy spirits instruct each other. It has not been revealed; and it is a subject which our limited powers cannot discover. For we are unacquainted with their language, their organs of speech, and their method of communicating ideas; but it must be absurd to suppose that they are less perfect in these things than mortal men in the present state of comparative ignorance. No doubt they excel, in every method that can be used, of communicating thought from one intellectual being to another. And can they be ignorant of each other? Will nothing be said, by any intellectual spirit, to bring to remembrance persons and things of former times? Scripture and reason are both at variance with this absurd opinion.

But what sweet and edifying conversations may be expected between kindred spirits in that happy world! and how amazingly will these be heightened by a perfect knowledge of each other, when all have passed through this world of sin and sorrow! One will ever be ready to teach another, and all will rejoice in the acquisition of knowledge. The mind of every one will be enlarged; truth will be unfolded; and all will be innocent and holy. The joy arising from a knowledge of each other will be mutual; and to know and be made known will produce pleasure that cannot be expressed. But if former things are to be forgotten, and if we are to remain strangers to each other, our bliss will be imperfect. The ties of friendship in this case will be weakened; and all its peculiar enjoyments considerably abridged.

THE BELIEF OF THE FATHERS.

ALL the ancient and pious fathers agreed to this. St. Cyprian owns, that our parents, brethren, children, and near relations, expect us in heaven, and are solicitous for our good. St. Jerome comforts a good lady on this account, that we shall see our friends, and know them. St. Augustine endeavors to mitigate the sorrow of an Italian widow with this consideration, that she shall be restored to her husband, and behold and know him.

DR. EDWARDS.

THE DEPARTED REMEMBER.

MANY suppose a certain kind of continuance of their thinking faculties after death, but do not believe that with these faculties they will remember their earthly existence. They dream of an existence that is entirely new, which is better than the present, but upon which this life has no influence, and with which it has no connection. This whole idea amounts to just the same as entire annihilation at death; for if I cannot recollect this life—its fortunes and misfortunes, my wife and children, my friends, my weaknesses and my good deeds,—in short, nothing at all, then I am no more the same *I*, no more the same person, but I will be a being entirely new! The Lord in mercy preserve us from such a future state! But thanks to his name forever, that the Bible, and the common sense and feeling of men in all ages and in all places, teach directly the contrary.

STILLING.

HEAVEN AND EARTH.

There are no shadows where there is no sun;
There is no beauty where there is no shade;
And all things in two lines of glory run,
Darkness and light, ebon and gold inlaid.

God comes among us through the shroud of ah,
And His dim path is like the silvery wake
Left by your pinnace on the mountain lake,
Fading and reappearing here and there.
The lamps and veils, through heaven and
Earth that move,
Go in and out, as jealous of their light,
Like sailing stars upon a misty night.
Death is the shade of coming life; and Love
Yearns for her dear ones in the holy tomb,
Because bright things are better seen in gloom.

F. W. FABER.

BUT A LITTLE WHILE.

IT is yet but a little while, and we shall be delivered from the burden and the conflict, and, with all those who have preceded us in the righteous struggle enjoy the deep raptures of a Mediator's presence. Then re-united to the friends with whom we took sweet counsel upon earth, we shall recount our toil, only to heighten our ecstacy; and call to mind the tug and the din of war, only that with a more bounding throb and a richer song, we may feel and celebrate the wonders of redemption,

NEVILL.

FRIENDS NOT LOST.

THOU hast lost thy friend:—say, rather, thou hast parted with him. That is properly lost which is past all recovery, which we are out of hope to see any more. It is not so with this friend thou mournest for: he is but gone home a little before thee; thou art following him; you two shall meet in your Father's house, and enjoy each other more happily than you could have done here below.

REV. ROBERT HALL.

THE SEPARATION SHORT.

I WONDER at the weakness of our minds, that they should be so much depressed with this short separation; for these very scriptures assure us we shall meet with them again; for they and we being with the Lord, we must be with each other. What a delightful thought is this! when we run over the long catalogue of excellent friends, which we are rash to say we have lost, to think, each of us, I shall be *gathered to my people;* to those whom my heart still owns under that character, with an affection which death could not cancel, nor these years of absence erase.

DR. PHILIP DODDRIDGE.

DANTE.

THE PLEASING HOPE OF RECOGNITION.

LET me be thankful for the pleasing hope that though God loves my child too well to permit it to return to me, he will ere long bring me to it. And then that endeared paternal affection, which would have been a cord to tie me to earth, and have added new pangs to my removal from it, will be as a golden chain to draw me upwards, and add one farther charm and joy even to paradise itself. Was this my desolation? this my sorrow? to part with thee for a few days, that I might receive thee forever, (Philam., v 15) and find thee as thou art? It is for no language but that of heaven, to describe the sacred joy which such a meeting must occasion.

Dr. Doddridge.

> Oh blissful scene! where severed hearts
> Renew the ties most cherished;
> Where naught the mourned and mourner parts;
> Where grief with life is perished.
> Oh! nought do I desire so well,
> As here to die, and there to dwell!

R. Huie.

A WELL FOUNDED HOPE.

My hope is that I shall shortly leave this valley of tears, and be free from all fevers and pain; and which will be a more happy condition, I shall be free from sin, and all the temptations and anxieties that attend it; and this being past, I shall dwell in the New Jerusalem; dwell there with men made perfect; dwell where these eyes shall see my Master and Savior Jesus; and with him see my dear mother, and all my relations and friends. But I must die, or not come to that happy place. George Herbert.

RECOGNITION IN HEAVEN A FACT.

REV. WM. MORLEY PUNSHON, D. D.

HEAVEN is not a solitude; it is a peopled city, a city in which there are no strangers, no homeless, no poor, where one does not pass another in the street without greeting, where no one is envious of another's minstrelsy or of another's more brilliant crown. When God said in the ancient Eden, "It is not good for man to be alone," there was a deeper signification in the words than could be exhausted or explained by the family tie. It was the declaration of an essential want which the Creator in his highest wisdom Has impressed upon the noblest of His works. That is not life—you don't call that life—where the hermit in some moorland glade drags out a solitary existence, or where the captive in some cell of bondage frets and pines unseen? That man does not understand solitude.

Life, all kinds of life, tends to companionship, and rejoices in it, from the larvæ and buzzing insect cloud, up to the kingly lion and the kinglier man. It is a social state into which we are to be introduced, as well as a state of consciousness. Not only, therefore, does the Savior pray for His disciples, "Father, I will that those whom thou hast given me be with me where I am, that they may behold my glory," but those who are in that heavenly recompense are said to have come "to the general assembly and church of the first-born written in heaven." Aye, and better than that, and dearer to some of us, "to the spirits of just men made perfect."

The question of the recognition of departed friends in heaven, and special and intimate reunion with them, Scripture and reason enable us to infer with almost absolute certainty. It is implied in the fact that the resurrection is a resurrection of individuals, that it is this mortal that shall put on immortality. It is implied in the fact that heaven is a vast and happy society; and it is implied in the fact there is no unclothing of nature that we possess, only the clothing upon it of the garments of a brighter and more glorious immortality.

Take comfort, then, those of you in whose history the dearest charities of life have been severed by the rude hand of death, those whom you have thought about as lost are not lost, except to present sight. Perhaps even now they are angel watchers, screened by a kindly Providence from everything about, that would give you pain; but if you and they are alike, in Jesus, and remain faithful to the end, doubt not that you shall know them again. It were strange, don't you think, if amid the multitude of earth's ransomed ones that we are to see in heaven, we should see all but those we most fondly and fervently long to see? Strange, if in some of our walks along the golden streets, we never happen to light upon them? Strange, if we did not hear some heaven song, learned on earth, trilled by some clear ringing voice that we have often heard before?

> The saints on earth, when sweetly they converse,
> And the dear favors of kind heaven rehearse,
> Each feels the other's joys, both doubly share
> The blessings which devoutly they compare,
> If saints such mutual joy feel here below,
> When they each others heavenly foretastes know
> What joys transport them at each other's sight,
> When they shall meet in empyreal height!
> Friends, even in heaven, one happiness would miss,
> Should they not know each other when in bliss.
>
> BISHOP KEN

> Our first-born and our only babe bereft!
> Too fair a flower was she for this rude earth!
> The features of her beauteous infancy
> Have faded from me, like a passing cloud,
> Or like the glories of an evening sky;
> And seldom hath my tongue pronounced her name
> Since she was summoned to a happier sphere.
> But that dear love, so deeply wounded then,
> I in my soul with silent faith sincere
> Devoutly cherish till we meet again.
>
> SOUTHEY.

RECOGNITION NO DAY-DREAM.

I count the hope no day-dream of the mind,
　No vision fair of transitory hue,
　The souls of those whom once on earth we knew,
And lov'd, and walk'd with in communion kind,
Departed hence, again in heaven to find.
　Such hope to nature's sympathies is true;
　And such, we deem, the holy word to view
Unfolds; an antidote for grief designed,
One drop from comfort's well. 'Tis true we read
　The Book of life: But if we read amiss,
By God prepared fresh treasures shall succeed
　To kinsmen, fellows, friends, a vast abyss
Of joy; nor aught the longing spirit need
　To fill its measure of enormous bliss.

BISHOP MANT.

LOVE INDESTRUCTIBLE.

They sin who tell us love can die;
With life all other passions fly,
　All others are but vanity.
In heaven ambition cannot dwell;
Nor avarice in the vaults of hell;
Earthly these passions of the earth,
They perish where they have their birth·
　But LOVE is indestructible.
Its holy flame forever burneth,
From heaven it came, to heaven returneth;
Too oft on earth a troubled guest,
At times deceived, at times opprest,
　It here is tried and purified,
Then hath in heaven its perfect rest.
It soweth here in toil and care,
But the harvest time of love is there.
Oh! when a mother meets on high
The babe she lost in infancy,
Hath she not then, for pains and fears,
　The day of woe, the watchful night,
For all her sorrows, all her tears,
　　An over-payment of delight?

ROBERT SOUTHEY.

HEATHEN VIEWS OF RECOGNITION.

REV. W. H. COOPER, D. D

THE philosophers of ancient Greece and Rome did not look upon their departed friends as lost. They believed that death only separated them from each other for a time; that soon they should meet, in more happy reunion, in the realms of Hades. *How* they became impressed with this notion, it were useless to enquire; as to the *fact* no one acquainted with classic story will deny it. The poets frequently alluded to it. Homer, the great Grecian, for example, represents the shades of his heroes as retaining all the characteristics, dispositions, habits, stations and peculiarities which belonged to them before death. (Book II, line 48, &c). The *Elysium* and the *Tartarus* of the poets correspond respectively to the *Paradise* and the *Hell* of our Sacred Scriptures, or rather, according to Dr. Campbell, as quoted by Bishop Hobart, the prison of Hades wherein criminals are kept until the General Judgment. Cicero says: "O glorious day! when I shall retire from this low and sordid scene, to associate with the divine assembly of departed spirits; and not with those only whom I have just mentioned, but with my dear Cato that best of sons and most valuable of men!" If, says Socrates, the common expression be true that death conveys us to those regions which are inhabited by the spirits of departed men, will it not be unspeakably happy to escape the hands of mere nominal judges to appear before * * such as Minos and Rhadamanthus, and to associate with all who have maintained the cause of truth and rectitude? * * Is it nothing to converse with Orpheus, and Homer, and Hesiod? * * With what pleasure could I leave the world to hold communion with Palamedes, Ajax and others, who, like me, have had an unjust sentence pronounced against them. The ancient Germans hoped to meet their friends again beyond death in a beautiful and peaceful valley. Antigione says," Departing, I strongly cherish the hope that I shall be fondly welcomed by my father, and by my mother, and by my brother." When the soul of Achilles is told of the glorious deeds of Neoptolemus, he goes away taking mighty steps through the meadow of asphodel in joyfulness, because he had heard that his son was very illustrious.

WHAT SHALL WE BE?

CHARLES J. P. SPITTA.

WHAT shall we be, and whither shall we go,
   When the last conflict of our life is o'er,
And we return from wandering to and fro
   To our dear home through heaven's eternal door.
When we shake off the last dust from our feet,
   When we wipe off the last drop from our brow,
And our departed friends once more shall greet,
   The hope which cheers and comforts us below?

What shall we be, when we ourselves shall see,
   Bathed in the flood of everlasting light,
And from all guilt and sin entirely free,
   Stand pure and blameless in our Maker's sight:
No longer from His holy presence driven,
   Conscious of guilt, and stung with inward pain;
But friends of God and citizens of heaven,
   To join the ranks of His celestial train?

What shall we be, when we drink in the sound
   Of heavenly music from the spheres above,
When golden harps to listening hosts around
   Declare the wonders of redeeming love;
When far and wide through the resounding air,
   Loud hallelujahs from the ransomed rise,
And holy incense, sweet with praise and prayer,
   Is wafted to the Highest through the skies?

What shall we be, when the freed soul can rise
   With unrestrained and bold aspiring flight
To Him who by His wondrous sacrifice
   Hath opened heaven, and scatter'ed sin's dark night;
When from the eye of faith the thin veil drops,
   Like wreaths of mist before the morning's rays,
And we behold, the end of all our hopes,
   The Son of God in full refulgent blaze?

What shall we be, when hand in hand we go
   With blessed spirits risen from the tomb,
Where streams of living water softly flow,
   And trees still flourish in primeval bloom;
Where in perpetual youth no cheek looks old
   By the sharp tooth of cruel time imprest,
Where no bright eye is dimm'd, no heart grows cold
   No grief, no pain, no death invades the blest?

NOT STRANGERS TO EACH OTHER.

WE shall most certainly carry our natural affections with us into the Eternal World, or Heaven were no Heaven to us. Shall we all who have fought the good fight together here below, meet again as *strangers* on the golden streets? Are there to be no rapturous recognitions there? Shall Luther not know Melancthon? Shall Ridley not recognize Latimer? Will that sorrowing mother who wept such scalding tears when they hid away her little darling with face of marble beneath that cold, damp mould, not clasp it to her arms again on reaching the farther shore? Shall I not meet my children? This is either fact or rhetoric, scripture or poetry. Which? And if mere fiction—if, after all, there is to be no recognition of friends in Heaven, what mean those consolations which the minister of religion *professes* to administer in the Master's name to bursting hearts in their hour of sorrow? If nothing, then he too is a sham and a fraud; but if not such, there must in his estimate be recognition.

Rev. W. H. Cooper.

No night shall be in heaven; no gathering gloom
Shall o'er that glorious landscape ever come;
No tears shall fall in sadness o'er those flowers
That breathe their fragrance through celestial bowers,

No night shall be in heaven! forbid to sleep,
These eyes no more their mournful vigils keep;
Their fountains dried, their tears all wiped away,
They gaze undazzled on eternal day.

No night shall be in heaven no sorrow reign,
No secret anguish, no corporeal pain,
No shivering limbs, no burning fever there,
No soul's eclipse, no winter of despair.

No night shall be in heaven, but endless noon;
No fast declining sun, no waning moon;
But there the Lamb shall yield perpetual light
'Mid pastures green and waters ever bright.

No night shall be in heaven. Oh, had I faith,
To rest in what the faithful witness saith,
That faith should make these hideous phantoms flee,
And leave no night henceforth on earth to me.

Angelic Ministry.

JACOB'S DREAM.

ANGELIC MINISTRY.

ANGELS THE ESCORT TO HEAVEN.

RT. REV. SAMUEL FALLOWS, D. D.

I SAW in my boyhood days the remnant of that brave regiment (the Royal Guards) if I remember correctly, that participated in the battle of Waterloo.

The left arm of each soldier was not in the regular sleeve of the uniform, for that hung empty by the side, but was in another sleeve specially made. I asked my father the reason. He replied, "When the command was given to form into line, these men had not time to thrust both arms into the sleeves of their jackets, and so they rushed to the conflict with only the right arm covered, and performed immortal deeds." And this was now their uniform.

Gray headed, scarred veterans, they had helped change the destinies of the world on that fateful field. Honored now their position as they escorted the monarch of England on the grand procession days of the realm.

Aye, honored too the sovereign, doubly honored, to be escorted by such men.

I saw men who had been officers of all grades from Lieutenants to Major-Generals in our army, rush forth by one spontaneous impulse and take from his feet, as he entered the spacious hall in the city of Boston where the society of the Army of the Potomac was gathered, that gallant cavalry leader, who has just become the General of the army of the United States. On their shoulders they bore him amid the wildest huzzas and placed him on the platform, where stood General Joe. Hooker and a number of other distinguished heroes to give him a comrade's soldierly welcome.

But one day a band who had participated in battles that affected the destiny of worlds, was sent to escort a sovereign in triumph to the metropolis of the Universe.

In joyous haste they sped on their mission. Round him gathered these squadrons of the skies. The men in the busy streets did not see *them.* Him they did see. A crowd had gathered round him as he lay there on the hard cold pavement. "What is the matter? Who is it?" was said. "It is only that beggar Lazarus," was the reply from some one who knew him. The suffering, starving, spurned beggar whose only sustenance was the rich man's crumbs, and whose only physicians the poor man's dogs, was there dying upon the earth.

Away with him to the Potter's field, in the spirit of the modern rhymes,

"Rattle his bones over the stones;
He's naught but a pauper, whom nobody owns."

But see! in their arms and on their shoulders, with shouts and songs, the Royal Guard of Heaven bear him in triumph home. That hand pierced on Calvary grasps his. A king and priest unto God, he now sits forever enthroned and crowned.

> Prophets, priests,
> Apostles, great reformers, all that served
> Messiah faithfully, like stars appear
> Of fairest beam: round them gather, clad
> In white, the vouchers of their ministry —
> The flock their care had nourished,
> Fed and saved.
>
> POLLOCK.

THE INTEREST OF ANGELS IN MEN.

BISHOP CYRUS FOSS, D. D.

THERE has been a great deal of curious speculation concerning the relation of angels to worldly affairs. Some think that the angels dwell in the immediate presence of God, and sing His praise, and that during the intervals of song they fly from star to star to refresh and regale their minds with the glories of the sky. Others think that the angels bear a direct relation to man, that they influence all of his affairs, and that everyone has his guardian angel who watches over him, and, to a certain extent, protects him. The truth respecting angels probably lies in the golden mean, half way between these two opinions. The angels are, doubtless, charged with ministering to man, and they are interested in all of his affairs. It may be that all of the stars are inhabited, and that Christ's blood was shed for the remission of the sins of those who dwell in them, as well as of the people on the earth. It may be, too, that, after flying from star to star, the angels stoop to consider this little planet, and to set their thoughts upon it, because they are interested in God's plan of salvation, and desire to inquire concerning it, and to see how it is regarded by man. The angels, then, must have a sympathetic curiosity about our salvation. They, like man, are the offspring of God, and, therefore, they have a fellow-feeling for men, and wish to inquire into their affairs. There is a similarity between men and angels, and this similarity enables angels to sympathize with men, and they do sympathize with them in all their struggles. They look upon each soul as the germ of souls to come, and they desire that each soul shall reach a state of elevated happiness. For thousands of years they have observed the actions of men; they know how much they can suffer and how much they can enjoy, and they look, therefore, with great solicitude to see whether men are living so as to attain happiness or sorrow in the world to come. They also are acquainted with the great plan of salvation; they know that Christ died for men, and that if men will believe in Christ and come to Him, they will be saved, and that if they reject Him they will be lost beyond redemption. From heavenly heights the angels look down upon a world struggling with sin, and they rejoice greatly whenever they are able to help men in their conflict with wickedness, and to assist in saving souls. They look to Calvary, and to the altar where the penitent is kneeling, and see that God is merciful, and that man can, if he will, be saved. And Oh! how earnestly they watch to see if more will come to Christ and avail themselves of His blood which was shed for them. If the pure angels are thus concerned for us, how much more should we sinful creatures be concerned for ourselves! May God help us to be concerned for our salvation and to come to Christ and be cleansed and purified in His blood!

THE ANGELS DESIRE TO LOOK INTO SALVATION.

BISHOP M. SIMPSON, D. D.

They "desire to look into it." With all their powers of investigation, with all their vast knowledge, here was a matter that they had not fathomed, and that they greatly desired to know. Yet scientists sometimes feel that they are so busy as to have no time to study this salvation. They are busy at studying the structures of crystals. Why angels know all about them. They saw the particles taking their positions. These men are busy in investigating the strata of the rocks. Why the angels saw the upheaval of the rocks which so diversified and distorted the strata. They were there at the formation of the earth and have witnessed all the changes. Only this last summer how deeply moved were these men in supposing that they had discovered an inter-Mercurial planet. If there be such a planet the angels have known it ages ago. The brightness of the sun does not baffle their vision. These men are busy unweaving the rays of light. The angels heard God when He spake, "Let there be light." All these things, which so deeply concern these scientists, are plain as A B C to these angels who, nevertheless, so desire to see into the plan of salvation, that subject which the scientists deem of so little importance.

WHY MEN DENY ANGELIC EXISTENCE.

THE tendency to deny angelic existence or angelic visitation is precisely the tendency to deny the existence and power of the invisible God. It is not given to man to see heaven-angels upon earth as in the olden time.

But it is no argument that they do not exist and exert a powerful influence because unseen. We cannot see the electric fluid which outstrips the lightning in its fleetness, and yet thought employs it as a messenger and servant.

The divine Savior is unseen. Does he not exist? Is he failing in fulfilling his promise? "Lo, I am always with you, even unto the end of the world!" because we do not see his blessed form as his disciples saw it, or heard his comforting words as they heard them.

Heaven and earth were once together in the old Jewish dispensation. Are they further apart under the Christian dispensation? Have angels ceased ascending and descending the ladder reaching from this world to the skies? When did they cease and why?

Where is the ground for such belief in the Holy Scriptures? Where in the teachings of Reason? Their work, it is true, has ended in making audibly known the revealed will of God. But who has the authority to assert that their mission as ministers of peace and mercy and helpfulness and suggestion and guidance and guardianship has ended?

The Old Testament dispensation was one of types and shadows of literal and material things. The New Testament dispensation is a spiritual one. Not now in material forms but in a spiritual manner do these celestial visitants communicate with man. But that communication is as real now as ever before.

BISHOP FALLOWS.

> For spirits when they please
> Can either sex assume, or both; so soft
> And uncompounded is their essence pure;
> Not tied or manacled with joint or limb,
> Nor founded on the brittle thread of bones,
> Like cumbrous flesh; but in what shape they choose,
> Dilated or condensed, bright or obscure,
> Can execute their airy purposes,
> And works of love or enmity fulfil.   MILTON.

THE POOR DYING GIRL.

WENT once, to see a dying girl whom the world had roughly treated. She never had a father, she never knew her mother. Her home had been the poor-house, her couch a hospital-cot, and yet, as she had staggered in her weakness there, she had picked up a little of the alphabet, enough to spell out the New Testament, and she had touched the hem of the Master's garment, and had learned the new song. And I never trembled in the presence of majesty as I did in the majesty of her presence as she came near the crossing. 'Oh, sir!' she said, God sends his angels. I have read in his word: "Are they not ministering spirits, sent forth to minister to them who shall be heirs of salvation?" And when I am leaning in my cot, they stand about me on this floor; and when the heavy darkness comes, and this poor side aches so severely, he comes, for he says, "Lo, I am with you," and I sleep, I rest.'"

Rev. C. H. Fowler, D. D.

VIEWS OF WESLEY, OBERLIN AND CLARK.

WESLEY has spoken of his own clear conviction that the strong impression on his own mind of the images of deceased friends at particular moments, was produced by their actual invisible presence. Oberlin supposed that for many years he enjoyed intimate communications with the dead. He says that the appearance, visible as well as invisible, of the dead, is possible, the instances related in the Bible are decisive. That they have ever appeared to the outward eye, except in those instances, can scarcely be proved from history, to the satisfaction of the skeptical or even the indifferent. That, however, the strongest sense of their influence as if they were present, has often been impressed upon the mind, in those states in which visible object have least control, is confirmd by ten thousand testimonies."

"Our separation will not be a complete one. I feel that I shall often be with you. I cannot speak words to you but God, in his tenderness and loving kindness will permit me to suggest beautiful thoughts to you, and lead your minds heavenward. This idea is very present with me."—BISHOP D. W. CLARK's dying words to his family:

"Good-bye, papa; good-bye, mamma," said a sweet eight-year old, dying in Baltimore, "the angels have come to carry me to heaven!' and sure enough, in a few moments the heavenly convoy were bearing his freed spirit upwards to the skies.

THE angels undoubtedly, wander away from the throne of God to this wordly sphere, to watch over the soul's welfare of those they have left behind. It may be that some angels are hovering over the souls here to-night, to see if some one will decide in favor of the Lord's side.

D. L. MOODY.

CHILDREN UNDER CARE OF ANGELS.

CHILDREN are under the care of God's angels. "Take heed, how ye despise one of these little ones; for in heaven their angels do always behold the face of my Father which is in heaven." Christ is the Lord of angels, Jehovah of Hosts; and he brings all his glorious retinue to serve him in his office of Savior; as the author of the Epistle to the Hebrews says of the angels: "Are they not all ministering spirits sent forth to minister them who shall be heirs of salvation?" (Heb. i, 14). In the Old Testament, angels were declared to be guardians of God's people (Ps. xci. 11, 12). Here our blessed Master confirms the truth. His angels are his people's angels standing ready before God to be sent upon any mission that concerns the welfare of his little ones; little children and child-like believers. Some find here the doctrine of particular guardian angels; whether that be true or not we are unprepared to say; but, certainly, all Christ's people are under the guardianship of Christ's angels. There is not one of all the radiant winged spirits who do God's will in providence, that is not ready to be a servant of those whom Jesus numbers among his little ones.

REV. DR. BETHUNE.

THE ANGEL ANNOUNCING THE BIRTH OF CHRIST.

EARTH-ANGELS AND HEAVEN-ANGELS.

Saints are to each other angels in a blessed sense,—though their services and sympathies no more shut out those of angels than the light of the moon is destroyed by the light of the stars which attend him and mingle their light with his, to lessen, if they cannot entirely disperse the earth's darkness. "No," exclaims the poet with emphasis, against the idea that earth has no angels, because their wings are not seen, and their songs are not heard—

> No: earth has angels, though their forms are moulded,
>   But of such clay as fashions all below;
> Though harps are wanting, and bright pinions folded,
>   We know them by the love-light on their brow.
>
> I have seen angels by the sick one's pillow;
>   Theirs was the soft tone and the soundless tread,
> When smitten hearts were drooping like the willow,
>   They stood "between the living and the dead."
>
> And if my sight, by earthly dimness hindered,
>   Beheld no hovering cherubim in air,
> I doubted not—for spirits know their kindred—
>   They smiled upon the viewless watchers there.
>
> There have been angels in the gloomy prison;
>   In crowded halls; by the lone widow's hearth;
> And where they passed, the fallen have uprisen—
>   The giddy paused, the mourner's hope had birth.
>
> I have seen one whose eloquence commanding,
>   Roused the rich echoes of the human breast;
> The blandishments of wealth and ease withstanding,
>   That hope might reach the suffering and opprest.
>
> And by his side there moved a form of beauty,
>   Strewing sweet flowers along his path of life,
> And looking up with meek and love-blent duty:
>   I called her angel, but he called her wife.
>
> O! many a spirit walks the world unheeded,
>   That, when its veil of sadness is laid down,
> Shall soar aloft with pinions unimpeded,
>   And wear its glory like a starry crown.

Rev. H. Harbaugh, D. D.

THE NATION'S GUARDIAN ANGELS.

IN all theologies it is believed that every individual has *a guardian angel* sent forth to protect, to defend and to foster. The Jewish rabbis say that Adam's guardian angel was named *Razaiel*, and that Abraham's guardian angel was *Raphael*, and that Jacob's guardian angel was *Peniel.* If every individual has a guardian angel, shall not a Christian nation have guardian angels? Who shall they be? Those who never knew us? Those who never fought in behalf of our institutions? Those who never suffered for our land? No, no. Descend, ye *spirits of the martyred presidents*, and ye mighty men of the councils of the past, ye who defended our country on land and sea. Descend, ye who preached and prayed as well as ye who fought! Mighty spirits of departed patriots, descend—come down out of the ineffable light into the shadows of earth, and lead the way. Washington and Everett, and Sumner and Garfield, and Lincoln and Burnside, and Lyon and Witherspoon, and Mason and Channing—descend, descend! Speak with lips once quieted. Strike with arms once palsied. *Ride down into this fight* in which earth and hell and heaven are in battle array. Thou mighty God of our fathers and brothers who fell at Lexington and Yorktown, and South Mountain, and Gettysburg, descend and strike back national evil, and bring national good, and prove thyself the same God who answered the prayers of Hezekiah, and of Elijah, and of Deborah, and of Joshua. Thine, O Lord, is the Kingdom! TALMAGE.

THE BODIES OF ANGELS.

THE bodies of angels are doubtless of a much finer mould than the bodies of men; but, although they were at all times invisible through such organs of vision as we possess, it would form no proof that they are destitute of corporeal frames. The air we breathe is a *material* substance, yet it is *invisible;* and there are substances whose rarity is more than ten times greater than that of the air of our atmosphere. Hydrogen gas is more than twelve times lighter than common atmospheric air. If, therefore, an organized body were formed

OR VIEWS OF HEAVEN.

of a material substance similar to air, or to hydrogen gas, it would in general be invisible; but, in certain circumstances, might reflect the rays of light, and become visible, as certain of the lighter gaseous bodies are found to do. This is, in some measure, exemplified in the case of *animalculæ*, whose bodies are imperceptible to the naked eye, and yet are regularly organized material substances, endowed with all the functions requisite to life, motion and enjoyment.

Rev. Dr. Dick.

AN ANGEL STANDING BY.

E have read of a certain youth in the early days of Christianity (those periods of historic suffering and heroic patience and legendary wonder, to which I call your attention),—we read of a Christian youth on whom his persecutors put in practice a more than common share of their ingenuity, that by his torments (let those who can or will go through the horrible details) they might compel him to deny his Lord and Savior.

After a long endurance of those pains they released him, in wonder at his obstinancy. His Christian brethren are said to have wondered too, and to have asked him by what mighty faith he could so strangely subdue the violence of the fire, as that neither a cry nor a groan escaped him.

"It was indeed most painful," was the noble youth's reply; "but an angel stood by me when my anguish was at the worst, and with his finger pointed to heaven."

O thou, whoever thou art, that art tempted to commit a sin, do thou think on death, and that thought will be an angel to thee! The hope of heaven will raise thy courage above the fire cast threatenings of the world; the fear of hell will rob its persuasions of all their enchantment; and the very extremity of their trial may itself contribute to animate thy exertions by thought that the greater will be thy reward hereafter.

Bishop Heber.

What if death my sleep invade?
Should I be of death afraid?

ANGELS ARE IN HEAVEN.

WILL you turn to the 18th chapter of Matthew, 10th verse; "Take heed that ye despise not one of these little ones; for I say unto you that in heaven their angels do always behold the face of my Father which is in heaven." So we shall have the company of angels when we go there. We find when Gabriel came down and told Zachariah that he should have a son, Zachariah doubted his word; and Gabriel replied: "I am Gabriel, that stands in the presence of God." It says in Luke, 2d chapter and 13th verse, that after one angel had proclaimed that Jesus was born in Bethlehem, there was a multitude of the heavenly host telling out the wonderful story. So, we have angels in heaven. We have God the Father, and Christ the Son, and angels dwelling there.

Moody.

ANGELIC SYMPATHY.

Millions of spiritual creatures walk the earth
Unseen, both when we wake, and when we sleep.
All these with ceaseless praise his works behold,
Both day and night. How often, from the steep
Of echoing hill or thicket, have we heard
Celestial voices to the midnight air,
Sole, or responsive each to others' note,
Singing their great Creator! Oft in bands,
While they kept watch, or nightly rounding walk
With heavenly touch of instrumental sounds,
In full harmonic numbers joined, their songs
Divide the night, and lift our thoughts to heaven.

Milton.

Oh, angel, lend me the shade of thy wing;
  I see the portals of light unrolled,
With songs of welcome their arches ring—
  The ransomed is safe in the heavenly fold.

THREE LITTLE ANGELS.

Three pairs of dimpled arms, as white as snow,
    Held me in soft embrace ;
Three little cheeks, like velvet peaches soft,
    Were placed against my cheek.

Three pairs of tiny eyes, so clear, so deep,
    Looked up in mine this even,
Three pairs of lips kissed me a sweet "good night,"
    Three little forms from heaven.

Ah, it is well that "little ones" should love us ,
    It lights our faith when dim.
To know that once our blessed Savior bade them
    Bring "little ones" to him.

And said He not, "of such is Heaven," and blessed,
    them,
    And held them to his breast ?
Is it not sweet to know that when they leave us,
    'T is there they go to rest ?

And yet, ye tiny angels of my house,
    Three hearts cased in mine !
How 'Twould be shattered, if the Lord should say
    "Those angels are not thine !"

THE ANGELS COMING FOR ST. CECILIA.

HELIODORUS PUNISHED IN THE TEMPLE.

IN the Apocryphal book of the Maccabees, we read that Seleucus, King of Asia, at the instigation of Simon, a renegade Jew, ordered his Treasurer, Heliodorus, to proceed to Jerusalem, go into the temple, and bring to him the sacred treasures of silver and gold, which it contained. Heliodorus made the attempt, in spite of the protestations of the high priest. Then the priests and the people supplicated heaven to interfere and prevent the money laid up for the relief of the widows and the fatherless from being thus taken. As soon as Heliodorus entered the treasury, a fierce horse, with a terrible rider, covered with golden armor, attacked him. The horse struck him with his fore feet, and two angels in the guise of young men, scourged him continually, "and gave him many sore stripes." He was carried out nearly dead, but was restored through the prayers of the priests. He went back to his master without the treasure, and reported the miraculous treatment he had received.

THE ANGELS COMING FOR ST. CECILIA.

ST. CECILIA, the patroness of music, it is said, was condemned to a martyr's death, in the year 230. Her persecutors first threw her into a boiling bath, but on the following day she was found unhurt. The executioner next attempted to cut off her head, but found it impossible. Three days later she died a natural and peaceful death. The angels, making sweet music, hovered over her dying bed, and when the spirit left the body, bore it with triumphant songs to its celestial home. The poets and the painters never grow weary in celebrating and representing her.

HELIODORUS PUNISHED IN THE TEMPLE.

HOOKER'S MEDITATION ON THE ANGELS.

WHEN the most majestic divine of the English Church, Richard Hooker, was on his death-bed, he was found deep in contemplation, and on being asked the subject of his thoughts he replied "that he was meditating upon the number and nature of angels, and their blessed obedience and order, without which peace could not be in heaven; and oh! that it might be so on earth?" It was a meditation full of the same grand thought which inspired the great work the thought of the Majesty of Law, "whose seat," as he says, "is in the bosom of God, and whose voice is the harmony of the universe." The very words by which the angelic intelligences are described, "thrones, principalities and powers," the very connection into which they are brought with the searching laws of nature, "maketh the winds His angels and the flames of fire His ministers"—bring before us the truth that by law, by order, by due subordination of means to ends, as in the material so in the moral world, the will of God is best carried out.

DEAN STANLEY.

THE HEAVENLY HOST OF ANGELS.

THE idea of the heavenly host of angels includes the operations of God in the vast movements of the universe, and his ministrations through the spirits of men, whether now or hereafter. It includes that ideal world to which the greatest of heathen philosophers fondly looked as the sphere in which reside the great ideas, the perfect images, of which all virtue and beauty are but the inperfect shadow. It includes the thought of that peculiarly bright and lovely type of Christian character to which, for want of any other word, we have in modern times given the name as angel or angelic—superhuman, yet not divine; not heroic, nor apostolic, nor saintly, yet exactly what we call seraphic, elevating, attating, with the force of inherent nobleness and beauty. "He who has seen in men or women," says Luther "a gentleness without art or effort penetrating the whole nature through and through, he has seen for himself the colors wherewith he may paint for himself what is meant by an angel." The idea belongs to that high region of thought where religion and poetry combine. Religions beleif has furnished the materials, but poetry wrought and transformed them into shapes which the latest religious culture of mankind can never cease to recognize.

DEAN STANLEY.

ANGELS ATTENDANT UPON MAN.

ANGELS are sent to be his attendants. They come to minister to him here, and to conduct him home 'to glory.' Kings and princes are surrounded by armed men, or by sages called to be their counsellors ; but the most humble saint may be encompassed by a retinue of beings of far greater power and more elevated rank. The angels of light and glory feel a deep interest in the salvation of men. They come to attend the redeemed; they wait on their steps ; they sustain them in trial; they accompany them when departing to heaven. It is a higher honor to be attended by one of those pure intelligences than by the most elevated monarch that ever swayed a sceptre or wore a crown ; and the obscurest Christian shall soon be himself conducted to a throne in heaven, compared with which the most splendid seat of royalty on earth loses its lustre and fades away.

How beautiful and truthful these words of Spenser :

> And is there care in heaven? and is there love
>   In heavenly spirits to these creatures base,
> That may compassion of their evils move?
>   There is :— else much more wretched were the case
>   Of men than beasts; But O! th' exceeding grace
>   Of Highest God that loves his creatures so,
> And all his works of mercy doth embrace,
>   That blessed angels he sends to and fro
>   To serve to wicked man, to serve his wicked foe?
>
> How oft do they their silver bowers leave,
>   To come to succor us that succor want!
> How do they with golden pinions cleave
>   The yielding skies, like flying pursuivant,

Against foul fiends to aid us militant!
  They for us fight, they watch and duly ward,
And their bright squadrons round about us plant;
  And all for love and nothing for reward;
O why should Heavenly God to men have such regard!
REV. ALBERT BARNES.

ANGELIC SYMPATHY NEEDED.

"Why come not spirits from the realms of glory,
  To visit the earth as in days of old—
The times of ancient writ and sacred story?
  Is heaven more distant, or has earth grown cold?

Oft have I gazed when sunset clouds, receding,
  Waved like rich banners of a host gone by,
To catch the gleam of some white pinion speeding
  Along the confines of the glowing sky.

And oft when midnight stars in distant chillness
  Were calmly burning, listened late and long;
But nature's pulse beat on in solemn stillness,
  Bearing no echo of the seraph's song.

To Bethlehem's air was their last anthem given
  When other stars before the One grew dim?
Was their last presence known in Peter's prison?
  Or where exulting martyrs raised their hymn?

And are they all within the veil departed?
  There gleams no wing along the Empyrean now;—
And many a tear from human eyes have started,
  Since angel touch has calmed a mortal brow."

This is a truly pathetic complaint, and one to which few hearts have not returned an ardent echo. But there is no need of making it. It is true, if we look for angels with our bodily eyes, or even with the eyes of a poet, we shall not see the gleam of white pinions speeding along the confines of the glowing sky; we shall not hear their songs as the shepherds of Bethlehem heared them. Yet they have not all retired forever behind the veil of the visible. They may still be seen heard by the eye and ear faith, though

"There gleams no wing along the empyrean now."
REV. H. HARBAUGH, D. D.

THE ANGELIC-HOST.

UNSEEN COMPANIONS.

IT was expedient, says Christ, for his disciples that he should go away. The coming of the helper or comforter depended on his going. We may not understand all the reasons, or perhaps the main reasons, why, in the economies of heaven, this necessity existed ; but we can surmise one reason. We may belive that Christ would be much nearer his disciples when absent in the body. The bodily senses sometimes hinder the appreciation of truth. The artist's ideal is always more perfect than his canvas. The Christian's view of Jesus, when not seeing him in the flesh (visible familiarity might beget blindness) is far deeper and broader and higher and truer than the beholding him with the physical sense; friends who have left us for the prepared home are nearer and dearer to us than ever; the heart recognizes and understands them better than ever before, and this power suggests their spiritual presence as a complementary fact. Our Lord told his disciples that he would be with them personally and really, though unseen. May it not be true—is it not likely—that all the Lord's redeemed and glorified ones come personally and really, though unseen and unnoticed by any material sense, into the society of those with whom affection has indissolubly joined them? They would only in this be followers of their Lord, who is their forerunner and example. "But why do they not communicate with us?" Because, (1) Spirit and sense *cannot* communicate, and our own spirits are too clogged with sense to know the free spiritual communication ; (2) A free communication with the other world would take away our interest in this world's necessary duties ; while (3) on the other hand, it would beget so great a familiarity with the other world as to diminish its influence upon our lives and characters. When our Lord said, "I go," he also added, "The world seeth me no more, but *ye* see me, *ye* shall know that I am in my Father, and ye in me and I in you." His going was only the going of the flesh, perceived by the sense. In the truest and most real sense, he was not about to leave them.

REV. HOWARD CROSBY, D. D.

GUARDIAN ANGELS.

THE fathers of the Christian Church taught that every human being, from the hour of his birth to that of his death, is accompanied by an angel appointed to watch over him. The Mahometans give to each of us a good and an evil angel; but the early Christian supposed us to be attended each by a good angel only, who undertakes that office, not merely from duty to God, and out of obedience and great humility, but as inspired by exceeding charity and love towards his human charge. It would require the tongues of angels themselves to recite all that we owe to these benign and vigilant guardians. They watch by the cradle of the new-born babe, and spread their celestial wings round the tottering steps of infancy. If the path of life be difficult and thorny, and evil spirits work us shame and woe, they sustain us; they bear the voice of our complaining, of our supplication, of our repentance, up to the foot of God's throne, and bring us back in return a pitying benediction to strengthen and to cheer. When passion and temptation strive for the mastery, they encourage us to resist: when we conquer, they crown us; when we falter and fail, they compassionate and grieve over us; when we are obstinate in polluting our own souls, and perverted not only in act, but in will, they leave us, and woe to them that are so left! But the good angel does not quit his charge until his protection is despised, rejected, and utterly repudiated. Wonderful the fervor of their love, wonderful their meekness and patience, who endure from day to day the spectacle of the unveiled human heart with all its miserable weaknesses and vanities, its inordinate desires and selfish purposes! Constant to us in death, they contend against the powers of darkness for the emancipated spirit. MRS. JAMESON.

SYMPATHY OF ANGELS.

OH! there are no tears in heaven; but, when angels come down to earth, it may be they can fall into companionship with human sadness, and even learn to weep; and where is the spectacle which shall wring tears from eyes which they were never meant to stain, if it be not that of the obstinate rejection of the gospel of reconciliation and of careless trifling with a thing so inestimably precious as the soul? Old men, buried with your gold, angels weep over you! Young men, frittering away your days in vanities and pleasures, angels weep over you!

REV. H. MELVILL, D. D.

ANGELS NOT UNEMBODIED SPIRITS.

"IN every instance in which angels have been sent on embassies to mankind, they have displayed *sensible* qualities. They exhibited a *definite form*, somewhat analogous to that of man, and *color and splendor*, which were perceptible by the organ of hearing—they emitted *sounds* which struck the organ of hearing—they produced the harmonies of *music*, and sung sublime sentiments, which were uttered in articulate words, that were distinctly heard and recognized by the persons to whom they were sent, Luke ii, 14—and they exerted their power over the sense of *feeling*. * * * In these instances, angels manifested themselves to men through the medium of three principal senses, by which we recognize the properties of material objects; and why, then, should we consider them as purely immaterial universe? We have no knowledge of angels but from revelation: and all the descriptions it gives of these beings, lead us to conclude that they are connected with the world of matter, as well as with the world of mind, and are furnished with organical vehicles, composed of some refined material substances, suitable to their nature and employments.

REV. DR. DICK.

When sorrowing o'er some stone I bend,
Which covers all that was a friend,
And from his voice, his hand, his smile,
Divides me for a little while;
Thou, Savior, see'st the tears I shed,
For thou didst weep o'er Lazarus dead.

UNKNOWN.

ATTENDANT ANGELS.

HOW LOVING ARE THE ANGELS TO MEN.

REV. C. H. SPURGEON.

OW loving are the angels to men; for they rejoice over *one* sinner that repenteth. There she is, in that garret, where the stars look between the tiles. There is a miserable bed in that room, with but one bit of covering, and she lieth there to die! Poor creature! Many a night she has walked streets in the time of her merriment; but now her joys are over; a foul disease, like a demon, is devouring her heart! She is dying fast, and no one careth for her soul! But there in the chamber she turns her face to the wall, and she cries, "O thou that savedst Magdalen, save me; Lord, I repent; have mercy upon me, I beseech thee." Did the bells ring in the street? Was the trumpet blown? Ah! no. Did men rejoice? Was there a sound of thanksgiving in the great congregation? No; no one heard of it; for she died unseen. But stay! There was one standing at her bedside who noted well that tear; an angel who had come down from heaven to watch over this stray sheep, and mark its return; and no sooner was her prayer uttered than he clapped his wings, and there was seen flying up to the pearly gates a spirit like a star. The heavenly guards came crowding to the gate, crying, "What news, O son of fire?" He said, "'Tis done." "And what is done?" they said. "Why, she has repented." "What! She who was once a chief of sinners? Has she turned to Christ?" "'Tis even so," said he. And then they told it through the streets, and the bells of heaven rang marriage peals, for Magdalene was saved, and she who had been the chief of sinners was turned unto the living God.

It was in another place. A poor neglected little boy in ragged clothing had run about the streets for many a day. Tutored in crime, he was paving his path to the gallows; but one morning he passed by a humble room, where some men and women were sitting together teaching ragged children. He stepped in there, a wild Bedouin of the streets; they talked to him; they told him about a soul and an eternity—things he had never heard before; they spoke of Jesus and of tidings of great joy to this poor friendless lad. He went another Sabbath, and another; his wild habits hanging about him, for he could not get rid of them. At last it happened that his teacher said to him one day, "Jesus Christ receives sinners." That little boy ran, but not home, for it was but a mockery to call it so—where a drunken father and a lascivious mother kept a hellish riot together. He ran, and under some dry arch, or in some wild unfrequented corner, he bent his little knee, and there he cried, that poor creature in his rags, "Lord, save me, or I perish;" and the little Arab was on his knees—the little thief was saved! He said—

"Jesus, lover of my soul, let me to thy bosom fly;"

And up from that old arch, from that forsaken hovel, there flew a spirit, glad to bear the news to heaven, that another heir to heaven was born to God. I might picture many such scenes; but will each of you try to picture your own? You remember the occasion when the Lord met with you. Ah! little did you think what a commotion there was in heaven. If the Queen had ordered out all her soldiers, the angels would not have stopped to notice them; if all the princes of earth had marched in pageant through the streets, with all their robes, and jewelry, and crowns, and all their regalia, their chariots, and their horsemen—if the pomps of ancient monarchs had arisen from the tomb—if all the might of Babylon, and Tyre, and Greece had been concentrated into one great parade, yet not an angel would have stopped in his course to smile at those poor tawdry things; but over you, the vilest of the vile, the poorest of the poor, the most obscure and unknown—over you angelic wings are hovering, and concerning you it was said on earth and sung in heaven, "Hallelujah, for a child is born to God to-day."

Behind the cloud the star-light lurks;
Through showers the sunbeams fall;
For God, who loveth all his works
Hath left his hope with all.

I cannot feel their touch, their faces see,
Yet my soul whispers, they do come to me.

MINISTERING ANGELS IN HOLY SCRIPTURES.

THAT angels have been engaged in communicating intelligence to men, is abundantly evident from the Bible. Their very name, which means a messenger or bearer of news, designates their office in this respect. The intelligence that God would destroy Sodom, was communicated to Lot, by two angels. They announced the coming of the Savior, and of his fore-runner, John the Baptist. To the Marys who went early to the tomb to seek Jesus, they brought the information that he had risen. Even the law is said to have been "ordained by angels in the hands of a mediator," and Stephen says that the Jews received it by the "disposition of angels." The Revelation which John received on Patmos, in a vision of those things which must shortly come to pass, were "sent and signified" by an angel. Cornelius, who was a devout man, "and prayed to God always," received from an angel the comforting intelligence that his prayers were heard. "Thy prayers and thine alms," said the angel, "are come up as a memorial before God." Daniel also received notice in the same way that his prayer was heard; for the angel Gabriel, being caused to fly swiftly, reached him about the time of the evening incense, before his prayer was ended, clothed with authority to answer his prayer, and to assure him of his acceptance before God.

What if death my sleep invade?
Should I be of death afraid?
Whilst encircled by Thy arm,
Death may strike but cannot harm.
With Thy heavenly presence blest,
Death is life, and labor rest.
Welcome sleep or death to me,
Still secure, if still with Thee.

PHILIP DODDRIDGE.

THE ANGEL OF PATIENCE.

A FREE PARAPHRASE OF THE GERMAN.

O weary hearts, to mourning homes,
God's meekest Angel gently comes;
No power has he to banish pain,
Or give us back our lost again,
And yet, in tenderest love, our dear
And Heavenly Father sends him here.

There's quiet in that Angel's glance,
There's rest in his still countenance;
He mocks no grief with idle cheer,
Nor wounds with words the mourner's ear;
But ills and woes he may not cure,
He kindly learns us to endure.

Angel of Patience! sent to calm
Our feverish brow with cooling balm;
To lay the storms of hope and fear,
And reconcile life's smile and tear;
And throbs of wounded pride to still,
And make our own our Father's will.

Oh! thou, who mournest on the way,
With longings for the close of day,
He walks with thee, that Angel kind,
And gently whispers,—" Be resigned!
Bear up, bear on, the end shall tell
The dear Lord ordereth all things well!"

WHITTIER.

THE REV. JOHN HALL, D. D.

FALLEN ANGELS.

REV. JOHN HALL, D. D.

THERE is a true God; there is a rival of His name, an enemy of His cause and people. Satan walketh about as a roaring lion, seeking whom he may devour. God has His interest in true worship; Satan, in getting men from this true worship. Satan and his followers, his fallen and allied spirits, aim at diverting to themselves, under this name and guise, the work that truly belongs to the Lord. The things which the Gentiles sacrifice, they sacrifice to demons, and not to God. "I would not," says the apostle, "have you allied with the worship of demons." This agency of evil spirits, this hostility to God and His Kingdom, the subtle forces that divert men at the beginning from true spiritual worship, have not become extinguished. Dear brethren, *they are at work still.* And they have not learned much through all these ages---they are lying spirits after all. Their policy is just the same. Human hearts are just the same. And so we may say to you, without the least hesitation, as Peter wrote down in his letter: "Be sober, be vigilant, because your adversary, the devil, walketh about, seeking whom he may devour." The process begins when you are fascinated and attracted by the lion, and when so fascinated, you reject the truth that God is presenting to you.

> Angels our march oppose,
> Who still in strength excel
> Our secret, sworn, eternal foes,
> Countless, invisible.
>
> CHARLES WESLEY.

> An angel's hand can't snatch me from the grave;
> Legions of angels can't confine me there.
>
> YOUNG.

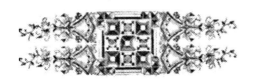

Saintly Sympathy.

WESTMINSTER ABBEY.

OUR BELOVED.

AND our beloved have departed,
While we tarry, broken-hearted,
   In the dreary, empty house;
They have ended life's brief story,
They have reached their home of glory,
   Over death victorious.

Hush that sobbing, weep more lightly,
On we travel, daily, nightly
   To the rest that they have found.
Are we not upon the river,
Sailing fast, to meet forever
   On more holy, happy ground?

Every hour that passes o'er us,
Speaks of comfort yet before us,
   Of our journey's rapid rate;
And like passing vesper bells,
The clock of time its chiming tells,
   At eternity's broad gate.

Ah! the way is shining clearer,
As we journey ever nearer
   To the everlasting home.
Friends, who there await the landing,
Comrades, round the throne now standing,
   We salute you, and we come.

INSEPARABLE FELLOWSHIP.

"There was, very early, a Christian custom which required that the memory of departed friends should be celebrated by their relations, husbands, or wives, on the anniversary of their death, in a manner suited to the spirit of the Christian faith and the Christian hope. It was usual on this day to partake of the communion under a sense of the *inseparable fellowship with those who had died in the Lord.* A gift was laid on the altar in their name, as if they were still living members of the church."

"While individual Christians and Christian families celebrated in this manner the memories of those departed ones who were especially near to them by the ties of kindred, *whole communities* celebrated the memory of those who, without belonging to their own particular community, died as witnesses for the Lord. The anniversary of the death of such individuals was looked upon as their birth-day to a nobler existence. Great care was bestowed in providing for their funeral obsequies, and at the repose of their bodies, as the sanctified organs of holy souls, which were one day to be awakened from the dead and restored to their birth-day (in the sense which has been explained) the people gathered round their graves, where the story was rehearsed of their confession and sufferings, and the communion was celebrated in the consciousness of a continued fellowship with them, now that they were united with Him for whom, by their sufferings, they had witnessed a good confession."

NEANDER.

I called on dreams and visions to disclose
That which is veiled from waking thoughts; conjured
Eternity as men constrain a ghost
T' appear and answer; to the grave I spake
Imploringly;—looked up, and asked the heavens
If angels traversed their cerulean floors,
If fixed or wandering star could tidings yield
Of the departed spirit—what abode
It occupies—what consciousness retains
Of former loves and interests.

COMMUNION OF THE DEAD WITH THE LIVING.

REV. PROF. A. P. PEABODY, D. D.

I am thy fellow-servant, and of thy brethren the prophets.—Revelation xxii, 9.

So said the angel that showed St. John the tree of life, and talked with him of the joys of heaven. He was an earth-born angel, trained by arduous duty and stern conflict for a holy and exalted ministry in God's nearer presence. It was in a *vision* that the apostle beheld him; and a *vision* denotes, with emphasis, *seeing;* that is, a clearer, deeper, truer insight than is enjoyed in the usual condition of the faculties. It was not fables or allegories, but realities and truths appertaining to spiritual world, that were unfolded to the seers of the Old and New Testament in vision. The inward eye was opened. They beheld things of which the external sense cannot take cognizance, and which they could describe only by images and symbols that feebly represented the impressions made upon their own minds. I have chosen this text in order to speak to you of the nearness of heaven to earth, and of our connection and communion with the great spiritual family. I cannot think of heaven as a separate, far-off mansion or city of the redeemed, but as in close connection with the world in which we live. I believe that the members of the heavenly society, even now, sympathize with us, rejoice in our virtue, and minister to our spiritual growth.

There are many sayings of Jesus, and incidents in his life, which imply the intimate communion of the dead with the living. One of the most striking features of his life is the frequency and nearness of his converse with the spiritual world: He never speaks of angels and just men made perfect, as if there were a weary distance to be crossed from them to us, or from us to them. They are often with him,—at his birth, in his temptation, and in his agony they come uncalled,—they watch by his sepulchre, and wait on his ascension. The spirits of the long-dead talk with him on the mountain. His voice to the widow's son, his powerful word at the tomb of Lazarus, seem addressed to souls not afar off, but within call,—near the scenes from which they had gone, and among the friends who thought them lost forever. He promises, also, his own spiritual presence with his followers, when he shall be no longer visible to the outward eye.

Among other touching allusions to the connection between the dead and the living, we cannot but assign a prominent place to that saying of our Savior,—"Joy shall be in heaven over one sinner that repenteth.' In this joy we cannot imagine the higher orders of the spiritually family as partaking, without its being shared by the penitent's kindred and friends in heaven. How intimate is the relation between the two worlds implied in the thought which these words suggest! The faint, lowly sigh of the contrite heart sweeps in glad harmony over the golden lyres, and wakes among the blessed a new song of thanksgiving. The first pulsations of spiritual life in the outcast sinner beat in the souls of the sinless, and every throb of godly sorrow on earth pours new joy through the ranks of the redeemed.

It is said that this near connection of heaven with earth must interfere with the perfect happiness of those in heaven, from their view of the painful discipline appointed to many of their nearest and best friends? I reply, that, whether they behold the trials of their friends or not, they must know, from their own remembered experience, that sorrow awaits all who enter into life. But they no longer dread for others the angel-ministries of adversity, which they now fully recognize for themselves. They behold universal Providence everywhere from seeming evil inducing the highest good, and thus can acquiesce with solemn joy in whatever afflictions are appointed for those whom they hope one day to welcome as their companions in glory, even as the Father himself, who loves us all better than we can love each other, dwells in serene and eternal happiness, while he mingles the cup of sorrow and agony for his children.

It is asked, how heaven can be thus near, and yet unseen? I reply, that the invisible presence of the children of God is no more mysterious than his own. They may be all around us, without our discerning them, because our spiritual vision is not strong and clear enough to behold them,—even as the minute creation, that fills air, earth, and sea, remained for ages unknown, for lack of a proper medium through which to view it. Our Savior saw the dead and talked with them; for in him the spiritual vision was clear and full. And when his religion shall become supreme and all-pervading, and generations shall come forward, as they will in the latter days, bathed from infancy in the light and love of his gospel, the free communion with heaven may be opened, the tabernacle of God be with men, and the union of the two worlds form as much a part of the distinct consciousness of every disciple as it did of the Savior himself.

I prize the belief of the communion of the dead with the living, on account *of the encouragement to religious effort* which their sympathy gives us. We all seek sympathy, and to secure it we often become followers of each other more than of Jesus. We walk slower than we need, that we may not part company with our halting fellow-pilgrims. We hang about our persons the same weights, and cherish the same easily besetting sins, as those who run the race at our side. And when, in any way, our consciences prompt us to walk otherwise or move on faster than our fellow-Christians, we cannot help looking back with a painful sense of solitude and desertion. But our friends in heaven are the more intimately associated with us, the farther we are in advance of the inert and sluggish. When we seem to be alone, we can say as did the prophet, when he saw himself environed and guarded by the host of heaven,—"They that be with us are more than they that be with them." Those of our friends who have entered the heavenly rest have enured what we must encounter, and know how severe are the conflicts through which we must struggle into the higher life. They themselves felt the loneliness and desolation which sometimes press so heavily upon our spirits. Their sensibilities are now touched to the finest issues. They are familiar with every mode of inward experience, and can enter into our hearts, where the closest sympathy of the living fails us.

Again, we can hardly entertain the idea of the communion of our departed friends with us, *without its prompting the desire for their continued approbation.* Can we bear their inspection, and willingly remain unworthy of their esteem? Can we cherish the thought that they are with us, and yet harbor principles and habits from which they would turn with disapproval and loathing? Shall they behold us clinging to the weights which we should lay aside, and hugging the sins which we should crucify? Our friends who have gone from us, perhaps, in the weakness of partial affection, could see no fault in us. Our parents were, it may be, blind to our failings. Our children looked up to us with unmingled reverence, as if we had been the incarnation of every virtue. Our gentle and loving fellow-Christians, while they were with us, threw over our weaknesses the beautiful mantle of their charity, and read our characters through the hazy medium of their own kindness. But the scales have now dropped from their eyes. If they see and know us, it is with a just appreciation of what we are. And have we fallen in their esteem? Do they find us less worthy of their love than they used to think us? Do they look upon us as less their companions and fellow-disciples than when they were here? As we, parents and children, neighbors and friends, hope to find the long lost, but unforgotten, still true and loving, still and forever ours, O, let us cut off these sources of alienation and disappointment on their part,—let us not break fellowship with them, by so living in negligence and sin, that they must often avert their eyes from our unprofitable lives to the eternal throne in pitying intercession for us.

The idea of this discourse appeals with peculiar power *to those who have never entered upon the spiritual life.* Is there a son who has a mother in heaven? Had God spared your mother, my young friend, would you not have held her happiness sacred, anticipated her desires, and shielded her from disappointment and sorrow? You can even now make her happier. Full as her joy is, it is not perfect, while you remain out of the circle of her communion. Your mother's soul still yearns for your salvation. Her intercessions, which first rose over your cradle, now ascend for you near the throne. Enter on the life of heaven, and you hang new jewels on her eternal crown of rejoicing. Is there a parent, still living without prayer and without the Christian's hope, who has committed a child to the grave in spotless infancy? How gladly, my friend, would you have guarded your child from peril and from grief, and born him in the arms of an all-enduring love along the rugged path of life! A work of love yet remains for you in that child's behalf. He prays that he may not be left an orphan spirit, though it be in heaven; and for your first steps in the footmarks of the Lord Jesus, the voice lost to earth, before it could say *My Father* or *My Mother*, will be lifted in glad thanksgiving for you. Brothers and sisters, from whose circle Heaven has chosen the pure and lovely, were you here united by cordial sympathy and deep affection? Their prayer is, that the divided household may again be made one. Are you the bond-slaves of gain, or pleasure, or self-indulgence? The spirits of the departed mark your downward steps, and turn away from the scenes of your levity or your guilt in earnest deprecation of the fatal issue to which they see you hastening. By a renewed heart and life, you can make yet happier those whom God has made happy, and satisfy the only longing of their souls which eternal love has left unfilled.

Finally, what a momentous interest is given to our whole earthly life by the thought that it is passed in the presence and communion of the great spiritual family! To my mind there is hardly a text of Scripture, or form of speech, that rolls on with such a depth and fulness of meaning as those words,—"Seeing that we are compassed about with so great a cloud of witnesses." Vast and bewildering is the philosophical speculation which tells us that we cannot lift a finger without moving the distant spheres. But far more grand and unspeakable solemn is the thought, that our daily lives, our conduct in lowly and sheltered scenes, our speech and walk in the retirement of our homes, are felt through the universe of ever-living souls,— that the laws of attraction and repulsion that reach through all orders of being extend to our least words and deeds,—that in every worthy, generous, holy impulse all heaven bears part,—that from the trail of our meanness and selfishness, our waywardness and levity, all heaven recoils. Let the august witnesses, the adoring multitude, in whose presence we dwell and worship, arouse us to growing diligence in duty, and awaken in us increasing fervor of spirit, that we may run with patience the race that is set before us, and, found faithful unto death, may receive the crown of life.

The world may change from old to new,
  From new to old againr
Yet Hope and Heaven forever true,
  Within man's heart remain.
The dreams that bless the weary soul,
  The struggles of the strong,
Are steps toward some happy goal,
  The story of Hope's song.

THE SAINTED DEAD LEAD US HEAVENWORD.

REV. H. HARBAUGH, A. M.

GOD graciously designs that the death of our friends, and our desire to meet them again, should lead us to piety "No one dieth to himself." Their death, as well as their life, is in this way to be of real service to us. It is most beautifully said—who can read it without tenderness?—

> Smitten friends
> Are angels sent on errands full of love ;
> For us they languish, and for us they die,
> And shall they languish, shall they die in vain ?
> Ungrateful shall we grieve their hovering shades,
> Which wait the revolution in our hearts?
> Shall we disdain their silent soft address ;
> Their posthumous advice, and pious prayer ;
> Senseless as herds which graze their hallowed graves,
> Tread under foot their agonies and groans,
> Frustrate their anguish, and destroy their deaths?

In many cases this sweet motive to piety has led to blessed results—no doubt much oftener than is known. "Several years ago,' says a pastor, "I was called to attend the funeral of a child *five* years of age. She had sickened and died suddenly. The father I knew not, except that he was an infidel. This child had attended my Sabbath school, and she had left behind some interesting conversation with several members of the church. This, after the child had died, was communicated to the bereaved mother for her consolation. At the funeral the mother appeared more deeply interested in the subject of her own salvation than that of the loss of her child. The next Sabbath this family were at my church, and requested prayers that their afflictions might be sanctified. They continued to attend may church Sabbath after Sabbath, and on the fifth Sabbath the father became hopefully pious. Soon after this his wife became pious, and then a sister, and then a yonug lady residing in the family; and the father, mother, sister, and young lady, all, on the same Sabbath, made a public profession of their faith in the Lord Jesus Christ. That father is now a pillar in the church. This great change in that family was produced instrumentally by the death of that child!" Following their sainted child into a holy world, they felt that they were not prepared to meet it there, and this led to deep and saving penitence. Thus,

> Heaven gives us friends to bless the present scene,
> Resumes them to prepare us for the next.

THE SAINTED DEAD INTERESTED IN US.

REV. H. HARBAUGH, A. M.

The same reasons which induce us to believe in a final reunion with our sainted friends, encourage and warrant us also in the belief that they now remember us and feel interested in us. This idea too is full of consolation! It is sweet to be remembered by friends on earth, but how much more so to be assured that we live in the memory of those who are now saints in light. Being raised higher, their interest in us must increase in proportion as they become acquainted with those heavenly joys which await us also, and which they already possess. As they approach towards their perfection, their benevolence and love must increase; and, when we consider that we think most about our friends when we ourselves are most blest, we cannot but believe that they regard us with special concern. To have friends in heaven, then, is to have an inheritance in which we may well delight, and after which we are sweetly constrained to long. We, who are heirs of such celestial treasures, may enter fully into the spirit of the Poet's holy boasting—

> My boast, is not, that I deduce my birth
> From loins enthroned, and rulers of the earth;
> But higher far my proud pretensions rise—
> The son of parents passed into the skies!

A babe in a house is a well-spring of pleasure,
A messenger of peace and love,
A resting place for innocence on earth; a link between angels and men.
M. F. TUPPER.

JACOB WRESTLING WITH THE ANGEL.

THE SHINING ONES.

JOHN BUNYAN.

NOW you must note, that the City stood upon a mighty hill; but the pilgrims went up that hill with ease, because they had these two men to lead them up by the arms; they had likewise left their mortal garments behind them in the river; for though they went in with them, they came out without them. They therefore went up here with much agility and speed, though the foundation upon which the city was framed was higher than the clouds; they therefore went up through the regions of the air sweetly talking as they went, being comforted because they safely got over the river, and had such glorious companions to attend them.

The talk that they had with the shining ones was about the glory of the place; who told them that the beauty and glory of it was inexpressible. There, said they, is "the Mount Sion, the heavenly Jerusalem, the innumerable company of angels, and the spirits of just men made perfect." You are going now, said they, to the paradise of God, wherein you shall see the tree of life, and eat of the never fading fruits thereof; and, when you come there, you shall have white robes given you, and your walk and talk shall be every day with the King, even all the days of eternity. There you shall not see again such things as you saw when you were in the lower region upon the earth; to wit: sorrow, sickness, affliction, and death; "for the former things are passed away." You are going now to Abraham, to Isaac, and to Jacob, and to the prophets, men that God hath taken away from the evil to come, and that are now resting upon their beds, each one walking in his righteousness. The men then asked, What must we do in the holy place? To whom it was answered, You must there receive the comfort of all your toil, and have joy for all your sorrow; you must reap what you have sown, even the fruit of all your prayers, and tears, and sufferings for the King by the way. In that place you must wear crowns of gold, and enjoy the perpetual sight and visions of the Holy One; for there you shall see him as he is. There also you shall serve him continually with praise, with shouting and thanksgiving, whom you desired to serve in the world,

THE GUARDIAN ANGEL.

though with much difficulty, because of the infirmity of your flesh. There your eyes shall be delighted with seeing, and your ears with hearing the pleasant voice of the Mighty One. There you shall enjoy your friends again that are gone thither before you; and there you shall with joy receive even every one that follows into the holy place after you. There also you shall be clothed with glory and majesty, and put into an equipage fit to ride out with the King of Glory. When he shall come with sound of trumpet in the clouds, as upon the wings of the wind, you shall come with him; and when he shall sit upon the throne of judgment, you shall sit by him; yea, and when he shall pass sentence upon all the workers of iniquity, let them be angels or man, you also shall have a voice in that judgment, because they were his and your enemies. Also, when he shall again return to the City, you shall go too with sound of trumpet, and be ever with him.

DEGREES OF BLISS IN HEAVEN.

THERE are to be different degrees of bliss in a future heaven. One star is to differ from another star in glory. There are to be rulers over five, and rulers over ten cities—those who are to be in the outskirts of glory, and those basking in the sunlight of the Eternal Throne! Is this no call on us to be up and doing?—not to be content with the circumference, but to seek nearness to the glorious centre— not only to have crowns shining as the brightness of the firmament, but to have a tiara of *stars* in that crown? It is the degree of holiness now that will decide the degree of happiness *then*—the transactions of *time* will regulate the awards of eternity.

REV. J. R. McDUFF, D. D.

It is little matter at what hour of the day
The righteous fall asleep. Death cannot come
To him untimely who has learned to die.
The less of this brief life, the more of heaven
The shorter time, the longer immortality.

DEAN MILLMAN.

SAINTED FRIENDS

REV. H. HARBAUGH, A. M.

WE think of heaven but vaguely unless we think of it as the abode of sainted freinds. Though our Savior is the chief attraction of the place, yet He, as the light of the upper temple, reveals to us also the saints as the happy worshipers; thus presenting to our minds these subordinate attractions, begetting in us a kind of familiar home-feeling, and giving to heavenly joys a definiteness which they would not otherwise have. When we hear of a distant country, especially if we hear much in praise of it, we think and speak of it it is true, yet not in the same way as we do when once some of our dearest friends have gone to dwell there; then our thoughts and feelings assume a definiteness in reference to it, which they had not before. So in regard to heaven, when once we regard it as the home of our sainted friends. Then it is, to us, no more heaven in a vague and general idea, but it is heaven as the abode of our departed freinds—it is heaven as the place where we expect soon to rejoin them;—this gives distinctness and intensity to all our thoughts of it. Then all our hearts transfer themselves to it, and live in it. Then, in faith,

> Our dying friends come o'er us like a cloud
> To damp our brainless ardors; and abate
> That glare of life, which often blinds the wise.

Much is gained as help to devout reverence and tender piety in thus drawing around us the solemn mysteries of eternity; especially so, if we can recognize by faith the alluring smiles of friends, looking out upon us through the cloudy veil which partly hides its mysteries like the golden light through the vista of clouds which hang along the evening sky. The love which we bear towards the saints in the triumphant church, draws us towards them with humble reverence. It is a sweet attraction, which causes us to linger, in affectionate longings, on the confines of the shadowy spirit land. It gives us an indescribable desire for their "silent company." It is said that the home-sickness of the Swiss soldiers in foreign lands was often so strong that they must return to their beloved home in the Alps or die; all was dreary and tasteless to them in absence, while the "sweet home" of their childhood hovered in smiles around them in visions of the day, and in dreams of the night. So it is with those to whom heaven is a Fatherland—the bright home-like abode of kindred and friends. It brings with it an unquenchable desire to leave this foreign land and return home. It familiarizes us with death as a narrow crossing. It keeps the power of eternal things near us; and, to a great extent, converts the valley of the shadow of death into gardens of the Lord, through which lies the Father's pleasant highway, by which His children return to him and to each other.

We very much need influences like these to break in upon the lower attachments of life, which are too prone to detain our thoughts and feelings. Even when we very well know, in theory, what value to set upon earthly things, we need also to learn the value of heavenly things, in order to enable us to feel practically the vanity of earth. The Poet has truly said:

"Tis, by comparison, an easy task
Earth to despise; but, to commune with heaven—
"Tis not so easy.

THE SAINTED WATCHERS.

Withdraw not your mysterious presence from me, ye sainted watchers! Ye have been an host around me, that came at the call of faith, in loveliest hours of my life. Look still on me through the veil, and let me still feel the calming influence of your blessed communion. Leave me not alone! The earth is gloomy and sad from the curse. It shines but as a cold moon, with a borrowed light. My soul is weary of these storm-swept solitudes outside of holy Eden. Hail! ye far-off lands of light. Hail! ye happy dwellers in the peaceful Salem of purity and love! "Oh that I had wings like a dove! for then would I fly away, and be at rest."

What remains eternity will reveal!

REV. H. HARBAUGH.

THE SAINTED DEAD INTERESTED IN THE LIVING.

BISHOP MATTHEW SIMPSON, D. D.

AND death does not change the nature, it does not destroy the affections. Think you those that clasped us in their arms but yesterday are careless of us because they have gone beyond the veil? Not at all. The purest affection is the holiest affection. The mother's love is taken as the type of heavenly love; but has that mother who watched over me for forty or fifty years, and was a mother always—now that she has just gone into the heavenly world, has she ceased to be a mother still? No; she is in the cloud. Gazing up into glory, she sees the face of Jesus; gazing down on earth, she sees the forms of those she loved. She is a witness. And it seems to me life would have more of its sacredness if we could only enter into the conviction that the departed ones are not away from us, not unmindful of us. We shall enter, it seems to me, into a higher conviction of the watchful providence of God, if we can think of the watchful care of our friends. And oh! to think, as you walk along the street, exposed to trials, temptations, sorrows, and cares, that dear, departed friends are looking at you! You who are tempted and likely to go wrong, think: "Mother sees me." You who are assailed and likely to be led astray, think: "The dear one that dropped from my bosom is looking at me, wishing for my triumph and escape." What a moral power it would give! And there is Jesus at the right hand his eye on us always, and his strength communicated to us always. Oh! it is these witnesses, a great company, their eyes upon us, that may have a powerful influence upon our hearts and lives and make us strain every nerve. There are some of you in this room who, when you took hold of that hand that was cold in the dying hour, promised you would live for Jesus and meet the dying one in glory. These loved ones are watching you; they are looking for you to turn; they are wondering what you are doing; they are astonished that you are living away from Jesus. And yet you do not see them, because your duties here, all your energies, are to be employed in doing what you can. You are to look at present duty. They are resting, and gaze down on you. It is time enough for you to enter upon that beautiful vision when you become victors.

COMMUNION WITH THE DEPARTED.

The *communion of saints* in the church of Christ with those which are departed, is demonstrated by their communion with the saints alive. For if I have communion with a saint of God, as such, while he liveth here, I must still have communion with him when he is departed hence; because the foundation of that communion cannot be removed by death. The mystical union between Christ and his church, the spiritual conjunction of the members to the head, is the true foundation of that communion which one member had with another, all the members living and increasing by the same influence which they receive from him. But death, which is nothing else but the separation of the soul from the body, maketh no separation in the mystical union, no breach of the spiritual conjunction; and, consequently, there must continue the same communion, because there remaineth the same foundation.   BISHOP PEARSON.

THE DEPARTED ANXIOUS FOR US.

Why should we lament and sorrow for *those among us who are departed?* Christ himself, our Lord and God, exhorts us, and He says: "I am the resurrection and the life; whosoever believeth in me, though he were dead, yet shall he live; and he that liveth and believeth in me, shall never see death!" Why hasten we not to see our country, to salute our parents? There a vast multitude of them that are dear to us, await our arrival, a multitude of parents, brethren, and children, who are now secure of their own salvation, *and anxious only about ours*. What a mutual joy will it be for them and us, when we come into their presence and receive their embrace!
     NEANDER.

I bent before Thy gracious throne
And asked for peace with suppliant knee;
And peace was given—nor peace alone,
But faith, sublimed to ecstacy!

THE MEMORY OF THE SAINTED DEAD.

REV. H. HARBAUGH, A. M.

THE memory of the sainted dead hovers, a blessed and purifying influence over the hearts of men. At the grave of the good, so far from losing heart, the spiritually minded find new strength. They weep, but as they weep, they look down into the sepulchre, and beholds angels sitting, and the dead come nearer, and are united to them by a fellowship more intimate than that of blood.

How soul-subduing is the thought, that but a thin veil, which a moment may lift, divides us from the conscious fellowship of our beloved dead! How solemn the thought that, being raised into a higher sphere, they may even now know much more of us than we do of them. How like devotion does the place become to us when we sit alone and summon around us their familiar faces; or, when we think of them in their white robes, with harps and palms, bending before the throne or walking in "heavenly pastime." It makes us feel almost like the Publican, who stood afar off, casting a wishful and reverent look towards the holiest place, but conscious of his unworthiness to enter it. A sweet penitence comes over our hearts, and we look immediately to Jesus for a fresh application of his cleansing blood, that we may be made more like those into whose holy society we expect soon to be introduced. When the spirit of earthliness and sense hangs too heavily upon our affections and thoughts, so that we cannot rise to the contemplation of heavenly attraction as we desire, the prayer of the Poet is excusable.

> Ye holy dead, now come around,
> In season more profound;
> And through the barriers of our sense
> Shed round your calming influence;
> In silence come and solitude,
> With thoughts that o'er the mourner brood

THE CLOUD OF WITNESSES.

The Old Testament saints are represented as a cloud of witnesses around us, like the crowd which bent down from all sides upon the race-ground in the Olympic games. According to this allusion of the Apostle, they are around us, not merely as examples, but as interested spectators. That we are not conscious of this, does not prove its improbability; for the lower orders of nature that are beneath us are not aware of our perfect knowledge of them, neither do they know us, and yet we know them—their nature, habits, prospects, and destiny. In like manner, we have reason, and also intimations of Scripture, to confirm in us the belief that our sainted friends are bending an interested eye of love over us in all our earthly pilgrimage—that they keep up a tender and affectionate acquantance with us who still struggle here below striving for immortality.

Rev. H. Harbaugh, D. D.

COMMUNION WITH THE DEPARTED.

"Those we loved on earth may be spectators at this moment of those they left behind them. The partition wall that separates Time from Eternity may be so thin that those on the other side may hear the voice of music and prayer lifted up to God from those on this side; the eye of saints in glory may have that penetrating power that it can see through the partition, and witness the countless races that are on their course to immortality and glory."

Rt. Rev. Geo. Burgess, D. D.

God's voice doth sometimes fall on us with fear;
More oft with music low yet clear

THE CLOUD OF WITNESSES.

BISHOP MATTHEW SIMPSON, D. D.

THERE is an intense interest in our gaining the victory, by the great cloud of witnesses; and these are they who themselves have gained. If you look at a gallery, stretching away back, higher, and higher, and higher, the aspect of a crowded gallery is like a cloud; and if you can fancy gallery above gallery, it seems like clouds piled upon clouds. Around us are gathered, not our associates merely, nor chiefly, for the racers have very little time to look up at the countenances of all and scan them—the race was before them and all their energies were there; but the witnesses, who had ended their race, and were through their conflicts, and were resting, had time to look down and witness the contest of those who were in the arena. The apostle goes back from the beginning to reckon, bringing, age by age, those who are in this cloud. Thus, he says, Abel, who being dead yet speaketh—that is, not only may a man have his influence and interest in the world, who has been dead a year, or a hundred years, or a thousand years, but that influence and that interest exist from the very beginning, for Abel is the first man that died, and he is yet speaking, and he yet feels an interest. Abel is in that cloud and is looking down on those who are running the race. He has not forgotten the world yet, though gone up to glory; he himself having died for his faith, having witnessed a good profession and triumphed, is looking down on earth. And Enoch, who walked in the midst of ungodly men and prophesied, and they thirsted for his life, and the descending cloud took him up toward heaven, and he was not, for God took him in the clouds of glory—that Enoch, holy, pure, triumphant—he is part of the cloud watching us still; he has not forgotten earth or its scenes; he is gazing down upon us. And Noah, who, warned of God, saved his family in the ark, saw that dreadful scene when the ocean, breaking over its boundary, being above hill and mountain, swept the earth of its inhabitants—Noah, having gained the reward, he is part of that cloud, and is looking down upon us, who are exposed to a deluge of sin worse than that deluge which swept the face of the earth. There is Abraham, who was called to part with his dearest son, as he supposed, the son of promise, to lay him on the altar; and when he sees father or mother struggling with the dearest of all affections, their hearts almost breaking at the sacrifice they may make, Abraham is looking down out of that cloud and trying to whisper: "Give them up for God. I gave up Isaac, and had him back again. Trust God. Be not afraid to sacrifice everything for Jesus." And Jacob, in his perilous pilgrimage—the poor boy, who laid his head upon a rock, and saw angels ascending and descending, and trusted God, and gave the tenth of his possessions to God's cause, and God blessed him abundantly—he is in that cloud, and he is looking down, as if to whisper to every poor boy who may be tempted to do wrong: "Do right and trust God. The angels of God are coming down to thee. Give what God has given thee, and He will give it back again."

Such are the voices that come whispering out of that cloud. And then there come Gideon and Samson, and Barak, and Jephtha, and host of others—prophets, apostles, patriarchs, martyrs—what say they, looking down from the cloud? Isaiah? I listen, but oh! what glorious visions had he! Down in the valley by that tree they had sawn him asunder, and I hear his voice speaking out of that cloud : "Better obey God and be sawn asunder, than live a life of sin and be saved here in health." Oh! what the voices speak! The martyrs who were stoned, the men who were torn of wild beasts those who passed through fire and blood, who conquered in the name of Jesus—they are in the cloud, and they are looking down upon us, and they are saying . " Trust God, and all shall be well. Death lasts only a little while ; glory comes afterward. Suffering is but a few years—the morning is breaking. Driven from the company of men to be in the company of angels. Driven from a life of suffering to be crowned with eternal glory before the throne of God." These are some of the voices out of the cloud.

But mark the peculiarity of expression. And it is to bring this great thought to your hearts to-day, if I can, that I have selected this passage. We are encompassed about by a great cloud of witnesses ; they are looking down on us, watching us. And Abel, and Enoch, and Noah, and Abraham, to-day, gaze even upon us, and they are anxious to see what shall be the results. Will we conquer, will we triumph, or will we fall by the way?

But the cloud of witnesses ends not here. If the thousands of years that have passed have not changed Abel, and Enoch, and Noah, and Abraham, but they are part of that cloud of witnesses looking down still on those who are running this race. What shall we say of those more recently gone out from our midst? They have passed out of our sight but they are in the cloud, just as Noah, and Abraham, and Jacob, and Samson are there; and though we are not witnesses of them, they are witnesses of us; we are surrounded by a cloud of witnesses. They are witnesses—that is, looking at, watching, gazing on us. And who are they, and what interest do they feel? Ah! there is no one here who has not witnesses just beyond the veil. You cannot see them, but they see you—grandfathers who clasped you in their arms; grandmothers who held you on their knees; fathers who counselled you and guided you in the days of your youth; mothers whose warm kiss you can still feel on your cheek, or whose warm tears dropped on your boyish head; husbands who walked by your side; wives who were your comfort and joy; brothers who stood, shoulder to shoulder, with you; sisters who talked with you by day and rested with you by night; children who were in your arms, and you talked to them of heaven and glory, and of the angels, and little thought how soon they should be called away, but they have gone up and they are in the cloud. And they are witnessing you, and they are witnessing to-day.

THEY ARE PERFECTLY BLEST.

They are perfectly blessed—the redeemed and the free—
Who are resting in joy by the smooth glassy sea;
They breathed here on earth all their sorrowful sighs,
And Jesus has kissed all the tears from their eyes.

They are happy at home! They have learnt the new song,
And warble it sweetly amid the glad throng:
No faltering voices, no discords are there—
The melodious praises swell high through the air.

There falls not on them the deep silence of night;
They never grow weary—ne'er fadeth the light;
Throughout the long day new hosannahs they raise,
And express their glad thoughts in exuberant praise.

E'en thus would we praise thee, dear Savior divine—
We too would be with thee—loved children of thine,
O teach us, that we may sing perfectly there
When we are called to that city so fair.

MARIANNE FARNINGHAM.

MY TWO ANGEL BOYS.

I may not see their features,
  Save in memory's faithful glass,
But I feel that they are with me,
  Each moment that doth pass.

I feel them in the promptings
  Of good which thrill my heart;
I hear them in the voices
  Which pleasures most impart.

When the sun beams bright around me,
  And my soul is full of joys,
I then discern the presence
  Of my two angel boys.

They whisper solace to me,
  When sorrow's cloud is dark,
They fan hope's fading embers
  When dwindled to a spark.

Their voice is sweetest music,
  But it greeteth not the ear;
The heart alone receives it,—
  The heart alone can hear.

As I lay me down to slumber
  Peace in my breast doth reign,
For I know my angel watchers
  Amid the gloom remain.

Spirit eyes gaze on me,
  Eyes that know not night;
Spirit hands unite to bless me
  Hidden from my sight.

Hidden, but, O, happiness!—
  Faith assurance brings!
Living, loving, still they're round me,
  Borne on willing wings.

B. P. Shillaber.

OUR COMING LIFE.

JOHN G. WHITTIER.

WE shape ourselves the joy or fear
   Of which the coming life is made,
And fill our future's atmosphere
   With sunshine or with shade.

The tissue of the life to be
   We weave with colors all our own,
And in the field of destiny
   We reap as we have sown.

Still shall the soul around it call
   The shadows which it gathered here,
And, painted on the eternal wall,
   The past shall reappear.

Think ye the notes of holy song
   On Milton's tuneful ear have died?
Think ye that Raphael's angel throng
   Has vanished from his side?

Oh, no! we live our life again;
   Or warmly touched, or coldly dim,
The pictures of the past remain—
   Man's works shall follow him.

To me there is an inexpressible sweetness in the thought that our friends who are asleep in Jesus may not be so distant from us as we had perhaps conceived. Should this be irreconcileable with the idea of confinement in a separate place, in expectation of the Resurrection, then will I give up that idea for the sake of this. To think that not only are we ministered to by God's angelic agents, and compassed about with that vast cloud of Old Testament witnesses of whom the Apostle makes mention, but that our own dear friends, a sainted mother or wife, for example, or a loving father, may be also with us in our sleeping and in our waking hours, suggesting thoughts —for aught I know—of purity and peace, oh! what harm can there be in that belief? Men may call it the romance, the enthusiasm, the exaggeration of religion, if they will. I do not think any will dare to call it "superstition."

REV. W. H. COOPER, D. D

THE GRAFTED BUD.

O brightly beautiful, so fair!
  So lovely in her tender years,
Ye might have known she could not bear
  To tarry in a life of tears.
Those long-fringed lashes never more
  With drops of sorrow shall be wet,
For she hath reached a blessed shore
  And only left us to regret,
And broken hearts and troubled care,
And garbs of grief that mortals wear.

The stricken father, desolate,
  Folding his arms on empty air,
Where erst his darling daughter sat,
  How will ye comfort his despair!
The sunshine and the dews of love
  Have nursed in vain his foreign flower,
And for her native soil above
  She early left his earthly bower;
She could not linger, save to bless
A little while his tenderness.

Then bear her to a quiet spot,
  And break for her the moistened earth,
The burden of each tender thought,
  The blessing of the household hearth:
And let the May flowers gently wave
  With life like hers, as brief, as fair,
In fragrant beauty on her grave,
  And o'er the dust that slumbers there:
While her pure spirit, from above
Bends o'er her home of earthly love.

Perchance before the Eternal Throne,
  The new-born angel bows her head,
With yearning heart and thrilling tone,
  Asks healing for the hearts that bled;
Asks from the Holy Comforter,
  Comfort for her loved ones here,
For her "sweet mother,' oh! for her
  Permission but to hover near,
To such, to cheer, to shield from ill:
Her child in heaven to bless her still.

HELP FROM THOSE FALLEN ASLEEP.

For all the recollections of help received from those who are now fallen asleep, I would ask you to give God hearty thanks to-day. I might apply to some of these—though they were never your ministers—those touching words of the great anonymous Epistle, "Remember these your guides, who spoke to you, in some past day, the word of God: whose faith follow, as you contemplate the end of their conversation"—their death, that is, in the faith of Jesus; remembering that One Person never dies—"Jesus Christ is the same yesterday and to-day and forever."

Who would not shrink with pain and horror from the thought of severing himself, by lukewarmness, unbelief, or apostacy, from the fellowship, from the sympathy, from the everlasting company, of these his young comrades once in the army of the living God? O, let many an earnest prayer go up this morning from us who "remain unto this present," that we may have grace to end well—to finish our race with joy.

Rev. C. J. Vaughn, D. D.

THE HEAVENLY HOST.

The mind recalls a venerable host whose names are written in heaven,—prophets, evangelists, patriots, apostles, benefactors of every kind, differing widely in power and grace, and the worth of their work, as one star differeth from another in glory; but all agreeing in this one trait, that they labored, not "for the meat that perisheth, but for that which endureth unto everlasting life." They gave themselves up with unwavering faith and uncalculating love to some worthy object in and for which they lived. Their creeds were many; but the same mind which was in Christ was in them all. They wrought with differences of administrations, but in them wrought one and the self-same spirit, asserting itself in all diversities of operations as holy and divine. We cannot think of these as dead and dust. They are with us still by the witness of the spirit that was in them: vital forces in the realms of faith,—the spirit's own, they live unto God and they live unto us, witnessing and working with us and for us until now.

Prof. Frederick H. Hedge, D. D.

ENTERING THE CELESTIAL GATE.

TAPPAN.

WOULD I were with them! they are free
   From all the cares they knew below,
And strangers to the strife that we
   Encounter in this vale of woe.
From storms of sorrow and of pain,
   Forever are they garnered in,
Secure from sad defilement's stain,
   The mildew and the blight of sin.

Would I were with them! They embrace
   The loved ones, lost, long years before;
What joy to gaze upon the face
   That never shall be absent more!
There friends unite who parted here,
   At Death's cold river, O how sadly!
Forgotten are the sigh and tear,
   Their hearts are leaping, O how gladly!

Would I were with them! They behold
   Their Savior, glorious and divine;
They touch the cups of shining gold,
   And in his kingdom drink new wine.
How flash, like gems, their brilliant lyres,
   Along the sparkling walls of heaven,
When from the radiance catching fires,
   The song of songs to Christ is given!

Would I were with them! While without
   Are sighs and weeping, they, within,
For every joy and gladness shout,
   And well they may, who're free from sin!
O this, indeed, is heaven above,
   This fills the bliss of every soul,
To grow in holiness and love,
   As age on age shall ceaseless roll.

REV. HENRY W. BELLOWS, D.D.

PERSONALITY AND CONSEQUENT SYMPATHY OF THE DEPARTED.

REV. H. W. BELLOWS, D. D.

IF man is the confessed summit of the visible creation—the noblest of creatures—it is equally true that his personality is the noblest and most dignified characteristic, nay, cause, of this superior nature. He is a thinking, reflecting, self-knowing, moral, and intellectual being only by force of this personality. The law does not call children under a certain age persons, because they are not responsible until self-consciousness, reflection, comparison, a distinction between themselves and their impulses, or force operating upon them, is felt and recognized. To this sense of personality belongs all moral life, all capacity of progress and improvement, all dignity and worth of character. Men are properly distinguished and graded by the degree in which personality, or the sense of it, is developed in them. What marks a man out as not one of the common herd only is the special force in and with which his personality exists and acts. You cannot lump him with his race. He is a person by eminence and genius, talents, achievements, and in the emphasis they give to this personality. It is the jeweled hilt of that sword whose shining blade, however keen and lustrous, weighty and fearful, falls useless and aimless when its handle is gone. Nay, it is the hand that grasps that hilt. It is the central principle of the man himself—the soul of his soul, the innermost and last recess and home of his being. Humanity, if it exists at all in any abstract essence, really exists not in a race, but in individual men and women. There is properly no human race, except a name or generality which comprehends all persons of that race, as there is no dodo or megalosaurus after the last dodo has died.

Nature is barren, unmoral, loveless, uninteresting in her mere forces; and only living, attractive, knowable, consummate, in the things, species, individual plants, animals, insects, flowers—above all, the persons she produces or attests. Now, is it possible or probable then, that the most sacred, venerable, awful, tender, central experience or manifestation she makes—the noblest characteristic of her noblest off-spring—the principle or fact of personality in man, has no permanency, contains no prophecy, has no future? If that lasts not, no matter what else endures, man is not immortal in the only sense in which it is of any interest to him to be immortal.

THE SYMPATHY OF THE TWO WORLDS.

REV. C. H. SPURGEON.

BUT I have no doubt the thought has sometimes struck us that our praise does not go far enough. We seem as if we lived in an isle cut off from the main land. This world, like a fair planet, swims in a sea of ether unnavigated by mortal ship. We have sometimes thought that surely our praise was confined to the shores of this poor narrow world, that it was impossible for us to pull the ropes which might ring the bells of heaven, that we could by no means whatever reach our hands so high as to sweep the celestial chords of angelic harps. We have said to ourselves there is no connection between earth and heaven. A huge black wall divides us. A strait of unnavigable waters shuts us out. Our prayers cannot reach to heaven, neither can our praises affect the celestials. Let us learn from our text how mistaken we are. We are, after all, however much we seem to be shut out from heaven, and from the great universe, but a province of God's vast united empire, and what is done on earth is known in heaven; what is sung on earth is sung in heaven; and there is a sense in which it is true that the tears of earth are wept' again in paradise, and the sorrows of mankind are felt again, even on the throne of the Most High.

"There is joy in the presence of the angels of God over one sinner that repenteth." It seems as if these words showed me a bridge by which I might cross over into eternity. It doth, as it were, exhibit to me certain magnetic wires which convey the intelligence of what is done here to spirits in another world. It teaches me that there is a real and wonderful connection between this lower world and that which is beyond the skies, where God dwelleth, in the land of the happy.

THE DEPARTED REMEMBER.

"Some suppose a certain kind of continuance of their thinking faculties after death, but do not believe that with these faculties they will remember their earthly existence. They dream of an existence that is entirely new, which is better than the present, but upon which life has no influence, and with which it has no connection. This whole idea amounts to just the same as entire annihilation at death; for if I cannot recollect this life—its fortunes and misfortunes, my wife and children, my friends, my weaknesses and my good deeds,—in short, nothing at all, then I am no more the same I, no more the same person, but I will be a being entirely new! The Lord in mercy preserve us from such a future state! But thanks to his name for ever, that the Bible, and the common sense and feeling of men in all ages and in all places, teach directly the contrary."

STILLING.

WHAT A MEETING IN HEAVEN.

What a meeting on the other shore! If we could see there this morning how our hearts would enlarge. Multitudes around the throne to-day. I am charmed with that thought. There's a central figure I am more charmed with—the Man on the Throne. His kingdom shall triumph over all. The time will come when every knee shall bow and every tongue confess.

I think of the men gone before—fathers, mothers, little children—that cloud up yonder. I think I can see them. Oh, there is a cloud of witnesses. I urge on my way, run my race, ever looking to Jesus, who is alone the finisher of faith. Oh, may this audience all follow Jesus and be a part of that grand gathering that shall meet on that other shore!

BISHOP M. SIMPSON, D. D.

THE DEAR LOVE OF OLD.

No comfort, nay, no comfort. Yet would I
In Sorrow's cause with Sorrow intercede.
Burst not the great heart,—this is all I plead;
Ah! sentence it to suffer, not to die.
'Comfort?' It Jesus wept at Bethany--
That doze and nap of Death--how may we bleed
Who watch the long sleep that is sleep indeed!
Pointing to Heaven I but remind you why
On earth you still must mourn. He who, being bold
For life-to-come, is false to the past sweet
Of mortal life, hath killed the world above.
For why to live again if not to meet?
And why to meet if not to meet in love?
And why in love if not in that dear love of old?

SYDNEY DOBELL

SAINTLY SYMPATHY.

When once we close our eyes in death,
  And flesh and spirit sever:
When earth and fatherland and home,
With all their beauty sink in gloom—
  Say, will it be forever?

Will we, in heaven, no more review,
  Those scenes from which we sever?
Or will our recollection leap
O'er death's dark gulf, at times, to keep
  With earth acquaintance ever?

In life we loved the blessed past,
  It clings upon us ever;
The songs of childhood and of home,
Like music when the minstrel's gone,
  Live in our hearts forever?

The child's included in the man,
  And part of him for ever;—
The Past still in the Future lives
And basis to its being gives,
  Not it, but of it, ever!

UNKNOWN

LOVE UNITES US AGAIN.

REV. JAMES FREEMAN CLARKE.

SOMETIMES people have a fear lest the friends who have gone before them may have gone on away from them; that progress may have removed them too far; that they will never be able to rise to their communion. But this is to forget, that, while progress tends to separate, love tends to unite again. The balance of the spiritual universe is maintained by these two antagonistic forces, just as the balance of the material universe is preserved by attraction on the one side, and the centrifugal force on the other. Does not a parent love a child, though the parent knows more, and is higher? Did not Christ love his disciples? When he went away, did not he say that he went to return again? It is the work of the highest angels to help the lowliest sinners; and love always tends to bring together extremes and opposites, in order that progress may not pull the universe of souls apart. Our angels do not love us less because they have gone into heaven; they love us more. They do not forget us because they have ascended to God; they remember us more. The higher they go up the lowlier they lean down; for every acquisition, elevation and attainment in God's heaven is used for the good of those who most need help, light and deliverance.

In thinking of the other world, we sometimes seem to consider it impossible that the myriads of human beings who pass into it from all lands, races, nations; of all habits, tastes, characters, opinions, ages; infants and old men, should be provided, each with his own home, sphere, surroundings; that a suitable place should be got ready beforehand to receive every one of them. But why should that be more strange than that the same provision has been made in this world; that the tens of thousands who are born daily are born each into a home, on the bosom of a mother, with fostering care and patient love around him? Each comes wholly helpless; each is helped fed, clothed, taught, by provided love. Not only so, but of the millions of insects, reptiles, animals, fishes, daily arriving, each one comes to find its blade of grass, its leaf, made ready for it; each with the climate, the home, the food it needs. "In my Father's house are many mansions; if it were not so I would have told you. I go to prepare a place for you." It may be part of the occupation of angels and higher spirits to prepare suitable circumstances for those who are to come after.

COME UP HITHER.

REV. F. W. P. GREENWOOD, D. D.

E hear other great voices from heaven, saying unto us, "Come up hither!" They are the voices of the "glorious company of the apostles," "the goodly fellowship of the apostles," "the noble army of martyrs," the innumerable multitude of saints and sealed servants of God, which no man can number, of all nations and kindreds and people and tongues. Come up hither! they cry, and witness our joys, and be encouraged by our success. Ages roll on, but our pleasures are never new. Your years come to an end, but we have put on immortality. Your days and nights succeed each other, but there is no night here. Faint not at your tribulations; if we had fainted, we had not conquered. Behold our crowns and our palms. Fight the good fight, as we did; and then come up hither unto us, and swell our song of praise and victory, and join with us in ascribing blessing and honor and glory and power unto him who sitteth upon the throne and unto the Lamb for ever and ever!

Where the spirits of all the just and good and pious and constant of all past times are assembled, shall not the spirit of every Christian, of every rational man desire to be, and strive to go? Shall not theirs be the society of his choice? Shall not their abode be the country of his own adoption? Will he refuse a little labor for such a rest? Will he repine at a light sorrow, which may work out for him such a weight of glory? He will rather say,

> "This is the heaven I long to know:
> For this, with patience I would wait,
> Till weaned from earth, and all below,
> I mount to my celestial seat,
> And wave my palm, and wear my crown.
> And, with the elders, cast them down."

"WILL YOU WRITE ABOUT ME, MOTHER?"

MRS. N. L. M. SANDERSON.

"WILL you write a piece 'bout me, mother?"
   And round my neck he twined
His arms with an earnest look
   His eyes gazed into mine.

And then I felt his loving kiss,
   Pressed close upon my brow;
As I to him the promise gave,
   To write one soon—not now!

Then joyously he bounded off,
   Laughing in boyhood's glee,
And soon I heard him, " Mother says
   She'll write a piece 'bout me."

*   *   *   *   *   *

A few short weeks have passed away—
   Once more I take my pen;
And with an aching, heavy heart,
   I strive to write again.

'Tis very strange! why comes he not
   To stand behind my chair?
In vain I wait and call his name—
   In vain! he is not here!

Perhaps he'll leave his spirit home
   To hover near to-night;
He'll stand just where he used to stand,
   And watch me while I write.

And when I've done, and read it loud,
   Will listen though unseen,
And smile that I've my promise kept,
   And written 'bout him.

Then closer comes and round my neck
   His phantom arms he'll twine,
And I shall feel, though all unseen,
   His spirit lips press mine.

Oh! often I shall take my pen,
   As I have done to night,
Then I shall know my boy is near,
   To watch me while I write.

A BLIND GIRL'S DREAM.

HAD a dream last night, Mother,—
   A dream replete with bliss;
I was in a world of light, Mother,
   Not dark and cold like this;
There were skies serene and cloudless,
   Sweet music filled the air,
And all was bright and beautiful,
   For Jesus Christ was there.

He wore a crown of glory,
   Containing pearls untold;
And "little children" sung to Him,
   And struck their harps of gold;
I wept to think I had no harp,
   That his praise I could not swell,
For he looked so pure and holy,
   That I loved him deeply well.

But brother William came to me,
   And bade me not to cry;
He said I soon should have a harp
   And dwell with him on high;
He wound his arms around my neck,
   And kissed me on my brow:—
His eyes they looked so bright, Mother,
   I can almost see them now.

This world has been all dark, Mother,
   My eyes have never seen
The skies, so bright and beautiful,
   The meadows, fresh and green—
And I have never gazed, Mother,
   Upon your loving smile,
As you've told me of the Savior,
   In tones so sweet and mild.

Dear Mother, I am going now
   Where little Willie's gone;
Nay, do not weep, I know, Mother
   You'll meet us very soon,
Your little Annie now will see,
   For all in heaven is bright;
I'm going, Mother, Willie's come
   To guide me there,—good-night.

THE TRANSLATION OF ELIJAH.

While she raised the dear, cold body, with lustrous white impearled,
Its little arms all helpless, its flaxen locks uncurled;
And as her lips clung to it, the heavenly guest knelt by,
And softly said to her spirit, "Their angels can never die."

THE SPIRIT RETAINS ITS HUMAN FORM.

BISHOP D. W. CLARK, D, D.

THE Scriptures most clearly recognize this grand truth ; for wherever the dead are spoken of or represented as making their appearance upon earth, they are uniformally referred to as being in their appropriate human form. Hence it is that recognition and identiffcation take place. This idea has prevailed in all ages. The heathen poets and philosophers thought and wrote of the shades of their departed friends appearing as when tabernacled in the flesh. It is the universal conception of human nature. It is an unconscious element of that faith in the heart of the Christian which exults in the confident expectation of seeing the loved ones who have gone into eternity, when he also shall have crossed over the irremeable flood. So does the Bible represent Dives to have seen and recognized Abraham and Lazarus, and them also to have recognized him ; so were seen Moses and Elias ; And so the great multitude around the throne of God were seen by St. John. Their form, their words, their actions, all marked them as having been once beings of earth, in spite of all the transformations of circumstance, and time, and place. They were disembodied ; new scenes enchanted them; new glories blazed upon them; everything was wondrously new; but through all the human and personal were visibly and distinctly marked.

The demand of this sentiment is met when we come to the recognition of the departed. Identity is what we want ; nature craves for identity, and scripture gives back the response that assures us this identity shall remain. All the anicipated glories of a reunion with the departed are enhanced by this prospect. The form may be vastly improved, infinitely more glorious, but it will be the same. Our friends or our children, who have been absent from us for a few years, sometimes become so changed that at first we do not recognize them, though their general form and identity are the same. So may it be with our friends in heaven. Our aged friends who totter with halting step and wasting frame to the grave, may there be rejuvenated and glowing with celestial life. Our children, nipped like the buds of Spring, may be so changed in the transition and rapid growth of heaven that it may be necessary for some attendant angel to point them out before we could recognize their beautiful forms. It shall gladden our eyes as we emerge from the gloom of the dark valley, to behold how glorious they have become, and to receive their welcome to the land of everlasting bliss.

> "And ere thou art aware, the day may be
> When to those skies they'll welcome thee."

THE DEAD ARE WITH US.

REV. S. IRENÆUS PRIME, D. D.

MILLIONS of spiritual beings walk the earth unseen, both when we wake and when we sleep. And we believe, with many others, that if we were suddenly divested of this mortal, we should find ourselves in a vast ampitheatre reaching to the throne of God, filled with spirits, the unseen witnesses, the cloud of witnesses of which we are encompassed continually. There is a place where the Most High dwells in light that no man can approach, where the darkness of excessive brightness hangs over and around his throne, making *Heaven*, as Heaven is not elsewhere in the Universe of God. But neither time nor place may with propriety be affirmed of spiritual existence. * * It is, therefore, scriptural and rational to suppose that the spirits of our departed friends are around by day and night; not away from God; his presence fills immensity; he is everywhere present. If an angel or the soul should take the wings of the morning, and dwell in the uttermost part of the sea, there to be with us or with those we love, even there the gracious presence of God would dwell, and the sanctified would find Heaven as blessed and glorious as in the temple of which the lamb is the Light.

THE DEPARTED STILL OURS.

REV. H. W. BEECHER, D. D.

THUS our friends are separated from us because they are lifted higher than our faculties can go. Our child dies. It is the last we can see of him here. He is lifted so far above us we cannot follow him. He was our child; he was cradled in our arms; he clambered upon our knees. But instantly in the twinkling of an eye, God took him, and lifted him up into his own sphere. And we see him not. But it is because we are not yet developed enough. We can not see things spiritual with carnal eyes. But they who have walked with us here, who have gone beyond us, and whom we cannot see, are still ours. They are more ours than they ever were before. We cannot commune with them as we once could because they are infinitely lifted above those conditions in which we are able to commune. We remain here and are subject to the laws of this realm. They have gone where they speak a higher language, and live in a higher sphere. But this silence is not the silence of vacuity, and this mystery is not the mystery of darkness and death. This is the glory; ours is waiting for it. There is the realization; ours is the hoping for it. Theirs is the perfection; ours is the immaturity striving to be ripe. And when the day comes that we shall disappear from these earthly scenes, we shall be joined to them again; not as we were—for we shall not then be as we were—but as they are, with God. We shall be like them and Him.

COWPER'S GRAVE.

ELIZABETH BARRETT BROWNING.

IT is a place where poets crowned
  May feel the heart's decaying,—
It is a place where happy saints
  May weep amid their praying:
Yet let the grief and humbleness,
  As low as silence, languish!
Earth surely now may give her calm
  To whom she gave her anguish.

O poets! from a maniac's tongue,
  Was poured the deathless singing!
O Christians! at your cross of hope,
  A hopeless hand was clinging!
O men! this man, in brotherhood,
  Your weary paths beguiling,
Groaned inly while he taught you peace,
  And died while ye were smiling.

And now, what time ye all may read,
  Through dimming tears his story,
How discord on the music fell,
  And darkness on the glory,
And how, when one by one, sweet sounds
  And wandering lights departed,
He wore no less a loving face
  Because so broken-hearted;

He shall be strong to sanctify
  The poet's high vocation,
And bow the meekest Christian down
  In meeker adoration;
Nor ever shall he be, in praise,
  By wise or good forsaken;
Named softly, as the household name
  Of one whom God hath taken.

With quiet sadness and no gloom,
  I learn to think upon him,
With meekness that is gratefulness
  To God whose heaven has won him—
Who suffered once the madness-cloud,
  To His own love to blind him;

But gently led the blind along
  Where breath and bird could find him,

And wrought within his shattered brain,
  Such quick poetic senses,
As hills have language for, and stars,
  Harmonious influences!
The pulse of dew upon the grass
  Kept his within its number;
And silent shadows from the trees
  Refreshed him like a slumber.

Wild timid hares were drawn from woods
  To share his home caresses,
Uplooking to his human eyes
  With sylvan tendernesses:
The very world, by God's constraint,
  From falsehood's ways removing,
Its women and its men became
  Beside him, true and loving.

But while in blindness he remained
  Unconscious of the guiding,
And things provided came without
  The sweet sense of providing,
He testified this solemn truth,
  Though frenzy desolated—
Nor man nor nature satisfy,
  Whom only God created!

Like a sick child that knoweth not
  His mother while she blesses
And drops upon his burning brow
  The coolness of her kisses,—
That turns his fevered eyes around—
  "My mother! where's my mother?"
As if such tender words and looks
  Could come from any other!—

The fever gone, with leaps of heart,
  He sees her bending o'er him;
Her face all pale from watchful love,
  The unweary love she bore him!—
Thus, woke the poet from the dream,
  His life's long fever gave him,
Beneath those deep pathetic eyes,
  Which closed in death to save him!

Thus? oh, not *thus*! no type of earth
  Could image that awaking,

Wherein he scarcely heard the chant
  Of seraphs, round him breaking,
Or felt the new immortal throb
  Of soul from body parted;
But felt *those eyes alone*, and knew
  My Savior! *not* deserted!

Deserted! who hath dreamt that when
  The Cross in darkness rested,
Upon the Victim's hidden face,
  No love was manifested?
What frantic hand outstretched have e'r
  The atoning drops averted,
What tears have washed them from the soul,
  That *one* should be deserted?

Deserted! God could separate
  From His own essence rather:
And Adam's sins *have* swept between
  The righteous Son and Father;
Yea, once, Immanuel's orphaned cry,
  His universe hath shaken—
It went up single, echoless,
  "My God, I am forsaken!"

It went up from the Holy's lips
  Amid His lost creation,
That, of the lost, no son should use
  Those words of desolation;
That earth's worst frenzies, marring hope,
  Should mar not hope's fruition,
And I, on Cowper's grave, should see
  His rapture, in a vision!

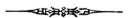

O mighty grace, our life to live
  To make our earth divine;
O mighty grace! Thy heaven to give,
  And lift our Life to Thine!

O strange the gifts and marvellous,
  By Thee received and given!
Thou tookest woe and death from us,
  And we receive Thy Heaven!

                              T. H. GILL.

DEPARTED FRIENDS NEAR US.

BISHOP M. SIMPSON, D. D.

HOW strange is this feeling of a spiritual world, an invisible realm, that gathers so closely around the Christian heart near the hour of death? All along through life we are in the midst of the invisible, stepping on its very verge. Bright forms are around us unseen; ministering angels guard our footsteps. But when the eye is clear, the ear is quick, the limbs are strong, the heart beats regularly, and the nerves are trained for intense action, the visible fills our thoughts, commands our time and energies. But when the charms of earth fade, the system loses its power, the hour of action has gone, how sweetly steals over the soul thoughts of the presence of unseen forms, and how near may man feel to the throne of God! When the work of Stephen was ended, though in the active hours of his strength, yet he saw the heavens opened, and Jesus standing on the right hand of God. Paul, in his prison hours, had glimpses of the glorious crown of righteousness reserved for him. Dying saints, in all ages, have felt a nearness to a glorious realm. But as we read of such scenes cheering the martyrs or the apostles, or the leading minds of earth, we may possibly fancy that such greetings do not meet the Christian in the ordinary walks of life: but when in our own circle of friends, we see the lovely, the frail, the delicate, as they pass away, grow strong in faith and love, and hope, as they listen to voices calling from the spirit land; as bright visions of the future rise before them, seems to draw near to earth, and we almost feel that we, too, have friends in light who may be hovering around us. To those of us who know the deep pang of parting with loved ones of our family, who know the shadow which grief casts over the household, and feel a loneliness because the voice of a loved one is no longer heard, what a consolation to think of the associations of heaven!

<blockquote>
Then in the living God we'll trust,
Who doeth all things well;
The body shall return to dust,
The soul in heaven shall dwell.
</blockquote>

BISHOP D. W. CLARK, D. D.

THE DEPARTED EMPLOYED ON MINISTRIES OF LOVE.

BISHOP R. S. FOSTER, D. D., LL. D.

WHAT, then, is this truth which we believe? The dead live. In the years gone we had them with us; they became very dear to us. They separated from the throng, and gave us their love. They grew into our being, and were a part of us. One day they became very weary and sick. We thought nothing of it at first; but morning after morning came, and they were more faint. The story of the dark days that followed is too sad. One dreary night, with radiant face, they kissed us, and said good-bye. They were dead. Kind neighbors came and carried them out of our homes, and we followed with dumb awe, and saw them lay them down gently beneath the earth. We returned to the vacant house, which never could be home again. Our hearts were broken. The earth and sky have been so dark since that day. We have searched through the long nights and desolate days for them, but we cannot find them; they do not come back. We listen, but we get no tidings. Neither form nor voice comes to us. The dark, silent immensity has swallowed them up. Are they extinct? No. They live; we cannot tell where, whether near us or remote; we cannot tell in what form, but they live. They are essentially the same beings they were when they went in and out among us. There has been no break in their life. It is as if they had crossed the sea. The old memories and old loves still are with them. New friends do not displace old ones. They are more beautiful than when we knew them, and purer, and holier, and happier. They are not sick or weary now. They have no sorrow. They are not alone. They have joined others. They think and talk of us. They make affectionate inquiries for our welfare. They wait for us. They are learning great lessons, which they mean to recite to us some day. They are not lonely; they are a glorious company. They have no envies or jealousies. They are ravished with the happiness of their new life. I do not know where it is, or how it is; but I am certain it is so. They are kings and priests unto God. They wear crowns that flash in the everlasting light. They wear robes that are spotlessly white.

They wave victorious palms. They sing anthems of such exceeding sweetness as no earthly choirs ever approach. They stand before the throne. They fly on ministries of love. They muse on tops of Mount Zion. They meditate on the banks of the river of life. They are rapturous with ecstasies of love. God wipes away all tears from their faces, and there is no more death, neither sorrow, nor crying, nor any more pain; for the former things are passed away. The glorious angels are their teachers and companions. But why attempt to describe their ineffable state? It hath not entered into the heart of man to conceive it.

WE DO NOT LOSE DEPARTED FRIENDS.

It is a hasty conclusion, and one which marks an inadequate apprehension of the nature of friendship to say that we lose a friend when he dies. Death is not only unable to quench the genuine sense of friendship between the living and the dead; it is also unable to prevent the going forth of a real feeling of friendship for the dead whom we have, it may be, never known at all. Goldwin Smith, in his new biography of Cowper, says of that poet: "There is something about him so attractive, his voice has such a silver tone, he retains, even in his ashes, such a faculty of *winning friends*, that his biographer and critic may be easily beguiled into giving him too high a place." Have we not an added help toward a kindly life in the thought that we may win new friends when our bodies are laid in the dust?

H. CLAY TRUMBULL.

> The sunshine and the trembling leaves,
>   The blue o'erarching sky,
> The music of the wandering winds
>   That float in whispers by—
> All speak in tender tones to me
> Of life's parted hours and thee.

THE VOICES OF THE DEAD.

WILLIAM AIKMAN, D. D.

THE dead speak by their lives, by their works, and by their words. They speak in the ear of memory and affections. The friends we have loved pass away from our sight, but they live in our memory and our hearts, while their voice comes back to us with a power that it never had when we saw their moving lips. To some there are more voices of the dead than of the living, and they are sweeter voices than the ear shall ever hear again. A little thing may wake them. Perhaps it is the tone of some friend who is speaking. It came and went, and was only for a moment, but in that moment memory was busy, and the old remembered voice comes up; you hear the living no more while you listen. Your look falls upon some memorial of the past: perhaps it is the little shoe that you took off once with a smile and a kiss, but which has been waiting ever since for the cushioned feet that shall fill it no more; perhaps it is the shawl that you once wrapped around the form that you could shield from the winter's wind, but not from the blast of death; perhaps it is a footfall that is wondrously like the tread, telling of a presence which was life and health to the home; perhaps it is the worn cane which once steadied uncertain steps; perhaps it is only a glove that you last saw in a sister's hand—anything may be enough. Straightway your gaze is fixed, you hold the token, but soon you see it not, your eye is looking far beyond through the door it has opened. Now the past is past no more, the dead are dead no more, nor are they silent. With the form comes the voice. You listen, and it begins to speak. It may be a little voice which prattles as in the other days; perhaps it is a mother's voice, and it calls your name, and then you listen to words of counsel and advice which you did not know before had so deep a meaning; perhaps it is a wife's voice, and it speaks in all the confidence of love. Whichever it may be, it is real now and has a more than living power. You only can tell what the voice is saying, your ear alone heard it and your heart alone interprets it.

Sometimes the dead speak reproachfully, and sometimes gladly and encouragingly. The voices are not all or always sad, nor always full of cheer. The long-hushed whisper never has in it anything of anger or of passion; it is very calm and low, but terribly distinct, and changes not. Oh, how many a weary, discouraged wayfarer has started up with another life, because a low, sweet call has reached his ear from the long departed.

THE CHILD AND THE MOURNERS.

CHARLES MACKAY.

A LITTLE child, beneath a tree
Sat and chanted cheerily
A little song, a pleasant song,
Which was—she sang it all day long—
"When the wind blows the blossoms fall;
But a good God reigns over all."

There passed a lady by the way,
Moaning in the face of day,
There were tears upon her cheek,
Grief in her heart too great to speak;
Her husband died but yester-morn,
And left her in the world forlorn.

She stopped and listened to the child
That looked to heaven, and singing, smiled
And saw not for her own despair,
Another lady, young and fair,
Who also passing, stopped to hear
The infant's anthem ringing clear.

For she but few sad days before
Had lost the little babe she bore;
And grief was heavy at her soul
As that sweet memory o'er her stole,
And showed how bright had been the past,
The present drear and overcast.

And as they stood beneath the tree
Listening, soothed and placidly

A youth came by, whose sunken eyes
Spake of a load of miseries;
And he, arrested like the twain,
Stopped to listen to the strain.

Death had bowed the youthful head
Of his bride beloved, of his bride unwed:
Her marriage robes were fitted on,
Her fair young face with blushes shone,
When the destroyer smote her low,
And changed the lover's bliss to woe.

And these three listened to the song,
Silver-toned, and sweet, and strong,
Which that child, the live-long day,
Chanted to itself in play.
" When the wind blows the blossoms fall,
But a good God reigns over all."

The widow's lips impulsive moved;
The mother's grief, tho' unreproved,
Softened as her trembling tongue
Repeated what the infant sung;
And the sad lover, with a start,
Conned it over to his heart.

And though the child—if child it were,
And not a seraph sitting there—
Was seen no more, the sorrowing three
Went on their way resignedly,
The song still ringing in their ears—
Was it music of the spheres?

Who shall tell? They did not know.
But in the midst of deepest woe
The strain recurred when sorrow grew,
To warn them and console them too:
" When the wind blows the blossoms fall,
But a good God reigns over all."

There s a beautiful face in the silent air
　Which follows me ever and near,
With its smiling eyes and amber hair,
With voiceless lips, yet with breath of pray'r,
　That I feel, but I cannot hear.

THE FAMILY IN HEAVEN AND EARTH.

'T IS but one family,—the sound is balm,
A seraph-whisper to the wounded heart,
It lulls the storm of sorrow to a calm,
And draws the venom from the avenger's dart.

T'is but one family,—the accents come
Like light from heaven to break the night of woe,
The banner-cry, to call the spirit home,
The shout of victory o'er a fallen foe.

Death cannot separate—is memory dead?
Has thought, too, vanished, and has love grown chill?
Has every relic and memento fled,
And are the living only with us still?

No! in our hearts the lost we mourn remain
Objects of love and ever-fresh delight;
And fancy leads them in her fairy train,
In half-seen transports past the mourner's sight.

Yes! in ten thousand ways, or far or near,
The called by love, by meditation brought,
In heavenly visions yet they haunt us here,
The sad companions of our sweetest thought.

Death never separates; the golden wires
That ever trembled to their names before,
Will vibrate still, though every form expires,
And those we love, we look upon no more.

No more indeed in sorrow and in pain,
But even memory's need ere long will cease,
For we shall join the lost of love again,
In endless bands, and in eternal peace.

EDMESTON.

THE HAPPIER SPHERE.

SHOULD yon bright stars which gem the night,
   Be each a blissful dwelling sphere,
Where kindred spirits re-unite,
   Whom death has torn asunder here,
How sweet it were at once to die,
   And leave this blighted orb afar—
Mix soul with soul, to cleave the sky,
   And soar away from star to star.

But oh! how dark, how drear, how lone
   Would seem the brightest world of bliss,
If wandering through each radiant zone,
   We failed to find the loved of this!
If there no more the ties should twine,
   Which death's cold hand alone can sever,
Ah! then these stars in mockery shine,
   More hateful as they shine forever.

It cannot be!—each hope and fear
   That blights the eye or clouds the brow,
Proclaims there is a happier sphere
   Than this black world which holds us now!
There is a voice which sorrow hears,
   When heaviest weighs life's galling chains;
'Tis heaven that whispers, "dry thy tears—
   The pure in heart shall meet again!"

TIES NOT BROKEN IN DEATH.

WE delight greatly in the hope that the ties which bind us to our sainted friends are not broken in death—that while we are loving them still, they love us too; and while we long to find them again they are watching with holy interest over us, and are alluring us, by sweet mysterious influences, into their holy society, and into a participation, with them, of celestial joys. Seeing we are compassed about with so great a cloud of witnesses, we are animated to lay aside every weight—even that of the body itself in death—that we may fly to their embraces, and be near them, as they are near the Lord.   REV. H. HARBAUGH.

THE HOME BEYOND

THE SAINTED DEAD.

HOW beautiful is the belief of man's immortality! The dead alive again and forever. "Earth to earth, ashes to ashes, dust to dust," is only spoken over the body, when consigned to "the house appointed for all the living." Not such the requiem of the soul. A refrain of immortality concludes earth's history and announces eternity's beginnings. "Not lost, but gone before." Such is the cherished and beautiful faith of man in all ages and lands; a mere glimmering indeed in minds unirridiated with divine truth; and only a power and a joy when God's voice audibly falls upon the ear in words of counsel and prophecy.

The sainted dead dwell in life; beholding "the king in his beauty;" shining "as the brightness of the firmament, and as the stars for ever and ever." They fade no more, nor realize pain; a wealth of love is theirs, a heritage of goodness, a celestial habitation; and in them thoughts, hopes, feelings expand and move forward in ceaseless progressions. We may feel sad because they are lost to us; but while we weep and wonder, they are wrapped in garments of light and warble songs of celestial joy. They will return to us no more, but we shall go to them; share their pleasures; emulate their sympathies; and compete with them in the path of endless development. We could not call them back. In the homes above they are great, and well-employed and blest. Shadows fall upon them no more; nor is life ruffled with anxious cares; love rules their life and thoughts; and eternal hopes beckon them forever to the pursuit of infinite good.

To whom are these thougths strange and dull? Who has no treasure in Heaven—well-remembered forms hallowed by separation and distance—stars of hope illumining with ever increasing beauty life's utmost horizon? What family circle has remained unbroken—no empty chair—no cherished mementoes—voices and footsteps returning no more—no members transferred to the illimitable beyond? Where is he who has stood unhurt amid the chill blasts, that have blighted mortal hopes, and withered mortal loves? Alas! the steps of death are everywhere; his voice murmuring in every sweep of the wind; his ruins visible on towering hill and in sequestered vale. We all have *felt* or *seen* his power. Beneath the cypress we rest and weep; our hearts riven with memories of the loved and lost; and yet hope springing eternal from earth's mausoleums to penetrate and posses the future.

Heaven is ours; for is it not occupied by our dead? Heaven and earth lay near together in the myths of the ancients; and shall it be otherwise in the institutions of Christianity? We need faith. Our paths are surrounded by the departed; our assemblies multiplied by their presence; our lives bettered by their ministries. From beneath light shadows we look forward into the approaching day; and while we gaze the beams of the morning spread light and loveliness over the earth. It is not otherwise, as from beneath the night of time we peer anxiously after the pure day of Heaven.

Faith penetrates the vail, and bids the invisible stand disclosed; while its magic wand wakens into life forms well-known, but holier and lovelier far than we knew them here. Such thoughts make us better, purer, gentler. We cannot keep society with the sainted dead, and with the great God in whose presence they dwell, without feeling a nobler life throbbing through us. They draw us upward. We grow less earthly, more heavenly; and God-like aspirations come to us, as we wander along the border land where dwell the sainted dead. Too little do we seek such communings. Our time is so absorbed with perishable and unsatisfying forms of good; and so we lose the image of the heavenly, and grow carnal. The beauty of our life fades; and we are left to hanker after passing shadows and unsubstantial dreams. Let us tear away oftener from these earthly moorings; let us walk more steadily in the light of celestial companionship; and so attain to the true and the good, as they have attained who roam the hills of immortality.

> "They dwell with thee—the dead;
> Pavilioned in auroral tents of light;
> Their spheres of heavenly influence round thee spread,
> Their pure transparence vailing them from sight,
> Angelic ministers of love and peace,
> Whose sweet solicitudes will never cease."

Communion by faith with the immortals can not fail to strengthen us for the stern conflicts of life. At once this earthly existence is seen in its true light; the opening of a day that shall never close; the spring-time of a year that will know no end, the initial chapter in a volume whose records shall find no final page nor incident. When life is thus truly gauged, we learn to place a proper estimate upon its passing pomps and pleasures; and we grow less sensitive to the world's smiles and frowns; more careful to seek after the eternal good. The example of the sainted dead, who toiled and endured till they now reign, affects us; and we feel strong for like conflicts, and ready for equal labors, till in us too the mortal shall put on the immortal. Divine ties spring up, and last forever, binding the heart to the good, the beautiful, the true, and making it strong for the work and trials of life.

And communion with the dead, whom we have known and loved on earth, will make Heaven more real and attractive to us; dissipating the vagueness of the notion with which it is too often regarded; begetting within us abiding attachments for celestial seats. God, who created the world, and whose providence is everywhere visible in promoting our welfare, is there; and Jesus, who died for us, and with whom we have grown familiar in his earthly history; and the Holy Spirit, the sanctifier of the church, and whose gentle influences we have felt within us. And our friends are there,—changeless, loving spirits now,—yet with lineaments familiar and forms well remembered. The homes of the blest are no longer vague, indistinct, poorly defined. We see them—the beautiful city, the outlined hills of immortality—the on-flowing river making glad the palaces of God. And we can have an idea of what they must be—how substantial in their foundations—how vast in their proportions—how rich in their furnishings—to be fitting habitations for the immortals. Heaven comes nearer to us, and grows more attractive, as we think of the loved ones who dwell there.

> "It was not, mother, that I knew thy face:
> The luminous eclipse that is on it now,
> Though it was fair on earth, would have made it strange
> Even to one who knew as well as he loved thee;
> But my heart cried out in me, Mother!"
>
> Cowper.